A TASTE of Georgia

Published by
Newnan Junior Service League, Inc.
Newnan, Georgia

For additional copies, send order to

A Taste of Georgia

P.O. Box 1433
Newnan, Georgia 30264

Conveninet order forms are located inside the back cover.

A Taste of Georgia
© Copyright, 1977
Newnan Junior Service League, Inc.
Newnan, Georgia

Library of Congress Card #77-79768
ISBN 0-9611002-2-2

First Printing	7,500 Books	October, 1977
Second Printing	10,000 Books	April, 1978
Third Printing	20,000 Books	February, 1979
Fourth Printing	20,000 Books	September, 198(
Fifth Printing	20,000 Books	August, 1981
Sixth Printing	20,000 Books	February, 1983
Seventh Printing	20,000 Books	November, 1984
Eighth Printing	25,000 Books	April, 1986
Ninth Printing	25,000 Books	May, 1988
Tenth Printing	25,000 Books	May, 1990
Eleventh Printing	15,000 Books	March, 1992
Twelth Printing*	15,000 Books	December, 1992
Thirteenth Printing	15,000 Books	July, 1993
Fourteenth Printing	10,000 Books	March, 1995

(*Southern Living® Hall of Fame edition)

A TASTE OF GEORGIA STAFF

EDITOR
Mrs. John N. White

ASSOCIATE EDITORS
Mrs. William R. Arnall, Jr.   Mrs. Robert L. Lee

RECIPE COLLECTION CHAIRMAN
Mrs. Charles M. Smith

RECIPE TESTING CHAIRMAN
Mrs. James W. Roberts

EDITING CHAIRMEN
Mrs. Herman E. Fletcher   Mrs. Dennis M. Simpson

TYPISTS	PROOFREADERS	RESEARCH
Mrs. Chip Barron	Mrs. Bob Hammock	Mrs. John Goodrum
Mrs. Major Boone	Mrs. Parnell Odom	Mrs. Joe McNabb
Mrs. Keith Brady	Mrs. Sidney Pope Jones	Mrs. Harry Tysinger
Mrs. Fred Gilbert	Mrs. Cliff Smith	
Mrs. Dan Umbach	Mrs. Boyce Thomas	

Design, Lay-Out, and Art Work
by
James Hoke Rutledge

Cover
by
John N. White

Typesetting by
Stanley's Little Type Shop

Printed in the United States of America
by

FATHER&SON
ASSOCIATES, INC.
4909 N. Monroe Street
Tallahassee, Florida 32303

NEWNAN JUNIOR SERVICE LEAGUE 1976-77
ACTIVE MEMBERS

Mrs. William Anderson
Mrs. William Arnall, Jr.
Mrs. Chip Barron
Mrs. Major Boone
Mrs. Keith Brady
Mrs. Danny Brown
Mrs. Warren Budd
Mrs. Ellis Crook
Mrs. Richard Day
Mrs. Ronald Duffey
Mrs. James Elrod
Mrs. Steve Fanning
Mrs. Tom Farmer
Mrs. Herman Fletcher
Mrs. G. A. Giddings, Jr.
Mrs. Fred Gilbert
Mrs. John Goodrum
Mrs. Benny Grant
Mrs. Bob Hammock
Mrs. Larry Hansen
Mrs. Carleton Jones
Mrs. Otis Jones
Mrs. Sidney Pope Jones
Mrs. Tom Jones
Mrs. Brantley Kemp
Mrs. Billy Lee
Mrs. Robert Lee

Mrs. Edwin Lee Lovett, Jr.
Mrs. Jim Luckie
Mrs. Joe MacNabb
Mrs. Bill McWaters
Mrs. Jimmy Mann
Mrs. Walker Moody
Mrs. Parnell Odom
Mrs. Oliver Reason
Mrs. James Roberts
Mrs. Al Robertson
Mrs. Leigh Sanders
Mrs. Bryan Sargent
Mrs. Brad Sears
Mrs. Eugene Secor
Mrs. Dennis Simpson
Mrs. Charles Smith
Mrs. Cliff Smith
Mrs. Larry Strickland
Mrs. John Stuckey
Mrs. Boyce Thomas
Mrs. Harry Tysinger
Mrs. Dan Umbach
Mrs. Phil Vincent
Mrs. John White
Mrs. Bruce Williams
Mrs. Joseph Williams
Mrs. John Woods

WE ARE GRATEFUL TO EACH CONTRIBUTOR
WHO DONATED RECIPES FOR USE IN

A Taste of Georgia

UNFORTUNATELY, LACK OF SPACE
PREVENTED US FROM INCORPORATING
ALL
THESE PRIZED RECIPES.

A Taste of Georgia
INTRODUCTION

Welcome to *A Taste of Georgia*! Within this unique volume we offer you insights into the delights and traditions that make Georgia a place of gracious hospitality and fine cooking. A special notation (★) beside many of the recipes signifies those which are typically Southern.

A Taste of Georgia is not only a collection of carefully selected, treasured recipes from Southern kitchens, it is also an illustrated guide to such special features as appetizer trees, cake decorating, punch rings, garnishes, napkin folding, and table settings. In addition, it presents one of the most extensive series of kitchen charts available in a community cookbook.

We were so determined to give our readers maximum exposure to cooking helps that we feature hundreds of valuable culinary hints throughout the entire book. These hints include cooking short-cuts, short recipes, new ideas, and old stand-by ways of solving kitchen problems. *A Taste of Georgia* may well stay near your favorite reading chair for many days before it finds its way into your kitchen!

A very discriminating system of selection was used in determining which recipes would appear in our cookbook. Literally thousands of recipes to be considered for inclusion in our cookbook were donated by many hundreds of skilled Southern cooks. All the recipes were kitchen-tested by our JUNIOR SERVICE LEAGUE members and League friends. Each recipe was then evaluated by at least three testers, and its rating was placed in one of four categories on our evaluation scale. Only those recipes receiving the TOP category rating were included in our book. We were determined to assure our readers of only the best of Georgian cookery!

Our cookbook is much larger than we originally envisioned. Its impressive size was dictated by our insistance on including a maximum number of superior recipes and by our unwillingness to compromise a large type style and easily readable format for the sake of economy.

The NEWNAN JUNIOR SERVICE LEAGUE is proud to share *A Taste of Georgia* with you. We are confident that it will soon become a treasured favorite.

Mrs. John N. White
EDITOR

Mrs. William R. Arnall, Jr.
Mrs. Robert L. Lee
ASSOCIATE EDITORS

CONTENTS

Appetizers

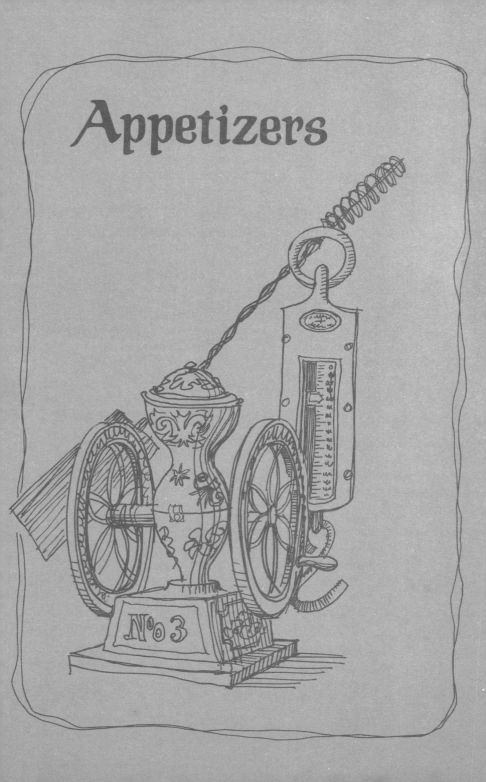

APPETIZERS

Appetizers Chapter Design: Spatula (1865), "Enterprise" Coffee Mill (1910), Chatillon's Ice Balance or Scale (1910)

ANTIPASTO I

Great cocktail party fare

Yield: 18 servings

1 (8-ounce) can mushrooms
1 (14-ounce) can artichoke
  hearts
1 (9-ounce) jar Spanish olives
1 (16-ounce) can ripe olives
1/4 cup bell pepper, chopped
1/2 cup celery, chopped
3/4 cup white vinegar
3/4 cup olive oil (may be
  half salad oil)
1/4 cup minced dry onion

2 1/2 teaspoons Italian
  seasoning
1 teaspoon onion salt
1 teaspoon salt
1 teaspoon seasoned salt
1 teaspoon garlic salt
1 teaspoon Accent
1 teaspoon sugar
1 teaspoon cracked pepper

Finely chop the first 6 ingredients, and place in a large jar with a tight-fitting lid. Combine and boil remaining ingredients. Pour over chopped vegetables. Refrigerate overnight at least or several days if possible. Give the jar a good shake several times a day to stir up ingredients. Serve as an hors d'oeuvre with wheat thins, as a relish on a meat sandwich, or as a salad dressing.

NOTE: An old Italian family recipe

Mrs. Robert K. Mayo (Betty)
Shreveport, Louisiana

****

Easy canapé: Cut out rounds of white bread. Dip each piece in melted butter, sprinkle with Parmesan cheese, and place on cookie sheet. Bake at 400° for a few minutes until crisp.

9

ANTIPASTO II
Easy!

Yield: 12 to 15 servings

1 (32-ounce) bottle catsup
1 (10½-ounce) can tomato purée
1 (6-ounce) can crabmeat, drained
2 (4½-ounce) cans shrimp, drained
1 (7½-ounce) can minced clams undrained

1 (6-ounce) can chopped ripe olives
1 (4-ounce) can diced green chili peppers
1 (4 or 8-ounce) can mushrooms
1/4 cup dehydrated chopped onions
Garlic salt to taste

Pick over crabmeat and shrimp; rinse and drain. In large bowl, thoroughly mix all ingredients. Chill at least 4 hours. Serve with crackers.

Mrs. Wallace Mitchell (Jeri)

HERBED BREAD STICKS

Oven: 250° 30 minutes

Yield: Approximately 8 dozen

1 (8-ounce) tub margarine
2 teaspoons parsley
1 teaspoon chives
1 teaspoon tarragon
1 teaspoon marjoram

1 teaspoon garlic salt
3 tablespoons sesame seed, toasted
1½ loaves very thin white Pepperidge Farm bread

Mix all ingredients except bread into the soft margarine. Spread on bread; cut each piece of bread into 4 slices. Bake at 250° for 30 minutes, then turn off oven. Leave in oven another 30 minutes. Keep several weeks in a sealed container.

Mrs. Gene Owen (Judy)

ARTICHOKE DIP

Oven: 350° 20 minutes   Yield: 12 to 15 servings

1 (14-ounce) can artichoke   Dash of garlic powder
   hearts   Dash of salt
1 cup mayonnaise   Lemon juice (optional)
1 cup grated Parmesan cheese

Drain artichokes well. Squeeze out all the juice. Break artichokes into small pieces and add mayonnaise and Parmesan cheese. Mix well. Add garlic powder and salt and mix lightly. Place in shallow baking dish (one that the dip can be served in) and bake at 350° for approximately 20 minutes or until brown on top. Blot excessive grease with paper towel. Serve hot with king-size Fritos, Melba toast rounds, or other crackers.

Mrs. Clark Hudson (Corille)

BROCCOLI DIP

Very popular!

Yield: 10 to 12 servings

1 medium onion, finely chopped
1 (4-ounce) can mushroom
   stems and pieces, drained
1 tablespoon butter
1 roll Kraft garlic cheese
1 (10¾-ounce) can mushroom
   soup

1 (10-ounce) box frozen chopped
   broccoli, cooked and drained
Dash worcestershire sauce,
   red hot sauce, and red
   pepper
Salt to taste

Sauté onion and mushrooms in butter in a saucepan. In a double-boiler, melt cheese. To cheese, add mushroom soup and all remaining ingredients. Serve warm in chafing dish with chips or Fritos.

Christy King
Atlanta, Georgia

11

HOT BROCCOLI DIP

Yield: 1 quart

1/2 cup chopped onion
1/2 cup chopped celery
1 cup chopped mushrooms
4 tablespoons melted butter
1 (10-ounce) package frozen chopped broccoli, cooked and
   drained
1 (10 3/4-ounce) can cream of mushroom soup
1 (6-ounce) package garlic cheese, diced

Sauté onion, celery, and mushrooms in butter until tender.
Combine broccoli, soup, and cheese; cook over low heat until
cheese melts, stirring occasionally. Add sautéed vegetables to
broccoli mixture. Serve hot.

NOTE: Serve with corn chips.

Mrs. Parnell Odom (Pat)

SPINACH DIP

Good relish dip

Yield: 1 quart

1 (10-ounce) package frozen
   chopped spinach
2 cups mayonnaise
1/2 cup chopped chives or
   grated onion
1/2 cup parsley, chopped
1 teaspoon salt
1 teaspoon pepper

Cook spinach for 3 minutes. Drain well. Combine all
ingredients and mix well.

Mrs. Lawrence Keith, Jr. (Jane)

CHEESE BALL I

Yield: 12 servings

12 ounces cream cheese
4 ounces blue cheese
1 stick butter

1 (3-ounce) can of black
olives, chopped
1/2 cup chopped nuts

Have first 3 ingredients at room temperature. Mix well. Add chopped olives. Wrap ball in waxed paper and chill. Roll in chopped nuts to cover. Allow ball to come to room temperature before serving.

Mrs. Larry Strickland (Mary)

CHEESE BALL II

Easy and a real taste treat

Yield: 12 to 14 servings

2 (8-ounce) packages cream cheese, softened
1 (.04-ounce) package Hidden Valley Ranch dressing mix, original or blue cheese flavor
Imitation bacon bits

Cream the cheese and dressing mix well with a fork or with an electric mixer. Form into a ball and roll in imitation bacon bits. Serve with Sociables crackers or Triscuits.

❊❊❊❊❊❊❊❊❊❊❊❊❊❊

Ring Tum Diddy: In the top of a double boiler, combine 2 cans of tomato soup and 1 cup grated sharp cheese. Add a dash of Tabasco. When soup is hot and cheese is melted, serve with crackers.

CORNED BEEF CHEESE BALL

Yield: 6 to 8 servings

1 (8-ounce) package cream
cheese, softened
1 teaspoon grated onion
3 teaspoons prepared
horseradish

3 to 4 drops Tabasco sauce
1/2 cup finely chopped beef
(Armour in a jar)
Parsley or chopped nuts

Mix all ingredients except parsley or nuts and roll into a ball. Refrigerate. Before serving, roll ball in fresh minced parsley or chopped nuts (or both). Let stand at room temperature about an hour before serving.

Mrs. Dennis Simpson (Jan)

CURRY CHUTNEY MOLD

Very unusual

Yield: 25 servings

1 (8-ounce) package cream
cheese
2 tablespoons heavy cream
1/2 to 1 tablespoon curry

3/4 cup Major Grey chutney,
very finely chopped
1/2 cup finely chopped pecans
Angel flake coconut

Combine all ingredients except coconut. Line bowl with clear wrap. Place cheese mold in bowl and chill thoroughly. Remove and cover with coconut. Serve with crackers.

NOTE: Softer than most cheese molds. Must be handled more carefully, but delicious for those who like curry.

Mrs. Lawrence Keith, Jr. (Jane)

CHEESE RICE KRISPIES

Oven: 375° 10 to 15 minutes   Yield: 5 dozen

3 sticks margarine, softened
8 to 10 ounces sharp cheese,
  grated
2 cups all-purpose or
  self-rising flour

Dash red pepper
2 1/4 to 2 1/2 cups Rice
  Krispies

Mix margarine and cheese. Add flour and pepper; mix well. Add Rice Krispies and shape into small balls. Bake on a greased cookie sheet at 375° for 10 to 15 minutes.

Mrs. Robert L. Lee (Pam)

Mrs. James P. Reese (Mary Ann)
Senoia, Georgia

★   MRS. FOSTER'S CHEESE STRAWS

Oven: 350° 10 to 12 minutes   Yield: 25 to 30 servings

3/4 cup butter, softened
1 pound New York State sharp
  cheese, grated

2 cups all-purpose flour
1 teaspoon salt
1 scant teaspoon red pepper

Mix softened butter with grated cheese. Add flour, salt, and pepper; combine thoroughly. Press dough onto ungreased cookie sheet using a star-shaped disc of cookie press. Bake at 350° for 10 to 12 minutes.

Mrs. John Goodrum (Marsha)

※※※※※※※※※※※※※

Always follow canning instructions carefully. Process fruits, pickles, and tomatoes in a waterbath according to a reliable guide.

★ ## CHEESE STRAWS I

Oven: 350°   Yield: 6 dozen 2-inch cheese straws

1 1/2 pounds cheese
2 sticks margarine or butter
2 3/4 cups all-purpose flour

1 teaspoon salt
3/4 teaspoon red pepper,
   or to taste
1/2 tablespoon baking powder

Grind cheese and margarine or butter and mix well with hand. Mix flour, salt, pepper, baking powder, and add to cheese mixture. Keep cool. Run mixture through cookie press and bake in a moderate 350° oven until light brown on edges.

Dr. W. Earnest Barron

★ ## CHEESE STRAWS II
Freezes well

Oven: 325° 10 minutes   Yield: 10 to 12 dozen

1 pound New York sharp
   cheese, grated
3 cups all-purpose flour

2 sticks margarine
1/4 teaspoon red pepper

Mix all ingredients together. Press through a cookie press onto cookie sheets. Bake at 325° for about 10 minutes.

Mrs. Marion Truitt (Pauline)

****

For quick ham cornucopias, cut cold sliced boiled ham into 2x3-inch retangles. Spread with softened cream cheese, plain or made zippy with horseradish, and roll meat securely into a cornucopia. Fasten with an hors d'oeuvre pick and refrigerate. Pick may be removed before slicing and serving.

CHEESE COOKIES

A great make-ahead appetizer

Oven: 375° 10 minutes   Yield: 6 to 8 dozen

1/2 pound grated Cheddar   3 cups flour
   cheese   1/2 cup chopped pecans
1/2 pound butter   (optional) ·
1/2 cup sifted powdered sugar

Soften cheese and butter. Add remaining ingredients and shape into a roll. Refrigerate or freeze until ready to bake. Slice very thinly and bake on a cookie sheet in a 375° oven for approximately 10 minutes.

Mrs. William E. Anderson (Dell)

CHEESE WAFERS I

Oven: 375° 12 minutes   Yield: 4 dozen

2 cups flour   1/4 pound butter
1/2 teaspoon salt   1 pound sharp American
1/2 teaspoon garlic salt   cheese, grated
1/4 teaspoon cayenne pepper

Mix and sift dry ingredients. Cut in butter. Add the cheese. Mix well. Thinly roll out and cut into desired shapes. Bake at 375° for 12 minutes.

Mrs. Otis Jones (Ann)

※※※※※※※※※※※※※※

When planning food for an afternoon party, allow 3 to 4 cups of punch, 2 to 3 cups of tea or coffee, and 10 "bites" (sandwiches, etc.) per person.

CHEESE WAFERS II

Oven: 350° 25 minutes

Yield: 6 dozen

3 cups all-purpose flour
1 heaping teaspoon salt
1/2 teaspoon cayenne pepper

1 pound Wisconsin cheese, grated
1 scant cup butter or margarine, softened

Measure flour before sifting. Sift flour, salt, and pepper. Add butter and cheese and work all ingredients together with hands. Shape into rolls 1 inch in diameter.

Roll in waxed paper and refrigerate for 24 hours. Cut into thin slices and bake in moderate oven about 25 minutes, or until light brown.

Mrs. B. S. Askew

JALAPEÑO COCKTAIL PIE

Can be made several days ahead — just reheat

Oven: 350° 30 minutes

Yield: 6 dozen 1-inch squares

3 to 4 Jalapeño peppers, seeded and chopped
1 large onion, finely chopped
1 garlic clove, minced

1 pound sharp Cheddar cheese, shredded
6 eggs, beaten

Sprinkle peppers, onion, and garlic in a well-greased 9-inch square pan. Cover with cheese. Pour eggs over cheese. Bake at 350° for 30 minutes or until firm. Cool and cut into 1-inch squares.

Mrs. Gene Owen (Judy)

****

The term "natural almonds" means almonds that have not been blanched but still have their brown skins.

PARMESAN CHEESE HORS D'OEUVRES

Also a good addition to one-dish meals

Yield: 18 servings

2 mini-loaves French bread,
  sliced
1/2 cup real mayonnaise
1/2 cup shredded Parmesan cheese

1 tablespoon minced onion
1/2 teaspoon garlic salt

Toast bread slices on one side. Mix ingredients together and spread thickly on untoasted side of bread. Broil until bubbly. A large loaf of French bread may be used; cut slices into hors d'oeuvre-size pieces.

Mrs. A. H. Verner (Alice)
Waupun, Wisconsin

ROLLED CHEESE FINGERS

Freezes well

Oven: 350° 8 to 10 minutes

Yield: 6 to 8 servings

1 (king-size) loaf of bread,
  fresh and soft
12 ounces New York sharp
  cheese, grated
1/2 cup margarine
1/2 cup mayonnaise
1/2 cup minced or dried onions

1 (2-ounce) jar pimiento,
  finely chopped
1/4 teaspoon Tabasco sauce
Italian dressing, package or
  bottle
Additional melted margarine

Mix cheese, margarine, mayonnaise, onions, pimiento, and Tabasco sauce well. Spread on soft, fresh bread from which crusts have been trimmed. Roll up to form fingers. Spread melted margarine on tops of rolls and then sprinkle each with Italian dressing. Bake at 350° for 8 to 10 minutes. (May take longer if frozen.)

Mrs. Joseph E. Williams, II (Nadine)

19

CHEESE PUFFS

Tastes like crab!

Oven: Broil 2 minutes   Yield: 40 servings

2 cups mayonnaise
1/2 cup Parmesan cheese,
  freshly grated
2 tablespoons onion, finely
  grated

2 teaspoons prepared hot
  mustard
40 toast rounds

Mix 2 cups mayonnaise with 1/2 cup freshly grated Parmesan cheese, 2 tablespoons finely grated onion, and 2 teaspoons prepared hot mustard. Using 1 heaping teaspoon per round, spread mixture on 40 toast rounds. Be careful to spread mixture to very edge of each round. Just before serving, broil puffs 6 inches from heat for 2 minutes, or until golden brown.

Mrs. Charles Woodroof (Minerva)

CHEESE-OLIVE BALLS

Freezes well

Oven: 400° 15 to 20 minutes   Yield: 36 servings

8 ounces sharp Cheddar
  cheese, grated
1 1/4 cups all-purpose flour

1/2 cup margarine, melted
1 jar pimiento-stuffed small
  olives (about 36)

Work cheese and flour together until crumbly. Add melted margarine and work with hands. Mold 1 teaspoon dough around each olive; shape into ball. Place on ungreased baking sheet. Cover and chill 1 hour or longer. Bake at 400° for 15 to 20 minutes. Serve hot. These may be frozen before or after they are cooked.

Mrs. Ellis Crook (Pat)

BLEU CHEESE DIP
Simple to make

Yield: 8 to 12 servings

1 pint mayonnaise
1/2 cup sour cream
1/2 tablespoon salt
1 tablespoon lemon juice
1/4 teaspoon Tabasco sauce
1 1/2 tablespoons white vinegar
1 tablespoon worcestershire sauce

1 teaspoon onion, finely grated
1/2 teaspoon black pepper
1 teaspoon garlic powder
2 (4-ounce) packages bleu
  cheese, crumbled

Place all ingredients in a bowl and mix thoroughly. Refrigerate until almost ready to serve. Use with any raw vegetables such as cauliflower, celery, carrots, mushrooms, bell pepper, and radishes.

NOTE: This dip may also be used as a dressing on a mixed salad.

Mrs. Joseph E. Williams, II (Nadine)

QUESO DIP
Great!

Yield: 10 to 12 servings

1 (11-ounce) can Cheddar
  cheese soup
1/4 pound American cheese,
  grated
1/2 (7½-ounce) can Jalapeño
  pepper relish

1 teaspoon chili powder
1 teaspoon cumin
1 tablespoon catsup

Combine all ingredients in the top of a double boiler. Cook and stir until well blended. Serve warm with chips or Fritos.

Mrs. Thomas R. Kerley (Lynda)
Lexington, Kentucky

SURPRISE CHEESE PUFFS
Freezes well

Oven: 400° 15 minutes   Yield: 50

1/2 cup butter or margarine   Dash of cayenne or red pepper
2 cups grated sharp cheese   1 cup sifted all-purpose flour
1/2 teaspoon salt   50 small stuffed green olives
1 teaspoon paprika

Allow butter to soften. Blend with cheese, salt, paprika, and cayenne. Stir in flour, mixing well. Mold 1 teaspoon of this mixture around each olive, covering it completely. Arrange on baking sheet and chill until firm. Bake in 400° oven for 15 minutes. Serve hot.

NOTE: These can be prepared ahead and frozen. Freeze on baking sheet to keep shape and then store in a plastic bag in freezer. Bake as needed.

Mrs. William F. Lee, Jr. (Susan)

SUMMER CHEESE APPETIZER
Very good with caviar

Yield: 10 servings

1/2 cup ripe olives   1 teaspoon grated onion
2 chicken bouillon cubes   1 teaspoon worcestershire
2 tablespoons hot water   sauce
1 (8-ounce) package cream cheese

Cut olives into small pieces. Dissolve bouillon cubes in hot water. Soften cheese and blend in bouillon mixture, onion, and worcestershire sauce. Stir in olives. Makes 1 1/2 cups. Serve with crackers.

Mrs. Lawrence Keith, Jr. (Jane)

CRAB AND CHEESE FONDUE

Yield: 4 to 6 servings

2 (16-ounce) jars Cheese Whiz
1 (6-ounce) package frozen
   crabmeat, or
1 (7-ounce) can crabmeat

2 1/2 tablespoons red wine,
   or to taste
Dash salt

Combine all ingredients in saucepan and cook over medium heat, stirring constantly until mixture is bubbly. Pour into fondue pot. Serve with cubed, toasted French bread.

Mrs. Gayle Golden
Valdosta, Georgia

CRABMEAT DIP
May be made ahead

Oven: 375° 30 minutes

Yield: 4 to 6 servings

1 (8-ounce) package cream
   cheese
1 (6½-ounce) can crabmeat
2 tablespoons grated onion
2 tablespoons milk

1/2 teaspoon horseradish
1/4 teaspoon salt
1/3 cup toasted, blanched
   almonds

Mix all ingredients except almonds. Put in 1-quart baking dish. Heat at 375° for 30 minutes. Sprinkle with almonds. This can be made ahead of time and heated in a chafing dish. Serve with crackers or Melba rounds.

Mrs. Eddie Lovett (Teresa)

❋ ❋ ❋ ❋ ❋ ❋ ❋ ❋ ❋ ❋ ❋ ❋ ❋

Homemade celery salt: thoroughly dry celery leaves, crush them to a powder or rub them through a sieve, then mix with salt.

MUSHROOMS STUFFED WITH CRABMEAT

Oven: 400° 10 minutes   Yield: 3 per person
      400° 20 minutes

1 pound large mushrooms,   1 (6-ounce) package frozen
  or 3 per person   crabmeat, thawed
Melted butter   1 tablespoon cognac
3 tablespoons butter   1 egg yolk
1 tablespoon flour   Tabasco sauce to taste
1/2 cup milk   1/4 cup grated Parmesan cheese
Salt and pepper to taste   3 tablespoons butter, melted
1/2 cup finely chopped
  scallions or onions

Remove stems from mushrooms and set aside. Place mushroom caps, hollow-side down, in a buttered baking dish. Brush with melted butter and bake 10 minutes at 400°. Make white sauce of 1 tablespoon butter, 1 tablespoon flour, and 1/2 cup milk. Stir until thickened and add seasonings. Sauté scallions or onions and chopped mushroom stems in 2 tablespoons butter for 4 minutes. Add crabmeat and cognac, mixing well. Add white sauce, egg yolk, and Tabasco sauce. Cook gently until mixture holds together well. Stuff mushroom caps with crab mixture. Sprinkle with Parmesan cheese and brush with melted butter. Bake at 400° for 20 minutes.

NOTE: These are also good served as a side dish with steak.

Mrs. Duke Blackburn (Julia)

****

Blend 1/2 cup grated Cheddar cheese, 1/2 stick butter, and 1 teaspoon chili powder for a tasty sandwich spread. Cut in strips and brown under broiler for a delectable canape.

CLAM DIGGER'S DIP
Inexpensive!

Yield: 4 to 6 servings

1 (10 3/4 ounce) can condensed New England clam chowder
  soup
1 (8-ounce) package cream cheese, softened
1 (4-ounce) can mushrooms, drained and chopped
1 tablespoon finely chopped onion
Dash of lemon-pepper seasoning
Dash of worcestershire sauce

With a mixer, gradually blend the soup into the cream cheese. Add mushrooms, onion, lemon-pepper seasoning, and worcestershire sauce; vary amounts according to taste. Chill and serve with crackers or chips.

Mrs. Ben C. Wetherington (Denise)
Valdosta, Georgia

CLAM DIP

Yield: 10 servings

1 (4 1/2-ounce) can minced   1 teaspoon lemon juice
  clams, drained   1 teaspoon seasoned salt
1 tablespoon worcestershire   1 (8-ounce) carton sour cream
  sauce

Mix ingredients well; chill and serve with chips or crackers.

Mrs. Otis Jones (Ann)

❊❊❊❊❊❊❊❊❊❊❊❊❊

When using the herb rosemary in cooking, measure it first, then crush it. A little goes a long way!

★ ## GLAZED NUTS

Oven: 325° 45 minutes   Yield: 15 to 20 servings

4 egg whites   1/2 pound margarine
2 cups sugar   1 pound slivered almonds
Pinch of salt   1 pound pecan halves

Beat egg whites and add sugar and salt slowly. Melt margarine in 3-quart casserole. Mix nuts into egg whites. Bake in melted margarine at 325° until all margarine is absorbed. Stir as they brown.

Mrs. Chuck Moates (Alice Ann)

PEPITAS
Save that Halloween pumpkin!

Pumpkin seeds   Salt
2 to 3 tablespoons butter

Wash pumpkin seeds. Let dry. Sauté in butter. Spread seeds on pan. Salt. Toast in 350° oven until slightly tan.

NOTE: Fun for the kids! Healthy snack.

Mrs. J. Littleton Glover, Jr. (Kathryn)

★ ## SUGARED PECANS
Delicious

Yield: 6 to 8 servings

1 1/2 cups sugar   1 teaspoon grated orange rind
1/2 cup orange juice   3 cups pecan halves

Boil sugar and orange juice together until soft-ball stage. Remove from heat and add grated orange rind and pecans. Beat until creamy. Pour out and break into pecan halves.

Mrs. C. A. Moody (Virginia)

SALMON BALL
Can be prepared the day before

Yield: 10 servings

1 (16-ounce) can salmon
1 (8-ounce) package cream
  cheese
2 tablespoons lemon juice
3 1/2 teaspoons grated onion
2 1/2 teaspoons horseradish
3/4 teaspoon salt

Dash of worcestershire sauce
Several dashes cayenne pepper
1/4 teaspoon liquid smoke
3/4 cup chopped pecans
3 tablespoons minced fresh
  parsley

Drain salmon, remove bones, and flake. In small bowl of electric mixer, cream cheese and blend in lemon juice, onion, horseradish, salt, worcestershire, cayenne, and liquid smoke. When well blended, gently stir in flaked salmon. Shape into a ball. Combine pecans and parsley and spread on sheet of waxed paper. Turn salmon ball in this mixture until well coated. Wrap in waxed paper and chill.

Mrs. Parnell Odom (Pat)

CHEESE AND SHRIMP FONDUE
Very easy and good for a cocktail party

Yield: 12 servings

1 (10¾-ounce) can cream
  of shrimp soup
1/2 pound grated Swiss cheese

2 tablespoons white wine
French bread

Combine all ingredients except French bread in either a double boiler or electric fondue pot until cheese melts. Serve in a chafing dish or fondue pot along with hunks of French bread for dunking.

Mrs. Gary R. Landsiedel (Marty)
Peachtree City, Georgia

SEAFOOD MOUSSE

Yield: 12 to 15 servings

1 (10¾-ounce) can cream of
mushroom soup
1 cup mayonnaise
2 (3-ounce) packages cream
cheese
1/2 teaspoon worcestershire
sauce
1/2 teaspoon seasoned salt
1 tablespoon grated onion

1 1/4 pounds cooked, cleaned
shrimp, finely chopped
1 (6½-ounce) can crabmeat
3 packages unflavored gelatin
1 cup cold water
Red food coloring

Cook first 6 ingredients in top of double boiler over medium heat. Stir until smooth. Add shrimp and crabmeat. Dissolve gelatin in cold water; blend into mixture. Add 2 to 3 drops red food coloring. Pour into 6-cup mold and chill until firm.

NOTE: For a zippier taste, add several drops Tabasco sauce and increase seasoned salt.

Mrs. Brooksie Knight (Linda)

SHRIMP DIP I

Yield: 4 to 6 servings

1 (4½-ounce) can shrimp
1 (8-ounce) package cream
cheese
1 teaspoon lemon juice

1 teaspoon onion salt
1 tablespoon worcestershire
sauce
1 tablespoon mayonnaise

Blend all ingredients with mixer. Chill and serve with chips or crackers.

Mrs. Otis Jones (Ann)

SHRIMP DIP II

Make ahead so flavors will blend

Yield: 4 to 6 servings

1 (4½-ounce) can shrimp
1 (3-ounce) package cream
  cheese, softened

4 tablespoons mayonnaise
1 grated onion
Tabasco sauce, to taste

Cut shrimp into tiny pieces with tines of a fork. Add softened cream cheese, grated onion, and mayonnaise. Mix well to get out lumps of cream cheese. Add Tabasco sauce to taste. Lemon juice also can be used.

Mrs. Gaston A. Green (Happy)

SHRIMP DIP OR SPREAD III

Yield: 1 1/2 cups dip or 2 to 3 dozen party sandwiches

1 (8-ounce) carton sour cream or
  1 (8-ounce) package
    cream cheese
1/2 cup cooked shrimp,
  finely chopped

1 teaspoon onion, minced
1 teaspoon catsup
Dash Tabasco

For dip: Use sour cream; mix all ingredients, and refrigerate for several hours.

For sandwich spread: Use cream cheese instead of sour cream.

Mrs. William Donald Tomlinson (Jane)

* * * * * * * * * * * * * *

No more torn or mashed bread for party sandwiches. Freeze bread before cutting into fancy shapes and spread with filling while bread is still stiff.

SHRIMP LOUISIANNE

Yield: 8 to 12 servings

3/4 cup hot mustard
  (Dijon or Creole)
3/4 cup salad oil
4 tablespoons catsup
1/2 cup vinegar

Hot pepper sauce to taste
1 bell pepper, diced
3 green onions, chopped
2 to 3 pounds cooked,
  cleaned shrimp

Combine all of the ingredients and chill. May be served with toothpicks as an hors d'oeuvre, on lettuce as a salad, or as an entrée.

Mrs. J. Littleton Glover, Jr. (Kathryn)

SHRIMP MOLD

Yield: 8 servings

1 envelope unflavored gelatin
1/2 cup cold water
2 cups cooked shrimp
3/4 cup chopped celery
1 1/2 cups mayonnaise

2 tablespoons grated onion
Dash of salt
1 (8-ounce) package cream
  cheese, room temperature

Heat gelatin in water until dissolved. Chop the shrimp and celery in blender. Mix the mayonnaise, onion, and salt together. Cream the cheese in mixer. Mix all ingredients together. Pour into oiled 4-cup mold and congeal in refrigerator. Serve as a spread on crackers or bread.

Coweta County Republican Women
Marie Johnson, President

❀❀❀❀❀❀❀❀❀❀❀❀❀❀

Pack lunch boxes with frozen sandwiches; they will thaw by lunch time.

★ ## ROASTED PECANS

Oven: 250° 1 hour   Yield: 8 servings

2 tablespoons oil   1 pound or 4 cups shelled
2 tablespoons butter   pecan halves
Salt

Melt oil and butter on large cookie sheet or broiler tray (cannot be sideless as the butter-oil mixture will run out). Sprinkle with salt. Spread pecans over pan in single thickness and stir to coat them with butter-oil mixture. Bake at 250° for 1 hour, stirring every 15 minutes. Add more salt if necessary.

Mrs. Howard F. Fairman (Donna)
Tucker, Georgia

TUNA MOUSSE

Yield: 10 to 12 servings

1/2 package unflavored gelatin   1/2 cup finely chopped celery
1/8 cup tap water   1 tablespoon grated onion
1 (3-ounce) package lemon-   1/2 cup chopped black olives
   flavored gelatin   1/2 cup slivered almonds
3/4 cup boiling water   1 (6½-ounce) can tuna, drained
1 tablespoon cider vinegar   Dash of dill and paprika
1 (10¾-ounce) can cream of   1/2 teaspoon curry powder
   chicken soup
3/4 cup mayonnaise

Soften unflavored gelatin in tap water; dissolve lemon-flavored gelatin and unflavored gelatin in boiling water and vinegar. Add remaining ingredients and pour into 5-cup mold. Chill until firm. Garnish with parsley before serving.

Mrs. William Dudley (Jakie)
Montgomery, Alabama

PIZZA BOCAS
Freezes well

Oven: 375°   Yield: 10 servings

1 pound ground hot sausage
1 medium onion, diced
1/4 to 1/2 teaspoon
  oregano
1 (8-ounce) can tomato sauce
2 loaves party rye bread

2 (8-ounce) packages sliced
  mozzarella cheese
Parmesan cheese
1 (4-ounce) can mushroom
  stems and pieces, finely
  chopped (optional)

Combine crumbled sausage, onion, and oregano in frying pan. Fry until sausage is done; drain well. Add tomato sauce and mix well. Place party rye bread on a large cookie sheet and broil until crisp and browned slightly. Turn bread over and place a slice of mozzarella cheese on the unbrowned side of each piece of bread. Top with sausage mixture and a sprinkling of Parmesan cheese. Bake at 375° until bubbly. If frozen, bake at 400° for about 20 minutes. If mushrooms are used, add them before spreading the sausage mixture on the bread. This mixture will keep in the refrigerator for several days. It is good for a quick lunch on any kind of bread.

Mrs. Robert L. Lee (Pam)

PARTY PIZZA

Oven: 400° 7 minutes   Yield: 6 dozen small pizzas

1 pound ground pork sausage
1 pound Cheddar cheese, grated
2 tablespoons worcestershire
  sauce

2 tablespoons catsup
2 1/2 loaves party rye bread
Oregano

Brown meat, then add other ingredients except oregano and cook until cheese melts. Spread mixture on each piece of bread, then sprinkle with oregano and place on cookie sheet. Bake at 400° for 7 minutes.

SHRIMP SANDWICHES

Yield: Approximately 10 dozen party sandwiches

1 (8-ounce) package cream
    cheese, softened
1 (4 1/2-ounce) can shrimp
Mayonnaise to moisten

Grated onion, to taste
Lemon juice, to taste
Extra shrimp or parsley to
    garnish

Beat all ingredients with mixer until well blended. Spread on bread. Garnish with tiny whole shrimp (there are approximately 75 per can) or parsley.

SAUSAGE APPETIZER

Oven: 375° 35 minutes   Yield 3 dozen

1/4 cup butter
1/2 cup water
1 1/2 cups herbed seasoned
    stuffing

1 egg, slightly beaten
1/4 pound mild bulk pork
    sausage
3/4 pound bacon

Melt butter in water. Remove from heat; stir into stuffing. Add egg and sausage, blending well. Chill for easier handling, then shape into small balls. Cut bacon strips into thirds, crosswise. Wrap one piece around dressing mixture and fasten with toothpick. Place on a rack in pan and bake at 375° for 35 minutes or until brown and crisp, turning at halfway point in cooking. Drain on paper towel and serve hot. May be made the day before baking.

Mrs. Eugene F. Secor (Martha)

※※※※※※※※※※※※※

When preparing party sandwiches for freezing, spread first with butter (never salad dressing), then spread with the filling. No more soggy bread. Fresh vegetables and hard-boiled eggs do not freeze well.

SAUSAGE PINWHEELS
Freezes well

Oven: 350° 15 to 20 minutes   Yield: 6 dozen

4 cups all-purpose flour   2/3 cup vegetable oil
1/4 cup cornmeal   2/3 cup milk
1/4 cup sugar   2 pounds hot sausage,
2 tablespoons baking powder   uncooked
1/2 teaspoon salt

Sift flour, cornmeal, sugar, baking powder, and salt together. Blend in vegetable oil. Add enough milk to make a stiff dough. Roll out thinly on lightly floured board. Spread sausage on dough and roll up lengthwise. Chill well and slice. Bake for 15 to 20 minutes at 350°.

Mrs. Danny Brown (Gail)

MARINATED CAULIFLOWER AND MUSHROOMS
Great as appetizer or vegetable dish

Yield: 8 servings

1 large head cauliflower
1 (8-ounce) can whole mushroom caps, drained
1 (16-ounce) bottle Italian dressing

Break cauliflower into flowerettes. Drop into boiling water for approximately 3 minutes. Drain. Add mushrooms. Pour Italian dressing over. Mix and let marinate at least one hour at room temperature. Drain off dressing and serve.

Mrs. Seth Osburn (Pat)

COCKTAIL MEAT BALLS
The sauce is the secret

Yield: Approximately 6 dozen small meat balls

Meat Balls:

2/3 cup fine, dry bread crumbs
1 1/2 pounds lean ground beef
2 eggs, beaten
3/4 cup tomato juice
1/8 teaspoon garlic powder

2 tablespoons instant minced
  onion
1 3/4 teaspoons salt
1/4 teaspoon pepper
1/4 teaspoon thyme
Oil for browning

Sauce:

1 1/2 cups catsup
3/4 cup red wine

6 teaspoons prepared mustard

MEAT BALLS: Combine all ingredients and mix well. Shape into desired size balls. Brown well in cooking oil and drain.

SAUCE: Combine all sauce ingredients and place in a chafing dish to serve. Add browned meat balls to sauce and simmer to heat thoroughly.

This sauce will pit aluminum foil, so do not store in foil or aluminum containers. Meat balls and sauce freeze very well.

Mrs. John P. Woods, Jr. (Elizabeth)

VEGETABLE SANDWICH FILLING

Yield: 3 to 4 dozen sandwiches

1 carrot, peeled
1 bell pepper, cut in slices
1 cucumber, sliced and cored

1 onion, peeled
2 (8-ounce) packages
  cream cheese

Put all vegetables through food grinder (don't use core of cucumber). Blend with cream cheese and spread on bread for sandwiches.

Mrs. William Donald Tomlinson (Jane)

SWEET AND SOUR MEATBALLS
Can be made a day ahead

Yield: 4 dozen

2 pounds lean ground beef
2 eggs, slightly beaten
1/2 cup bread crumbs
1/2 cup water
Salt, pepper, and garlic powder
  to taste

1 (12-ounce) bottle chili sauce
1/2 cup grape jelly
Juice of 1 lemon

Combine ground beef, eggs, bread crumbs, water, salt, pepper, and garlic powder. Shape into walnut-size balls. Combine chili sauce, grape jelly, and lemon in a large sauce pan. Heat until jelly melts. Drop uncooked meatballs into sauce and simmer for 45 minutes. (Refrigerate until excess grease is easily removed.) Reheat and serve in a chafing dish.

Mrs. Gary R. Landsiedel (Marty)
Peachtree City, Georgia

CURRIED VEGETABLE DIP

Yield: 4 to 6 servings

1 cup mayonnaise
2 teaspoons tarragon vinegar
1/2 teaspoon salt
1/8 teaspoon thyme

1/2 teaspoon curry powder
3 teaspoons chopped chives
1 tablespoon grated onion
Dash of pepper

Mix together and chill. Serve with assorted raw vegetables.

Mrs. Phil Thompson (Julie)
Atlanta, Georgia

****

Always thaw food in the refrigerator, not at room temperature.

HAWAIIAN NUT SANDWICHES

Yield: Approximately 12 dozen party sandwiches

1/4 cup evaporated milk
2 (8-ounce) packages cream
   cheese, softened

1 cup pineapple, crushed and
   drained well
1/4 cup chopped pecans

Blend milk and cheese together well. Add pineapple and nuts. Blend well. Good on orange or raisin bread as well as white bread.

Mrs. William Dudley (Jakie)
Montgomery, Alabama

CHICK PEA DIP

Yield: 10 servings

1 (1-pound) can chick peas
   (garbanzos), drained
1/4 cup sesame sauce (tahini)
1/8 cup liquid from chick peas

1/2 cup fresh lemon juice
1 clove garlic, crushed
1/2 teaspoon salt or to taste

Heat the chick peas and liquid in a saucepan. In blender put 1/8 cup heated liquid, 1/4 cup sesame sauce, and 1/2 cup lemon juice. Blend on high speed for 10 seconds. Then, gradually add drained chick peas until a smooth paste is achieved. Add crushed garlic and salt. Blend at high speed for 10 seconds. Place in closed container and chill in refrigerator until ready to serve.

When serving, dribble a few drops of olive oil on top of dip and garnish with 1 tablespoon of fresh chopped parsley. Serve with carrot and celery sticks or cocktail crackers.

Mayme B. Mansour

SWEDISH COCKTAIL MEATBALLS

Yield: 2 dozen large meatballs or 4 dozen small meatballs

Meat Balls:

1 pound ground beef
1/2 cup Italian seasoned
   bread crumbs
1 egg
2/3 cup milk

1 tablespoon finely chopped
   onion
1 teaspoon salt
1/8 teaspoon pepper
1/8 teaspoon nutmeg

Sauce:

1 (12-ounce) bottle chili sauce
1 (6-ounce) jar sweet pickle relish

1 can beer

Mix the first eight ingredients together and then form into small balls. Brown the meat balls well in cooking oil.

Mix all the sauce ingredients together; then add all the browned meat balls. Simmer on a low heat for approximately 30 minutes.

To double recipe, 3 pounds of meat are required.

Mrs. Eugene F. Secor (Martha)

VEGETABLE DIP

Yield: 4 to 6 servings

1 (8-ounce) package cream
   cheese
2 tablespoons cream
2 tablespoons Thousand Island
   dressing
1 tablespoon onion, grated

1/4 teaspoon salt
Dash of worcestershire sauce
Dash of Tabasco sauce

Mix all ingredients well.

Mrs. Ronald F. Wassenberg (Betty)

Beverages

BEVERAGES

Beverage Chapter Design: Left to right: Cocoa Dipper (1910), Teakettle (1898), Teapot (1898)

HOT CRANBERRY APPLE CIDER
A quick cider made in a percolator

Yield: 24 servings

1 1/2 quarts cranberry juice
2 (1-quart) bottles apple
   juice
4 cinnamon sticks

1/3 cup brown sugar
1/2 teaspoon salt
2 teaspoons whole cloves

Put cranberry juice and apple juice in bottom of a percolator. Place remaining ingredients in the basket. Perk approximately 10 minutes.

Mrs. Dennis M. Simpson (Jan)

MULLED CIDER
Pour this winter treat over clove-studded orange wedges.

Yield: 8 to 10 servings

1/2 cup brown sugar
1 teaspoon whole allspice
1 teaspoon whole cloves
1/4 teaspoon salt

Dash nutmeg
1 (3-inch) cinnamon stick
2 quarts apple cider

Combine all ingredients in a saucepan and bring slowly to a boil. Cover and simmer for 20 minutes. Strain before serving.

Mrs. John N. White (Martha)

❋❋❋❋❋❋❋❋❋❋❋❋❋

To make large ice cylinders for pitchers of cold drinks, fill empty frozen orange juice cans with water and freeze.

INSTANT COCOA

1 (8-quart) package nonfat
  dry milk
1 (6-ounce) jar nondairy
  coffee creamer

1 pound box Nestle's Quick
1 1/3 cups powdered sugar

Mix together in large container. Store airtight. To serve, put 1/3 cup mix in cup and add hot water to fill.

Mrs. W. Earnest Barron (Carolyn)

★   EGGNOG I

Well worth the trouble for the traditional holiday celebration

Yield: 25 servings

25 eggs, separated
1 1/2 cups bourbon
1 quart whipping cream

1 1/2 cups sugar, divided into
  2 equal portions

Beat yolks for 10 minutes; then add 1 1/2 cups of bourbon, a drop at a time, to the yolks. In another bowl, beat 1 quart whipping cream, slowly adding 3/4 cup sugar to cream while beating. Fold egg mixture into cream. Whip egg whites, add 3/4 cup sugar, and fold into yolk and cream mixture. Top with nutmeg, if desired, and serve.

Mrs. Charles J. Smith (Martha)

❋❋❋❋❋❋❋❋❋❋❋❋❋

When making iced tea, pour boiling water **over** the tea bags; do not add the bags to the water.

EGGNOG II

An inexpensive, non-alcoholic version

Yield: 10 servings

2 eggs, well beaten
1 (14-ounce) can sweetened
   condensed milk
1 teaspoon vanilla extract
1/4 teaspoon salt

1 quart homogenized milk
1/2 pint whipping cream,
   whipped
Nutmeg

Combine eggs, condensed milk, vanilla, salt, and homogenized milk. Fold in whipped cream. Sprinkle each individual serving with nutmeg. Liquor may be added, if desired.

Mrs. Carl E. Williams (Eddy)

★   ## EGGNOG III

Yield: 16 servings

4 eggs, whites and yolks
   beaten separately
3/4 cup bourbon
1 quart whipping cream
   (whipped in large bowl)

1 2/3 cups sugar
Extra: 2 envelopes of un-
   flavored gelatin

Beat yolks of eggs until whitish. Alternately add bourbon and sugar to beaten egg yolks. Stir thoroughly. Beat egg whites until stiff. Whip cream and gently fold the egg whites into the whipped cream. Add egg yolk mixture, 1 tablespoon at a time, to cream mixture. This can be served "as is" in glasses or put into deep pan to freeze.

To make Charlotte, add 2 envelopes of gelatin that have set in 1 cup cold water, then dissolved over hot water.

Mrs. Hugh A. Farmer (Zoe)

43

★ EGGNOG IV

One of the best!

Yield: 20 (8-ounce) servings

6 egg yolks
1 cup blended whiskey
1/4 to 1/2 cup rum
1/4 cup sugar
1 quart dairy eggnog, or
   1 quart half and half

6 egg whites, stiffly beaten
1/2 gallon eggnog ice cream
   or vanilla ice cream
Dash nutmeg (optional)

Beat egg yolks. Slowly add whiskey and rum. This cooks the yolks. Add sugar and blend well. Add the eggnog or half and half. Pour into chilled punch bowl; fold in beaten egg whites and scoops of ice cream.

NOTE: If there is any left over, this eggnog keeps well in the refrigerator for a few days. After that, freeze for a great ice cream.

Mrs. John P. Woods, Jr. (Elizabeth)

INSTANT RUSSIAN TEA

Simple and delicious; keeps well

Yield: 1 1/2 quarts dry mix

1 (18-ounce) jar Tang instant
   breakfast drink
2 (3-ounce) packages instant
   lemonade mix
2 teaspoons cinnamon

2 teaspoons cloves, ground
3/4 cup instant tea
2 1/2 cups sugar

Mix all ingredients together thoroughly. Place in tightly covered jars and use as needed. To make each cup of tea, place 2 heaping teaspoons in cup and add boiling water. Stir well.

Mrs. Joseph E. Williams, II (Nadine)

HOT SPICED TEA
A substitute for coffee

Yield: 3 1/2 quarts

3 quarts water
1 1/2 cups sugar
5 cinnamon sticks
20 whole cloves
5 individual-size tea bags

2 cups orange juice
1/2 cup lemon juice

Bring water, sugar, cinnamon sticks, and cloves to a boil. Remove from heat and add tea bags. Let stand for 15 minutes. Remove tea bags. Add orange juice and lemon juice. Strain. Serve hot.

Mrs. Walker Moody (Sally)

BETTY'S PUNCH
Excellent ladies' punch

Yield: Approximately 3 quarts

1 (46-ounce) bottle white
    grape juice
1 (32-ounce) bottle ginger ale
    with lemon

1 (36-ounce) bottle Pina Colada
    Mix
Rum to taste

Combine all ingredients at serving time. Pour into a large punch bowl. May use with an ice mold.

Mrs. James W. Roberts (Sue)

* * * * * * * * * * * * *

Instead of water, use ginger ale to reconstitute frozen grape juice.

45

CHAMPAGNE PUNCH

Yield: Approximately 20
(5-ounce) servings

Juice of 12 lemons
1/2 pint brandy
1 (32-ounce) bottle club
  soda

2 bottles champagne
Powdered sugar to taste

Chill liquids and combine at serving time. Sprinkle a little powdered sugar over just to sweeten slightly.

John F. Herbst
Kansas City, Missouri

FRENCH 75 CHAMPAGNE PUNCH

Yield: 35 to 40 small servings

3 bottles champagne, preferably
  pink
2 teaspoons powdered sugar
5 (12-ounce) cans ginger ale

3 ounces creme de cacao
2 ounces brandy

Pour all ingredients into a punch bowl and stir. Float an ice ring (decorated for the season or occasion) in the punch.

Mrs. Charlie Jordan (Carmine)
Lookout Mountain, Tennessee

❋❋❋❋❋❋❋❋❋❋❋❋❋

For zippy hot chocolate, add a cup of strong coffee to hot chocolate. Top with whipped cream to which almond and vanilla extracts have been added.

MIDGE'S PUNCH

Yield: 2 gallons

4 (6-ounce) cans frozen orange
juice concentrate
2 (6-ounce) cans frozen lemon
juice concentrate
1 (46-ounce) can pineapple
juice

1 fifth vodka
1 quart ginger ale

Dilute orange and lemon juice according to directions on cans. Add pineapple juice and vodka. Add ginger ale at serving time.

NOTE: Freeze some of the punch in a mold with fruit to float in the punch bowl.

Mrs. Bennett Baxley (Mildred)
East Point, Georgia

SANGRÍA

2 bottles Bordeau wine or
a California wine such as
Cabernet Sauvignon
1 cup lemonade concentrate
1/4 cup brandy
1 cup Cointreau
1 bottle soda

1/2 cup sugar
Oranges
Lemons
Limes
Bananas and/or strawberries

Combine all of the above ingredients in a large container. Strength may be adjusted. Use fruits in season, sliced. Add ice. Chill and serve.

Mrs. J. Littleton Glover, Jr. (Kathryn)

TURNER COUNTY PUNCH

Yield: 8 to 10 servings

1 (6-ounce) can undiluted frozen
orange juice
6 ounces lemon juice
1 tablespoon bitters
2 tablespoons powdered sugar
1 (8-ounce) jar cherries and
juice

1 orange, sliced
1 lemon, sliced
10 ounces bourbon
1 (20-ounce) bottle whiskey sour
mix
6 ounces club soda

Mix all ingredients except bourbon, sour mix, and club soda. Chill overnight. At serving time add other ingredients (bourbon, sour mix, and club soda). Serve over ice.

Mrs. Herman Fletcher (Anne)

BRIDE'S PUNCH

Yield: 1 gallon

1 (12-ounce) can frozen orange
juice, undiluted
1 (6-ounce) can frozen
lemonade, undiluted
2 cups tea, strong, unsweetened, and chilled
2 cups sugar, or to taste

1 (46-ounce) can pineapple
juice, chilled
1 quart ginger ale, chilled

Put all ingredients except ginger ale into a gallon container; finish filling the container with water. Store in refrigerator. At serving time, add 1 quart ginger ale to punch mixture.

NOTE: This was a recipe from Miss Onetta Varner, a home economics teacher at Newnan High School for many years.

Mrs. Robert H. Shell (Mary)

WASSAIL

Yield: 50 punch cup servings

2 cups water
1 tablespoon ginger
1 tablespoon nutmeg
6 whole cloves
6 whole allspice
2 sticks cinnamon
1 gallon apple cider

3 cups sugar
1 1/2 cups firmly packed brown
  sugar
1 cup brandy or to taste

Cook first six ingredients in 6-quart boiling pot or even better, cook them in a crock pot, letting the spices simmer all day. Next add the following three ingredients and heat, stirring the sugar to be sure that it dissolves. Simmer over low heat for 5 to 10 minutes. Be sure it's hot before the party. Pour into punch bowl and add the 1 cup brandy, or whatever amount is desired. Leave whole spices in the punch bowl. It adds originality.

NOTE: Historically, "Wassail" was a salutation of wishing health and happiness to a person in England. The wassail bowl adds distinction to every party.

Mrs. Jack Camp, Jr. (Elizabeth)

****

Make milk more appealing to children by adding something tasty. For banana milk, add a mashed banana and 1/3 cup sugar or corn syrup to 1 quart milk. For peanutty milk, add 1/3 cup peanut butter, a pinch of salt, and 1/3 cup sugar or corn syrup to 1 quart milk.

FROSTED COFFEE

Yield: 50 servings

1 gallon water
1 pound coffee
2 cups sugar
1 pint whipping cream,
   whipped

2 gallons vanilla ice cream

It is best to use a glass or porcelain container for making coffee. Make 1 gallon strong coffee, using 1 gallon water and 1 pound (34-35 tablespoons) of coffee. Tie coffee in a loose bag and boil in the water for 6 to 10 minutes. Remove bag and discard. Add 2 cups sugar while coffee is hot. Cool. Add 1 pint whipped cream. This mixture may be stored in the refrigerator for 1 to 2 days.

About 30 minutes before serving, cut the ice cream into big pieces and add to the coffee. Continue stirring coffee-ice cream mixture while serving.

NOTE: Since all measurements are even, it is easy to cut down the recipe to serve fewer. Optional additions: add a little milk if the punch has too strong a coffee flavor; add 2 or 3 teaspoons vanilla extract for extra flavoring.

Mrs. George T. Hull (June)
Paducah, Kentucky

****

Make fancy sugar lumps for tea by dropping tiny bits of lemon juice on the sugar cubes. Be careful not to dissolve the sugar! Instead of lemon juice, try orange juice, lime juice, or brandy.

SALLY'S BANANA PUNCH

Yield: 25 servings

6 large bananas, mashed
1 (6-ounce) can frozen lemon
juice, undiluted
1 (6-ounce) can frozen orange
juice, undiluted

7 cups water
4 cups sugar or to taste
3 quarts ginger ale
Assorted frozen fruit

Mix first five ingredients well and freeze until serving time. Crush enough to fill punch bowl one-half full. Add ginger ale to fill bowl 3/4 full and fizz punch. Float frozen mixed fruit on top.

NOTE: Can be frozen in ice trays for children to enjoy as snacks.

Mrs. Thomas R. Kerley (Lynda)
Lexington, Kentucky

SURPRISE PUNCH
Delightfully refreshing

Yield: Approximately 25 servings

1 to 2 quarts reconstituted
orange juice, chilled
2 large bottles Wink, chilled

Strawberries, sliced

Placed sliced strawberries in the bottom of a punch bowl. Add orange juice and Wink. Stir and serve immediately.

NOTE: A frozen punch ring containing strawberries is a lovely addition to this sparkling punch.

Mrs. Ronald Duffey (Lynn)

51

SLUSH

Yield: Approximately 20 (8-ounce) servings

1 (46-ounce) can pineapple
   juice
1 (46-ounce) can pineapple-
   grapefruit juice
1 (6-ounce) can frozen
   lemonade concentrate
1 lemonade can full of water

2 quarts ginger ale, or 1 quart
   ginger ale and 1 quart Sauterne or champagne, chilled
Food coloring (optional)

Mix first 4 ingredients. Place in freezer 8 to 10 hours, stirring often. Do not freeze hard; it should be "slushy." When ready to serve, pour in chilled ginger ale and/or Sauterne. Pour into punch cups. If served in a punch bowl, ice is unnecessary as long as it does not have to stand too long. If using unsweetened fruit juices, add 1/4 to 1/2 cup sugar.

NOTE: This is a delightful way to welcome luncheon guests on a hot day — with a silver cupful. It is equally good as an appetizer beverage in any type of weather.

Mrs. John P. Woods, Jr. (Elizabeth)

BANANA BANSHEE

Yield: 1 serving

1 jigger crème de banana
1 jigger white crème de cacao

1 jigger light coffee cream

Shake with ice and strain into chilled glass, or serve over ice.

TANGY FRUIT PUNCH

Yield: 40 (6-ounce) servings

2 (6-ounce) cans frozen
  lemonade concentrate
1 (46-ounce) can pineapple
  juice
1 (46-ounce) can orange
  juice
2 quarts water
2 cups sugar
1 tablespoon almond extract

1 teaspoon vanilla extract
1 to 2 (28-ounce) bottles
  ginger ale

Combine the first seven ingredients; chill. Add ginger ale when ready to serve.

Mrs. J. R. Vaughn
Doraville, Georgia

ALEX-NOG
A potent after-dinner drink

Yield: 27 servings

2 ounces Benedictine
19 ounces crème de cocoa
16 ounces rum

24 ounces brandy
48 ounces whipping cream

Prepare one day ahead. Mix all ingredients and store in refrigerator. Pack glasses with ice and put in freezer. Shake drink mix and serve in the iced glasses.

NOTE: Half and half may be substituted for whipping cream in part or totally.

Mrs. John Killebrew (Candy)
Lookout Mountain, Tennessee

WEDDING PUNCH

Yield: 50 servings

3 gallons water
3 (3-ounce) packages lemon-
flavored gelatin (straw-
berry may be used instead)
6 cups sugar
3 (46-ounce) cans pineapple
juice

5 (6-ounce) cans frozen orange
juice
3 (6-ounce) cans frozen lemonade
3 quarts ginger ale

DO NOT MAKE IN A METAL CONTAINER. USE A CHURN OR GLASS CONTAINER.

Measure water in gallon jugs. Take out 3 cups of water and bring to a boil. Add gelatin and sugar and stir until dissolved. Add all the juices. Add remainder of the water. Mix well. Let set for 3 to 4 hours. Add ice and ginger ale when ready to serve.

Mrs. Ellis Crook (Patricia)

BILL'S BLOODY MARY

Yield: 8 servings

1 (46-ounce) can V-8 juice
1 1/2 cups vodka
6 ounces lemon juice
1 ounce worcestershire
sauce

1/2 ounce Tabasco
8 dashes lemon pepper
4 dashes salt

Mix all ingredients. Pour over ice and sprinkle with salt.

William E. Anderson

BLUE TAIL FLY I

Yield: 1 serving

2 jiggers blue curacao
1 jigger white crème de
cacao

1 jigger coffee cream

Shake and strain into chilled glass.

BLUE TAIL FLY II

Yield: 2 servings

2 jiggers blue curacao
1 jigger white crème de
cacao

1/2 cup soft vanilla ice cream
1/2 cup crushed ice

Put all ingredients into blender and process until slushy.

DAIQUIRIS FOR A CROWD

Yield: 18 to 20 servings

2 (6-ounce) cans frozen
lemonade
2 (6-ounce) cans frozen
limeade

2 (46-ounce) cans pineapple
juice
1 quart rum

Combine all ingredients and freeze in freezer until slushy.
Serve with a sprig of mint.

Mrs. Toby Silberman (Betsy)
Lookout Mountain, Tennessee

FROZEN WHISKEY SOUR
Do ahead-freezes well

Yield: 20 small or
10 generous
servings

1 (12 ounce) can frozen
lemonade
1 (6-ounce) can frozen
orange juice
3/4 cup sugar

2 cups bourbon
5 cups water

Combine all ingredients and mix well to dissolve juices and sugar. Put in freezer. Remains slushy for days in freezer. Garnish with cherry and orange slice to serve.

Pamela Hough
Fort Lauderdale, Florida

SNOW CAP

Yield: Any number desired

Equal parts of each:
Whipping cream (or
substitute half and half)
Gin

Crème de cacao

Make a day ahead and chill. Pack mint julep cups with ice and chill in freezer. Shake drink well and pour over ice to serve. So easy a husband can fix it!

Mrs. John Killebrew (Candy)
Lookout Mountain, Tennessee

★ ## MINT JULEP OR TEA SYRUP

Syrup will keep for weeks in the refrigerator

Yield: 4 1/2 quarts

Rinds of 12 lemons,
  juice removed
4 quarts water
2 handfuls fresh mint

Juice from the 12 lemons
2 1/2 to 3 cups sugar

SYRUP: Simmer the first 3 ingredients for 15 minutes, but do not boil. Strain and discard the mint and rinds. To the remaining syrup add the juice from 12 lemons and 2 1/2 to 3 cups sugar.

MINT JULEPS: Add a small amount of bourbon to syrup and pour into chilled julep cups packed with ice.

ICED TEA: Add syrup to taste to unsweetened tea.

PUNCH: Mix syrup with strong, unsweetened tea and pineapple juice. Adjust amounts of each to taste.

Mrs. Rob Healy (Betsy)
Lookout Mountain, Tennessee

BLUE MOON

Yield: 3 servings

1 cup vanilla
  ice cream
4 ounces blue curacao
2 ounces gin

5 drops bitters
3 to 4 drops blue food
  coloring

Blend all ingredients. Garnish drinks with a cherry.

HOT BUTTERED RUM
Fantastic!

Yield: 36 servings

1 pound butter, no
   substitute
1 pound box dark brown
   sugar
1 pound box powdered sugar

1 quart vanilla ice cream

Cream butter, brown sugar, and powdered sugar. Add ice cream, mixing gently. Put into freezer containers. Freeze. To serve; in a mug put 2 to 3 tablespoons butter rum batter and 1 jigger rum. Add boiling water to fill. Stir and serve.

NOTE: Recipe may be halved or quartered.

Mrs. H.G. Boone (Nancy)

STRAWBERRY DAIQUIRI

Yield: 6 to 8 servings

1 (6-ounce) can frozen
   lemonade
1 can rum (use lemonade
   can)
Crushed ice to
   fill blender

Powdered sugar to taste
Strawberries-fresh or
   1 (10-ounce) package frozen

Put all ingredients in blender and process. Garnish each drink with an additional fresh strawberry if available.

Mike Brazeal
Columbia, South Carolina

INSTANT SPICED TEA MIX

Yield: Approximately 2 cups
dry mix

1 (9-ounce) jar Tang
1/2 cup sugar
1/2 package lemonade
    mix (dry)
1/2 teaspoon cinnamon

1/4 teaspoon ground cloves
1/4 cup instant tea

Mix ingredients and store in moisture-proof container. To serve: mix 1 1/2 to 2 teaspoons mix with a cup of hot water.

Mrs. Carl E. Williams (Eddy)

SPICED TEA

Yield: 3 quarts

1 1/2 quarts boiling water
1 cup sugar
2 cups apple juice
3 cups pineapple juice
Juice of 2 lemons
(approximately 4 table-
    spoons)

Juice of 3 oranges (approxi-
    mately 1 cup)
1 teaspoon whole cloves
3 to 4 sticks cinnamon
3 tea bags

Combine all ingredients in saucepan. Simmer 15 minutes. Remove tea bags, strain, and serve hot. Makes 3 quarts.

Mrs. John Goodrum (Marsha)

※※※※※※※※※※※※※

Add celery salt, lemon juice, basil, and worcestershire sauce to tomato juice. Serve ice cold with celery stirrers.

FROSTED ORANGE

A nutritious, refreshing drink for children and adults!

Yield: 4 (10-ounce) servings

1 (6-ounce) can frozen
  orange juice
1 cup water
1 cup milk

1/2 cup sugar
1/4 to 1/2 teaspoon vanilla
  extract

Put all ingredients into blender. Fill rest of blender with ice cubes. Blend until ice is crushed and drink is frothy.

Mrs. William F. Lee, Jr. (Susan)

MARY KATE'S TOMATO JUICE

Tangy

Yield: 4 quarts

1 gallon tomato juice
2 teaspoons celery salt
1/2 teaspoon Tabasco sauce
1/2 teaspoon worcestershire
  sauce

4 teaspoons salt
1 teaspoon onion salt
1/2 cup sugar

Combine all ingredients in a large pot. Bring to a boil and seal in jars or freeze.

Mrs. Mike Spitler (Rita)

※※※※※※※※※※※※※※

Save the juices from canned fruits. Combine several kinds and add orange juice and/or ginger ale to make a great punch for children.

Breads

BREADS

Breads Chapter Design: "Universal" Bread Maker (1910), Burl Bread Bowl (circa 1800)

ANGEL BISCUITS I

Can store covered in refrigerator for days

Oven: 400° 12 minutes   Yield: Approximately 4 dozen biscuits

5 cups flour
1 teaspoon baking soda
1 teaspoon salt
1 tablespoon baking powder
2 tablespoons sugar

3/4 cup shortening
1 yeast cake, or 1 package
yeast, dissolved in 1/2 cup
lukewarm water
2 cups buttermilk

Mix dry ingredients. Cut in shortening and add yeast and buttermilk, mixing well. Roll dough out on lightly floured surface. Cut with small biscuit cutter. Bake on greased sheet in pre-heated 400° oven for 12 minutes or until golden brown.

Mrs. Chuck Moates (Alice Ann)

ANGEL BISCUITS II

Very light

Oven: 450° 10 minutes

Yield: Approximately 4 dozen
2-inch biscuits

5 cups sifted self-rising flour
1/3 cup sugar
1 teaspoon baking soda
1 cup shortening

2 packages yeast dissolved in
1/4 cup warm water
2 cups buttermilk

Combine flour, soda, and sugar; cut in shortening and stir in yeast and buttermilk. Be sure to mix well. Keep covered in refrigerator at least an hour or two before using. Roll out and cut as desired. Place on greased pan. Let rise for 2 hours. Bake at 450° for about 10 minutes.

NOTE: Dough will keep in refrigerator as long as a week.

Mrs. M. H. Holden
Dublin, Georgia

ANGEL BISCUITS III

Perfect for party ham biscuits because they won't crumble

Oven: 400° 20 minutes

Yield: 4 to 5 dozen large biscuits or 6 dozen small biscuits

1 1/2 packages yeast
5 tablespoons warm water
5 cups sifted all-purpose flour
2 tablespoons baking powder
1/4 teaspoon soda

2 tablespoons sugar
1/2 teaspoon salt
1 cup shortening
1 1/2 cups buttermilk

Dissolve yeast in warm water. Sift dry ingredients together, then cut shortening into the flour mixture. Add buttermilk and yeast. Knead lightly—**do not let rise**. Roll out and cut with a round biscuit cutter. Cut almost through center of biscuit with a knife and fold over to form a pocketbook shape. Bake for 20 minutes at 400°. Brush with melted butter after baking.

Mrs. Irwin H. Pike (Helen)

CHARLOTTE'S CHEESE BISCUITS

Oven: 450° 10 to 15 minutes

Yield: Approximately 4 dozen

2 1/2 to 3 cups sifted self-rising flour
1 1/2 cups grated New York State sharp cheese
1 cup vegetable shortening
1 cup milk

Sift 2 1/2 cups flour into a large bowl, add other ingredients in order, mixing after each addition. Dough should be sticky. Add more flour if necessary. Turn out onto floured surface. Roll 1/2 inch thick and cut with biscuit cutter. Place on ungreased cookie sheet. May be frozen at this point and kept in bags in freezer. Bake at 450° for 10 to 15 minutes or until **very lightly** browned. May be baked frozen — adjust time accordingly, but should not take longer than 15 minutes.

Mrs. Dennis Simpson (Jan)

LEMON BREAD
Great to wrap and give at Christmas instead of fruitcake; freezes well

Oven: 350° 1 hour   Yield: 1 loaf

1/2 cup solid shortening   1/2 teaspoon salt
1 cup sugar   1/2 cup milk
2 eggs, beaten   1/2 cup nuts
1 2/3 cups all-purpose flour   Grated peel of 1 lemon
1 teaspoon baking powder

Topping:

1/4 cup sugar   1/4 cup lemon juice

Cream shortening with sugar; add eggs. Sift flour, measure, and sift again with baking powder and salt. Alternately add flour mixture and milk to shortening mixture, blending well. Stir in nuts and lemon peel. Pour into 9x5-inch loaf pan. Bake at 350° for 1 hour.

Combine 1/4 cup sugar with 1/4 cup lemon juice and pour over loaf while hot. Let cool and remove from pan. Will have a nice lemony crust!

Mrs. William Donald Tomlinson (Jane)

❉❉❉❉❉❉❉❉❉❉❉❉❉

Buy 1 pound of any inexpensive margarine and soften it in a bowl. With a hand mixer, whip the margarine until it changes color. Add 1 cup buttermilk and continue to whip. This will make 1 1/2 pounds of really fluffy, fresh, and tasty whipped margarine.

For different breakfast biscuits, fry several pieces of bacon until crisp. Crumble the bacon and stir into the dry ingredients of a basic biscuit or muffin recipe. Mix and bake as recipe directs; then serve hot with butter.

★
SWEET POTATO BISCUITS
Good with ham

Oven: 400° 25 to 30 minutes   Yield: 1 1/2 to 2 dozen

1 cup all-purpose flour
1/2 teaspoon salt
3 teaspoons baking powder
4 tablespoons solid shortening

1 cup cooked sweet potatoes,
   mashed
1/2 cup milk

Sift dry ingredients together. Cut in shortening. Add mashed potatoes. Add enough milk to make firm dough but not too stiff. Roll out on floured cutting board, then cut with biscuit cutter. Place in greased biscuit pan and bake at 400° for 25 to 30 minutes until browned.

Mrs. C. B. Cochran (Louise)

DATE NUT BREAD

Oven: 350° 1 hour   Yield: 1 loaf

1 cup chopped dates
1 cup sugar
2 tablespoons shortening
1 cup boiling water
2 1/4 cups all-purpose flour

1 teaspoon soda
1 teaspoon salt
1 teaspoon baking powder
1 cup chopped nuts
1 egg

Put dates, sugar, and shortening into a bowl. Pour boiling water over mixture and cool. Sift flour with soda, salt, and baking powder. Mix with dates. Add nuts and mix well. Add egg last, mix thoroughly, and pour into a greased 9x5x3-inch loaf pan. Bake one hour at 350°.

Mrs. Everett Bryant (Mary)

❊❊❊❊❊❊❊❊❊❊❊❊

Bananas give pancakes a mellow delectable flavor. Add 2 cups diced bananas to pancake batter and bake as usual.

PORTUGUESE SWEET BREAD

Oven: 350° 25 minutes   Yield: 3 to 5 loaves

2 packages dry yeast
1 1/2 cups sugar
1 cup scalded milk
1 stick butter
1 1/4 teaspoons salt

3 eggs, beaten
1/4 teaspoon lemon juice
Yellow food coloring
6 to 7 cups flour

Dissolve yeast in 1/3 cup lukewarm water. Combine sugar, milk, butter, and salt in a sauce pan until butter is melted. Cool to lukewarm, then add beaten eggs. Add lemon juice and food coloring and blend well. Add this mixture to flour and knead until smooth, about 10 minutes. The dough should turn loose from side of bowl. Let dough rise, covered, until doubled. Place in pans and let it rise until doubled again. For variation, dough may be made into pie tin loaves, small rolls, or braided in wreath shape then topped with powdered sugar. Bake at 350° about 25 minutes.

NOTE: My husband's mother came from the Azores Islands as an immigrant. She brought this recipe with her. At Easter, she places a coin in one loaf and the person who finds it has good fortune.

Mrs. Joseph M. Fagundes (Betty Ann)
Senoia, Georgia

※※※※※※※※※※※※※

To make croutons, melt 6 tablespoons of butter with 1/2 teaspoon seasoned salt. When butter is hot, sauté 1 cup bread cubes until lightly browned on all sides. Drain on paper towel.

Melt 1 stick butter, then add 1/2 teaspoon garlic powder and 1/4 teaspoon each of thyme, oregano, and basil. Simmer 20 minutes; then brush on 2 loaves of French bread.

BANANA BREAD

Delicious breakfast bread; very moist

Oven: 300° 1 hour   Yield: 1 large loaf or 2 small loaves

1 stick butter	2 cups flour
1 cup sugar	1/2 teaspoon soda
2 eggs	1/2 teaspoon vanilla extract
3 bananas, mashed	1 cup nuts

Cream butter and sugar together. Add eggs and beat well. Add mashed bananas, flour, soda, vanilla, and nuts. Grease and flour 1 large or 2 small loaf pans. Pour dough into pan. Bake for 1 hour or until brown at 300°.

Mrs. Irwin H. Pike (Helen)

PUMPKIN BREAD I

Oven: 350° 1 hour   Yield: 2 regular-size loaves or 4 small loaves

4 eggs	1 cup nuts (optional)
1 cup cooking oil	3 cups sugar
2/3 cup water	2 teaspoons baking soda
1 (1-pound) can pumpkin	1 1/2 teaspoons salt
3 1/2 cups flour	1 1/2 teaspoons cinnamon
Pinch of cloves (optional)	1 1/2 teaspoons nutmeg

Beat eggs; add oil, water, and the can of pumpkin. Mix well. Add the dry ingredients and mix well. Pour into generously greased and floured pans. Bake at 350° for at least 1 hour. Test with toothpick. If still moist, try another 15 minutes. Let cool 20 minutes in pans, then remove onto cake racks until completely cool.

Mrs. Jack Slavin (Ruth)
New York, New York

PUMPKIN BREAD II
Men love this!

Oven: 300° 1 hour   Yield: 2 loaves

1 (16-ounce) can pumpkin   1 1/2 teaspoons salt
   (2 cups)   1 1/2 teaspoons ground
1 cup oil   allspice
4 eggs   1 1/2 teaspoons nutmeg
3 1/2 cups flour   2 teaspoons cinnamon
3 cups sugar   1/2 cup chopped nuts
1/2 teaspoon baking soda   (optional)

Combine pumpkin, oil, and eggs. Sift together dry ingredients. Combine two mixtures, blending thoroughly. Pour into 2 greased 9x5x3-inch loaf pans and bake at 300° for 1 hour. For variation, add 1/2 cup chopped nuts per loaf.

Mrs. Charles F. Colbert, III (Pat)
Pittsburgh, Pennsylvania

ZUCCHINI BREAD
Enjoy one loaf today; freeze the second for later.

Oven: 325° 1 hour   Yield: 2 loaves

3 eggs   1 teaspoon salt
1 cup cooking oil   1 teaspoon baking soda
2 cups sugar   3 1/2 teaspoons cinnamon
1 teaspoon vanilla extract   1/4 teaspoon baking powder
2 cups raw zucchini, peeled,   1/2 cup nuts, chopped
   grated, and drained
3 cups all-purpose flour, sifted

Beat eggs until foamy. Add oil, sugar, and vanilla. Mix well; stir in grated zucchini. Sift flour with salt, soda, cinnamon, and baking powder. Add to egg mixture and blend well. Fold in nuts. Pour into 2 greased 9x5x3-inch loaf pans and bake in a preheated oven at 325° for 1 hour.

Harry C. Tysinger

69

SWEDISH LIMPA BREAD
A traditional Christmas bread

Oven: 375° 30 to 35 minutes

Yield: 2 loaves

2 packages active dry yeast
1 1/2 cups warm water
 (105° to 115°)
1/2 cup molasses
1/3 cup sugar
2 teaspoons salt
1 tablespoon shortening

1 1/2 teaspoons anise seed
2 tablespoons grated orange
 peel
2 1/2 cups medium rye flour
2 1/2 cups all-purpose flour
Corn meal

Dissolve yeast in warm water in mixing bowl. Stir in molasses, sugar, salt, shortening, anise seed, orange peel, and rye flour. Beat until smooth. Stir in enough all-purpose flour to make dough easy to handle (dough will be sticky).

Turn dough onto slightly floured surface. Cover; let rest 10 to 15 minutes. Knead until smooth and elastic, about 5 minutes. Place in greased bowl; turn greased side up. Cover, let rise in warm place until double, about 1 hour. Dough is ready if an indentation remains when touched. Punch down dough; round up and let rise until double, about 40 minutes.

Grease baking sheet; sprinkle with corn meal. Punch down dough; divide in half. Shape each half into a round, slightly flat loaf. Place loaves in opposite corners of baking sheet. Let rise 1 hour.

Heat oven to 375°. Bake until loaves sound hollow when tapped, 30 to 35 minutes, remove from baking sheet; cool on wire racks.

Mrs. Eugene F. Secor (Martha)

❋❋❋❋❋❋❋❋❋❋❋❋❋

To substitute in a recipe calling for "lard," use 1 1/4 cups vegetable shortening for 1 cup lard.

MORAVIAN SUGAR CAKE
An original Moravian recipe that is very special

Oven: 375° 20 to 30 minutes   Yield: 2 (9x13x2-inch) cakes

1 package dry yeast	1 cup water that potatoes
1/2 cup warm water	were cooked in
1 cup unseasoned mashed	2 eggs, well-beaten
potatoes	5 cups all-purpose flour, sifted
1 cup sugar	1 cup butter
1/4 cup butter	Brown sugar
1/2 cup shortening	Cinnamon (optional)
1 teaspoon salt	Pecan pieces (optional)

Dissolve 1 package yeast in 1/2 cup warm water. Mix 1 cup mashed potatoes, sugar, 1/4 cup butter, 1/2 cup shortening, and 1 teaspoon salt. When lukewarm, add 1 cup potato water and yeast mixture.

Set first mixture aside and let rise in warm place until spongy. Beat in 2 well-beaten eggs and sifted all-purpose flour to make a soft dough. Let rise until double in bulk. Punch down and divide dough in half.

Spread dough evenly into 2 greased 9x13x2-inch pans. Let rise until double in bulk. Make holes with fingers in rows down dough. Fill with dots of butter (about 1 cup) and brown sugar. Be generous. Dust with cinnamon and pecan pieces if desired.

Bake at 375° for 20 to 30 minutes. Remove cakes from pans and cool on racks. Serve cakes, cut into squares, either warm or cold. If preferred, 4 (9-inch) cake pans may be substituted for the 2 (9x13x2-inch) pans. Cakes may be frozen after baking.

Mrs. James W. Roberts (Sue)

QUICK COFFEE CAKE

Oven: 375° 30 minutes   Yield: 20 to 24 servings

Filling and Topping:

4 tablespoons butter, melted   4 tablespoons flour
1 cup walnuts, chopped   1 teaspoon cinnamon
1 cup light brown sugar

Cake:

1/4 cup butter, softened   2 teaspoons baking powder
1 cup sugar   Pinch salt
2 eggs   1/2 cup milk
1 1/2 cups flour

FILLING AND TOPPING: Mix all ingredients and set aside.

CAKE: Cream butter and sugar together; then beat in eggs, one at a time. After measuring flour, take out 1/4 cup of the measured amount and add the baking powder to it, mixing together. Alternately add milk and the rest of the flour and salt. Fold in the flour and baking powder mixture last. Pour half of the batter into a greased 8x12-inch baking dish. Sprinkle half the nut mixture over the top, pour on remaining batter, and top with remaining nut mixture. Bake at 375° for 30 minutes.

Mrs. Benny N. Grant (Diane)

✸✸✸✸✸✸✸✸✸✸✸✸✸

Children are fascinated with food served in unusual shapes. Cut bread with a rabbit or other shaped cookie cutter for a fun sandwich. Keep a supply in the freezer ready to use at any time.

SOUR CREAM BREAKFAST CAKE

Oven: 350° 45 minutes   Yield: 1 bundt cake

1/2 cup butter or margarine
1 cup sugar
1 cup sour cream
2 eggs

1 teaspoon baking powder
1 teaspoon baking soda
2 cups all-purpose flour
1 teaspoon vanilla extract

Topping:

1/2 cup brown sugar
1 teaspoon cinnamon

1/4 cup chopped nuts

Cream first 4 ingredients well. Add baking powder, soda, flour, and vanilla extract. Combine thoroughly. Pour half the batter into a greased bundt pan. Combine the topping ingredients and sprinkle half over the batter in the pan. Pour on remaining batter and the rest of the topping. Bake at 350° for 45 minutes. Cool in pan for 10 minutes.

Mrs. Dan B. Umbach (Marie)

★   CAJUN HUSH PUPPIES
Great with fried catfish

Yield: 4 servings

1 1/2 cups plain corn meal
1/2 cup flour
1 teaspoon baking powder
1/2 teaspoon baking soda
1 teaspoon salt

1 egg
1 onion, chopped
1 cup buttermilk
1 large Jalapeño pepper,
   finely chopped (optional)

Mix all ingredients in a large bowl. Drop with a large spoon into **hot** oil in a deep fat fryer. Cook until golden brown, turning with a long wooden spoon.

NOTE: This is a recipe originating in the South Louisiana Bayou Country.

Benny N. Grant

★ **CRACKLIN' CORNBREAD**
Necessary with a Southern vegetable dinner!

Oven: 425° 15 to 20 minutes   Yield: 24 muffins

2 cups cornbread batter
2 tablespoons sugar (omit if using a sweet cornbread mix)
1 1/2 cups cracklins

Make cornbread by usual recipe. Stir in sugar and cracklins, making mixture quite thick with cracklins. Fill muffin cups and bake according to cornbread directions or 425° approximately 15 to 20 minutes until browned.

Mrs. John P. Woods, Jr. (Elizabeth)

SOUR CREAM COFFEE CAKE I

Oven: 350° 40 minutes   Yield: 8 servings

1 cup sour cream
1/2 teaspoon baking soda
1 cup butter or margarine
1 cup sugar

2 eggs
1 teaspoon vanilla extract
1 1/2 cups flour
1 1/2 teaspoons baking powder

Filling and Topping:

1/2 cup brown sugar
1/2 cup nuts, chopped

2 teaspoons cinnamon

Mix together sour cream and soda; set aside for 1 hour. Cream butter and sugar, then add eggs and vanilla. Beat well. Add sour cream mixture, then stir in flour and baking powder which have been sifted together. Beat well. Batter will be fluffy. Combine brown sugar, nuts and cinnamon. Put half of batter in a greased 9-inch layer pan, then top with half of the filling; put remainder of batter on top of this, then remainder of topping. Bake at 350° for 40 minutes.

Mrs. Frank H. Barron (Ruth)

SOUR CREAM COFFEE CAKE II

Oven: 350° 25 to 30 minutes   Yield: 12 servings

Cake:

1 stick margarine
1 cup sugar
2 large eggs
1 teaspoon vanilla extract
2 cups all-purpose flour
1 teaspoon soda

1 teaspoon baking powder
1 cup sour cream
1/3 cup brown sugar
1/2 cup chopped nuts
1 teaspoon cinnamon

Icing:

1 tablespoon milk
1 teaspoon vanilla extract

Powdered sugar

CAKE: Cream margarine and sugar well. Add eggs, one at a time, beating after each. Add vanilla extract. Add flour, baking powder, and soda, which have been sifted together alternately with the sour cream. Put into greased 9x12-inch pan. Mix together the brown sugar, nuts, and cinnamon and sprinkle over the batter. Bake at 350° for 25 to 30 minutes.

ICING: In a small bowl, add milk, vanilla extract, and enough powdered sugar to make an icing which can be drizzled over the cake while it is still warm.

Mrs. Ellis Crook (Pat)

****

To save time and make muffins uniform in size, use an ice cream scoop to measure muffin batter.

The cover of the cake saver is just the right thing to cover a pan of rolls while they are rising.

★ ## DIXIE CORN BREAD

Oven: 450° 20 to 25 minutes   Yield: 3 to 4 servings

1 1/2 cups enriched white   2 cups buttermilk
  corn meal   1 egg
3 tablespoons all-purpose flour   2 tablespoons bacon drippings
1 teaspoon salt   or butter, melted
1 teaspoon soda

Sift together dry ingredients; add buttermilk, egg, and drippings, mixing just until dry ingredients are moistened. Pour into a greased, hot 10-inch oven-proof skillet.

Bake in preheated hot oven (450°) 20 to 25 minutes. Serve warm, with butter.

Mrs. William F. Lee, Jr. (Susan)

MEXICAN BREAD

Oven: 350° 45 to 60 minutes   Yield: 10 to 12 servings

1 1/2 cups self-rising corn meal   1 teaspoon salt
3 eggs, beaten   3 Jalapeño peppers, seeded
1 cup creamed corn   and chopped
1 cup buttermilk   1 1/2 cups grated sharp cheese
2/3 cup oil   1 (4-ounce) can taco sauce

Mix all ingredients except cheese. Pour half of mixture into greased 10-inch square container. Spread half of cheese on top. Spread remaining mixture on top, ending with remaining cheese. Bake at 350° for 45-60 minutes or until done.

Mrs. Gayle Golden
Valdosta, Georgia

MEXICAN CORN BREAD I

Oven: 350° 25 minutes

Yield: 6 to 8 servings

3 cups self-rising corn meal
1 teaspoon salt
2 teaspoons baking powder
1 1/2 cups grated sharp cheese
1 cup cooking oil
3 eggs, slightly beaten

1 1/2 cups milk
1 large onion, chopped
1 (8-ounce) can whole kernel
    corn, drained
2 Jalapeño peppers, chopped

Combine all ingredients. Bake 25 minutes at 350° in an iron skillet or large Pyrex dish.

Mrs. John Goodrum (Marsha)

MEXICAN CORN BREAD II
A favorite with men

Oven: 325° 1 hour

Yield: 8 servings

1 1/2 pounds ground beef
1 1/2 cups self-rising corn meal
1 (16-ounce) can yellow
    cream-style corn
2 eggs
2 tablespoons chopped bell pepper

2 tablespoons chopped onion
3 Jalapeño peppers
1 cup sour cream
2/3 cup cooking oil
1 1/2 cups grated cheese

Brown beef and drain on paper towel. Mix all other ingredients together and add browned beef. Place in 1 large or 2 small well-greased skillets. Bake at 325° for 1 hour or until golden brown.

Mrs. Bobby Shell (Jean)
Senoia, Georgia

❊❊❊❊❊❊❊❊❊❊❊❊

Do not wriggle the cutter or glass around while cutting biscuits. This will cause the biscuits to topple while baking.

SPANISH CORNBREAD
May be prepared in advance

Oven: 400° 40 minutes   Yield: 6 servings

1 1/2 cups self-rising corn meal
1 medium onion, chopped
2 eggs
1 (8-ounce) carton sour cream
1 (8-ounce) can cream-style corn
3/4 cup cooking oil
Chopped Jalapeño peppers (optional)

Mix all ingredients together in a bowl. Coat a 9-inch square pan with bacon drippings and pour in mixture. Bake at 400° for 40 minutes.

Mrs. Howard G. Boone (Nancy)

★   ## SOUTHERN HOE CAKE
Perfect with fresh vegetables

Yield: 2 servings

2 rounded tablespoons self-rising corn meal
1 rounded tablespoon self-rising flour
1/4 cup water, or enough to make a thin batter
3 tablespoons cooking oil

Mix dry ingredients, then add water and mix well. Put cooking oil in small fryer or skillet (about 6 inches in diameter) and heat until it will cause the batter to fry. Pour batter into hot fryer, reduce heat to medium high and brown. When brown, turn with an egg turner and let other side brown. Take up and serve hot.

Mrs. V. J. Bruner (Ethel)

★ ## OLD-FASHIONED SPOON BREAD

Oven: 325° 45 minutes   Yield: 6 to 8 servings

1 pint milk   1/2 teaspoon salt
3/4 cup corn meal   3 eggs, separated
1 tablespoon butter

Scald milk; add meal and simmer until thick, about 5 minutes. Add butter and salt. Let cool. Add egg yolks, then fold in stiffly beaten egg whites. Put into a greased 1 1/2-quart casserole dish. Set casserole in a pan of warm water and bake in 325° oven for 45 minutes. Serve hot.

Mrs. James P. Reese, Jr. (Mary Ann)
Senoia, Georgia

★ ## SPOON BREAD I

Oven: 325° 45 to 60 minutes   Yield: 6 servings

1/2 cup corn meal   4 egg yolks, beaten
Dash of salt   4 egg whites, beaten
2 cups hot milk

Mix corn meal, salt, and milk. Cook until thick. Add egg yolks. Remove from heat. Fold in beaten whites. Pour into 8-inch square buttered pan. Bake 325° for 45 to 60 minutes.

Mrs. Warren Budd (Courtenay)

❋❋❋❋❋❋❋❋❋❋❋❋❋

Homemade baking powder: Combine 6 ounces cream of tartar, 2 2/3 ounces bicarbonate of soda, and 4 1/2 ounces flour in a bowl and mix well. Store in a tightly covered container.

★ **SPOON BREAD II**

Oven: 350° 35 minutes   Yield: 8 servings

1 1/3 teaspoons sugar   4 tablespoons butter
1 1/2 teaspoons salt   3 eggs
1 cup corn meal   1 tablespoon baking powder
  (waterground type)   1 1/3 cups milk
1 1/3 cups boiling water

Mix sugar and salt with corn meal and blend well. Pour boiling water over meal, stirring constantly. Add butter; let stand until cool. Beat eggs until light. Add eggs and baking powder to corn meal mixture. Add milk and pour mixture into a 2-quart buttered pan or baking dish. Place in a shallow pan of hot water in 350° (preheated) oven. Bake approximately 35 minutes.

NOTE: This recipe is from Christiana Campbell's Tavern in Williamsburg, Virginia.

Mrs. Will Haugen (Evelyn)

APPLE DRESSING
Delicious with roast turkey or other fowl

Oven: 350° 1 hour   Yield: 12 servings

2 quarts stale bread,   1 teaspoon salt
  shredded   1 teaspoon cinnamon
1 large jar applesauce   1 cup turkey or chicken broth
  (at least 2 pounds)   1 cup raisins
1/2 cup sugar   2 eggs, beaten

Mix all ingredients well in large pan. Mixture should be quite moist. Bake in large buttered pan or shallow casserole for 1 hour at 350°.

Mrs. Mike Spitler (Rita)

★   CHICKEN OR TURKEY DRESSING

Oven: 350° 30 minutes   Yield: 10 to 12 servings

6 cups corn bread crumbs   1/2 teaspoon salt
2 cups bread crumbs   1/4 teaspoon pepper
8 cups poultry stock   4 eggs, beaten
2 large onions, chopped   1/4 teaspoon garlic salt
1 cup celery, chopped

Mix cornbread and bread crumbs with poultry stock. Add rest of ingredients, mixing well. Pour into greased 9x13-inch baking dish. Bake at 350° for 30 minutes or until lightly brown.

Mrs. James T. Arnold (Flossie)

BRAN MUFFINS

Oven: 400° 20 minutes   Yield: 3 dozen

1 cup Nabisco 100% Bran   2 1/2 teaspoons soda
1/2 cup shortening   1/2 teaspoon salt
1 1/2 cups sugar   2 cups buttermilk
3 eggs   2 cups Kellogg All-Bran
2 1/2 cups all-purpose flour,   1 cup raisins
   sifted   1 cup chopped nuts

Pour 1 cup boiling water over 100% Bran and allow to cool. Cream shortening and sugar; add eggs one at a time, beating after each addition. Add flour, soda, salt, and buttermilk; mix well. Add cereal, raisins, and nuts. Stir only until well mixed. Half fill lightly greased muffin tins and bake at 400° for 20 minutes. This mixture will keep in the refrigerator for 5 weeks in a closed container. Just dip mixture out as needed; do not stir.

Miss Carrie May McElroy

ICEBOX MUFFIN MIX
A good breakfast bread

Oven: 400° 15 minutes   Yield: 3 dozen

1 cup Nabisco 100% Bran
1 cup boiling water
1 cup solid shortening
1 1/4 cups sugar
2 eggs
2 cups buttermilk

2 1/2 cups unsifted all-purpose
flour
2 1/2 teaspoons soda
1/2 teaspoon salt
2 cups Kellogg All-Bran

Soften 100% Bran in hot water and set aside. Blend shortening, sugar, and eggs in a large bowl, preferably with a cover. Add buttermilk, bran mixture, flour, soda, salt, and All-Bran. Mix well. Fill number of muffin tins needed and bake at 400° for 15 minutes. Cover remaining mixture and refrigerate. Never stir again even though ingredients seem to have settled. Just dip out amount needed. This mixture keeps well up to 6 weeks in the refrigerator.

Mrs. Lannie Hoyle (Derryl)
Macon, Georgia

GERMAN PANCAKES
Very light!

Yield: 2 servings

1 cup flour
1 cup milk
2 eggs

2 tablespoons sugar
1 teaspoon baking powder

Mix all ingredients well. Melt butter in large iron skillet. Pour in approximately 1/2 cup batter; tilt skillet to coat bottom. When top of pancake is set, turn and brown other side. Remove from pan. Fold pancake in half, then in half again. Stack on platter until all batter is cooked. Serve topped or filled with fresh or frozen berries.

Mrs. Wallace Mitchell (Jeri)

★ ## SWEET CORN MUFFINS
These tasty muffins freeze well

Oven: 450° 9 to 12 minutes   Yield: 1 1/2 dozen large muffins
                                      or 3 dozen small muffins

1 cup all-purpose flour   1/2 teaspoon salt
1/2 cup yellow corn meal   2 eggs
1/2 cup sugar   1/2 cup milk
1/2 cup butter, melted   1/2 teaspoon corn syrup
2 teaspoons baking powder

Mix first six ingredients. Combine eggs, milk, and syrup separately; mix the flour mixture and the milk mixture together. Grease muffin tins and fill each cup half full of batter. Bake 9 to 12 minutes or until brown at 450°.

Mrs. Walker Moody (Sally)

BETTY'S HOT CAKES

Yield: 10 servings

3 eggs   4 teaspoons baking powder if
3 cups buttermilk   flour is all-purpose or
1 teaspoon salt   2 teaspoons baking powder
3 tablespoons sugar   if flour is self-rising
Flour   6 tablespoons vegetable oil
1/2 teaspoon soda

Beat eggs. Add milk, salt, and sugar. Beat thoroughly. Add enough flour to make a batter consistency. Do not beat well. Hot cake batter should be slightly lumpy. Add soda and baking powder. Stir in oil.

NOTE: If any batter is left over, use batter to fry onion rings! Substitute corn meal for flour and use this recipe for egg bread.

Mrs. Elton Wall (Betty)
Macon, Georgia

83

BLUEBERRY PANCAKES

Yield: 4 servings

1 cup flour
2 teaspoons baking powder
3 eggs
1/2 teaspoon salt
3 tablespoons sugar

2 cups milk
1/2 stick margarine
1 (16-ounce) can blueberries
2 tablespoons powdered sugar

Sift flour with baking powder. Separate eggs. Mix egg yolks with salt, sugar, and milk. Add to flour. Stir until smooth. Very carefully stir in whipped egg whites. In large skillet, fry 4 big pancakes, one at a time, in hot margarine. Fold pancakes over and fill with heated blueberries. Sprinkle with powdered sugar.

Mrs. Thomas C. Jones (Carmen)

CRÊPE BATTER

Crêpes freeze well

Yield: 32 to 36 crêpes

4 eggs
1/4 teaspoon salt
2 cups flour

2 1/4 cups milk
1/4 cup butter, melted

In mixing bowl, combine eggs and salt. Gradually add flour alternately with milk, beating with electric mixer or whisk until smooth. Beat in melted butter. Refrigerate batter at least one hour. In a lightly greased crêpe pan over medium-high heat, pour 2 to 3 tablespoons batter. Turn crêpe when lightly browned and cook about 30 to 45 seconds on other side. Cool crêpes in a single layer on absorbent paper. When freezing, it is best to put a square of waxed paper between each crêpe and place them in freezer bags. To prevent breaking or cracking, "sandwich" the freezer bag of crêpes between two paper plates and staple or tape around the edge.

Mrs. Dan B. Umbach (Marie)

VELVET WAFFLES

Yield: 7 to 8 (7-inch) waffles

2 cups sifted all-purpose flour
3 teaspoons baking powder
3/4 teaspoon salt
2 tablespoons sugar, if desired

3 eggs, separated
1 3/4 cups milk
1/2 cup cooking oil

Sift flour with baking powder, salt, and sugar. Beat egg whites until stiff. Beat egg yolks; add milk and oil; pour into flour mixture. Beat until smooth. Fold in egg whites lightly, but thoroughly. Use 1/2 cup batter for each waffle.

Mrs. Welborn Davis (Mary)

ALL-BRAN ROLLS
Freezes very well

Oven: 400° 10 to 15 minutes

Yield: 6 dozen

3/4 cup sugar
1 cup shortening
1 1/2 teaspoons salt
1 cup All-Bran cereal
1 cup boiling water

2 eggs, well beaten
2 packages yeast
1 cup lukewarm water
6 1/2 cups flour

Put sugar, shortening, salt, and All-Bran in bowl and pour 1 cup of boiling water over them; stir until shortening is melted. Let stand until warm. Add eggs and mix well. Add yeast which has been dissolved in the lukewarm water. Add half the flour and beat until smooth, then add the rest of the flour and beat. Let rise about 1 hour; then chill in refrigerator several hours, preferably overnight. Roll our dough, cut and fold into pocketbook shape. Place on greased cookie sheet. Let rise until double in size — about 2 hours, or longer. Bake at 400° for 10 to 15 minutes.

Mrs. William F. Lee (Parky)

COUNTRY CINNAMON ROLLS
Delicious with morning coffee

Oven: 375° 12 to 15 minutes   Yield: 1 dozen rolls

Rolls:

1 package dry yeast
1/2 cup warm water
  (105° to 115°)
1 egg
1 tablespoon sugar
3 cups Bisquick baking mix

2 tablespoons butter or
  margarine, softened
1 tablespoon sugar
1 teaspoon cinnamon
3/4 cup raisins

Icing:

1 cup powdered sugar
1 tablespoon water

1/2 teaspoon vanilla extract

ROLLS: Dissolve yeast in warm water. Stir in egg, 1 tablespoon sugar, and the baking mix; beat vigorously. Turn dough onto well-floured board. Knead until slightly blistered, about 50 times. Roll dough into a rectangle, 12x10-inches; spread with butter. Mix 1 tablespoon sugar and the cinnamon; sprinkle over rectangle. Sprinkle raisins over sugar-cinnamon mixture. Roll up tightly, beginning at wide side. Seal well by pinching edge of dough into roll. Cut into 1-inch slices. Place slices cut side down in well-greased muffin cups. Cover; let rise 30 minutes. Heat oven to 375°. Bake 12 to 15 minutes. Immediately remove from pan. Let stand 5 minutes. Frost with icing and serve warm.

ICING: Mix ingredients until smooth.

Mrs. Brad Sears (Carolyn)

※※※※※※※※※※※※※

For great peanut butter and jelly sandwiches, cream the 2 ingredients together well, then spread. Children are happier when the peanut butter doesn't glue bread together.

SWEET ROLLS
Freezes well. Also good as dinner rolls.

Oven: 425° 10 to 15 minutes   Yield: Approximately 4 dozen

1/4 cup sugar	1/2 cup shortening
1/2 teaspoon salt	1 package yeast
1 egg	1/2 cup warm water
1/2 cup milk	3 3/4 cups all-purpose flour

Filling:

Melted margarine	Cinnamon
Brown sugar	Raisins

Icing:

1/2 to 3/4 box powdered sugar   Water
Vanilla extract to taste

In large mixing bowl, combine sugar, salt, and egg. Beat slightly. Heat milk (do not boil) and dissolve shortening in it. Dissolve yeast in warm water. Add liquids to mixing bowl and beat 1 to 2 minutes. Add flour gradually, beating well after each addition. Cover bowl and let rise in warm place about 1 hour or until doubled in bulk. Divide dough into 3 portions. Roll each out to 1/4-inch thickness in rectangular shape.

FILLING: Brush surface with melted margarine, sprinkle with brown sugar, cinnamon, and raisins. Roll up jellyroll-fashion, seal edges well, and cut each roll into 1-inch slices. Place slices on greased cookie sheet, cover, and let rise 1 hour. Uncover; bake at 425° for 10 to 15 minutes.

ICING: Mix powdered sugar, vanilla extract, and small amount of water for a thick icing. Frost each roll with 1 teaspoon icing. Serve warm or wrap and freeze.

NOTE: For dinner rolls, follow directions but omit filling and icing. After dough has risen, divide into manageable portions and roll to 1/4-inch thickness. Cut into desired shapes, brush with melted butter, place on greased cookie sheet, cover and let rise 1 hour. Bake at 425° for 10 to 15 minutes.

Mrs. Ewing Barnett (Ann)

EASY YEAST ROLLS
Can be refrigerated until ready to use

Oven: 350° 10 to 15 minutes   Yield: 24 medium rolls

1 cup boiling water   1 package yeast
1/4 cup shortening   1 egg
1/4 cup margarine   1 teaspoon salt
1/3 cup sugar   2 to 3 cups all-purpose flour

In a mixing bowl, pour the boiling water over the margarine and shortening. When the shortening and margarine have melted, add sugar. When liquid has cooled to lukewarm, add yeast and stir until dissolved. Add egg and salt to liquid. Sift flour into liquid, about 3/4 cup at a time. Add enough flour to make a soft dough. Let rise or put into refrigerator until ready to use. Make rolls. Let rise. Bake about 10 to 15 minutes at 350°.

Mrs. Ferrell Parrott (Emily)
Senoia, Georgia

HERB ROLLS
Great for buffet dinner

Oven: 425° 12 minutes   Yield: 6 servings

1/4 cup butter, melted   1/4 teaspoon onion flakes
1 1/2 teaspoons parsley flakes   1 (8-ounce) package refrig-
1/2 teaspoon dill seed   erated buttermilk biscuits

Preheat oven to 425°. Put butter, parsley flakes, dill seed, and onion flakes in a 9-inch pie pan. Blend well. Cut biscuits in quarters and swish each one in melted mixture. Arrange pieces touching in the pie pan. Bake in 425° oven for 12 minutes or until brown. Let stand a short time to absord the butter and seasonings.

Mrs. R. O. Jones II (Evelyn)

MASHED POTATO ROLLS
Foolproof!

Oven: 400° 8 minutes   Yield: 3 to 4 dozen

1 package dry yeast   1 teaspoon salt
1/2 cup lukewarm water   2/3 cup salad oil
1 cup mashed potatoes   1 cup milk, scalded
1/2 cup sugar   5 to 6 cups flour
2 eggs

Soak yeast in lukewarm water. In large bowl place potatoes, sugar, eggs, salt, salad oil, and milk. Mix together. Add yeast and flour to make a stiff dough. Place in greased bowl and cover. Place in refrigerator and use within 4 days. Punch down and knead slightly. Shape and let rise 1 1/2 hours or until double in bulk. Bake for 8 minutes at 400°.

Mrs. Irwin H. Pike (Helen)

QUICK DELICIOUS ROLLS

Oven: 450° 10 minutes   Yield: 1 dozen

2 cups self-rising flour   1 cup milk
4 tablespoons mayonnaise   1 teaspoon sugar

Mix all ingredients in a mixing bowl about 2 minutes. Fill muffin tins 2/3 full; bake 10 minutes or until golden brown at 450°. Delicious!

Victoria P. Hanson

❊ ❊ ❊ ❊ ❊ ❊ ❊ ❊ ❊ ❊ ❊ ❊ ❊

When making bread or rolls that call for scalded milk, use canned evaporated milk diluted with equal parts hot water. Saves time and is economical, too.

AUNT ELLIE'S REFRIGERATOR ROLLS

Oven: 400° 10 minutes

Yield: Approximately 3 dozen medium rolls

1/2 cup shortening
1/3 cup sugar
3/4 to 1 teaspoon salt
1/2 cup boiling water

1 package yeast
1/2 cup warm water
1 large egg, beaten
3 cups all-purpose flour, sifted

Blend shortening, sugar, salt, and water; let cool. Mix yeast with 1/2 cup warm water and let stand 5 minutes. Mix egg with flour; then combine all ingredients and mix well. Cover and refrigerate until thoroughly cooled, preferably overnight. Roll out a small amount of dough at a time. Cut with floured biscuit cutter, brush rounds with melted margarine, and fold over, pocketbook style. Place on a baking sheet and cover with wax paper. Let rise 1 to 1 1/2 hours or until double in size. Bake at 400° approximately 10 minutes or until lightly browned. These freeze well. To freeze, bake but do not brown well; when ready to use, thaw and bake until golden.

Mrs. John P. Woods, Jr. (Elizabeth)

VARIATION: Brush rolls with melted butter before baking. Dough will keep 2 weeks in refrigerator.

Mrs. Jeanne Benson
Athens, Georgia

****

For a glossy crust on bread, brush the top lightly with a mixture of one whole egg, an egg yolk, or egg white, plus 1 or 2 tablespoons of water immediately before baking. For a soft crust, brush the top with melted butter as soon as the bread is removed from the oven.

REFRIGERATOR ROLLS

Oven: 425° 12 to 15 minutes   Yield: 8 dozen small rolls

1 cup boiling water   2 eggs, beaten
1 cup solid shortening   2 packages dry yeast
1 cup sugar   1 cup lukewarm water
1 1/2 teaspoons salt   6 cups all-purpose flour, unsifted

Pour boiling water over shortening, sugar, and salt. Blend and cool. Add beaten eggs. Sprinkle yeast on lukewarm water and stir until dissolved. Combine with egg mixture, add flour, and blend well. Cover and place in refrigerator at least 4 hours, preferably overnight. Use a large bowl, for dough will rise. Dough will keep in refrigerator for a week to 10 days. About 3 hours before serving, roll into desired shape, using only enough extra flour for easy handling. Place on greased cookie sheet and allow to rise at room temperature, about 3 hours or until double in bulk. Bake at 425° for 12 to 15 minutes.

Mrs. Lindsey Barron (Genet)

ROLLS

Oven: 400° 25 minutes   Yield: 4 dozen

1 cup milk, heated   1 egg
3 tablespoons solid shortening   1 package yeast, dissolved in
1/2 cup sugar   1/2 cup warm water
1 teaspoon salt   4 cups all-purpose flour

To heated milk, add shortening, sugar, and salt. Cool. Add egg and yeast cake which has been dissolved in warm water. Add flour to make a soft dough and cover. After it has risen slightly, put covered dough in refrigerator (dough will continue to rise). Leave for 3 to 4 hours before working out for rolls. Cut with biscuit cutter, brush tops with butter, and fold over. Place in greased pan and bake at 400° about 25 minutes or until brown.

Mrs. Bob B. Mann (Frances)

91

YEAST ROLLS
Do ahead . . . freezes well!

Oven: 400° 15 minutes   Yield: 6 dozen

3/4 cup shortening
1/3 cup sugar
1 cup hot water
2 eggs, well beaten

2 packages yeast
1 cup cold water
6 cups flour
2 teaspoons salt

Cream shortening and sugar together. Add 1 cup of boiling water. Cool. When lukewarm, add beaten eggs and yeast dissolved in 1 cup cold water. Add flour; then add salt. Mix well Put into a greased bowl in refrigerator to rise. Cover. Let dough chill thoroughly, overnight if possible. Make rolls into desired shape and place on a greased cookie sheet. Brush with margarine. Let rise at least 2 hours or until rolls double in bulk. Bake at 400° for 15 minutes.

Mrs. William F. Lee (Parky)

CHEESE SQUARES
Great luncheon bread

Oven: 375° 15 minutes   Yield: 10 serving

1/2 pound butter
1/2 pound sharp yellow cheese
1 tablespoon cream
1/2 teaspoon salt

1 unbeaten egg white
Dash Tabasco sauce
1 loaf unsliced bread

Cream cheese and butter until smooth. Add unbeaten egg white, cream, salt, and Tabasco, and blend. Chill until mixture can be easily spread. Remove the crust from one loaf of unsliced bread and cut into one-inch cubes. Spread 5 sides with the cheese mixture and place 6th side down on cookie sheet Bake in 375° preheated oven for 15 minutes or until golden

Mrs. William E. Anderson (Dell

HERBED FRENCH BREAD

Oven: 350° 10 minutes   Yield: 4 to 6 servings

1/2 cup margarine
1 teaspoon parsley
1/4 teaspoon oregano
1/4 teaspoon dill

1 clove garlic, crushed, or
  garlic salt to taste
1 loaf French bread
Parmesan cheese

Cream margarine with seasonings. Spread in between slices of bread; sprinkle top with Parmesan cheese. Wrap bread in a blanket of foil, top uncovered. Bake 10 minutes at 350°.

Mrs. Billy Arnall (Linda)

MICKEY LIKES IT BREAD
Very nutritious

Oven: 350° 35 to 45 minutes   Yield: 4 loaves

4 cups milk
1/2 cup molasses
1/2 cup honey
1 cup wheat germ
1/2 cup salad oil

2 tablespoons salt
1/2 cup warm water
3 packages yeast
1 teaspoon sugar
12 cups whole wheat flour

Scald the milk. When it has cooled, add next 5 ingredients. Mix well and let stand 5 minutes. In a separate bowl, combine water, yeast, and sugar. Add to milk mixture and mix well. Stir in flour until dough is stiff enough to be kneaded on a floured surface. Put in large bowl, cover with damp tea towel and let rise until double in bulk (about 2 hours). Turn onto floured surface again and knead. Divide dough into four 9x5-inch loaf pans and let rise again until double in bulk. Bake at 350° 35 to 45 minutes or until loaves sound hollow when tapped. Let cool 10 minutes; turn onto wire rack to completely cool.

Mrs. J. B. Kopp (Lynn)
Corbin, Kentucky

WHITE BREAD

Oven: 375° 15 minutes
      350° 10 to 15 minutes

Yield: 4 to 5 loaves

2 teaspoons salt
1/2 cup melted butter
3/4 cup sugar
2 cups milk

2 packages yeast, softened in
   3/4 cup warm water
10 cups all-purpose flour,
   sifted and divided
3 eggs

Combine salt, butter, and sugar in a large bowl. Scald milk and pour over mixture. Stir; cool mixture to lukewarm. Soften yeast in warm water and stir until dissolved. Add to milk mixture. Add 5 cups flour and eggs to make a thick batter. Beat thoroughly. Add 3 cups flour and continue to beat. Dough should be a little sticky. If too sticky, stir in more flour. Let rest 5 to 10 minutes.

Sift some of remaining flour onto board. Sprinkle a little flour over dough ball and knead on floured surface with floured hands until satiny and smooth, about 10 minutes. Put in a greased bowl and turn to grease entire ball. Cover with a warm, damp cloth and let rise in a warm place until double in bulk, about 1 hour 15 minutes.

Punch down dough. With greased fingers, pull off enough dough to fill 4 (8 1/2 x 4 1/2 x 2 5/8-inch) loaf pans 1/3 full. Pull and shape each portion until smooth. Press gently to spread out in pans. Brush each loaf with melted margarine or shortening. Cover as before and let rise again until double in bulk, about 45 to 60 minutes.

Bake at 375° until brown on top, about 15 minutes. Lower heat to 350° and cook 10 to 15 minutes longer. Cool on wire racks.

NOTE: This bread freezes well. Wrap tightly in foil or freezer wrap.

Mrs. Charles M. Smith (Lynn)

Cakes & Frostings

CAKES

FROSTINGS

Cakes & Frostings Chapter Design: Round Cake Box (1883), Dodecahedral Cake Mould (1890)

APPLE CAKE
Serve with ice cream, whipped cream, or cheese slices

Oven: 350° 1 hour

Yield: 1 (9x13-inch) cake

1 cup corn oil
2 eggs
2 cups sugar
2 1/2 cups all-purpose
   flour
1 teaspoon salt

1 teaspoon soda
2 teaspoons baking powder
1 teaspoon vanilla extract
3 cups apples, peeled and
   chopped
1 cup chopped pecans

Mix oil, eggs, and sugar, and beat until creamy. Sift dry ingredients together and add to oil mixture. Add vanilla extract, apples, and pecans. Mix well. Bake in a greased and floured 9x13-inch pan at 350° for 1 hour.

Mrs. William V. Headley (Anita)

VARIATION: Substitute 1 1/2 cups cooking oil and 3 eggs for similiar ingredients above.

Mrs. S.S. Vincent
Milledgeville, Georgia

❋❋❋❋❋❋❋❋❋❋❋❋❋

To make chocolate leaves for a cake, wash and dry rose leaves. Melt semisweet chocolate squares. Using a small paint brush, coat the underside of the leaves with chocolate, then refrigerate. When chilled, carefully peel off leaf using a knife. Store chocolate leaves on waxed paper in refrigerator until ready to use. Keep decorated cake refrigerated, also.

For cream cheese frosting, cream 1/2 cup butter and 1 (8-ounce) package cream cheese until well blended. Gradually add 1 (1-pound) box powdered sugar, stirring until thoroughly combined.

97

FRESH APPLE CAKE I

Oven: 325° 45 minutes   Yield: 1 (9x13-inch) cake

Cake:

1/2 cup margarine
2 cups sugar
2 eggs
2 cups self-rising flour
1 teaspoon soda
3/4 teaspoon salt
1/2 teaspoon nutmeg
1/2 teaspoon cinnamon

1/4 teaspoon allspice
1/4 teaspoon cloves
1 1/2 cups chopped nuts
4 cups finely chopped apples

Topping:

1 cup sugar
1 stick margarine
1/4 teaspoon salt
1/2 cup evaporated milk

1 1/2 teaspoons vanilla extract

CAKE: Cream margarine and sugar. Add eggs and beat until smooth. Sift dry ingredients and spices and add to egg mixture. Stir in apples and nuts. (This mixture will seem dry, but the apples make it moist as it bakes.) Bake in greased 9x13-inch pan at 325° for approximately 45 minutes.

TOPPING: Combine all the topping ingredients in a saucepan and cook over low heat, stirring constantly for 10 minutes. Remove from heat and add 1 1/2 teaspoons vanilla extract. Spread over warm cake in the pan.

Mrs. Carl Williams (Eddy)

❉❉❉❉❉❉❉❉❉❉❉❉❉

Heavy cakes are sometimes caused by too slow an oven, or by the use of too much sugar or shortening. Coarse-grained cakes are the result of too much leavening ingredients, too slow an oven, insufficient creaming of shortening and sugar, or insufficient beating of batter before addition of egg whites.

FRESH APPLE CAKE II
Freezes well

Oven: 350° 40 to 45 minutes

Yield: 1 (8-inch) square cake

3 tablespoons margarine
1 cup sugar
1 egg, beaten
1 cup plus 2 tablespoons
  sifted, all-purpose flour
1/2 teaspoon baking powder
1/2 teaspoon soda

1/2 teaspoon cinnamon
1/2 teaspoon nutmeg
1 teaspoon vanilla extract
3 cups diced raw apples, peeled
1/2 cup chopped pecans

Cream margarine and sugar together. Add beaten egg. Sift flour, baking powder, soda, and spices together and add to shortening mixture. Add vanilla extract, diced apples, and nuts. Turn into greased and floured 8-inch square pan. Bake 40 to 45 minutes at 350°. Serve warm with ice cream or whipped cream.

Mrs. John Goodrum (Marsha)

NUT CAKE
A Christmas favorite

Oven: 350° 1 hour

Yield: 1 (10-inch) cake

1 quart chopped pecans
2 (8-ounce) boxes chopped
  dates

2 (7-ounce) cans coconut
2 (14-ounce) cans sweetened
  condensed milk

Mix all ingredients in large bowl; add a little water if mixture seems dry. Heavily grease a 10-inch cast iron skillet and pour in mixture. Bake at 350° for 1 hour. Let cool before flipping it out of pan.

Mrs. Dan Rainey (Lynn)

DRIED APPLE CAKE
Stays moist for days

Oven: 350° 1 hour and 10 minutes   Yield: 1 tube cake

2 cups dried or evaporated
  apples
1 cup sugar
1 cup cane sugar syrup
1 cup shortening
1 cup milk
1 teaspoon soda
3 cups all-purpose flour

1/2 teaspoon salt
1 teaspoon allspice
1 teaspoon cinnamon
2 cups raisins
1 cup chopped pecans
1 egg, beaten

Soak apples in water until soft, approximately 1 hour. Drain, cut in small pieces, and measure out 2 cups. Place diced apples in a 4-quart saucepan, add sugar and syrup; bring to a rolling boil and cook for 20 minutes, stirring frequently. Remove from heat; add shortening, milk, and soda. Stir until shortening is melted. Add spices and salt to sifted flour and stir into batter until thoroughly mixed. Add raisins and nuts. Fold in beaten egg. Pour into well-greased and slightly floured tube pan. Bake at 350° for 1 hour and 10 minutes. When done it will pull away from sides of pan. Remove from oven and cool on rack. Then turn pan upside down on rack; remove pan and let cake continue to cool. Store wrapped in foil.

Mrs. B. R. Miller, Jr. (Caroline)
Atlanta, Georgia

****

For a simple maple sugar frosting use 1 cup each of maple and granulated sugar and 1 teaspoon of butter and 3 teaspoons cream. Boil 5 minutes and stir until slightly thickened.

APPLESAUCE CAKE

Very moist, keeps for 10 days to two weeks

Oven: 250° 2 1/2 hours   Yield: 1 tube cake

4 level teaspoons soda
2 1/2 cups hot, cooked apples
1 cup butter
2 cups brown sugar
2 eggs
4 cups all-purpose flour
1 pound raisins
2 cups walnuts

1 teaspoon nutmeg
1 teaspoon allspice
1 teaspoon cinnamon
1/2 teaspoon cloves
1 teaspoon vanilla extract
2 tablespoons cocoa
2 tablespoons white sugar

Stir soda into hot apples and let cool. Cream butter and sugar. Add eggs. Mix in flour. Add raisins, walnuts, spices, vanilla extract, and apples. To cocoa and 2 tablespoons sugar, add enough warm water to melt. Add to mixture; mix well. Bake in greased tube pan for 2 1/2 hours at 250°.

Mrs. Oliver P. Reason (Annette)

APPLE BUTTER CAKE

Oven: 325° 1 1/2 hours   Yield: 1 tube cake

1 cup butter or margarine,
    melted and cooled
2 cups sugar
2 eggs
2 cups sifted all-purpose
    flour
1 1/2 teaspoons soda

2 teaspoons cinnamon
1 teaspoon cloves
1 teaspoon nutmeg
1/2 teaspoon salt
2 teaspoons vanilla extract
1 cup chopped pecans
3 cups chopped, peeled apples

Combine melted, cooled butter and sugar. Add eggs, then flour, soda, spices, salt, and vanilla extract. Fold in pecans and apples. Bake in well-greased and floured tube pan for 1 1/2 hours at 325°.

Mrs. Henry L. Camp, Jr. (Susan)

CHEESECAKE

Epicures say this is the most elegant cheesecake ever tasted

Oven: 350° 25 minutes   Yield: 1 (8-inch) cake
      475° 5 minutes

3 (8-ounce) packages cream
   cheese
4 egg whites
1 cup sugar
1 teaspoon vanilla extract
2/3 cup Zwieback crumbs
2 cups thick sour cream
2 tablespoons sugar

1/2 teaspoon vanilla extract
1/3 cup shaved, blanched almonds or chopped pecans

Stir cream cheese until softened. Beat egg whites until stiff, then blend in 1 cup sugar and combine with cheese. Add 1 teaspoon vanilla extract. Butter an 8-inch spring-form pan and dust with Zwieback crumbs. Leave all crumbs in bottom of pan. Pour cream cheese mixture on top of crumbs. Bake at 350° for 25 minutes.

Mix together sour cream, sugar, and vanilla extract; spread over top. Sprinkle 1/3 cup toasted shaved, blanched almonds or chopped pecans on top. Bake 5 minutes longer at 475°. Chill 2 hours. If desired, garnish with fresh fruit.

Mrs. Carl E. Williams (Eddy)

✲✲✲✲✲✲✲✲✲✲✲✲✲

Toast pound cake slices and top with applesauce and cinnamon. Sprinkle with nuts.

To make gumdrop flowers, roll gumdrops between 2 sheets of sugared waxed paper. Cut into petals and leaves and arrange on cake in the shape of flowers.

FANNY BARRANCO'S CHEESECAKE

Oven: 350° 1 hour 15 minutes   Yield: 1 cake

Filling:

1 pound cottage cheese
2 (8-ounce) packages cream
  cheese
1/4 cup corn starch
1 1/2 cups sugar
Grated rind of 1 lemon
2 teaspoons lemon juice

Fruit for topping

1 teaspoon vanilla extract
5 eggs
1 cup sour cream
1 stick melted butter

Crumb Crust:

1 1/4 cups graham cracker
  crumbs
1/4 cup sugar

Dash cinnamon

Beat together first 8 ingredients, adding eggs one at a time. Beat well. Add sour cream, then melted butter. Beat well. Butter sides and bottom of spring-form pan. Mix crumb crust and shake around sides of buttered pan. Spread remaining crumbs evenly on bottom. Pour cheese batter over crumbs and bake at 350° for 1 hour and 15 minutes. Turn oven off and leave cake in oven for another hour. After cake has completely cooled, remove from spring pan and add favorite fruit topping.

SUGGESTIONS: Strawberries, pineapple, or blueberries may be used. To make a thick syrup when using fresh fruit, add 1 tablespoon corn starch to each cup of fruit juice. Cook over medium heat until thick. Let cool and pour over fruit topping on cooled cake.

Mrs. Ellis A. Mansour (Melinda)

HOLIDAY NUT CAKE

Oven: 275° 1 hour 30 minutes

Yield: 2 loaf cakes

1 pound margarine
1 pound light brown sugar
6 eggs
1 ounce lemon extract
4 cups all-purpose flour, sifted

3 cups pecans, coarsely chopped
1/2 pound candied red cherries
1/2 pound candied pineapple

Cream margarine and sugar. Add eggs one at a time; beat well. Add flavoring and 3 1/2 cups flour. Sift remaining flour over nuts and fruits and add to batter. Bake in 2 greased 9x5x3-inch loaf pans at 275° for 1 hour 30 minutes.

Mrs. C. A. Moody (Virginia)

MY FAVORITE NUT CAKE

Oven: 250° 3 hours

Yield: 1 tube cake

1 pound butter
2 cups sugar
6 eggs, beaten
4 cups cake flour
1 teaspoon baking powder
1/4 teaspoon salt

1/2 pound candied cherries, cut up
1/2 pound candied pineapple, cut up
1 pound pecans, chopped
2 teaspoons vanilla extract

Cream butter and sugar. Add beaten eggs. Add 3 cups flour sifted with baking powder and salt. Mix remaining flour with cherries, pineapple, and chopped pecans; stir into batter. Add vanilla. Pour into tube pan, greased and double lined with waxed paper. Bake at 250° for 3 hours. Cool in pan.

Mrs. Charles Connally (Rosa)

GERMAN SWEET CHOCOLATE CAKE
Delicious!

Oven: 350° 30 to 40 minutes   Yield: 1 (3-layer) cake

 ounces German chocolate   2 1/2 cups sifted all-purpose
/2 cup boiling water   flour
 cup butter or margarine   1 teaspoon baking soda
 cups sugar   1 cup buttermilk
 egg yolks   4 egg whites, stiffly beaten
 teaspoon vanilla extract

Melt chocolate in boiling water; let cool. Cream butter
and sugar, add egg yolks, vanilla extract, and chocolate,
beating well after each addition. Add flour with soda sifted in,
alternately with buttermilk. Fold in egg whites. Pour batter
into 3 greased and floured 8 or 9-inch cake pans. Bake at
350° for 30 to 40 minutes. When cool, frost with Coconut
Pecan Icing.

Mrs. Annie Pearl Cook

COCONUT PECAN ICING

Yield: Icing for 3-layer cake

 cup evaporated milk   1 1/3 cups coconut
 cup sugar   1 cup pecans, chopped
 egg yolks
 teaspoon vanilla extract

Cook milk, sugar, egg yolks, and vanilla extract until
thickened. Add coconut and pecans. Cool, then beat until
it is of spreading consistency. Makes 2 1/2 cups, enough
for a 3-layer cake.

Mrs. Annie Pearl Cook

NEW ORLEANS DOBERGE CAKE

An easy version of the famous Gambino Bakery's delight!

Oven: 350° 12 to 15 minutes   Yield: 1 (6-layer) cake

1 (17 or 18-ounce) package   **Chocolate frosting**
yellow cake mix
2 (4 1/2-ounce) packages
instant chocolate pudding

Prepare cake batter according to package directions. Grease and flour 6 cake pans (8 inches round). Divide batter and spread evenly in each pan. Layers may be baked 2 or 3 at a time, then repeated. Bake at 350° about 12 to 15 minutes. Small layers need less baking time, so don't let them overcook! Cool baked layers. Prepare pudding according to package directions. Spread each layer with pudding as the cake is stacked. Frost sides and top of cake. Refrigerate an hour or so for easier slicing.

NOTE: For a tasty variation, substitute lemon or vanilla pudding for the chocolate, and ice with a lemony icing. Garnish top of cake with a lemon twist and mint sprigs.

Mrs. Robert L. Lee (Pam)

****

Add a pinch of baking powder to powdered sugar icings. Icing will not get hard or crack and will stay moist.

Add a little cream of tartar to 7-minute icing to prevent it from drying and cracking.

SOUR CREAM CHOCOLATE CAKE
Very moist

Oven: 325° 1 hour   Yield: 1 tube cake

Cake:

1 cup sour cream   2 1/2 cups all-purpose flour
2 teaspoons soda   1/4 teaspoon salt
1 cup butter, softened   1 cup boiling water
2 cups sugar
2 eggs
2 (1-ounce) squares unsweetened
  chocolate, melted and cooled
2 teaspoons vanilla extract

Frosting:

1 (6-ounce) package semi-sweet   1 1/2 to 2 cups powdered sugar
  chocolate chips
1/3 cup evaporated milk

CAKE: Combine sour cream and soda. Let stand. Cream butter and sugar. Add eggs, one at a time, mixing well after each addition. Add cooled chocolate and vanilla extract; add sour cream mixed with soda. Combine flour and salt; add flour mixture alternately with boiling water. Bake at 325° for 1 hour to 1 hour and 10 minutes in a greased and floured tube pan. Cool completely before removing.

FROSTING: Heat chocolate chips and milk in top of double boiler until chocolate melts. Add powdered sugar and mix well. Spread on cooled cake.

Mrs. Wayne Honeycutt (Tanya)
Hickory, North Carolina

* * * * * * * * * * * * * *

To help prevent cake layers from sticking to the pans, place the pans on a wet towel as soon as they come out of the oven.

DEVIL'S FOOD CAKE
Simple, inexpensive, and foolproof!

Oven: 325° 25 minutes   Yield: 1 (2-layer) cake

1 1/2 cups flour
1 1/4 cups sugar
1/2 cup cocoa
1 1/4 teaspoons soda
1/4 teaspoon cream of tartar
1 teaspoon salt

2/3 cups vegetable shortening
1 cup buttermilk or sour milk
1 teaspoon vanilla extract
2 eggs

Sift flour, sugar, cocoa, soda, cream of tartar, and salt together into mixing bowl. Add vegetable shortening, 1/3 cup milk, and vanilla extract. Beat together. Add eggs and rest of milk and beat well. Grease and flour two 8-inch pans. Pour batter into the prepared pans. Bake at 325° for 25 minutes. Cool to ice. Use a chocolate filling between layers and frost sides and top with 7-minute icing. For a Valentine's Day cake, add 1/2 to 3/4 cup crushed peppermint candy to the 7-minute frosting before icing cake.

Mrs. Irwin H. Pike (Helen)

※ ※ ※ ※ ※ ※ ※ ※ ※ ※ ※ ※ ※

Unless the recipe specifies otherwise, cool cake in the pan for 5 to 10 minutes before turning it out on a wire rack to cool.

Cake should be completely cool before spreading with frosting.

For cholesterol watchers: substitute 2 egg whites, stiffly beaten and folded into cake batter, for each whole egg called for in the recipe.

MOCHA-DEVIL'S FOOD CAKE
Very rich, very good

Oven: 375° 25 minutes   Yield: 1 (2-layer) cake

Cake:

1/4 pound butter or margarine	1 1/2 cups milk
2 cups sugar	1/4 pound (4-squares) unsweetened chocolate, melted
2 eggs, separated	1 teaspoon vanilla extract
2 cups all-purpose, sifted flour	2 teaspoons baking powder

Icing:

1/4 pound butter or margarine	1 teaspoon cocoa or 1 square unsweetened chocolate, melted
1 (16-ounce) box powdered sugar	Cold liquid coffee

CAKE: Cream butter and sugar. Beat in egg yolks. Mix flour and milk into batter alternately. Add melted chocolate and vanilla extract. Sift in baking powder and fold in. Add stiffly beaten egg whites and fold in. Bake in two 9-inch prepared layer pans at 375° for about 25 minutes.

ICING: Cream butter and sugar. Add chocolate. Use enough cold coffee to make spreading consistency.

Mrs. A.M. Bowen (Julia)

❋❋❋❋❋❋❋❋❋❋❋❋❋

No more sticky cake squares in the lunch box! Cut frosted cake squares in half and place the 2 icing sides together. The frosting becomes the filling.

To any yellow or white cake mix, add 1 teaspoon each of vanilla extract and lemon extract for a much-improved flavor.

109

BROWNSTONE FRONT CAKE
Great!

Oven: 300° 1 hour   Yield: 1 tube cake

1 cup buttermilk
1 teaspoon baking soda
2 sticks margarine
2 cups sugar
3 egg yolks

2 envelopes readi-melt
  chocolate or 2 squares
  (1-ounce) unsweetened chocolate, melted
3 cups cake flour
1/2 teaspoon salt
1 teaspoon vanilla extract
3 egg whites, stiffly beaten

Mix buttermilk and soda together; let stand to expand. Cream margarine and sugar. Add yolks and chocolate; mix. Add buttermilk mixture, then sifted dry ingredients. Add vanilla extract and beat well. Fold in egg whites. Bake in greased, lined tube pan at 300° for 1 hour.

NOTE: This cake is delicious unfrosted or, for a special touch, frost with Icing for Brownstone Front Cake.

Mrs. John W. Anderson (Nancy)
Florence, South Carolina

ICING FOR BROWNSTONE FRONT CAKE

Yield: Approximately 3 1/2 cups

2 sticks margarine or butter
2 cups sugar
1 (5 1/3-ounce) can
  evaporated milk

1 1/2 teaspoons vanilla
  extract

In saucepan, combine margarine, sugar, and milk. Dissolve over low heat. Bring to boiling point and simmer 45 minutes uncovered. Remove from heat; add vanilla extract. Cool to room temperature, then beat well. Spread on cake.

Mrs. John W. Anderson (Nancy)
Florence, South Carolina

★

COCONUT CAKE
A very special treat

Oven: 325° 30 minutes   Yield: 1 (3-layer) cake

Cake:

1 cup butter or margarine	1/4 teaspoon almond extract
2 cups sugar	1 cup chopped pecans
4 eggs	1 cup chopped walnuts
3 cups sifted all-purpose	1 cup golden raisins
flour (reserve 1 cup to mix	1 cup grated coconut (see
with fruit and nuts)	Filling ingredients)
1 teaspoon salt	1/2 cup cherries (optional)
3 teaspoons baking powder	
1 cup milk	
1/2 teaspoon vanilla extract	

Filling:

4 coconuts, grated (use 1 cup	Juice of all 4 coconuts
in batter)	
4 cups sugar	
3 tablespoons cornstarch	

CAKE: Cream butter and sugar until very fluffy. Add eggs, one at a time, beating well after each. Sift 2 cups flour with salt and baking powder three times. Add flour and milk alternately to egg mixture. Add extracts. Mix pecans, walnuts, raisins, coconut, and cherries with the reserved cup of sifted flour, and stir into batter. Pour into 3 (9-inch) cake pans that have been greased and floured. Bake at 325° until straw tester comes out clean, about 30 minutes. Cool in pans about 10 minutes and then completely cool on rack.

FILLING: Mix all ingredients together and cook until thick on low heat. Stir frequently. Place filling on top and sides of each cake layer. Frost sides with 7-minute frosting, if desired.

Delilia Marie Jeter
Grantville, Georgia

111

★ **FRESH COCONUT CAKE**
Well worth the time involved

Oven: 325° to 350° 20 to 30 minutes   Yield: 1 (3-layer) cake

Cake:

1 cup butter	1 teaspoon salt
2 cups sugar	2 1/2 teaspoons baking powder
6 large eggs (use 3 whites	1 teaspoon vanilla extract
for filling)	
1 cup milk	
3 cups cake flour	

Frosting:

1 (16-ounce) bottle light corn	1 grated coconut (do not use
syrup	canned coconut)
3 egg whites	
1 teaspoon vanilla extract	

CAKE: Cream butter and sugar. Add eggs and beat well. Add milk. Sift together dry ingredients and add along with vanilla extract. Line 3 (9-inch) cake pans, grease, and dust with self-rising flour. Divide cake batter evenly among the prepared pans. Bake 20 to 30 minutes at 325° to 350°. Cool completely before icing. If desired, sprinkle 1 teaspoon coconut milk over each layer before icing.

FROSTING: Bring syrup to a boil. In bowl of electric mixer, beat egg whites to soft peaks. Very slowly add boiling syrup to whites while continuing to beat. (Keep syrup at boiling point while adding.) Add vanilla extract. Ice cake and sprinkle with fresh, grated coconut.

Mrs. John P. Woods, Jr. (Elizabeth)

STIRRING FRUIT CAKE
Unusual procedure

Oven: 375° 1 hour   Yield: 1 tube or 2 loaf pans

2 sticks butter or margarine
1 cup sugar
4 large eggs
1 cup self-rising flour
2 teaspoons apple pie spice
   mix
2 teaspoons vanilla extract
2 teaspoons almond extract

1 pound red candied cherries,
   chopped
1/2 pound white candied pineapple, chopped
1/2 pound green candied pineapple, chopped
1/4 pound raisins
6 cups pecans, chopped

Cream butter and sugar. Add eggs, one at a time, and beat well. Add flour and spice. Add vanilla and almond extracts. Add fruits and nuts which have been coarsely chopped. Put into large greased pan and place in 375° oven. After mixture has cooked 15 minutes, stir it. Do this 3 times. After the third time, have tube pan or 2 loaf pans greased and lined with brown paper. Pack cake into pan(s) very well and bake 15 minutes more. Cool at least 15 minutes before removing from pan.

Mrs. Hubert Yarbrough (Mary)
Cusseta, Alabama

✿✿✿✿✿✿✿✿✿✿✿✿✿

Substitute powdered sugar for flour when preparing buttered cake pans. There will be less sticking.

To keep chocolate cakes brown on the outside, grease pans and dust with cocoa instead of flour.

★   ## SOUR CREAM COCONUT CAKE
Stays moist for days

Oven: 350° 25 minutes   Yield: 1 (3-layer) cake

Cake:

1 cup shortening
2 cups sugar
5 eggs
1 cup all-purpose flour

1 cup self-rising flour
1 cup milk
1 teaspoon vanilla extract

Icing:

2 cups sugar
1 cup sour cream

1 (12-ounce) package frozen coconut
1 teaspoon lemon extract

CAKE: Cream shortening and sugar together. Add eggs. Add flour and milk alternately, mixing well. Add vanilla extract. Put into 3 greased and floured 8-inch cake pans and bake at 350° for approximately 25 minutes or until done. Frost while the cake is still warm.

ICING: Mix all ingredients together. Do Not Cook.

Mrs. Lester Morgan (Vora)
Senoia, Georgia

JAPANESE FRUIT CAKE
Freezes nicely

Oven: 350° 25 to 30 minutes   Yield: 2 (3-layer) cakes

Cake:

2 1/2 cups sugar
1 cup butter
6 eggs (save 2 whites for icing)
4 cups cake flour (after sifting)
4 teaspoons baking powder

1/4 teaspoon salt
1 teaspoon vanilla extract
1 cup milk (or 1 cup buttermilk plus 1 teaspoon soda)
1 (8-ounce) box seeded raisins
1 teaspoon cinnamon
1 teaspoon allspice

Light Layer Optional Ingredient:

1 (8 1/4-ounce) can crushed pineapple in heavy syrup

Dark Layer Optional Ingredients:

1/2 cup chopped nuts or citron
2 ounces fig preserves, drain syrup
2 ounces blackberry wine

Filling:

4 oranges
1 grated coconut
1 tablespoon fresh lemon
  juice
2 cups sugar
4 heaping tablespoons all-
  purpose flour

2 cups water (use coconut milk,
  if it is sweet)
1 (20-ounce) can crushed pineapple in heavy syrup
2 cups chopped pecans
2 cups candied cherries

LAYERS: Cream sugar and butter until smooth. Add eggs, one at a time, beating until light. Sift flour, baking powder, and salt together. Add alternately with milk to batter. Add vanilla extract and mix well. Divide mixture in half. Add optional ingredients as desired to each half of batter. Add raisins and spices to dark half of batter only. Pour into 6 layer pans that have been greased and floured. Bake at 350° for 25 to 30 minutes or until done. Use 2 dark layers and 1 light layer for one cake and 2 light layers and 1 dark layer for the other cake. Alternate color of layers.

FILLING: Cut oranges and scoop out segments. Add rest of ingredients except nuts and cherries. Bring to boil and cook until thick, stirring continuously. Add nuts and cherries. This goes between all layers and on top of cakes. Frost sides of each cake with 7-minute icing.

NOTE: This is a seasonal cake. In order to make it at times other than Christmas, omit cherries from filling and instead of fresh coconut, use 1 cup canned coconut.

Mrs. John W. Anderson (Nancy)
Florence, South Carolina

★ ## SWEET POTATO FRUIT CAKE
A moist, economical cake

Oven: 250° 2 1/2 hours   Yield: 1 tube cake

2 cups granulated sugar
1 1/2 cups cooking oil
4 eggs, separated
4 tablespoons hot water
2 1/2 cups sifted cake flour
3 teaspoons baking powder
1/4 teaspoon salt
1 1/2 cups grated raw sweet
  potatoes

4 cups chopped pecans
1 cup dark raisins
1 cup light raisins
4 ounces red cherries
4 ounces green cherries
8 ounces candied mixed fruit

Blend sugar and oil. Add yolks, beat well. Add hot water. Sift dry ingredients together. Add to sugar and yolk mixture. Beat well. Add potatoes. Fold in stiffly beaten egg whites. Stir in nuts and fruit. Pour into a greased and floured tube cake pan. Cook at 250° for 2 1/2 hours; cake is done when it pulls away from pan sides. Let cool. Remove from pan. Wrap in plastic wrap and foil. Store in refrigerator. It might pull apart when slicing. Just piece back together. Requires a very large bowl to mix in.

Alice Reese

✳✳✳✳✳✳✳✳✳✳✳✳✳✳

Glass, enamel, and dark metal pans absorb more heat then shiny ones; therefore, oven temperatures should be lowered 25° when using them.

The creaming process for a cake may be shortened by rinsing the mixing bowl out with hot water, then wiping dry.

TINY CHRISTMAS FRUIT CAKES

Oven: 300° 30 to 35 minutes   Yield: 36 tiny fruitcakes

1/4 pound candied cherries,   1 (14-ounce) can sweetened
   chopped   condensed milk
3 candied pineapple slices,   3 tablespoons butter (do not
   chopped   melt)
2 1/4 cups chopped pecans   2 teaspoons vanilla extract
1 (6-ounce) can coconut

    Cut or chop fruit and nuts. Add fruit, nuts, and coconut to milk, butter, and vanilla extract; mix well. Grease tiny muffin tins very well and fill three-fourths full. Bake at 300° for 30 to 35 minutes or until golden on top. Remove carefully when cool.

Mrs. Wayne Honeycutt (Tanya)
Hickory, North Carolina

CHIP AND CHERRY CAKE
A "fruit cake" your family will love!

Oven: 350° 1 hour 10 minutes   Yield: 1 loaf cake

3 eggs   2 cups pecans or walnuts,
1 cup sugar   chopped
1 1/2 cups sifted all-purpose   1 cup chopped dates
   flour   1 cup halved candied cherries
1 teaspoon baking powder   1 cup chopped candied pine-
1/4 teaspoon salt   apple
1/4 pound chocolate chips

    Beat eggs well. Gradually add sugar and beat well. Sift dry ingredients together. Add chocolate chips, nuts, dates, cherries, and pineapple to flour. Fold into the egg-sugar mixture. Pour into a wax paper-lined, oiled loaf pan. Bake at 350° for 1 hour and 10 minutes.

Mrs. Robert D. Royal (Sue)

117

THREE LAYER CAKE

Use Japanese Fruit Cake Filling with this delicious cake

Oven: 350° 25 to 30 minutes   Yield: 1 (3-layer) cake

1 cup shortening or 1/2 cup
   butter and 1/2 cup
   shortening
2 cups sugar
4 eggs

3 cups cake flour
2 teaspoons baking powder
1 teaspoon salt
1 cup milk
1 teaspoon vanilla extract

Cream shortening and sugar. Add eggs, one at a time, and beat well. Sift flour once, measure 3 cups, then sift twice more with baking powder and salt. Add flour and milk alternately with vanilla extract, beating until smooth. Divide batter evenly into 3 greased and floured (8-inch) round cake pans. Bake at 350° for 25 to 30 minutes. This makes a big cake, and it freezes well.

Mrs. Floyd Bowie (Frances)
Madras, Georgia

JAPANESE FRUIT CAKE FILLING

1 quart pecans
1 pound candied mixed
   fruit
1 fresh coconut, meat
   removed

1/2 pound light raisins
1/2 pound dark raisins
1 cup orange juice, fresh or
   frozen (this may be increased)

Grind all ingredients in a food grinder or blender. Add orange juice until filling is easily spreadable. This makes a generous amount of icing, enough for 3 or 4 layers. If desired, decorate the cake top with pecan halves and candied cherries.

Mrs. Floyd Bowie (Frances)
Madras, Georgia

1-2-3-4 CAKE

A wonderful basic recipe handed down from generation to generation

Oven: 325° 25 to 30 minutes   Yield: 1 (3-layer) cake

1 cup butter
2 cups sugar
4 eggs
3 cups all-purpose flour
   (sift, then measure)
1 teaspoon salt

3 teaspoons baking powder
1 cup milk
1/2 teaspoon vanilla extract
1/4 teaspoon almond extract

Cream butter and sugar until very fluffy. Add eggs one at a time, beating well after each addition. Sift flour, salt, and baking powder three times. Add flour and milk alternately to creamed mixture, beating well after each addition. Add extracts. Divide evenly in three greased and floured 9-inch cake pans. Bake in a 325° preheated oven until straw tester comes out clean (approximately 25 to 30 minutes). Cool in pans 5 to 10 minutes. Remove from pans and cool on cake racks. Make sure cake bottom is next to rack.

If white layers are desired, substitute 6 egg whites for whole eggs and solid shortening for butter. Beat whites until soft peaks form and fold into cake batter LAST.

NOTE: For an especially velvety cake, use 2 duck eggs and 2 hen eggs instead of 4 hen eggs.

Rachel S. Jenkins

❊❊❊❊❊❊❊❊❊❊❊❊❊

Whipped butter cannot be substituted for butter in cake and cookie recipes. Air has been whipped into the butter and there is actually less butter in the whipped product.

LADY BALTIMORE CAKE

*Combine 1-2-3-4 cake layers and the following
procedure to prepare this delicious, moist cake*

Icing:

3 cups sugar
Juice of 2 oranges
Juice of 2 lemons
Juice from drained pineapple
Water added to juices to equal 1 1/2 cups total liquid
3 egg whites

1 1/2 cups walnuts, coarsely chopped
1 (8-ounce) can crushed pineapple, drain well and reserve juice
2/3 cup maraschino cherries, chopped
2 (3-ounce) cans coconut
1/2 cup raisins (optional)

2/3 cup lightly floured raisins (optional addition to 1-2-3-4 cake
batter)

ICING: Bring sugar and the 1 1/2 cups total liquid to a boil in a heavy saucepan over LOW heat. Stir constantly and cook very slowly until a boil is reached, and the sugar is dissolved. Continue to cook and stir until a very heavy syrup forms. Meanwhile beat egg whites until stiff peaks form. Pour heavy syrup VERY slowly over egg whites, beating constantly with electric mixer until mixture is cool and very thick.

Place bottom cake layer on serving plate. Stick generously with broken nuts. Sprinkle with 1/3 of crushed pineapple, chopped cherries, coconut, and raisins. Spoon icing over all (icing will SOAK into cake). Repeat procedure on top of second and third layers.

Rachel S. Jenkins

* * * * * * * * * * * * *

Form doughnuts, then let them stand 15 minutes before frying. They'll absorb less fat.

SHERRY NUT CAKE

Quick and easy

Oven: 325° 30 minutes

Yield: 1 (9x13-inch) cake

1 (18 1/2-ounce) box yellow
  cake mix
1 (3 5/8-ounce) package
  regular vanilla pudding
1/4 cup sherry

3/4 cup cooking oil
4 eggs
1 cup pecans, chopped

Glaze:

1 tablespoon margarine, melted
2 cups powdered sugar
1/3 cup sherry

Mix dry ingredients together. Add sherry, oil, and eggs. Beat at medium speed until well mixed. Add nuts and mix. Pour into a greased and floured 9x13-inch pan. Bake at 325° for 30 minutes.

GLAZE: Melt margarine, add powdered sugar and sherry. Mix until well blended. While cake is still hot, punch holes all over and pour on glaze.

Mrs. Warren C. Budd (Courtenay)

****

Grease only the bottom of cake pans unless recipe directs otherwise.

121

ORANGE CAKE

Good for brunch or coffee

Oven: 350° 40 to 45 minutes   Yield: 1 bundt or tube cake

1 orange	2 eggs
1/2 cup sugar	2 cups flour
1 cup dates or raisins	1 teaspoon soda
1/2 cup nuts, chopped	1/2 teaspoon salt
1/2 cup margarine	1 cup buttermilk
1 cup sugar	1 teaspoon vanilla extract

Juice orange. Add 1/2 cup sugar to juice. Cook to thin syrup. Set aside. Grind orange rind and pulp with dates in food mill. Set aside. Prepare nuts and set aside. Cream margarine and sugar. Add eggs. Sift together dry ingredients. Add alternately with buttermilk. Add vanilla extract, fruit, and nuts. Bake at 350° for 40 to 45 minutes in a greased and floured bundt, loaf, or tube pan. Pour syrup over cake while warm.

Mrs. T. Leigh Sanders, Jr. (Martha)

* * * * * * * * * * * * *

Any frosting can be used for almost any double-layer cake. Here's the difference between the basic frostings:

Butter cream: uncooked frosting made with butter, powdered sugar, flavoring, and a little liquid; smooth consistency.

7-minute (Double-Boiler):   cooked frosting, made with egg whites, corn syrup, and water, beaten at high speed; fluffy consistency.

Royal: not cooked; hardened by an acid such as lemon juice; almost always used for decorating.

PIG LICKIN' CAKE

Also called Mandarin Orange Cake

Oven: 350° 20 to 25 minutes   Yield: 1 (3-layer) cake

Cake:

1 (18 1/2-ounce) box butter
  yellow Duncan Hines cake
  mix
3/4 cup cooking oil

4 eggs
1 (11-ounce) can mandarin
  oranges and juice

Icing:

1 (3 3/4-ounce) box instant
  vanilla pudding mix
1 (15 1/2-ounce) can crushed
  pineapple, undrained

1 (9-ounce) container frozen
  whipped topping, thawed

CAKE: Beat all ingredients together for 4 minutes. Bake at 350° in 3 layers for 20 to 25 minutes. The layers will be thin. This cake is best done in 3 layers, but it may be baked in only 2 layers or in a tube pan; bake the cake longer, however, Cool to ice.

ICING: Mix all ingredients by hand. Do not use an electric mixer. Iced cake is best kept refrigerated. Keeps well.

NOTE: This icing could be used on almost any cake. It is so delicious and stays soft.

Mrs. George Neff (Ruth)
Metropolis, Illinois

Mrs. John Goodrum (Marsha)

※ ※ ※ ※ ※ ※ ※ ※ ※ ※ ※ ※ ※

To soften hard butter quickly, fill a bowl with very hot water for 3 minutes. Drain and dry bowl and invert it over the sticks of butter.

ORANGE SLICE CAKE

Excellent alternate to fruitcake

Oven: Tube pan-300° 2 hours
    9x13-inch pan-250° 2 1/2 hours

Yield: 1 tube cake

1 cup butter or margarine
2 cups sugar
4 eggs
1 teaspoon soda
1/2 cup buttermilk
3 1/2 cups all-purpose
   flour

1 pound dates, cut into
   small pieces
1 pound candy orange slices,
   cut into small pieces
2 cups pecans or black walnuts,
   chopped
1 (4-ounce) can coconut

Topping:

1 cup orange juice

2 cups powdered sugar

Cream butter and sugar well. Add 4 eggs, one at a time. Mix 1 teaspoon soda with 1/2 cup buttermilk and add to cake alternately with 3 1/2 cups flour. Stir in dates, orange slices, and nuts that have been dredged in a small amount of flour. Add coconut. Bake cake in either a greased and floured tube pan in a 300° oven for 2 hours or a greased and floured 9x13-inch pan in a 250° oven for 2 1/2 hours.

TOPPING: Combine orange juice and powdered sugar. Pour over hot cake and let stand overnight.

Mrs. Wheeler Roberts (Bess)
Spring City, Tennessee

Mrs. Fred R. Smyre (Martha)
Hickory, North Carolina

VARIATION: Substitute 1 1/2 cups sugar, 2 cups flour, 8 ounces coconut, and 8 ounces dates for similiar ingredients in recipe above.

Mrs. Ellis R. Truett
Jackson, Tennessee

POUND CAKE I

Oven: 325° 1 hour 15 minutes   Yield: 1 tube cake

2 sticks butter or margarine
  at room temperature
1/2 cup solid shortening at
  room temperature
3 cups sugar
5 large eggs

3 cups all-purpose flour
1/2 teaspoon baking powder
1 cup milk
1 teaspoon vanilla extract
1 teaspoon lemon extract

Cream butter and shortening. Add sugar, beating until well mixed. Add eggs one at a time. Sift flour and baking powder. Add alternately with milk to creamed mixture. Add flavorings. Pour into a large tube pan which has been greased. Bake in a 325° oven for 1 hour 15 minutes.

Mrs. Ray Sewell (Edith)

VARIATION: Substitute whipped margarine for regular margarine.

Mrs. Harvey E. Roberts (Carolyn)

❋ ❋ ❋ ❋ ❋ ❋ ❋ ❋ ❋ ❋ ❋ ❋

Bake a "homemade" tasting cake when using a boxed cake mix by substituting the following ingredients instead of what is specified on the box:
  To **Our Pride** cake mix, add 3 eggs and 1 1/4 cups milk.
  To **Duncan Hines Deluxe II** cake mix, add 3 eggs, 1 1/3 cups buttermilk, and a few drops (less than 1 teaspoon) of butter flavoring.
Bake cake as directed on package.

POUND CAKE II

Good alone or as base for shortcake and ice cream

Oven: 325° 1 hour   Yield: 1 tube cake

3 sticks butter or margarine
1 (1-pound) box powdered
   sugar
4 large eggs or 5 small eggs
1/3 cup water

1/2 teaspoon salt, scant
3 cups sifted cake flour
1 teaspoon vanilla extract
1/4 to 1/2 teaspoon almond or
   rum extract

Cream butter. Add sugar and continue to cream. Add eggs, one at a time, beating between additions. Add water, then sifted dry ingredients. Mix well. Add extracts. Bake in greased, lined tube pan for 1 hour at 325°.

NOTE: This recipe may be doubled. It stays fresh for at least a week.

Mrs. John W. Anderson (Nancy)
Florence, South Carolina

POUND CAKE III

Oven: 350° 1 hour   Yield: 1 tube cake

1 cup butter
2 cups sugar
6 eggs, room temperature
3 tablespoons brandy or
   brandy extract

2 cups cake flour, sifted
Dash of salt
1/2 cup chopped and floured
   pecans (optional)

Cream butter and sugar. Add eggs one at a time; beat one minute after adding each one. Add brandy, flour, and salt. Add nuts. Mix well. Pour in prepared pan. Bake in tube pan, bundt pan, or 2 loaf pans at 350° for 1 hour or until done.

Mrs. E. Victor Hanson (Joe Ann)

ALMOND POUND CAKE
Easy

Oven: 325° 55 minutes   Yield: 1 bundt cake

1 1/2 cups solid shortening   6 eggs
1/4 pound butter   1 teaspoon vanilla extract
1 3/4 cups sugar   1 teaspoon almond extract
2 cups all-purpose flour

Cream shortening, butter, and sugar. Add flour and eggs (begin and end with flour). Add flavorings and bake in a buttered and lightly sugared bundt pan for 55 minutes at 325°. NOTE: Buttering and sugaring the pan makes a sweet, crisp crust.

Mrs. Robert A. Blackwood, III (Lorene)
Peachtree City, Georgia

CHOCOLATE POUND CAKE
Very moist!

Oven: 325° 1 hour 45 minutes   Yield: 1 tube cake

2 sticks butter or margarine   1/2 cup cocoa
1/2 cup solid shortening   1 teaspoon salt
3 cups sugar   1/2 teaspoon baking powder
5 eggs   1 1/4 cups milk
3 cups cake flour   1 tablespoon vanilla extract

Cream butter, shortening, and sugar. Beat in eggs one at a time. Sift flour, cocoa, salt, and baking powder together. Add to cream mixture alternating with milk. Stir in vanilla extract and blend well. Pour batter into greased and floured tube pan. Bake at 325° for 1 hour 45 minutes. Wrap in foil to keep.

Mrs. Red Breed (Ruby)
Hogansville, Georgia

127

MERIWETHER POUND CAKE

Larger than most pound cakes

Oven: 300° 2 hours   Yield: 1 tube cake

1 pound butter
1 pound sugar (2 1/4 cups)
9 eggs
1 pound all-purpose flour
   (4 cups)

1 teaspoon baking powder
1/2 teaspoon salt
1/2 cup milk
2 teaspoons lemon extract

Cream butter and sugar. Add eggs, one at a time. Beat well. Add sifted dry ingredients alternately with milk. Add lemon extract. Put into greased, lined tube pan. Bake 2 hours at 300°.

Georgia H. Long

WHIPPED CREAM POUND CAKE

Oven: 275° to 300° 1 hour 20 minutes   Yield: 1 tube cake

1/2 pound butter or margarine
2 1/2 cups sugar
6 eggs

3 cups sifted cake flour
1/2 pint whipping cream
1 teaspoon vanilla extract

Cream butter and sugar. After adding one egg at a time, beating 1 minute after each, reduce speed of mixer and add flour and cream (not whipped) alternately. Add vanilla extract. Pour into greased, lined tube pan. Put into cold oven and bake at 275° to 300° for 1 hour without opening the door. Then turn the cake around and cook 20 minutes more or until done.

Mrs. George W. Fleming (Sarah)

ORANGE-COCONUT POUND CAKE
Quick and easy-stays moist for days

Oven: 350° 1 1/2 hours   Yield: 1 tube cake

Cake:

2 cups solid shortening   1/2 teaspoon coconut extract
3 1/3 cups sugar   1 cup orange juice
10 large eggs   1/2 teaspoon lemon extract
4 cups all-purpose flour

Icing:

1 stick margarine   5 tablespoons orange juice
2 cups powdered sugar   1 cup coconut

CAKE: Cream shortening and sugar together with electric mixer until fluffy. Add eggs, one at a time beating well after each addition. Add flour alternately with orange juice. Mix well after each addition. Add extracts. Pour into greased and floured tube pan. Bake at 350° for 1 1/2 hours.

ICING: Cream margarine. Add sugar and orange juice alternately. Beat to spreading consistency. Spread on top and sides; sprinkle with coconut.

Mrs. Mary Ann Reese

❋ ❋ ❋ ❋ ❋ ❋ ❋ ❋ ❋ ❋ ❋ ❋ ❋

To get the most volume from egg whites, whip them in an unlined copper utensil because of the reaction between the raw copper and the egg whites. Or use a stainless steel or glass bowl and add a dash of salt, lemon juice, or cream of tartar to achieve the same effect. Do not use an aluminum bowl; it will discolor the whites and keep them from reaching the right volume.

★   **PEANUT BUTTER POUND CAKE**

Oven: 350° 45 minutes   Yield: 1 tube cake
          325° 15 to 20 minutes

2 1/2 sticks butter   2 cups all-purpose flour
2 cups sugar   1 teaspoon baking powder
6 eggs   1/4 teaspoon salt
1 teaspoon vanilla extract   1/3 cup peanuts, finely chopped
1/2 cup peanut butter,   (optional)
   smooth or crunchy

Cream butter and sugar until light yellow. Beat in eggs, one at a time, until thoroughly blended. Add vanilla extract and slowly beat in peanut butter. Sift flour with baking powder and salt. Add flour mixture, a little at a time, until well blended. Line a 9 or 10-inch tube pan on the bottom with wax paper. Spoon in batter and bake at 350° for 45 minutes; reduce heat to 325° and bake 15 to 20 minutes longer, until cake tests done. Cool in pan on wire rack for 10 minutes, then remove from pan and cool cake completely. If desired, toward the end of baking, while cake is still soft, sprinkle about 1/3 cup finely chopped peanuts onto batter to give it a crunchy topping.

Mrs. Jimmy Carter (Rosalynn)
Plains, Georgia, and Washington, D.C.

※※※※※※※※※※※※※

For perfectly even cake layers, put the batter into the cake pans with an ice cream scoop. Alternate from one pan to the other until batter is gone.

Adding sugar too soon to whipped egg whites will result in a thin marshmallowy sauce that will never thicken. Wait until whites stand in soft peaks to add sugar.

7-UP CAKE I

Oven: 350° 20 minutes   Yield: 1 (3-layer) cake

Cake:

1 (3 5/8-ounce) box vanilla   3/4 cup cooking oil
  instant pudding   4 eggs
1 (18 1/2-ounce) package   1 (10-ounce) 7-Up
  Duncan Hines white or
  yellow cake mix

Filling:

1 1/2 cups sugar   1 (8-ounce) can crushed pine-
2 tablespoons flour   apple, drained
2 eggs   1 (4-ounce) can coconut
1 stick butter or margarine   1/2 cup nuts

CAKE: Combine pudding mix, cake mix, and cooking oil. Add eggs, one at a time, beating well after each addition. Blend 7-Up into batter. Pour into three 9-inch cake pans that have been greased and floured. Bake at 350° for 20 minutes. Remove from oven, let stand for 10 minutes. Remove layers from pans and cool on racks. Place filling between layers and on top of cake.

FILLING: Mix sugar and flour. Add slightly beaten eggs and butter or margarine. Place in top part of double boiler and cook until consistency of syrup. Add remaining three ingredients.

Mrs. Bruce Williams (Sandra)

❋❋❋❋❋❋❋❋❋❋❋❋❋

Bananas give a special interest to grilled sandwiches. Place a slice of ham on a slice of bread, spread with peanut butter, top with sliced bananas, add a second slice of bread, and spread with margarine. Grill in skillet over low heat, turning once, until bread is golden.

7-UP CAKE II

Oven: 325° 30 minutes   Yield: 1 (3-layer) cake

Cake:

1 (18 1/2-ounce) box lemon   4 eggs
   cake mix   3/4 cup vegetable oil
1 (3 5/8-ounce) box instant   1 (10-ounce) bottle 7-Up
   pineapple pudding mix

Filling:

1 (20-ounce) can crushed   2 eggs
   pineapple   2 tablespoons flour
1 1/2 sticks margarine   1 (3 1/2-ounce) can coconut
1 1/2 cups sugar

CAKE: Put all ingredients in bowl and mix well. Bake in 3 greased and floured 8-inch layer pans at 325° for 30 minutes.

FILLING: Cook first 5 ingredients until thick; add coconut. Cool and spread on cool cake layers.

Mrs. Duke Daniel (Sonya)
Franklin, Georgia

※※※※※※※※※※※※※

Luminaries make a useful, festive lining along a walk, driveway, or stairway for a summer evening party. Buy plumber's candles from a hardware store and medium-size paper bags from a grocery. Roll the bags down to 8 to 10 inches in height, fill with 2 inches of sand, then insert a candle in each bag. Use long matches to light the candles.

PINEAPPLE STACKED CAKE
Very moist and light

Yield: 1 (3-layer) cake

Cake:

1 (18 1/2-ounce) box Duncan
Hines Butter Cake Mix

Filling:

1 (20-ounce) can crushed
    pineapple in heavy syrup
1/4 cup sugar

2 egg yolks
3 level tablespoons flour

Icing:

2 egg whites
1 1/2 cups sugar
2 tablespoons white corn
    syrup

5 tablespoons water
1/8 teaspoon cream of tartar
1 teaspoon vanilla extract

CAKE: Prepare cake according to directions on cake package, pouring batter into 3 prepared pans. Bake as directed on package, but adjust time for three layers.

FILLING: Mix pineapple, egg yolks, flour and sugar. Place over medium heat and cook until thick, stirring constantly. Use filling between layers.

ICING: Cook all ingredients in top of a double boiler over boiling water. Mix with hand mixer until icing will stand in a peak. Ice top and sides of cake.

Mrs. V. J. Bruner (Ethel)

★ ## SWEET POTATO CAKE
Freezes well as individual, unfrosted layers

Oven: 350° 25 to 30 minutes   Yield: 1 (3-layer) cake

1 1/2 cups cooking oil
2 cups sugar
4 eggs, separated
2 1/2 cups sifted cake flour
3 teaspoons baking powder
1/4 teaspoon salt
1 teaspoon ground cinnamon

1 teaspoon ground nutmeg
1/3 cup water
1 1/2 cups grated raw sweet
   potato
1 cup chopped nuts
1 teaspoon vanilla extract

Combine cooking oil and sugar and beat until smooth. Add egg yolks one at a time. Sift dry ingredients and add to first mixture alternately with water, beating well after each addition. Stir in potatoes, nuts, and vanilla extract. Fold stiffly beaten egg whites into mixture. Pour batter into 3 greased and floured 8-inch cake pans. Bake at 350° for 25 to 30 minutes. Cool and frost.

Mrs. H.C. Tysinger (Judy)

FROSTING FOR SWEET POTATO CAKE

1 (13-ounce) can evaporated
   milk
1 cup sugar
3 egg yolks

1 stick margarine
1 teaspoon vanilla extract
1 1/3 cups flaked coconut

Combine milk, sugar, egg yolks, margarine, and vanilla extract in a saucepan. Cook over medium heat about 12 minutes, stirring constantly until mixture thickens. Remove from heat and add coconut. Beat until cool and of spreading consistency.

Mrs. H.C. Tysinger (Judy)

ITALIAN CREAM CAKE

Oven: 350° 20 to 30 minutes   Yield: 1 (3-layer) cake

Cake:

1 stick margarine, softened
1/2 cup cooking oil
1 teaspoon vanilla extract
2 cups sugar
5 eggs, separated

1 cup buttermilk
1 teaspoon baking soda
2 cups all-purpose flour
1 cup pecans, chopped
1 (3-ounce) can coconut

Icing:

1 stick margarine at room
   temperature
1 (1-pound) box powdered
   sugar

1 (8-ounce) package cream
   cheese
1 teaspoon vanilla extract

CAKE: Combine first 4 ingredients by hand. Do not over-beat. Slightly beat egg yolks and add to mixture. Add remaining ingredients, then fold in stiffly beaten egg whites. Bake in 3 (8-inch) greased and floured pans at 350° for 20 to 30 minutes or until done. Cool before icing.

ICING: Mix all ingredients with a fork and apply to cooled cake.

Mrs. Al Moody (Linda)

✱✱✱✱✱✱✱✱✱✱✱✱✱✱

Go to the yard for unusual placecards. Pick undamaged, medium to large ivy leaves. Rinse and dry thoroughly; then write each guest's name on the leaf with opaque white ink and a stylus (purchased from an art supply store.) Use magnolia leaves in a similar manner, or use chalk to write the names.

LEMON GOLD CAKE

Oven: 325° 30 minutes

Yield: 1 (4-layer) cake

Cake:

2 1/4 cups cake flour
1 1/2 cups sugar
1 tablespoon baking powder
1 teaspoon salt
1/2 cup salad oil
6 eggs, separated

3/4 cup cold water
2 teaspoons lemon juice
1 teaspoon grated lemon rind
1/2 teaspoon cream of tartar

Frosting:

1 cup sugar
3 tablespoons all-purpose
  flour
1/3 cup lemon juice
Grated rind of 1 lemon
1 teaspoon lemon extract

4 egg yolks, beaten
1/2 cup water
3 tablespoons butter
Dash salt
1 cup coconut (optional)

CAKE: Sift together flour, sugar, baking powder, and salt. Make a well and add in order the oil, egg yolks, water, lemon juice, and rind. Beat well. Add cream of tartar to egg whites and beat until very stiff. Pour egg yolk mixture gradually over the egg whites and blend thoroughly. Pour into 4 greased and floured (8-inch) pans. Bake at 325° approximately 30 minutes, or until top springs back when lightly touched.

FROSTING: Mix sugar and flour. Add lemon juice, rind, and extract. Beat well. Add well-beaten egg yolks. Add water, butter, and salt. Cook in top of double boiler until mixture thickens. Cool. Spread on layers and sides of assembled cake. If desired, sprinkle layers and sides with coconut.

Mrs. Red Breed (Ruby)
Hogansville, Georgia

PLUM CAKE

Oven: 350° 1 hour   Yield: 1 bundt cake

2 cups all-purpose flour   1 teaspoon vanilla extract
2 1/2 teaspoons baking powder   1 teaspoon cinnamon
1/2 teaspoon salt   1 teaspoon nutmeg or cloves
2 cups sugar   2 (4 3/4-ounce) jars baby food
1 cup oil   plums
1 1/2 cups chopped pecans   3 eggs

Dump everything into a large bowl and mix well. Bake in a greased and floured bundt pan for 1 hour at 350°.

Mrs. Thomas G. Kerley (Florence)
Paducah, Kentucky

FAVORITE VANILLA WAFER CAKE
A delightfully different cake

Oven: 350° 60 minutes   Yield: 1 tube cake

1 cup chopped pecans   2 cups sugar
1 (8-ounce) can coconut   6 eggs
14 ounces vanilla wafers   1/2 cup milk
1 cup margarine

Preheat the oven to 350°. Chop the pecans into small pieces. Pour into a bowl. Add the coconut. Crush the vanilla wafers in a blender and add them to the above and mix well. Cream the softened margarine and sugar. Add eggs, one at a time, to the margarine and sugar, beating well. Fold the dry ingredients into the egg mixture and add 1/2 cup milk. Pour the cake batter into a well-greased tube pan. Bake at 350° for an hour. Remove from tube pan when cool. Slice and serve topped with whipped cream or vanilla ice cream.

NOTE: This cake freezes beautifully.

Mrs. Tom Smith (Ann)

BROWN SUGAR CAKE

Oven: 325° 1 1/2 hours   Yield: 1 tube cake

1 cup shortening
1 stick margarine
1 (16-ounce) box light brown
  sugar
1 cup white sugar
5 eggs

3 cups sifted all-purpose flour
1/2 teaspoon baking powder
1 cup milk
1 teaspoon vanilla extract
1 cup nuts, finely chopped

Cream shortening, margarine, and brown and white sugars.
Add eggs, one at a time, beating well after each addition. Add
flour and baking powder (sifted together) alternately with milk.
Add vanilla extract, then nuts dredged in flour. Pour into a
greased and floured 10-inch tube pan, and bake 1 1/2 hours
at 325°.

Mrs. Annie Pearl Cook

DR. BIRD CAKE
Freezes well

Oven: 350° 1 hour 20 minutes   Yield: 1 tube cake

2 cups mashed bananas
3 cups self-rising flour
2 cups sugar
1 teaspoon cinnamon
1 (8-ounce) can crushed
  pineapple

1 1/4 cups cooking oil
1 1/2 teaspoons vanilla extr
3 eggs
1 cup nuts, chopped

Mash 3 to 4 (2 cups) small bananas. Sift dry ingredients
and to it add undrained pineapple, cooking oil, vanilla extract
eggs, and bananas. Mix well until blended. Do not beat. Stir
in nuts. Pour batter into a greased tube pan and bake at 350°
for 1 hour and 20 minutes.

Mrs. Tony Wilson (Erni

DUMP CAKE

Oven: 350° 45 to 50 minutes   Yield: 1 (9x13-inch) cake

1 (20-ounce) can crushed pineapple with juice
1 (21-ounce) can blueberry
  pie filling

Cinnamon
2 sticks butter or margarine
1 cup chopped nuts
1 (18 1/2-ounce) package yellow
  cake mix

In a greased 9x13-inch baking dish, spread layers of pine-apple, pie filling, and dry cake mix. Be careful not to mix layers. Sprinkle with cinnamon. Top with thin pats of butter and chopped nuts. Bake at 350° for 45 to 50 minutes.

NOTE: Use spice cake mix with apple pie filling or yellow cake mix and cherry pie filling.

Mrs. Chuck Moates (Alice Ann)

★   CARAMEL CAKE

Oven: 325° 45 minutes   Yield: 1 (3-layer) cake .

1 pound margarine, softened
3 1/4 cups sugar
10 eggs

4 cups all-purpose flour
2 teaspoons vanilla extract

Cream margarine and sugar well in very large bowl. Alternately add eggs, one at a time, and flour. Beat well. Add flavoring. Bake in 3 (9-inch) prepared pans at 325° for 45 minutes. Cool; frost with caramel frosting.

Winnie Cook

★ **CARAMEL FROSTING**

Yield: Icing for 3 (9-inch) layers

3 cups sugar
3/4 cup evaporated milk,
   undiluted

3/4 cup margarine
1 tablespoon white corn syrup
1 teaspoon vanilla extract

Brown 1/2 cup of the sugar in heavy skillet. Add remaining ingredients. Cook 5 minutes. After mixture begins to boil, remove from heat and beat until thick enough to spread.

Winnie Cook

SHERRY CAKE

Yield: 1 tube or loaf cake

4 eggs
1 cup sugar
1/2 cup sherry
1 envelope unflavored gelatin

1/2 cup milk
1 pint whipping cream, whippe
1 small purchased angel food c

Separate the eggs. Beat the 4 egg yolks thoroughly with 1/2 cup sugar and 1/2 cup sherry. Put in double boiler and cook over boiling water until thick. Remove from heat. Soak envelope of unflavored gelatin in 1/2 cup cold milk. Add gelatin mixture to hot custard. Whip whites of 4 eggs until stiff. Reserve. Whip 1/2 pint cream until stiff. Fold remaining 1/2 cup sugar into cream. Carefully fold stiff egg whites and whipped cream into hot custard.

Tear angel cake into bite-size pieces. Layer angel cake pieces and custard in a tube or loaf pan, beginning and ending with the cake pieces. Let stand overnight in the refrigerator.

Turn out of pan and ice with the additional 1/2 pint whipped cream flavored with sherry and sugar.

Sarah Parrott

BASIC FROSTING

Perfect for cake decorating—so easy!

Yield: Approximately 2 cups

1 (1-pound) box powdered sugar
1/3 to 1/4 cup Crisco
1/2 teaspoon salt
1 scant teaspoon cream of tartar

1/4 cup water
1/2 teaspoon vanilla extract, or any flavoring desired

Mix all ingredients together and beat at medium speed with mixer for 7 to 8 minutes, or until smooth and lump-free. Stop, then beat again. If too thick, add drops of water while beating until of desired consistency. Tint icing the color desired using a cake coloring such as Wilton. Regular food coloring tends to run. Icing or icing leftovers will keep indefinitely in refrigerator. To use later, beat again to make smooth. A little water may need to be added. Icing may be spread directly on cake or piped through decorative tips.

Mrs. Stephen C. Bohannon (Carlene)

★ **CARAMEL BUTTER NUT ICING**

Yield: Icing for 2-layer cake

1/3 cup buttermilk
1/2 cup butter
1 cup light brown sugar
2 cups powdered sugar

1 cup pecans, finely chopped
1/4 cup pecans (optional)

Heat buttermilk and butter. Add sugars. Bring to a boil and continue boiling until the soft ball stage is reached. Add finely chopped pecans and beat until of spreading consistency. After the cake is iced, sprinkle 1/4 cup pecans over the top.

Mrs. Annie Pearl Cook

★ ## OLD-FASHIONED CARAMEL ICING

Yield: Icing for 2-layer cake

3 cups sugar
3/4 cup milk
1 cup sugar

3 tablespoons butter or margar
1 teaspoon vanilla extract

Boil 3 cups sugar and milk for 3 minutes. In a skillet melt 1 cup sugar over medium heat, stirring. Add the sugar and milk mixture, stirring quickly. Add the margarine and vanilla extract. Stir vigorously until of spreading consistency. If mixture seems too thick, add a little milk.

Mrs. Sam O. Candler (Betsy)
Sharpsburg, Georgia

CHOCOLATE FROSTING
Very creamy

Yield: Frosting for 2-layer cake

1 stick margarine or butter
3/4 cup brown sugar, loosely
  packed
2 heaping tablespoons cocoa
1 shake salt

1/3 cup water
2 cups powdered sugar
1 1/2 teaspoons vanilla or ru
  extract

Mix first 5 ingredients and bring to a boil. Boil 1 minute, stirring. Remove from heat. Beat in sugar, then add extract. Quickly ice cake before frosting cools.

Recipe doubles with good results; make a double batch if a thick icing is desired.

NOTE: Add additional powdered sugar and nuts to make a creamy fudge.

Mrs. John P. Woods, Jr. (Elizabeth)

CHOCOLATE ICING
Best ever!

Yield: Icing for 2 or 3-layer cake

3 cups sugar
3/4 cup cocoa
3/4 cup evaporated milk
3/4 cup margarine

Put all ingredients in large saucepan. When mixture comes to a boil, cook 1 minute. Remove from heat and set on cooling rack. Let cool until hand temperature on bottom of pan. Beat to spreading consistency.

NOTE: This icing was always a favorite at family gatherings. It was a specialty of Cecile Lipford of Franklin, Georgia.

Mrs. Billy Arnall, Jr. (Linda)

MOTHER'S CHOCOLATE ICING OR FUDGE

Yield: 24 pieces of fudge or icing for 2-layer cake

2 (1-ounce) squares unsweetened chocolate, finely chopped
2 cups sugar
2/3 cup milk
1 stick butter
1 pinch salt
1 teaspoon vanilla extract

Bring first 5 ingredients to a boil, stirring constantly. Boil gently about 3 minutes. Let cool for about 2 minutes. Beat until lukewarm. Add 1 teaspoon vanilla extract. Beat until thick enough to spread.

Mrs. Duke Blackburn (Julia)

143

LEMON CHEESE ICING

Yield: Icing for 2-layer cake

8 egg yolks
3 tablespoons all-purpose flour
3 to 4 tablespoons butter

Juice of 2 lemons
Grated rind of 1 lemon
1 1/2 cups sugar

Cook all ingredients in top of double boiler until thick.

Mrs. Bryan Sargent (Ellen)

SEVEN MINUTE ICING
Never fails

Yield: Icing for 3-layer cake

2 egg whites
1 1/2 cups granulated sugar
1 1/2 teaspoons white corn syrup
5 tablespoons water

1/8 teaspoon salt
1 1/2 teaspoons vanilla extra
3 marshmallows

Place all ingredients except marshmallows and vanilla extract into the top of a double boiler over hot or boiling water and beat with a rotary beater for 7 minutes or until mixture holds a peak.

Remove from heat. Add extract and 3 cut-up marshmallows. Continue to beat until well blended and apply to cake.

Mrs. Mary Ann Reese

* * * * * * * * * * * * * *

Silver polish on a pipe cleaner will easily clean between fork tines or other small, hard to reach places.

Cookies &
Candies

COOKIES

CANDIES

Cookies & Candies Chapter Design: Easley's Glass Lemon Squeezer (1910)
    Quackenbush Nut Crack (1910)

BROWNIES

Oven: 350° 20 to 25 minutes   Yield: 2 dozen

1 1/2 cups all-purpose flour
1/2 teaspoon salt
1 teaspoon baking powder
1 cup butter or margarine
2 cups sugar
4 eggs
4 (1-ounce) squares unsweetened chocolate, melted
2 teaspoons vanilla extract
2 cups chopped English walnuts or toasted pecans

Sift the flour, salt, and baking powder three times. Set aside. Cream the butter and gradually add the sugar. Cream until fluffy. Add the eggs, one at a time, and mix well. Blend in melted chocolate and vanilla extract. Add flour mixture and beat well. Fold in chopped nuts. Pour into greased and floured 9x13-inch pan. Bake at 350° for 20 to 25 minutes. Cool in pan and frost or remove from pan and cut into squares. Frost with chocolate frosting, if desired.

Mrs. S. L. Horvat (Theresa)
Fairburn, Georgia

CARAMEL BROWNIES

Oven: 325° 35 minutes   Yield: 2 dozen

1 (1-pound) box light brown sugar
3/4 cup butter or margarine
3 eggs
1 1/2 cups all-purpose flour
1 1/2 teaspoons baking powder
1 cup chopped pecans
2 teaspoons vanilla extract
Chocolate morsels (optional)

Blend all ingredients. Pour into 9x13x2-inch greased and floured baking dish, and bake for about 35 minutes at 325°.

Mrs. Ray Sewell (Edith)

147

FUDGE BROWNIES

Oven: 350° 15 to 20 minutes   Yield: 2 dozen

Brownies:

1 1/2 squares unsweetened chocolate
1 stick butter or margarine
2 eggs
1 cup sugar

3/4 cup flour
3/4 teaspoon baking powder
1 cup chopped nuts

Marshmallow creme or miniature marshmallows

Frosting:

1/2 stick margarine
4 tablespoons milk

2 cups powdered sugar
1/3 cup cocoa

BROWNIES: In small pan, melt chocolate and margarine together. Beat eggs and sugar well. Mix together the flour, baking powder, and chopped nuts. Combine chocolate mixture, egg mixture, and flour mixture. Stir until thoroughly mixed. Spread in a greased 11x7-inch pan; bake 15 to 20 minutes at 350°. Remove from oven and immediately top with marshmallows or creme.

FROSTING: Bring the margarine and milk to a boil. Mix together the powdered sugar and cocoa; add to milk mixture. Stir until the mixture is a good spreading consistency. While frosting is still hot, pour over brownies and marshmallows in pan. Let cool and store in refrigerator.

Mrs. Jeanne Benson
Athens, Georgia

❋❋❋❋❋❋❋❋❋❋❋❋❋

Make a badly discolored cookie sheet shine like new. Apply spray or brush-on oven cleaner to the cookie sheets, the same way as for cleaning an oven. Let it stand for the recommended length of time. Rinse the sheet, using paper towels; then use a soapy steel wool pad to bring back the shine.

PEANUT-BUTTERSCOTCH BROWNIES

Peanuts may be omitted

Oven: 350° 25 to 30 minutes   Yield: 2 dozen

2 cups brown sugar
1/2 cup oil
2 eggs
1 cup Spanish peanuts
1 teaspoon vanilla extract

1 teaspoon almond extract
1 1/2 cups flour
2 teaspoons baking powder
1 teaspoon salt

Mix all ingredients well. Bake in an ungreased 9x13-inch pan 25 to 30 minutes in 350° oven.

Mrs. Oliver P. Reason (Annette)

DATE NUT BARS

Oven: 275° 1 hour 15 minutes   Yield: 3 dozen

1 1/3 cups brown sugar
1 stick margarine
2 eggs
1 cup unsifted flour

1 teaspoon vanilla extract
1 teaspoon orange extract
8 ounces chopped dates
1 cup chopped nuts

Cream sugar and margarine. Add eggs, flour, and extracts. Beat well. Stir in dates and nuts. Bake in greased and floured 9x13-inch pan. Bake 1 hour 15 minutes at 275°. Cool in the pan and cut into small squares.

Mrs. Frank Bridges (Martha)

✳✳✳✳✳✳✳✳✳✳✳✳✳

When making cookies, if there is only 1 egg in the house and the recipe calls for 2 eggs, use 1 egg plus 1 tablespoon water.

Always use a shiny cookie sheet. Dark or stained cookie sheets absorb heat and may over-brown cookie bottoms.

DATE-NUT SQUARES
Recipe doubles nicely

Oven: 350° 20 to 30 minutes   Yield: 2 1/2 dozen

1 stick butter or margarine,   1 cup self-rising flour
  melted   1 cup dates, chopped and
1 cup sugar   floured
2 large eggs   1 cup pecans, chopped

Mix ingredients in order given. Pour into an 8x8-inch pan which has been greased, floured, and lined with wax paper. Bake at 350° 20 to 30 minutes. It will fall when removed from oven. Cool on wire rack before cutting.

Mrs. John W. Anderson (Nancy)
Florence, South Carolina

CHOCOLATE CHIP BARS

Oven: 350° 30 to 35 minutes   Yield: 2 dozen

1/3 cup soft shortening   1/4 teaspoon salt
2 eggs   1 1/4 teaspoons baking powder
1 1/4 cups brown sugar   1 cup chocolate chips
1 1/4 cups flour   1/2 cup nuts, chopped

Mix shortening, eggs, and brown sugar thoroughly. Sift together the flour, salt, and baking powder; stir into shortening mixture. Stir in chocolate chips and nuts. Spread in greased 9x9-inch pan. Bake at 350° for 30 to 35 minutes. When almost cool, cut into bars.

Mrs. B. M. Enger (Imogene)
Mobile, Alabama

CHOCOLATE SNOWBALLS
Freeze well

Oven: 350° 20 minutes   Yield: 6 dozen cookies

1 1/4 cups margarine or butter   1/8 teaspoon salt
2/3 cup sugar   1/2 cup cocoa
1 teaspoon vanilla extract   2 cups chopped pecans
2 cups all-purpose flour   1/2 cup powdered sugar

Cream butter and sugar until light and fluffy. Add vanilla extract. Add sifted flour, salt, cocoa, and nuts. Mix thoroughly. Chill several hours. Form into balls like marbles. Place on ungreased cookie sheet. Bake 20 minutes at 350°. Cool. Roll in powdered sugar.

Mrs. Edwin L. Wyrick (Lois)

JANE'S CHOCOLATE CHIP COOKIES
So easy!! Don't use mixer!

Oven: 350° 8 minutes   Yield: 4 to 5 dozen

1/2 stick margarine   4 cups Bisquick
1/4 cup solid shortening   1 teaspoon vanilla extract
2 eggs, beaten   1 (12-ounce) package
2/3 cup light brown sugar   chocolate chips
2/3 cup granulated sugar   1/2 cup nuts, chopped

Melt margarine and shortening and add sugars. Stir in eggs and mix well. Stir in Bisquick, then vanilla extract, chocolate chips, and nuts. Drop by teaspoonfuls onto baking sheet and bake at 350° for about 8 minutes. Do not overbake or cookies will be hard. Cookies should be slightly soft and chewy; they won't be brown on top, only light brown on bottom.

Mrs. William Donald Tomlinson (Jane)

151

MOCK BABY RUTH BARS
A chocolate lover's delight

Oven: 400° 12 minutes   Yield: 2 dozen

4 cups oatmeal	1/4 cup peanut butter
1 cup brown sugar	1 teaspoon vanilla extract
1/4 cup light corn syrup	3/4 cup butter, softened

Topping:

6 ounces chocolate chips	2/3 cup peanut butter
3 ounces butterscotch bits	

Combine oatmeal, brown sugar, corn syrup, 1/4 cup peanut butter, vanilla extract, and butter. Spread in a greased 9x13-inch pan. Bake in a 400° oven for 12 minutes. Remove from oven and immediately spread with mixture of chocolate chips, butterscotch bits, and 2/3 cup peanut butter. Cut into squares.

Mrs. John N. White (Martha)

SEVEN LAYER COOKIE
Very rich

Oven: 350° 30 minutes   Yield: 2 dozen

1/4 pound margarine, melted
1 cup graham cracker crumbs
1 cup shredded coconut
1 (6-ounce) package chocolate chips
1 (6-ounce) package butterscotch chips
1 (14-ounce) can sweetened condensed milk
Chopped pecans

Pour melted margarine into a 9x13-inch pan, making sure sides of pan are greased. Layer other ingredients in order. Bake at 350° for 30 minutes. Cool before cutting into squares.

Mrs. Phil S. Vincent (Mary Anna)

ROCKY ROAD FUDGE BAR
Incredibly delicious!!

Oven: 350° 25 to 35 minutes   Yield: 3 dozen

Bar:

1/2 cup butter
1 ounce unsweetened chocolate
1 cup sugar
1 cup all-purpose flour
1/2 to 1 cup chopped nuts
1 teaspoon baking powder
1 teaspoon vanilla extract
2 eggs

Frosting:

2 cups miniature marshmallow
1/4 cup butter
1 ounce unsweetened chocolate
Remaining 2 ounces cream
  cheese
1/4 cup milk
1 pound powdered sugar
1 teaspoon vanilla extract

Filling:

8 ounces cream cheese, softened
  (reserve 2 ounces for frosting)
1/2 cup sugar
2 tablespoons flour
1/4 cup butter, softened

1 egg
1/2 teaspoon vanilla extract
1/4 cup chopped nuts
1 (6-ounce) package semi-sweet
  chocolate pieces

BAR: Preheat oven to 350°. Grease and flour a 9x13-inch pan. In large saucepan, over low heat, melt 1/2 cup butter and 1 ounce chocolate. Add remaining bar ingredients. Mix well. Spread in prepared pan.

FILLING: In small bowl, combine 6 ounces cream cheese with next 5 ingredients. Blend until fluffy and smooth. Stir in nuts and spread over chocolate mixture. Sprinkle with chocolate pieces. Bake at 350° for 25 to 35 minutes until toothpick in center comes out clean.

FROSTING: Sprinkle with marshmallows and bake 2 minutes longer. Over low heat, in large saucepan, melt 1/4 cup butter, 1 ounce chocolate, remaining 2 ounces cream cheese, and milk. Stir in powdered sugar and vanilla extract until smooth. Immediately pour over marshmallows and swirl together. Store in refrigerator.

Mrs. Charles Byrd (Ruby)

153

CARAMEL CHOCOLATE SQUARES
A very rich brownie-type bar

Oven: 350° 20 to 25 minutes   Yield: 60 small square

1 (14-ounce) package light caramels
1/3 cup evaporated milk, undiluted
1 package German chocolate cake mix
3/4 cup margarine, melted
1/3 cup evaporated milk, undiluted
1 cup chopped nuts
1 cup chocolate chips

In heavy saucepan, combine caramels and 1/3 cup evapo
rated milk. Cook over low heat, stirring constantly until caramel
are melted. Set aside.

Combine dry cake mix, margarine, 1/3 cup milk, and nuts
Stir by hand until dough holds together. Press one half of dough
into a 9x13-inch pan or Pyrex dish which has been greased
and floured.

Bake at 350° for six minutes. Remove from oven and spread
caramel mix over baked layer. Then sprinkle chocolate chip
over the caramel layer. Crumb remaining cake mixture over top
of chips. Bake 15 to 18 minutes longer. It may appear not to
be thoroughly cooked, but once it cools, it will be soft and
chewy. Cut into small bars.

Mrs. John Goodrum (Marsha

※※※※※※※※※※※※※※

Mix ginger cookies with cold coffee instead of water for a
delightful change in flavor.

Store soft cookies in airtight container and place a slice of bread
in the container to keep them soft. Store crisp cookies in con
tainers with loose-fitting tops.

VANCOUVER SQUARES
Rich!

Yield: 16 to 20 bars

First Layer:

1 egg	28 single graham crackers,
1/4 cup sugar	crushed
1/2 cup margarine	1 cup coconut
4 tablespoons cocoa	1/2 cup nuts, chopped
1 teaspoon vanilla extract	

Second Layer:

1/4 cup margarine,	2 tablespoons vanilla pudding
softened	powder
3 tablespoons milk	1 1/2 cups powdered sugar

Icing:

4 (1-ounce) squares semi-sweet	1 tablespoon margarine
chocolate	

FIRST LAYER: Cook first 5 ingredients in a double boiler over boiling water until the consistency of custard. Mix last 3 ingredients and add to custard. Pour into a 9x9-inch pan.

SECOND LAYER: Cream margarine and add milk blended with pudding powder. Add powdered sugar; mix well. Spread over contents of pan and refrigerate for 15 minutes.

ICING: Melt chocolate and margarine together and mix well. Spread over contents of pan. Refrigerate until set.

Mrs. Ronald Wassenberg (Betty)

* * * * * * * * * * * * * *

To keep boiled sugar from crystallizing, add a pinch of baking soda.

In candy making, the weather is a huge factor. On a hot humid day, cook candy 2° higher than in cold, dry weather.

155

MYSTERY MACAROONS
Unconventional ingredients result in a special, quick cookie.

Oven: 350° 10 to 15 minutes   Yield: 3 dozen

1 (5 1/2 to 6 1/4-ounce) package buttermilk biscuit mix
1 (2 3/4-ounce) package instant potatoes
1 cup sugar
1 egg
1 stick margarine, melted
1 teaspoon coconut extract

Mix dry ingredients and set aside. Beat egg and slowly add melted margarine and extract. Combine dry ingredients and egg mixture. Roll into small balls, place on ungreased cookie sheets and press each ball with a fork. Bake at 350° for 10 to 15 minutes. Let cool a few minutes before removing from pan.

Mrs. John N. White (Martha)

OATMEAL MACAROONS
Keeps well

Oven: 325° 13 to 15 minutes   Yield: 4 to 5 dozen

4 cups quick-cooking oatmeal   1 teaspoon vanilla extract
1 cup salad oil   1 teaspoon almond extract
2 cups dark brown sugar   1 teaspoon salt
2 eggs, beaten   Chocolate chips (optional)

At least 6 hours before baking, mix oatmeal, oil, and brown sugar. When ready to bake, mix in remaining ingredients. Drop by rounded teaspoonfuls 2 inches apart on a greased cookie sheet and bake at 325° for 13 to 15 minutes. Remove at once to cooling rack. These keep well in a covered container for several weeks.

Mrs. Bryant M. Smith, Jr. (Betty)

CHOCOLATE CHIP OATMEAL COOKIES

Oven: 375° 13 to 15 minutes   Yield: 4 dozen

1 cup brown sugar
1 cup granulated sugar·
3/4 cup shortening
2 eggs, well beaten
1 1/2 cups all-purpose flour
1 teaspoon salt

1 teaspoon soda
2 tablespoons water
3 cups oatmeal
1 (6-ounce) package
   chocolate chips

Cream together the sugars and shortening. Add the beaten eggs. Sift together the dry ingredients and add to creamed mixture alternately with the water. Mix in the oatmeal and chocolate chips. Drop by spoonfuls onto ungreased cookie sheets and bake at 375° for 13 to 15 minutes.

Mrs. Charles Bradley (Joyce)

OATMEAL ROCKS
A family favorite since 1918

Oven: 375° 12 to 15 minutes   Yield: 6 dozen

1 cup shortening
2 cups brown sugar
2 eggs
1/3 cup sour cream*
2 teaspoons cinnamon
1 teaspoon nutmeg
1 teaspoon soda
1/2 teaspoon salt
3 cups sifted flour

1 teaspoon vanilla extract
1 cup black walnuts
   (may use other nut meats)
1 cup raisins
1 cup rolled oats
* 1/3 cup canned evaporated
   milk combined with 1 teaspoon vinegar may be used

Cream shortening and brown sugar. Add eggs and beat well for 2 minutes. Combine dry ingredients. Then alternate with sour cream and add to creamed mixture. Add vanilla extract. Add raisins, oats, and nuts and mix with spoon. Drop by teaspoon on cookie sheet. Bake 12 to 15 minutes in a 375° oven. Remove from pan to cooling racks immediately.

Mrs. Edwin L. Wyrick (Lois)

157

ORANGE COOKIES

Oven: 350° 25 minutes   Yield: 3 dozen

Cookie:

1/2 cup shortening
1 cup sugar
2 eggs
3 cups sifted all-purpose flour

1/2 teaspoon soda
1/2 teaspoon salt
3/4 cup orange marmalade
1 cup chopped nuts

Icing:

1 tablespoon margarine, melted
1 (16-ounce) box powdered
  sugar

Juice and grated rind of
  1 orange

COOKIE: Cream shortening and beat in sugar and eggs. Add flour which has been mixed with soda and salt; add marmalade and nuts. Cut a piece of waxed paper to fit a 13x10-inch pan; grease and flour the paper. Pour dough into pan; bake at 350° for 25 minutes. Cool.

ICING: Combine ingredients. Spread on cookies and cut into squares.

Mrs. C. A. Moody (Virginia)

※※※※※※※※※※※※※※

For no-fail fudge and candy: always begin cooking very slowly until all sugar is melted. Test to feel granulation: if there are any granules, continue cooking slowly. All sugar **has** to be melted! Once melted, turn up heat and continue with recipe. Do this and always use a candy thermometer — the results will be super.

MADELEINES
A classic French pastry

Oven: 400°   Yield: Approximately 2 dozen

2 eggs
3/4 cup sugar
1 teaspoon grated lemon rind
1/2 teaspoon vanilla extract
1 teaspoon orange flower water (optional)
1 cup all-purpose flour
3/4 cup butter, melted

Combine eggs, sugar, and lemon rind in a large bowl. Heat over hot water, stirring occasionally until warm to the touch, about 5 to 10 minutes. Beat with electric beater for 15 minutes until tripled in bulk. Add vanilla extract and orange flower water; fold in flour. Fold in melted butter. Spoon into well-buttered madeleine molds, filling 2/3 full. Bake in 400° oven until pale brown.

Mrs. Walter Sanders (Clara Berry)

ALMOND COOKIES

Oven: 350° 12 minutes   Yield: 6 dozen

1 stick margarine, softened
1 cup sugar
1 egg
1 teaspoon almond extract
1 (2 3/4-ounce) package instant potatoes
1 1/2 cups Bisquick
Almond slices (optional)

Cream margarine; add sugar gradually. Beat in egg and almond extract. Add instant potato flakes and Bisquick, beating until well mixed. Roll dough into marble-size pieces; make slight indentation in top. Bake on a greased cookie sheet at 350° approximately 12 minutes. A sliced almond may be pressed into each cookie before baking.

Mrs. G. J. S. Cappelmann (Sara)
Jesup, Georgia

IMPERIAL LEMON SQUARES

Extremely easy

Oven: 350° 20 minutes
      350° 20 minutes

Yield: Approximately 2 dozen

2 cups flour
1/2 cup powdered sugar
2 sticks butter or margarine
1/4 teaspoon salt
4 eggs
1 cup granulated sugar

2 small whole lemons,
   quartered and seeded
1 cup sugar
1/4 cup flour
1 teaspoon baking powder

Blend first 4 ingredients in mixer. Spread in 9x13-inch pan and bake at 350° for 20 minutes.

Combine 4 eggs, 1 cup sugar, and 2 lemons (peel and all) in blender. Add last 3 items. Mix well. Pour over crust. Bake for 20 minutes at 350°. After removing from oven, sprinkle with additional powdered sugar while warm.

Mrs. William V. Headley (Anita)

BUTTER COOKIES I

Oven: 300° 10 to 15 minutes

Yield: 4 to 5 dozen

3 sticks butter, softened
1 cup sugar
1 egg yolk
Dash salt

4 cups all-purpose flour
1 teaspoon vanilla extract
Pecan halves

Cream butter and sugar; add other ingredients and mix thoroughly. Pinch off in small balls, flatten, and top each with a pecan half. Place on a lightly greased sheet; bake at 300° for 10 to 15 minutes, or until golden brown.

NOTE: Do not roll out, or cookies will be hard.

Mrs. Welborn Davis (Mary)

BUTTER COOKIES II
Freezes well

Oven: 350° approximately 15 minutes   Yield: 8 dozen

1 pound sweet butter
2 cups powdered sugar
4 cups all-purpose flour

1 teaspoon vanilla extract
1 cup pecan halves

Cream butter and sugar gradually. Add flour; mix. Add vanilla extract. Roll into balls and flatten with fingers. Place half pecan on top of each cookie. Bake at 350° for approximately 15 minutes or until lightly browned. Cool on absorbent paper until crisp. (This recipe can be halved.)

Mrs. Lanier Harrell (Evelyn)
Jesup, Georgia

CARAMEL COOKIES

Oven: 375° 10 to 12 minutes   Yield: 6 dozen

1 cup shortening
1/2 cup brown sugar
1 cup granulated sugar
2 eggs, beaten
2 teaspoons vanilla extract

3 3/4 cups sifted all-purpose
flour
1 teaspoon salt
1/2 teaspoon soda

Cream shortening; gradually add sugars and cream thoroughly. Add eggs and vanilla extract. Sift flour, salt, and soda; gradually add to creamed mixture, mixing well. Press from a cookie press or drop by teaspoonfuls onto ungreased cookie sheets. Bake at 375° for 10 to 12 minutes.

Mrs. T. W. Tillman (Annie-Laura)

ORANGE HONEY BARS
Good for lunchboxes

Oven: 350° 35 minutes   Yield: 3 dozen bars

Bar:

3/4 cup honey
1 cup packed brown sugar
1/2 cup salad oil
2 eggs
1 teaspoon vanilla extract
1 teaspoon grated orange peel

1 1/2 cups unsifted all-purpose
   flour
2 teaspoons baking powder
1 teaspoon salt
1 cup chopped nuts

Icing: (optional)

1 1/2 cups powdered sugar
2 tablespoons milk or
   orange juice

1/2 teaspoon grated orange
   peel

BAR: Beat honey, brown sugar, oil, and eggs until smooth. Add vanilla extract and orange peel. Sift together dry ingredients and stir into honey-orange mixture. Add nuts and mix well. Pour into greased and floured 9x13-inch pan. Bake at 350° for 35 minutes or until done.

ICING: Mix sugar with milk or orange juice. Add orange peel. Frost when bars are cool.

Mrs. Mike Spitler (Rita)

****

Fudge placed in an airtight container for 24 hours will be softer and more velvety.

To keep chocolate glossy for candy-dipping and glazes, always place it over hot water and heat only until partially melted; then remove from the water and stir until chocolate is entirely melted.

GINGER SNAPS

Oven: 350° 8 to 10 minutes   Yield: 8 to 9 dozen cookies

3/4 cup shortening
1 cup sugar
1 egg
1/4 cup molasses
2 cups flour, sifted

1 1/2 teaspoons soda
1 teaspoon ground cloves
1 teaspoon cinnamon
1 teaspoon ginger
1/2 cup sugar

Cream together shortening and 1 cup sugar. Add whole egg and molasses and beat until smooth. Sift dry ingredients together and add to mixture, beating until smooth. Make into teaspoon-size balls and roll in 1/2 cup sugar. Bake at 350° for 8 to 10 minutes on ungreased cookie sheet.

Mrs. George Bull, Jr. (Helen)
Cameron, South Carolina

SUGAR COOKIES

Oven: 350° 8 to 10 minutes   Yield: 6 dozen

1 cup butter, softened
1 cup sugar
1 egg, slightly beaten
1/4 cup sour cream

3 cups flour, sifted
1/2 teaspoon nutmeg
1 teaspoon baking soda
1/4 teaspoon salt

Beat butter until creamy. Blend in sugar gradually; beat until fluffy. Add egg and sour cream; mix well. Sift together flour, nutmeg, soda, and salt. Add to creamed mixture and beat thoroughly. Chill 2 hours. On a floured surface, roll out a small amount of dough to 1/4-inch thickness. Cut with a Christmas cookie cutter or other appropriate shape. If desired, sprinkle with sugar, colored sugar crystals, or chopped nuts. Bake on a greased cookie sheet at 350° for 8 to 10 minutes or until very lightly browned.

Mrs. Benny Grant (Diane)

★ **ORVILLE'S TEA CAKES**

Freezes well

Oven: 400° 9 minutes   Yield: 10 dozen

3 2/3 cups cake flour, sifted
2 1/2 teaspoons baking powder
1/2 teaspoon salt
2/3 cup butter
1 1/2 cups sugar
2 eggs

1 teaspoon vanilla extract or
1/4 teaspoon vanilla extract
and 3/4 teaspoon almond
extract
4 teaspoons milk

Mix together cake flour and baking powder. Add salt. Sift again. Cream butter thoroughly; add sugar gradually, creaming well. Add eggs, one at a time, beating thoroughly after each addition. Add vanilla extract, then add flour alternately with milk. Blend. Chill dough. Roll 1/8-inch thick. Cut with a floured, 2 1/4-inch scalloped cutter and sprinkle with white sugar. Bake on a greased baking sheet in hot oven at 400° for 9 minutes.

NOTE: For Christmas, sprinkle with red or green sugar crystals instead of white sugar.

Mrs. E. Herben Turner (Orville)
Griffin, Georgia

❋ ❋ ❋ ❋ ❋ ❋ ❋ ❋ ❋ ❋ ❋ ❋ ❋

Making chocolate curls: the chocolate should be at room temperature. For larger curls, carefully pull a swivel-bladed vegetable knife across the broad, flat side of the chocolate square. For small curls, pull the peeler across the side of the square. Lift the fragile curls with a toothpick.

Minted sour cream and fruit make a deliciously refreshing summer dessert. Slice fresh fruit, such as nectarines, into each serving dish. Mix together 1 cup sour cream, 2 tablespoons finely chopped fresh mint, 2 teaspoons sugar, 1 teaspoon lemon juice, and a dash of salt. Spoon over fruit. Makes enough topping for 4 or 5 servings.

SAND TARTS
A delicious, rich favorite

Oven: 300° 45 minutes   Yield: 3 dozen

1 cup butter
1/4 cup sugar
2 cups pecans, finely chopped
2 cups sifted all-purpose flour
Powdered sugar

Cream butter until soft. Add sugar, pecans, and flour, mixing well. Shape into balls or crescents and bake in a 300° oven on ungreased baking sheets for 45 minutes. While hot, roll balls or crescents in powdered sugar. Roll again after all have been rolled once.

Mrs. Thomas G. Kerley (Florence)
Paducah, Kentucky

THUMB PRINT COOKIES
These mail well

Oven: 350° 15 minutes   Yield: 8 dozen cookies

3 sticks margarine or butter,   1/4 teaspoon salt
  softened   1 teaspoon vanilla extract
1 cup sugar   Plum preserves or any tart
2 egg yolks   preserves
3 3/4 cups all-purpose flour

Cream butter and sugar. Add egg yolks. Sift flour and salt, and blend into butter mixture. Add vanilla extract. Chill dough well. Shape into 1-inch balls and place on ungreased cookie sheet. Make indentation in center with thumb; fill with preserves, jelly, or pecan half. Bake at 350° for 15 minutes or until lightly browned. Cool slightly; remove to rack to finish cooling. These keep well in a tightly closed container.

Mrs. John P. Woods, Jr. (Elizabeth)

165

FORGOTTEN COOKIES
Quite tasty

Oven: Preheat to 350°   Yield: 2 dozen

3/4 cup sugar
2 egg whites, beaten
1/2 teaspoon vanilla extract
Pinch of salt
3/4 cup (6 ounces) semi-sweet chocolate chips or mint-
   flavored chips, if preferred
1/2 cup nuts (optional)

Preheat oven to 350°. Beat sugar into egg whites. Add vanilla extract and salt, beating until egg whites are stiff. Fold in chips and nuts. Drop by small spoonfuls onto a sheet of foil that has been placed on a cookie sheet. Place cookie sheet in oven and TURN OVEN OFF. Leave overnight or 6 to 8 hours without opening door.

NOTE: Be sure to make spoon drops small (almost bite-size).

Mrs. John T. Glover (Sandra)
Atlanta, Georgia

MINI-MERINGUES

Oven: 250° 50 minutes   Yield: Approximately 4 dozen

2 egg whites
1/2 cup sugar
1 teaspoon almond extract
1/2 cup pecans, finely chopped, or 1/2 cup coconut

Beat egg whites until stiff. Gradually add sugar. When mixture stands in peaks, add extract. Carefully fold in nuts or coconut. Drop by tiny spoonfuls onto a cookie sheet lined with wax paper. Bake at 250° for 50 minutes.

Mrs. E. Victor Hanson (Joe Ann)

CHEESE TARTS

Oven: 350° 15 to 20 minutes   Yield: 75

2 sticks butter, room temperature
1 heaping cup grated New York State cheese, room temperature
2 cups flour
Salt to taste
2 teaspoons half and half cream
Apple jelly

Mix softened butter and cheese. Sift together flour and salt; add to cheese along with half and half. Roll the dough to 1/4-inch thickness, cut with small round cutter. Place 1/4 teaspoon apple jelly in the center of each round, then fold in half and seal edges with a fork. Bake at 350° for 15 to 20 minutes.

Mrs. Murdoch MacLennan
Charleston, South Carolina

JELLY JEWELS

Oven: 325° 15 minutes   Yield: Approximately 2 dozen

1/2 cup butter   1 egg yolk, beaten
1/4 cup brown sugar   1 egg white, beaten
1 cup flour   Ground nuts
1 teaspoon vanilla extract   Jelly

Cream butter and sugar well. Add flour; mix. Add vanilla and egg yolk. Refrigerate for 30 minutes or more, then form into small balls, roll in beaten egg white and then in nuts. Cook 5 minutes at 325°. Take out and make a hole in center. Cook 10 minutes longer. Remove from oven, cool, and fill with jelly.

Mrs. W. A. Hart

PEANUT BUTTER STICKS
Fun and easy for children to make

Oven: 200° 45 to 60 minutes   Yield: 3 1/2 dozen

6 slices day-old white bread
1 cup peanut butter (smooth or crunchy)
3 tablespoons salad oil
2 1/2 tablespoons sugar

Trim crusts from day-old bread and cut bread into narrow strips. Place strips and crusts on a cookie sheet in a 200° oven for 45 minutes to 1 hour or until bread is crisp. Remove and cool. Mix peanut butter, oil, and sugar. Crush crusts of bread finely (bread ends can also be baked and crushed). Dip bread strips into peanut butter mixture, making sure strips are completely covered. Roll in crushed bread crumbs and shake off excess. Serve.

Mrs. H. C. Tysinger (Judy)

CREOLE PORCUPINES

Oven: 300° 25 minutes   Yield: 4 dozen small cookies

3 tablespoons butter
(no substitute)
1 cup brown sugar,
firmly packed
2 eggs, well beaten

1 1/2 cups chopped pecans
1 cup chopped dates
3 cups shredded coconut

Melt butter and stir into sugar. Beat in eggs. Add pecans, dates, and 1 cup of the coconut. Form into small balls and roll in the remaining 2 cups of coconut. Place on greased baking sheet and bake at 300° until cookies just begin to brown lightly or about 25 minutes.

Mrs. Norman Douglas McGowen (Sandy)
Atlanta, Georgia

★   **PRALINE COOKIES**

Oven: 350° 12 minutes   Yield: 3 1/2 dozen
Cookies:

1 2/3 cups all-purpose flour   1 1/2 cups brown sugar, packed
1/2 teaspoon salt   1 egg
1 1/2 teaspoons baking powder   1 1/2 teaspoons vanilla extract
1/2 cup butter   1 1/2 cups pecans

Frosting:

1 1/2 cups brown sugar, packed   1 1/2 cups powdered sugar
3/4 cup whipping cream

COOKIES: Sift flour with salt and baking powder; set aside. Cream butter; add sugar, egg, vanilla extract, and dry ingredients. Mix well. Drop by teaspoonfuls onto ungreased baking sheet. Bake at 350° for 12 minutes. Cool. Break nuts into pieces and place on top of cookies. Spoon frosting over top.

FROSTING: Combine brown sugar and cream in a small sauce pan. Bring to a boil, stirring constantly. Boil 2 minutes. Remove from heat and add powdered sugar. Beat until smooth. If frosting thickens, thin with a little cream.

Mrs. B. M. Enger (Jean)
Mobile, Alabama

DATE BALLS

Yield: 3 dozen

1/2 pound chopped dates   2 cups Rice Krispies
1 stick and 1 tablespoon   1/2 cup chopped nuts
   margarine   Sifted powdered sugar
3/4 cup sugar

Cook dates, margarine, and sugar over medium heat until thick. Add cereal and nuts. Roll into small balls and coat with sifted powdered sugar.

Carrie May McElroy

DOUBLE COOKIES

Oven: 350° 40 minutes   Yield: 16 to 20 servings

First Layer:

3/4 cup butter   1/2 cup all-purpose flour
3 tablespoons sugar

Second Layer:

3 egg yolks, beaten   3/4 cup coconut
2 1/4 cups brown sugar   3 egg whites, stiffly beaten
1 cup pecans, chopped   Powdered sugar

FIRST LAYER: Cream butter and sugar. Add flour. Blend thoroughly. Pat the mixture into a well-greased 9-inch baking pan. Bake about 15 minutes at 350°.

SECOND LAYER: Beat egg yolks, add brown sugar, nuts, and coconut. Fold in beaten egg whites. Pour over hot baked mixture, return to oven and bake 25 minutes, or until done. Cut and dust with powdered sugar.

Mrs. Everett Bryant (Mary)

CHINESE CHEWS

Oven: 350° 15 to 20 minutes   Yield: 4 to 5 dozen bars

4 eggs
1 (16-ounce) package brown sugar
2 cups sifted self-rising flour
2 cups chopped pecans
1 teaspoon vanilla extract

Beat eggs and mix with brown sugar in top of double boiler. Cook over boiling water until syrupy, about 15 to 20 minutes, stirring several times. Pour into bowl containing sifted flour, stirring constantly. Add chopped nuts and vanilla extract. Pour into greased and floured 13x9x2-inch pan and cook at 350° for 15 to 20 minutes. Cool. Cut into small bars.

Mrs. Lindsey Barron (Genet)

ICE BOX COOKIES
Can freeze prepared rolls for "slice and bake" cookies at any time

Oven: 350° 10 to 15 minutes   Yield: 9 dozen

1 cup butter	Scant teaspoon soda
1 cup granulated sugar	2 1/2 teaspoons cinnamon
1 cup light brown sugar	1 1/2 teaspoons nutmeg
2 eggs	1 teaspoon vanilla extract
3 1/2 to 4 cups self-rising	1 1/2 cups pecans,
flour	finely chopped

Cream butter and sugars. Add eggs, one at a time, beating well. Beat in flour, which has been sifted with soda, cinnamon, and nutmeg until the dough is stiff. Add vanilla, blending well, and stir in pecans. Shape into 2 or 3 long rolls, and refrigerate until firm. Slice thinly and place on greased cookie sheet. Bake 10 to 15 minutes in 350° oven, or until brown. Remove from cookie sheet and let cool on flat surface.

Mrs. Michael T. Wilson (Gwyn)
Sharpsburg, Georgia

CARAMEL CORN
A delicious snack any time of the year

Oven: 250° 40 to 45 minutes   Yield: 25 servings

7 large poppings of corn	1 cup white corn syrup
2 cups brown sugar	1 teaspoon vanilla extract
1 cup margarine	1/2 teaspoon soda
1 teaspoon salt	

Bring brown sugar, margarine, salt, and corn syrup to a boil. Remove from heat and stir in vanilla extract and soda. Slowly pour over popped corn and mix thoroughly. Bake on greased cookie sheets at 250° for 40 to 45 minutes. When corn is cool enough to handle, break into pieces.

Mrs. Carl E. Williams (Eddy)

171

CANDIED GRAPEFRUIT PEEL
Don't try to make these in one day!

Yield: Approximately 3 dozen

6 grapefruit halves
4 cups sugar
2 1/2 cups water
Red and green food coloring
Sugar

Scrape grapefruit shells clean and cut into 2-inch strips. Cover with water and boil for 30 minutes. Pour off water and rinse with cold water. Repeat 6 times. At any point, strips may be kept for several days in a bag in the refrigerator. Make a syrup of the sugar and water. Divide; color half red and half green. Cook peel a few at a time, until the peel is clear. Spread on foil and allow to dry overnight. Cut into small strips, roll in sugar and store in airtight container. These keep for weeks. It may be necessary to make extra syrup.

NOTE: This is an old recipe — Martha Washington made it at Mount Vernon.

Mrs. Walter Sanders (Clara Berry)

CREAM CHEESE CANDY
Easy; great for parties

Yield: 4 dozen

1 (8-ounce) package cream cheese
1 (1-pound) box powdered sugar
1 1/2 cups chopped pecans or walnuts
1 teaspoon vanilla extract

Melt cream cheese in double boiler. Mix in sugar, nuts, and vanilla extract. Drop immediately by spoonfuls onto a large sheet of wax paper.

Mrs. Bill McWaters (Linda)

EASY FUDGE

A quick and yummy treat

Yield: 3 dozen

3 (1-ounce) squares
  unsweetened chocolate
1/4 cup butter
3 cups sifted powdered sugar

1 egg
1 teaspoon vanilla extract
1 cup chopped nuts

Melt chocolate and butter over low heat. Blend half of powdered sugar into the melted chocolate. Beat in egg and extract. Add remainder of the sugar and nuts. Press fudge into an 8 or 9-inch square pan lined with waxed paper. Chill until firm.

Mrs. Robert L. Lee (Pam)

★   **GEORGIA PEANUT BRITTLE**
Use a candy thermometer and the brittle will be perfect!

Yield: 2 1/2 to 3 pounds

3 cups sugar
1 cup white corn syrup (Karo)
1/2 cup water
3 cups raw Georgia peanuts

3 teaspoons margarine
1 teaspoon salt
2 tablespoons soda

Grease two long pieces of aluminum foil and have them ready on counter top. Combine sugar, syrup, and water in heavy 5 to 6-quart pan. On medium heat, stir until sugar melts, then add peanuts. Leave on medium to medium-high heat and stir occasionally. Cook until candy thermometer reaches 300° — hard crack stage. Syrup will be golden and peanuts will "pop" because they have roasted. Remove from heat and add margarine, salt, and soda, stirring well. Candy will "puff up". Pour candy on pieces of prepared, greased aluminum foil. Pour candy quickly and stretch, using a fork or hands, when cool enough. Cool and break into pieces.

Mrs. William Donald Tomlinson (Jane)

173

MEXICAN ORANGE CANDY
A Christmas specialty

Yield: 2 dozen squares

1 cup sugar
1 1/2 cups milk
2 cups sugar
Grated rind of two oranges

Pinch of salt
1/2 cup butter
1 cup nuts

Melt the first cup of sugar in a large vessel over medium heat, while the milk is scalding in another boiler. When the sugar is melted (stir continually and watch to keep from scorching), add the hot milk, all at once, stirring. Add the other two cups of sugar to this mixture. This will cause a hard ball in the mixture, but keep stirring until dissolved. Cook until it forms a hard ball in water or use a candy thermometer. Just before it is done, add grated orange rind, salt, butter, and nuts. Remove from heat and beat until creamy and pour into a buttered 9x9-inch pan to cool. Cut into squares when cooled.

Mrs. Arthur Thornton (Catherine)

★ ## ALABAMA PRALINES

Yield: 2 dozen

1 cup buttermilk
2 cups granulated sugar
1 teaspoon soda

Dash salt
1 1/2 cups chopped pecans
1 teaspoon vanilla extract

In ·saucepan, combine buttermilk, sugar, soda, and salt. Bring to a boil and simmer slowly until mixture forms a hard ball when dropped into cold water. Do not stir more than necessary during this cooking period. Remove from heat; add pecans and vanilla extract. Beat until dull. Drop by tablespoons onto foil. Let stand at least 30 minutes to cream and harden.

NOTE: Humidity will cause pralines to become sugary.

Mrs. H. C. Tysinger (Judy)

★

PRALINES I

Foolproof recipe—creamy and good

Yield: 6 to 6 1/2 dozen

5 cups sugar
1 (14-ounce) can condensed
  milk
1 cup milk
5 cups pecans

1 teaspoon salt
1 stick margarine
1 tablespoon vanilla extract

Combine sugar and milks in a large, heavy saucepan. Stir until melted. Add pecans and let the mixture come to a boil. Boil for 20 minutes, stirring constantly. Add salt, butter, and vanilla extract. Remove from heat and beat a few more strokes. Spoon onto waxed paper and let cool.

This recipe can be halved.

Mrs. Tom Smith (Ann)

★

PRALINES II

Yield: 2 to 2 1/2 dozen

3 cups firmly packed
  light brown sugar
1/4 teaspoon cream of tartar
1/8 teaspoon salt

1 cup evaporated milk
2 tablespoons butter
1 teaspoon vanilla extract
2 1/4 cups pecan halves

In saucepan, combine sugar, cream of tartar, salt, and milk. Stir over low heat until sugar dissolves. Cook to 236° or 238° on a candy thermometer, or soft ball stage. Cool to 220°. Add butter, flavoring, and pecans. Beat by hand until creamy. Drop onto waxed paper and let harden.

Mrs. John Dunn (Teresa)

SUGARED NUTS

Oven: 250° 2 1/2 to 3 hours   Yield: 1 1/2 quarts

1 egg white   1/4 teaspoon salt
1/2 cup sugar   1 teaspoon ginger
3/4 teaspoon cinnamon   1 quart pecan halves
3/4 teaspoon cloves

Beat egg white until stiff; add all other ingredients and stir until pecans are well coated. Pour onto buttered baking sheet. Bake at 250° for 2 1/2 to 3 hours. Break apart when cool and store in airtight container.

Mrs. Ellis Crook (Pat)

NUTS AND BOLTS WITH WHITE CHOCOLATE
Easy, easy — good!

Yield: 3 dozen

5 squares Candiquick   1 handful Cheerios
  (white chocolate)   1 handful mixed nuts
1 handful Rice Chex   2 handfuls small pretzels
1 handful Froot Loops

Melt Candiquick in double boiler. Mix all other ingredients. Pour melted chocolate over small amount of mixture at a time. Shape into cookies and place on waxed paper.
Stores well in tins. Freezes well.

Mrs. John Goodrum (Marsha)

❋❋❋❋❋❋❋❋❋❋❋❋❋

For creamier and smoother fudge, add 1 teaspoon cornstarch to each cup of sugar used in making fudge.

Desserts

DESSERTS

Desserts Chapter Design: Left to right: Cross Toaster (1890), "Crescent" Waffle Iron (1910)

APPLE CRISP

Oven: 375° 40 to 45 minutes   Yield: 6 to 8 servings

1 cup sugar
2 teaspoons lemon juice
1/2 teaspoon cinnamon
1/4 cup water

6 tart apples, peeled and sliced
3/4 cup flour
6 tablespoons margarine
1/4 teaspoon salt

Combine 1/2 of sugar, lemon juice, cinnamon, and water in bottom of greased 2-quart baking pan. Mix with apples. Blend rest of sugar, salt, flour, and margarine. Sprinkle on top. Bake at 375° about 40 to 45 minutes. If it doesn't brown well, turn on broiler for a few minutes at end of baking period.

NOTE: More apples can be used, especially if apples are small.

Mrs. James W. Roberts (Sue)

APPLESAUCE GINGERBREAD

Oven: 350° 20 to 30 minutes   Yield: 12 to 15 servings

1 cup sweetened applesauce
1 teaspoon nutmeg
2 tablespoons shortening
1/4 cup sugar
1/4 cup molasses
1 egg, beaten
1/3 cup sour milk

1 cup flour
1/2 teaspoon soda
Pinch of salt
1/2 teaspoon ginger
Whipping cream, whipped
  (optional)

Spread applesauce in bottom of a greased 9x13-inch cake pan. Sprinkle with nutmeg. Cream shortening and add sugar. Add molasses, beaten egg, sour milk, and flour sifted with dry ingredients. Pour batter over applesauce and bake at 350° for 20 to 30 minutes or until done. Serve hot with whipped cream.

Mrs. Phil S. Vincent (Mary Anna)

BANANAS FOSTER
Very easy to prepare several servings at the same time

Yield: 1 serving

2 tablespoons brown sugar
1 tablespoon butter
1 ripe banana, peeled and
   sliced lengthwise
Dash cinnamon

1/2 ounce banana liqueur
1 ounce white rum
1 large scoop vanilla ice cream

Melt sugar and butter in flat chafing dish. Add banana and sauté until tender. Sprinkle with cinnamon. Pour in banana liqueur and rum over all and flame. Baste with warm liquid until flame burns out. Serve immediately over ice cream.

Brennan's of Atlanta
Atlanta, Georgia

BREAD PUDDING
Easy and quick

Oven: 350° 1 hour

Yield: 4 to 6 servings

1/2 cup raisins
5 slices white bread, sliced
   into strips
1/2 stick margarine, melted

3/4 cup sugar
2 eggs
1 teaspoon vanilla extract
2 cups milk

Put raisins in bottom of a greased 1-quart casserole. Dip bread slices in melted margarine and place on top of raisins. Mix sugar, eggs, vanilla extract, and milk and beat well. Pour over bread and raisins. Place casserole in pan of hot water and bake 1 hour at 350 degrees.

Mrs. Everett Gardner (Lillian)

BREAD PUDDING WITH BOURBON SAUCE
Somethin' special

Oven: 350° 45 minutes   Yield: 8 to 10 servings

Pudding:

1 loaf French bread
1 quart milk
3 eggs
1 1/2 cups sugar

2 tablespoons vanilla extract
1 cup raisins
3 tablespoons butter or
    margarine

Sauce:

1 stick margarine
1 cup sugar
1 egg, beaten

1 jigger whiskey, or to taste

PUDDING: Break bread into small pieces, add to milk in bowl, and soak; use hands to crush bread and mix well. Add eggs, sugar, vanilla extract, and raisins and stir well. Grease a thick pan with butter, pour in pudding and bake 45 minutes in 350° oven or until very firm. Let cool. Place on individual dessert plates and when ready to serve, add sauce and heat under broiler.

SAUCE: Put sugar and butter in double boiler and cook until well dissolved. Add well-beaten egg and whip rapidly so egg doesn't curdle. Allow to cool and add whiskey to taste.

Mrs. Richard L. Day (Gayle)

❋❋❋❋❋❋❋❋❋❋❋❋❋

A gelatin dessert will not congeal if frozen pineapple is added. Bring the pineapple to a boil and cook it a minute or two, then it will work perfectly.

LEMON REFRIGERATOR CAKE

Yield: 10 to 12 servings

1 1/2 envelopes unflavored
gelatin dissolved in 1/4
cup cold water
1 cup sugar
3/4 cup lemon juice
1 tablespoon grated lemon
rind
6 egg whites

1/4 teaspoon salt
6 egg yolks
2 dozen lady fingers, split in
half
1 cup heavy cream, whipped
1 3/4 cups grated coconut

Soften gelatin in cold water. In double boiler, heat egg yolks, lemon juice, rind, and sugar. Cook slowly over hot, not boiling, water. Stir in gelatin until dissolved. Beat egg whites and salt until they stand in peaks. When cooked mixture cools, add to whites. Line large mold with split lady fingers. Pour in mixture. Refrigerate overnight. At serving time cover with sweetened whipped cream; sprinkle with coconut.

CHOCOLATE CRISP

Oven: 325° 35 minutes

Yield: 1 (8 or 9-inch) pie

3 egg whites
3/4 cup sugar
1/2 teaspoon vanilla extract
1 package Nabisco chocolate
snaps, crumbed

1 teaspoon baking powder
1/2 cup chopped nuts

Beat egg whites until stiff, gradually adding sugar. Add vanilla. Mix crumbed snaps with baking powder and nuts. Fold into whites. Put into greased pie plate and bake at 325° for 35 minutes. Cut into wedges and top with whipped cream.

Mrs. Charles Woodroof (Minerva)

FRUIT TRIFLE
Delicious and easy

Yield: 8 servings

1/4 pound plain cake
1 (3-ounce) package peach-
 flavored gelatin
1 (20-ounce) can crushed
 pineapple
Milk, with pineapple juice,
 to equal 2 cups

1 (3-ounce) package instant
 vanilla pudding
3 bananas
1 cup frozen non-dairy whipped
 topping, thawed

Slice plain cake and place in bottom of glass 8-inch dish. Mix 1/2 cup boiling water with gelatin. When dissolved, pour over cake. Drain juice from crushed pineapple and reserve. Place pineapple over cake and gelatin. Combine pineapple juice with enough milk to equal 2 cups and mix with instant pudding. Pour over cake, gelatin, and pineapple. Slice the bananas, covering top. Place the non-dairy whipped topping over bananas and spread to cover entire pie.

Mrs. Clifford W. Flud (Virginia)

****

Soften vanilla ice cream and stir into it chopped cashews or peanuts and a little almond extract. Serve with hot fudge sauce.

Thaw a package of frozen raspberries and spoon it over individual servings of orange sherbet. Serve with plain cookies.

Spoon drained canned or frozen peach slices into sherbet glasses. Pour on chilled champagne and ginger ale and top with a scoop of pineapple sherbet.

BLUEBERRY TORTE

Easy dessert and very tasty; can be made a day ahead

Yield: 8 to 10 servings

Crust:

1/2 (13 1/2-ounce) package
   graham cracker crumbs
1 stick margarine

1/2 cup sugar

Filling:

1 (3-ounce) package cream
   cheese
3 tablespoons milk
1/2 cup sugar

1/4 cup pecans
1 pint whipping cream
1 (21-ounce) can blueberry pie
   filling

Mix together the cracker crumbs, margarine, and sugar, and press into the bottom of a 9x13-inch dish.

Blend together the cream cheese, milk, and sugar. Spread over crust layer. Sprinkle nuts on top of cheese layer.

Whip the cream and sweeten to taste. Spread over pecans. Top with a can of blueberry pie filling swirled into the whipped cream. Chill well, then cut into squares and serve.

Mrs. Nathan G. Knight (Ann)

****

For a quick Cherries Jubilee sauce, stir 1/4 cup brandy into a small jar of cherry preserves. Warm and serve. This is also delicious over ice cream.

Make a quick sauce for ice cream or cake by heating maple corn syrup. Just before serving, add 1/2 cup of toasted pecans or other nuts to the syrup.

YUMMY JELL-O CAKE

Marvelous, light summer dessert

Yield: 10 to 12 servings

1 (6-ounce) package strawberry-banana flavored gelatin
1 (29-ounce) can sliced peaches, drained and cut into smaller pieces
3 or 4 bananas, sliced
1 (9-ounce) carton frozen non-dairy whipped topping, thawed
1 loaf-style angel food cake, broken into walnut-size pieces

Make gelatin according to package directions. Line bottom of tube pan or spring-form pan with wax paper. Place half of fruit in bottom of pan, spread on half of whipped topping, then half of cake pieces. Repeat layers. Pour cooled gelatin over ingredients. Refrigerate for several hours before serving. Invert onto serving plate and carefully peel off wax paper.

NOTE: This recipe may be varied by using other fruits and other flavors of gelatin.

Mrs. Carl E. Williams (Eddy)

CHOCOLATE DESSERT

Yield: 6 servings

12 ounces chocolate semi-
  sweet morsels
4 tablespoons sugar
2 eggs
Pinch of salt

1 teaspoon vanilla extract
1 1/2 cups scalded milk
1 (9-ounce) carton non-dairy
  whipped topping

Combine all ingredients including whipped topping and place in blender. Blend. Pour into 9x13-inch dish. Refrigerate overnight. Top with more whipped topping at serving time, if desired.

Mrs. Larry Strickland (Mary)

★ TIPSY SQUIRE

Oven: 350° 20 to 30 minutes   Yield: 8 to 10 servings

Sponge Cake:

3 eggs, separated   1/2 teaspoon baking powder
1/2 cup sugar   1 teaspoon vanilla extract
1/2 cup flour

Custard:

1 quart milk   Sherry, to taste, for flavoring
3 eggs   custard and whipped cream
1/2 cup sugar
1/4 teaspoon salt

Raisins, chopped
Sliced almonds or pecan quarters
1 pint whipping cream, whipped

SPONGE CAKE: Beat the egg whites until stiff, then add
half the sugar. Beat the yolks and add to them the remainder
of the sugar. Combine the two mixtures. Stir in the flour and
the vanilla extract. Bake in one 9-inch layer at 350° for 20 to
30 minutes, or until top springs back when lightly touched.
CUSTARD: Heat milk over low heat or in a double boiler.
Do not boil. Add sugar when thoroughly heated. Beat the eggs
and add to hot milk. Stir constantly until mixture thickens
and flavor with sherry to taste.
Break sponge cake into bite-size pieces. Layer pieces in a
large serving bowl. Sprinkle each layer with nuts and raisins,
then pour custard over. Continue the layers until all cake has
been used. Cover the top with a generous layer of whipped
cream, also flavored with sherry to taste. Refrigerate until
served.

Mrs. J.O. St. John (Virginia)

186

CHARLOTTE I

Good for luncheon, dinner, or dessert bridge

Yield: 8 to 10 servings

1 tablespoon or 1 envelope
    unflavored gelatin
3/4 cup milk or sherry
1 pint whipping cream, whipped

2 egg whites
1 cup sugar
Pecan halves (optional)

Dissolve gelatin in milk or sherry in top of double boiler over hot water, stirring until dissolved. Set aside. Whip cream until stiff; set aside. Beat egg whites until stiff, adding sugar slowly. When gelatin is cool, but not cold, fold gelatin mixture into whipped cream and egg whites. The secret of smooth Charlotte is in the mixing of the gelatin mixture with the cream and egg whites. Put combined mixture in a loaf pan to slice or in compotes. May be tinted with food coloring. Pecan halves may be put on top.

Mrs. W.Y. Ellis (Ida Lee)

CHARLOTTE II

Yield: 6 to 8 servings

1 envelope unflavored gelatin
1/4 cup cold water
1/2 cup milk
1 pint whipping cream

1 cup sugar
4 egg whites, stiffly beaten
Sherry to taste

Soak gelatin in cold water. Heat milk and dissolve gelatin in it. Cool but do not let mixture congeal. Whip the cream, then add sugar and stiffly beaten egg whites. Add sherry. Slowly beat in gelatin until well mixed. Pour into mold or 1 1/2-quart casserole and congeal.

Mrs. James T. Pike (Helen)

CHERRY YUM YUM

Oven: 350° 20 minutes

Yield: 10 to 12 servings

1 1/2 cups all-purpose flour
1 1/2 sticks margarine,
   softened
1/2 cup chopped pecans
2 envelopes Dream Whip
   (prepared)

1 (8-ounce) package cream
   cheese, softened
1 cup powdered sugar
1 (21-ounce) can cherry pie
   filling

Combine flour, softened margarine, and pecans. Press into the bottom of a 9x13-inch pan. Bake 20 minutes at 350°. Cool.

Prepare Dream Whip according to package directions. Beat together the softened cream cheese and powdered sugar. Add the prepared Dream Whip and mix thoroughly. Spread 1/2 of this mixture over the cooled crust. Top with the cherry pie filling. Cover the pie filling with the remaining half of the Dream Whip mixture. Chill at least 3 hours before serving.

NOTE: Strawberry or blueberry pie filling may be substituted for the cherry filling.

Mrs. John Goodrum (Marsha)

****

Spread slightly softened ice cream between chocolate-covered graham crackers. Wrap in foil and freeze.

To a jar of marshmallow cream add a few drops of mint extract. Serve dollops on top of brownie squares.

Ice cream-liqueur combinations:
1) Vanilla ice cream topped with 1 jigger of créme de cacao
2) Lemon sherbet topped with 1 jigger of créme de menthe
3) Toffee ice cream topped with 1 jigger of Kahlúa

CHEESE BLINTZES

Yield: 12 to 14 blintzes

2 cups small curd cottage
  cheese
1 egg yolk
2 tablespoons sugar
3 teaspoons lemon juice

12 to 14 crêpes, cooked
2 tablespoons butter
Powdered sugar
Sour cream
Strawberries, sweetened

Drain the cottage cheese for at least 1/2 hour, then gently press out any excess liquid with the back of a spoon. In a bowl, mix the cottage cheese with the egg yolk, sugar, and lemon juice. Spoon this filling into center of cooked crepes. Fold over bottom, both sides, and top. Melt butter in skillet. Lightly brown blintzes on both sides. Sprinkle with powdered sugar. Serve warm with sour cream and top with sweetened strawberries.

Mrs. Dan B. Umbach (Marie)

EASY CHERRY COBBLER

Oven: 350° 55 minutes

Yield: 6 servings

1 (21-ounce) can cherry pie
  filling
1/2 teaspoon almond extract
1/2 (18-ounce) package cake
  mix (about 2 cups)

Chopped pecans (optional)
1/4 to 1/2 cup melted butter

Mix cherry pie filling with almond extract and pour into buttered 9x9-inch pan. Sprinkle cake mix and nuts over pie filling. Drizzle melted butter over all. Bake in a 350° oven for 55 minutes. Serve warm with ice cream.

Mrs. Eugene F. Secor (Martha)

CHOCOLATE DREAM PIE
Rich and yummy!

Oven: 350° 15 minutes   Yield: 12 to 16 servings

First Layer:

1 cup self-rising flour
1 cup nuts, chopped
1 stick butter, softened

Second Layer:

1 (8-ounce) package cream cheese, softened
1 cup non-dairy whipped topping
1 cup powdered sugar

Third Layer:

2 (6 3/4-ounce) packages instant chocolate pudding
3 1/2 cups milk

Mix ingredients for first layer; spread in a 9x13-inch baking dish. Bake at 350° for 15 minutes. Cool. Mix ingredients for second layer and spread on top of crust. Mix ingredients for third layer and spoon on top. Refrigerate. Serve topped with additional whipped topping.

Mrs. William V. Headley (Anita)

※※※※※※※※※※※※※※

Arrowroot is a useful thickener for desserts because it is clear and almost tasteless.

How to flame a dessert or other dish without using brandy: simply sprinkle drops of fresh lemon extract over the dish and flame!

★   **BLACKBERRY COBBLER**

Oven: 400°   Yield: 6 to 8 servings

Pastry for 1 pie   **4 tablespoons flour**
4 cups blackberries   **3/4 cup water**
1 1/4 cups sugar   **1/4 stick margarine**

Wash and cap berries; drain. Combine berries, sugar, flour, and water, and place in oven-proof baking dish. Prepare pastry and cut into strips. Place small side pieces of pastry into berry mixture. Arrange rest of pastry strips on top of berries and top with pats of margarine. Bake at 400° until crust is golden brown. Serve hot with ice cream or sweetened whipped cream. Raspberries, dewberries, or boysenberries may be substituted for blackberries.

Mrs. H.C. Tysinger (Judy)

FLAN DE LECHE

Oven: 350° 30 minutes   Yield: 6 servings

1/2 cup water   **1 teaspoon vanilla extract**
3 cups sugar   **Pinch of salt**
6 eggs   **1 pint boiling milk**

Boil water and 1 cup sugar until brown. Pour caramel into 6 molds or custard cups. Beat eggs, add remaining sugar, vanilla extract, and salt and beat again. Gradually add milk; strain through cloth. Pour into custard cups; set cups in water-filled pan. Bake 1/2 hour at 350°. Do not let water boil or custard will have bubbles. Cool in refrigerator. To serve, press edges of custard with spoon to break away from mold and invert. Caramel then tops the custard.

Mrs. Gaston W. Green (Happy)

BOILED CUSTARD
Very easy and good with your favorite cookie!

Yield: 8 servings

1 quart milk
4 eggs
1 cup sugar
2 tablespoons cornstarch

Flavoring (vanilla, rum, or nutmeg)

Pour milk into the top of a double boiler to heat. Mix 4 egg yolks and 3 egg whites, setting aside one of the egg whites. Mix thoroughly with sugar and cornstarch. Gradually add this mixture to the heated milk in the top of the double boiler and keep stirring. The contents are ready when the mixture covers the spoon. Mixture should be thicker than buttermilk but not as thick as pudding. Remove from heat. Beat the remaining egg white with a beater until it peaks. Then mix a little bit of egg white into the mixture and stir. Keep mixing a little of the egg white in and stirring until it is all gone. Flavor with vanilla, rum, or nutmeg.

Serve either hot or cold in bowls, along with your favorite cookie.

Mrs. Jack Camp (Sophia Stephens)
Moreland, Georgia

****

Fill drained canned pear halves with a scoop of vanilla ice cream. Drizzle chocolate syrup over ice cream and top with pecan halves.

Easy Cherries Jubilee: bake frozen patty shells as package directs and cool. In a saucepan combine one 16-ounce can of cherry pie filling with 1/4 cup brandy **or** 2 tablespoons brandy-flavored extract **or** 2 tablespoons orange extract. Heat until warm. Scoop vanilla ice cream into patty shells and spoon cherries over ice cream.

HORNS ·
Indescribably delicious!

Oven: 375° 30 minutes   Yield: Approximately 5 dozen

sticks butter
cup sour cream
tablespoon sugar
1/2 cups flour

Filling:

1/2 cup (more, if needed)		**1/2 cup (more, if needed)**
apricot jam	**OR**	**strawberry jam**
1/2 cup chopped walnuts		**1/2 cup chopped pecans**

Powdered Sugar

Blend butter, sour cream, and 1 tablespoon sugar. Gradually mix in flour using fork or fingers. Form into balls. Wrap in wax paper and refrigerate 3 hours.

Combine jam and nuts for filling. Remove small amount of chilled dough from refrigerator. Roll chilled dough on well-floured board into a 6-inch circle approximately 1/8 inch thick. Divide circle in half, then in fourths – making 4 equal triangles per circle. Place 1/2 to 1 teaspoon of filling in center of each triangle. Fold the two side corners of each triangle to the center. Roll.

Place seam down on ungreased baking sheet and bake at 375° for 1/2 hour or until lightly browned. Roll in powdered sugar.

Mrs. Jack Slavin (Ruth)
New York, New York

※※※※※※※※※※※※※

Quickie Spumoni: stir 1 tablespoon rum and 1/4 cup chopped candied fruits into 1 pint of softened vanilla ice cream. Spoon into 8 paper baking cups in muffin tins and freeze until firm.

FROZEN MINT LIME DESSERT

Yield: 16 serving

1 cup butter mints
1 (8-ounce) can crushed
   pineapple
1 (20-ounce) can crushed
   pineapple
1 (3-ounce) package lime-
   flavored gelatin

1 package (3 1/2 cups) tiny
   marshmallows
1 (9-ounce) carton frozen
   whipped dessert topping,
   thawed

In large bowl combine mints, both cans undrained pine apple, dry lime gelatin, and marshmallows. Cover and refrigerat for several hours or until mints are dissolved. Fold in desser topping. Spoon mixture in 16 paper baking cups in muffi pan. Cover and freeze 6 hours or overnight.

Mrs. Paul R. McKnight, Jr. (Totsie
Senoia, Georgi

FROZEN LEMON DESSERT
Low in calories and delicious

Yield: 12 serving

1 cup graham cracker crumbs,
   divided
1 (13-ounce) can evaporated
   skimmed milk, chilled

3/4 cup sugar
Juice and grated rind of
   lemons
4 drops yellow coloring

Place half the crumbs in a 12x8x2-inch pan. Whip th milk; add slowly the sugar, lemon juice, rind, and food coloring Pour mixture over the crumbs and top with remaining crumbs Freeze. This keeps well for 2 weeks. It may be made witl regular evaporated milk.

Mrs. Joseph S. Adams (Myrtice

DATE BARS

Oven: 350° 15 minutes   Yield: 32 (1x2-inch) bars
      300° 30 minutes

Bar:

1/2 cup shortening
3 tablespoons light brown
  sugar
1 cup sifted all-purpose flour

1/2 teaspoon salt
1 (8-ounce) package pitted
  dates, pressed flat

Topping:

3 eggs
1 cup light brown sugar,
  firmly packed
2 tablespoons all-purpose flour
1/2 teaspoon baking powder

1/2 cup chopped pecans
1 1/2 cups coconut
1 teaspoon vanilla extract

Icing: (optional)

2 cups sifted powdered sugar
2 tablespoons melted butter

2 tablespoons milk

BAR: Cream shortening and sugar until light and fluffy. Add flour and salt. Press mixture into paper-lined 8x8-inch pan. Bake at 350° for 15 minutes or until delicately brown. Remove from oven and place dates on top of mixture.

TOPPING: Beat eggs until light and fluffy. Add light brown sugar and beat until dissolved. Add flour and baking powder, sifted together. Mix until smooth. Fold in chopped nuts, coconut, and vanilla extract. Spread over baked mixture and return to oven and continue baking at 300° for about 30 minutes.

ICING: Cream ingredients and spread on top of cooled date bars which have been cut into squares. Place a pecan half on each bar.

Mrs. Thomas A. Luckie (Pollye)

195

DATE DESSERT
Never fails

Oven: 375° 20 minutes

Yield: 20 to 30 servings

1 3/4 cups quick oats
1 3/4 cups all-purpose flour
1 teaspoon soda
1/4 teaspoon salt
1 teaspoon vanilla extract

3/4 cup butter
1 cup brown sugar
1/2 pound chopped dates
1 cup water
1 cup sugar

Cook the last three ingredients in a saucepan until thick. While cooking the last three, mix the first seven ingredients in a mixing bowl. Mix dry ingredients very well, but be sure to keep an eye on the date mixture so it will not stick. Press half of crumbly mixture into a 9x9-inch pan, patting down firmly. Pour thick date mixture over this, then add remaining rolled oats mixture on top, patting down somewhat, but do not mash down. Bake about 20 minutes in a 375° oven, or until brown. Wait until thoroughly cool to cut into bars.

Mrs. Jack T. Camp, Jr. (Elizabeth)

ICE CREAM DESSERT
Freezes well

Yield: 10 to 12 servings

1/2 gallon vanilla ice cream, softened
1 (13 1/2-ounce) carton non-dairy whipped topping
1 dozen coconut macaroons, crumbled
1/4 cup sherry or rum

Soften ice cream. Crumble macaroons and pour sherry or rum over these and let stand until soft. Add whipped topping to ice cream and then macaroon crumbs. Pour into 9x13-inch casserole dish and freeze.

Mrs. C.A. Moody (Virginia)

ROBBYE'S CHOCOLATE DESSERT

Yield: 12 to 14 servings

1 (10 or 12-ounce) box vanilla
   wafers
1 quart vanilla ice cream
3 eggs, separated
3 cups powdered sugar

1 1/3 sticks margarine, softened
5 (1-ounce) squares semi-sweet
   chocolate, melted
2 teaspoons vanilla extract
1 cup chopped pecans

Butter sides and bottom of 9x13-inch pan. Crush all vanilla wafers; mix a very small amount of ice cream with wafers to soften. Press half of the wafers into the bottom of the pan. Beat egg yolks, sugar, margarine, and chocolate. Add vanilla extract. Beat egg whites until stiff, adding a little extra sugar. Blend together the chocolate mixture and egg whites. Spread on top of crumbs. Spread pecans on top, then a layer of softened ice cream. Sprinkle on remainder of crumbs and freeze. Cut with sharp knife into squares. Remove from freezer 15 minutes before serving.

Mrs. Thomas R. Kerley (Lynda)
Lexington, Kentucky

★   **PEACH ICE CREAM**
Very rich

Yield: 12 to 16 servings

1 quart peach purée
2 cups sugar
1 1/2 quarts half and half

Purée fresh peaches in blender or processor. Add sugar and whirl again. Mix in half and half and freeze in crank or electric freezer.

Mrs. Charles B. Woodroof, Jr. (Amelia)

197

ICE CREAM
Very easy with many variations

Yield: 1 gallon

Basic Recipe:

4 whole eggs	3 pints (approximately) half-
3 cups sugar	and-half cream
1 (13-ounce) can evaporated	Vanilla
milk	

Beat together ingredients in Basic Recipe. Add ingredients listed under one of the following variations:

PEACH: To the Basic Recipe add 6 or 7 finely chopped (or put in blender) ripe peaches.

BANANA: To the Basic Recipe add 3 mashed, ripe bananas.

CHOCOLATE: In the Basic Recipe substitute 1 can Hershey syrup for 1 cup of sugar.

CHOCOLATE CHIP: Partially freeze chocolate ice cream; then add 1/2 cup finely grated baking chocolate, chocolate candy bar, or chocolate chips.

CHERRY: To the Basic Recipe add 1/4 cup finely chopped maraschino cherries and 2 tablespoons cherry juice.

STRAWBERRY: To the Basic Recipe add 1 1/2 cups strawberries. When this mixture is partially frozen, add 1/2 cup finely chopped strawberries.

NOTE: Add only enough half-and-half cream in Basic Recipe to fill freezer 2/3 full.

Mrs. Robert L. Lee (Pam)

This recipe is used by the Sisters of Lourdes Hospital, Paducah, Kentucky.

※※※※※※※※※※※※※

When scalding milk, rinse the pan in cold water before heating to prevent sticking.

CHOCOLATE ICE CREAM

Yield: 1 or 1 1/2 gallons

For 1-gallon freezer:

3 eggs
1 1/2 cups sugar
1 (14-ounce) can sweetened
  condensed milk
1 quart milk

1 tablespoon vanilla extract
1/4 (16-ounce) can chocolate
  syrup (or more to taste)
1/2 pint whipping cream,
  whipped

For 1 1/2-gallon freezer:

4 large eggs
2 cups sugar
2 (14-ounce) cans sweetened
  condensed milk
1/2 gallon milk

2 tablespoons vanilla extract
1/2 (16-ounce) can chocolate
  syrup
1/2 pint whipping cream,
  whipped

Have all ingredients cold. Mix eggs and sugar with a beater or in blender. Pour into ice cream freezer. Add remaining ingredients, whipped cream last. Freeze in electric or crank-style freezer.

Mrs. Holden Thompson (Elsie)
Atlanta, Georgia

❊❊❊❊❊❊❊❊❊❊❊❊❊

For easy party serving, scoop ice cream ahead of time into paper muffin cups; place on a baking sheet in the freezer. When the candles are on the cake, bring out the ice cream. Ready to serve. No removing paper lids or last minute dipping!

Make an easy, colorful, no-cook dessert. Layer sliced fresh peaches, strawberries, melon balls or slices, and berries with sour cream and brown sugar in a pretty crystal bowl. Refrigerate until ready to serve.

BASIC ICE CREAM
Economical and very good

Yield: 1 gallon

4 eggs, separated
2 1/2 cups sugar
1 tablespoon vanilla

2 (13-ounce) cans evaporated
milk
3 quarts homogenized milk

Beat egg whites until stiff, but not dry. Set aside. Thoroughly combine egg yolks, sugar, and vanilla. Gradually add the evaporated milk to the mixture. Gently fold in the stiff egg whites. Put mixture into the cylinder of the ice cream freezer. Finish filling the cylinder with homogenized milk until it is approximately 3/4 full. Stir and freeze.

NOTE: **Sweetened** fruit may be added before filling the cylinder with homogenized milk.

Mrs. G.A. Giddings, Jr. (Rita)

★ ## HOMEMADE PEACH ICE CREAM
Peachy perfect

Yield: 16 servings

3 cups mashed peaches
3 cups sugar
4 eggs, well beaten
2 teaspoons vanilla extract

1 (13-ounce) can evaporated
milk
1/2 gallon milk, approximately

Mix peaches and sugar. Add beaten eggs and mix thoroughly. Add vanilla and evaporated milk. Stir well and pour into ice cream freezer. Finish filling freezer with milk. Freeze.

Mrs. Jim Luckie (Sandra)

★ **FRESH PEACH ICE CREAM**

Yield: 10 to 12 servings

1 1/3 cups sugar
1/8 teaspoon salt
2 tablespoons flour
2 eggs, slightly beaten
1 1/2 cups milk

2 cups heavy cream or evaporated milk
1/2 teaspoon almond extract
2 teaspoons vanilla extract
2 cups crushed peaches

Mix dry ingredients. Blend into eggs. Add milks and flavorings. Stir in peaches. Put in ice cream freezer and churn.

Mrs. John W. Anderson (Nancy)

STRAWBERRY ICE CREAM

Yield: 1 gallon

3 large eggs
1 cup sugar
Juice of 1 lemon
1 package Junket strawberry
  ice cream mix
1 (13-ounce) can evaporated
  milk

1 teaspoon vanilla extract
1 can sweetened condensed milk
Milk (approximately 1 3/4
  quarts)
1 (10-ounce) package frozen
  strawberries, thawed

Beat eggs until frothy. Gradually add sugar and lemon juice beating constantly. Add ice cream mix and vanilla. Add evaporated milk and condensed milk, stirring well. Next, add 1 cup milk and thawed strawberries. (If a pinker color is desired, a drop or two of red food coloring may be added.) Pour mixture into a 4-quart ice cream freezer. Add enough additional milk to fill freezer 3/4 full. Freeze.

Mrs. Fred Gilbert (Ann)

ICE CREAM DELIGHT
May be stored several days in freezer

Yield: 12 servings

1 stick or 1/4 pound
margarine
1 cup brown sugar
2 1/2 cups crushed Rice
Chex cereal
1/2 cup slivered almonds,
slightly toasted

1 (3 1/2-ounce) can moist
coconut
1 half gallon peppermint ice
cream
1 pint whipping cream or non-
dairy whipped topping
(optional)

Melt margarine and mix with the brown sugar. Cook over a low heat until well mixed. In a large bowl mix the Rice Chex, coconut, and almonds. Pour the butter-sugar mixture over the coconut mixture and mix well. Cover the bottom of a 9x13-inch pan with 1/2 of the mixture. Cover with the sliced ice cream. Pour other half of the coconut mixture over the ice cream. Freeze overnight. When serving, cut into squares and top with cream whipped with 2 tablespoons sugar or non-dairy whipped topping. A topping of hot fudge sauce may also be used.

Mrs. Karl Nixon (Mary)

✳✳✳✳✳✳✳✳✳✳✳✳✳✳

Keep all cream-filled desserts refrigerated.

Mix 3/4 cup sugar, 1 cup water, and a dash of lemon juice in a saucepan; boil 5 minutes. Add dried currants or raisins and allow them to stand until they plump up. Serve this sauce hot or cold over ice cream. This sauce keeps almost indefinitely in the refrigerator.

If custard curdles during cooking due to high heat, pour immediately into a cold bowl and beat hard with a whisk.

CHOCO-MINT FREEZE

Lengthy but well worth the time

Yield: 8 servings

1 1/4 cups vanilla wafer crumbs
  (or graham cracker)
4 tablespoons margarine, melted
1 quart peppermint ice cream,
  softened
2 ounces unsweetened
  chocolate
1 stick margarine

1 1/2 cups powdered sugar
3 egg yolks, well beaten
1/2 cup chopped pecans
1 teaspoon vanilla extract
3 egg whites

Combine the crumbs and margarine; reserve 1/4 cup. Press remaining cup of crumb mixture in 9x9x2-inch baking dish. Spread ice cream on top of crumb mixture. Melt the chocolate and butter over low heat. Gradually stir the powdered sugar into the egg yolks; add nuts and vanilla extract. Combine the chocolate mixture and the sugar mixture. Cool thoroughly. Beat egg whites until stiff peaks form. Beat chocolate mixture until smooth; fold in egg whites. Spread chocolate mixture over ice cream. Top with the reserved 1/4 cup crumbs. Freeze.

Mrs. Joe W. Wray (Sara)
Atlanta, Georgia

✳✳✳✳✳✳✳✳✳✳✳✳✳

Tomato juice-31 to 43 calories per 6 ounces
Club soda-0 calories
Tonic-12 calories per ounce

Gin, rum, vodka, whiskey:
1 jigger (1 1/2 ounces) 80 proof   97 calories
1 jigger 86 proof   105 calories
1 jigger 90 proof   110 calories
1 jigger 94 proof   116 calories
1 jigger 100 proof   124 calories

203

CREME AU GRAND MARNIER
May be frozen ahead

Yield: 6 to 8 servings

6 egg yolks at room
temperature
3/4 cup sugar (scant)
2 cups whipping cream

1 1/2 ounces Grand Marnier
3/4 cup whipping cream,
whipped

Beat egg yolks and sugar until very thick. Whip the cream until it is the same consistency as the egg yolks; gradually add Grand Marnier. Fold the 2 mixtures together until thoroughly combined. Pour into demitasse cups and freeze at least 2 hours. Decorate with the 3/4 cup cream, whipped. Sweeten cream, if desired.

NOTE: Optional garnishes include: chocolate curls, orange rind curls, or crystallized violets. If mixture is prepared and frozen ahead, let stand at room temperature until only slightly frozen.

Mrs. George C. Bull, Jr. (Helen)
Cameron, South Carolina

****

Soufflé tips:
1. If the whites are overbeaten and the base is too thick, a soufflé will split. If the base is too thin, a soufflé will run.
2. A soufflé should be baked at a moderate temperature so the heat can penetrate uniformly and make it rise evenly.
3. Speed is all important. Combine the beaten egg whites with the base sauce as fast as possible. Egg whites that stand after being beaten rapidly become grainy and break down-resulting in a soufflé that splits while baking.
4. A soufflé may be combined up to 2 hours before baking. Whipped egg whites must not be held, but once combined with the base sauce, the mixture will be safe for a few hours.
5. A soufflé should go from the oven immediately to the table!

CHOCOLATE MOUSSE
Freezes well

Yield: 10 servings

1 package lady fingers
1 (6-ounce) package chocolate
  chips
2 tablespoons margarine
5 eggs, separated

3 tablespoons water
1 (13 1/2-ounce) container
  non-dairy whipped topping,
  thawed

Butter an 8-inch spring form pan and line the edges with lady fingers. Melt chocolate chips with margarine and cool. Separate eggs; beat the yolks with water, then slowly add to chocolate mixture. Beat egg whites until stiff, then fold in the whipped topping. Add three-fourths of this mixture to the chocolate mixture. Pour into the pan, gently filling the center of the lady finger wall. Top with the remaining one-fourth of the egg white mixture. Chill until serving time.

Mrs. Marion Truitt (Pauline)

****

Different coolers! Top a glass of chilled cranberry-apple juice with a scoop of frozen raspberry or boysenberry yogurt. Or top chilled apple juice with frozen strawberry yogurt.

Reduce calories in mixed drinks:
1 teaspoon lemon juice- 1 calorie
1 teaspoon lime juice- 1 calorie
Unsweetened grapefruit juice-12 calories per ounce
Bouillon or beef broth-6 calories per cube
                6 calories per 4 ounces
                   canned broth

ELEGANT CHOCOLATE MOUSSE
A delectable, do-ahead dessert for a special dinner

Yield: 8 to 10 servings

3 egg whites
2 cups heavy cream, whipped
8 ounces German sweet
   chocolate

1 cup powdered sugar
Additional whipping cream,
   whipped and sweetened
   for topping
Chocolate curls

Let egg whites warm to room temperature-about 1 hour. Whip cream until very thick. Refrigerate until needed. In top of double boiler over hot, not boiling, water, melt chocolate, stirring constantly. Whip egg whites until they peak. Gradually add sugar and continue beating until very stiff. Carefully fold egg whites into whipped cream. Very, very slowly, dribble melted chocolate into mixture, gently folding just enough to combine. Carefully turn into an attractive serving dish. Refrigerate overnight. Several hours before serving, decorate mousse with additional whipped cream and chocolate curls.

To make chocolate curls, warm chocolate bar in wrapper until slightly soft. Then, with vegetable peeler pressing lightly, pare along bar in a long, thin stroke. Refrigerate until used.

Mrs. John N. White (Martha)

****

Gelatin tips:
   To substitute plain gelatin for a 3-ounce package of flavored gelatin in a recipe, add about 1/4 cup sugar to one envelope of unflavored gelatin.

   One envelope of plain gelatin or one 3-ounce package of flavored gelatin sets 2 cups each of liquid and of drained fruit.

★ ## PEACH MOUSSE

Yield: 10 to 12 servings

1 (16-ounce) package frozen
fresh peaches, preferably
home-frozen
1 envelope unflavored gelatin
4 eggs, separated
1/2 cup juice, drained from
peaches
1 tablespoon lemon juice

1/2 cup water
1/8 teaspoon salt
1/4 teaspoon almond extract
1/2 cup sugar
1/2 pint whipping cream,
whipped

Drain juice from peaches and set peaches aside. Sprinkle gelatin on juice to soften. Beat egg yolks and water together and add to gelatin mixture. Cook in double boiler until gelatin is dissolved and mixture is somewhat thickened. Remove from heat; add lemon juice, salt, and almond extract. Chill slightly. Puree peaches and add to cooled mixture. Beat egg whites until thick and add sugar gradually, beating until stiff. Fold into peach mixture. Whip the cream. Reserve some for garnish; fold remainder into mixture. Place in dessert dishes and chill overnight. Garnish with whipped cream.

Mrs. Charles B. Woodroof, Jr. (Amelia)

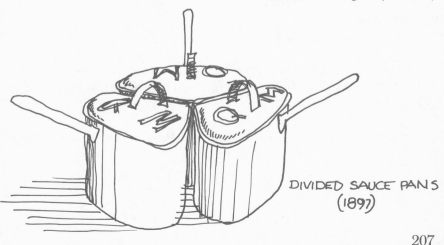

DIVIDED SAUCE PANS
(1897)

MERINGUE SHELLS

Oven: 250° 45 minutes

Yield: 50 very small shells or 25 larger shells

12 egg whites
2 1/2 cups sugar
2 teaspoons vanilla extract

Beat egg whites until stiff, gradually adding small amounts of sugar. Add vanilla extract and mix. Prepare cookie sheets with brown paper. Scoop meringue mixture onto sheets in small mounds. Make an indentation with back of spoon for filling. Cook at 250° for 45 minutes; turn oven off and let cool for 30 minutes. These keep well in a tightly closed container. If shells become tacky in humid weather, cook for 10 minutes at 150° to dry them out. Fill with Lemon Cheese Sauce.

Mrs. W. Earnest Barron (Carolyn)

LEMON CHEESE SAUCE
Delicious filling for meringue shells

12 egg yolks, well beaten
1 cup lemon juice, bottled
4 cups sugar
1 cup butter or margarine

Combine ingredients and cook over hot, not boiling, water in a double boiler. Stir frequently and cook until thick (45 to 60 minutes).

Mrs. W. Earnest Barron (Carolyn)

LEMON DELIGHTS

Oven: 250° 25 to 30 minutes　　Yield: Approximately 35 shells

Meringue:

4 egg whites
1/4 teaspoon cream of tartar
1 cup sugar

Filling:

4 egg yolks
1/2 cup sugar
1/4 cup bottled lemon juice
1 (4 1/2-ounce) container whipped topping

MERINGUES: Add cream of tartar to egg whites. Beat at high speed until soft peaks form. Gradually add 1 cup sugar; beat until stiff. Shape with spoon on foil-lined cookie sheet, using 1 level tablespoon for each shell. Bake at 250° for 25 to 30 minutes. Turn off oven and allow to dry thoroughly in oven. Store in closed container.

FILLING: Beat egg yolks and add sugar, continuing to beat until sugar is dissolved. Blend in lemon juice. Cook in small saucepan or double boiler over low to moderate heat, stirring constantly, until mixture is thick. Remove from heat, cool, and store in covered container in refrigerator up to 2 days. When ready to serve, remove sauce from refrigerator and beat until fluffy. Blend in whipped topping and fill meringue shells.

Mrs. John G. Wilkinson (Elizabeth)

❋❋❋❋❋❋❋❋❋❋❋❋❋

Use potato water (water in which potatoes were boiled) to make yeast breads. The potato water keeps the bread fresh longer and gives it a slightly greater volume but coarser texture.

FRENCH PUDDING
Very rich and delicious

Yield: 10 servings

2 cups vanilla wafers, crushed
1 stick margarine, melted
1 (1-pound) box powdered
    sugar
2 eggs
2 sticks margarine
1 (8-ounce) can crushed pine-
    apple, drained

1 (10-ounce) package frozen
    strawberries, drained
1 cup chopped nuts
1/2 pint whipping cream,
    whipped

    Combine vanilla wafers and melted margarine; make a crust with this mixture in a greased, oblong, 2-quart casserole. Mix the powdered sugar, eggs, and 2 sticks margarine, and beat for 15 minutes—no less! Spread this pudding over the crust. Layer the thoroughly drained pineapple over the pudding; next, layer the strawberries. Sprinkle nuts over fruit. Top with layer of whipped cream. Refrigerate. Cut into squares to serve.

    NOTE: For variety, substitute 3 to 5 sliced bananas and 1 bottle of chopped cherries over pineapple for strawberries.

Mrs. William Donald Tomlinson (Jane)

✻✻✻✻✻✻✻✻✻✻✻✻✻

Use a metal ice cube rack to cut biscuit dough quickly into squares.

Whole wheat flour can usually be substituted cup for cup for all-purpose flour in any recipe, but the final product will be heavier. Try using a mixture of white flour and whole wheat for a lighter product.

Stir whole wheat flour before measuring it; do not sift it-the grains will clog the sifter and the flavorful, nutritious particles will not pass through.

LEMON ICE BOX PUDDING

Yield: 8 to 10 servings

3 eggs, separated
1/2 cup sugar
Juice of 2 lemons or 1/4 cup
    lemon juice

4 tablespoons sugar
1/2 pint whipping cream,
    whipped
Vanilla wafers

Beat 3 egg yolks until creamy, adding 1/2 cup sugar gradually. Add juice of 2 lemons, or 1/4 cup juice. Put in top of double boiler, cook until thick, stirring all the time.

Whip 3 egg whites until stiff. Add 4 tablespoons sugar. Add beaten egg whites to yolk mixture. Whip 1/2 pint cream until thick and add to egg mixture. Mix well. Crush vanilla wafers. Put layer of custard in 2-quart flat casserole. Cover with layer of cracker crumbs and repeat layers.

Mrs. Jimmy Mann (Sallie)

CORNFLAKE AND NUT MERINGUES

Low cholesterol

Oven: 300° 20 minutes

Yield: Approximately 2 dozen

1 egg white
1/2 cup sugar
1/4 teaspoon salt
1/2 teaspoon vanilla extract

1/2 cup chopped walnuts
1 cup cornflakes or Special K

Preheat oven to 300° Beat egg white until stiff in large bowl. Beat in sugar gradually, then add salt and vanilla extract. Add nuts and cornflakes. Drop by teaspoonfuls onto a well-oiled (corn oil) baking sheet. Bake for approximately 20 minutes at 300°. Meringues should be dry but not brown. Remove from baking sheet while still warm.

Mrs. John M. Stuckey (Sandy)

NUT PUDDING

A very special family favorite!

Oven: 380° 19 minutes   Yield: 12 to 16 servings

6 eggs, separated
1 1/2 cups sugar
1 1/2 cups finely chopped
  nuts
1 teaspoon vanilla extract
1 teaspoon baking powder

2 heaping tablespoons all-
  purpose flour
1 1/2 pints whipping cream,
  whipped
Vanilla extract to taste
Sugar to taste

Beat egg yolks. Add sugar, then fold in the stiffly beaten egg whites. Add nuts, vanilla, and baking powder mixed with flour. Bake in 3 cake pans lined with paper, greased, and floured, at 380° for 19 minutes. Turn out of pans to cool. Meanwhile, whip cream and add vanilla and sugar to taste. Stack layers with whipped cream several hours before serving. Keeps 2 or 3 days in refrigerator.

Mrs. Charles W. Farmer, Jr. (Elsie)

RUM PUDDING

A real holiday dinner treat.

Yield: 12 to 15 servings

1 box vanilla wafers
2 egg yolks, lightly beaten
1/2 cup sugar
4 tablespoons rum

1 pint whipping cream,
  whipped
2 egg whites, stiffly beaten
1 (6-ounce) bottle red cherries
1 cup pecans, chopped

Crush vanilla wafers and line 3 ice trays which have been slightly buttered. To egg yolks, slowly add sugar and rum, mixing well. Add stiffly beaten egg whites to whipped cream. Add egg mixture to cream mixture. Add cherries and pecans. Put into ice trays and cover with a layer of crushed vanilla wafers. Freeze overnight.

Mrs. Hugh A. Farmer (Zoe)

CHOCOLATE-ALMOND SOUFFLÉ
WITH VANILLA SAUCE

Oven: 375° 45 minutes   Yield: 4 servings

Soufflé:

1 to 2 tablespoons soft butter	1/3 cup sugar
2 tablespoons all-purpose flour	3 egg yolks
4 ounces German chocolate	5 to 6 egg whites
2 tablespoons strong coffee or	2 tablespoons sugar
1 tablespoon coffee, 1	1/2 cup ground almonds
tablespoon cognac	2 tablespoons vanilla extract
2 tablespoons flour	or cognac
1 cup half and half or	1/2 tablespoon almond extract
1 cup milk or evaporated milk	

Vanilla Sauce:

1/3 cup sugar	2 tablespoons butter
1 tablespoon cornstarch	1 tablespoon brandy
1 cup milk	Dash salt

SOUFFLÉ: Generously butter a 6-cup straight-sided baking dish. Flour it and knock out the excess. In a heavy saucepan or double boiler melt the chocolate with the coffee/cognac. Make a smooth paste of the flour and some of the milk. Beat in remaining milk and sugar. Cook several minutes until very thick. After removing from the heat, stir in chocolate mixture. Let cool somewhat, add yolks, and beat well. Beat egg whites with sugar. Add almonds and flavorings. Beat some of the egg white mixture into the chocolate mixture to lighten it. With a spatula fold in the remaining egg whites. Be sure to leave big lumps of whites throughout to assure puffiness. Pour into mold. Cover with a cake tin lid or heavy pan of some kind if not baked immediately. Remove cover and bake in a 375° oven for 45 minutes. Try not to open the door during cooking. Serve immediately after removal with vanilla sauce.

VANILLA SAUCE: Stir first three ingredients in heavy saucepan or double boiler until thick. Remove from heat, add butter, brandy, and salt. Serve hot over soufflé.

Mrs. Charles B. Woodroof, Jr. (Amelia)

213

DAIQUIRI SOUFFLÉ

A nice summer treat that may be frozen

Yield: 8 to 10 servings

10 eggs, separated
2 cups sugar
1/2 cup lime juice
1/2 cup lemon juice
Grated rind of 2 lemons
   and 2 limes
Pinch of salt

2 tablespoons unflavored
   gelatin
1/2 cup rum
3 cups whipping cream
Green food coloring
Pistachio nuts

Beat egg yolks. Add 1 cup sugar. Add lime and lemon juices, rinds, and salt. Cook in double boiler over hot water until thick. Soak gelatin in rum. Stir into hot custard. Cool. Beat the 10 egg whites until stiff. Add the other cup of sugar. Gradually fold whites into **cool** custard. Whip 2 cups of cream, and fold into custard mixture. Add enough green food coloring to color a delicate green. Pour into 6-cup soufflé dish, using collar if necessary.

To serve, remove collar from soufflé dish. Whip the remaining cup of cream. Put on top of soufflé. Decorate top with pistachio nuts and lime curls. Candied violets and lime twists served on the top as garnishes are also very pretty. Serve from dish.

Mrs. W. R. Arnall (Louise)
Luthersville, Georgia

****

Biscuits will split open more easily if the dough is rolled thin and folded over once before cutting.

Slice bagels thinly with a meat slicer and toast under a broiler for a diet treat. 1/5 of a bagel has only 20 calories.

Whole wheat flour will become rancid if improperly stored. Keep the flour in a moisture-proof plastic bag in the refrigerator or freezer to protect its flavor and ensure a long shelf life.

CHOCOLATE SOUFFLÉ
Very rich, very elegant, and very easy!

Yield: 4 servings

1 (6-ounce) package semi-sweet
  chocolate bits
1 egg
1 teaspoon vanilla extract
2 1/2 teaspoons sugar

Pinch of salt
3/4 cup hot milk
Kahlúa
Whipping cream, whipped

Put first six ingredients into blender, milk last. Mix on low for one minute. Pour into pot de crème pots or small custard cups. Put into refrigerator. Top each serving with one teaspoon of Kahlúa and whipped cream, if desired.

Mrs. Tom F. Farmer (Mary Anne)

CHOCOLATE TARTS

Yield: 8 to 10 servings

3 egg yolks
1 cup sugar
2 tablespoons flour
1 cup milk
1/2 stick butter

2 1/2 squares unsweetened
  chocolate, melted
1 cup nuts, toasted
8 to 10 baked tart shells or
1 (9-inch) baked pie shell

Beat egg yolks until they are very light. Mix sugar and flour and sift together. Add flour and sugar mixture to egg yolks. Add milk and butter. Cook over hot water in double boiler until thick. Add melted chocolate and cook 15 to 20 minutes, stirring often. Add 1 cup toasted nuts to filling just before filling tart shells. Top with whipped cream.

Mrs. Raleigh Arnall (Susan)

LEMON CUSTARD TARTS

A light, delicious dessert

Yield: 12 to 15 servings

6 large egg yolks
3/4 cup sugar
3/4 cup fresh lemon juice
2 teaspoons grated lemon rind
1 envelope unflavored gelatin
1/4 cup cold water
6 egg whites, at room temperature

3/4 cup sugar
1 cup whipping cream,
  whipped and flavored to
  taste with vanilla and sugar
Cherries to garnish

In small bowl, beat egg yolks with 3/4 cup sugar until thick and lemon-colored. Blend in juice and rind. Transfer to double boiler. Cook over hot, not boiling, water until mixture coats a spoon, stirring to be sure it cooks evenly. Remove from heat. Sprinkle gelatin over cold water; let stand 5 minutes. Stir into hot mixture and cool to room temperature. Beat egg whites. Add sugar and beat until stiff. Fold into cooled custard. Refrigerate. Let mixture come almost to room temperature before serving. Stir gently and fill tart shells or custard cups. Garnish with whipped cream and cherries.

NOTE: For easy tart shells, use pie crust mix. Roll out a small amount of dough, shape foil around the dough to form the desired size shell, and bake.

Mrs. John P. Woods, Jr. (Elizabeth)

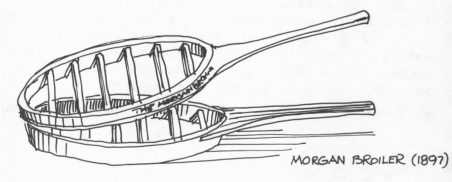

MORGAN BROILER (1897)

★ ## PECAN TARTS

Oven: 350° 20 to 30 min.   Yield: 5 dozen

Crust:

1 stick margarine
1 (3-ounce) package cream cheese
1 1/2 cups all-purpose flour

Filling:

1 stick margarine
1 cup sugar
2 eggs, unbeaten
1 teaspoon vanilla extract
1 cup chopped pecans

CRUST: Mix together margarine and cream cheese. Add flour. Roll very thinly; cut with a biscuit cutter. Place in very small tins.

FILLING: Melt margarine. Add sugar, eggs, and vanilla. Add nuts and mix well. Put 1 teaspoon in each uncooked pastry. Cook 20 to 30 minutes at 350°.

Carrie May McElroy

✳✳✳✳✳✳✳✳✳✳✳✳✳

Add 1 teaspoon molasses to pancake batter for well-browned pancakes.

Cool nut bread several hours or overnight or put it in the freezer for an hour before slicing. It crumbles and is hard to cut when fresh.

NOTES:

INDURATED FIBREWE
DURABLE
LIGHT
NO HOOP

Eggs, Cheese, Rice & Pasta

EGGS

CHEESE

RICE

PASTA

Eggs, Cheese, Rice, Pasta Chapter Design: Left to right: Butter Churn (1855), Butter Mould (1886), Indurated Fibre Ware Star Water Pail (1898)

CHEESE BAKED EGGS
This recipe can be doubled easily

Oven: 350° 10 minutes   Yield: 4 servings

2 medium onions, chopped   Sliced Cheddar cheese to
3 tablespoons butter   cover
Salt and pepper   2 tablespoons bread crumbs
4 eggs   or stuffing mix

Sauté the onions in butter until tender. Arrange in a pie plate; salt and pepper to taste. Carefully break eggs over onions. Top with cheese and sprinkle with bread crumbs. Bake uncovered 10 minutes at 350° or until eggs are of desired firmness. Plan on 2 eggs per person for brunch.

Mrs. William E. Anderson (Dell)

C.K.'S EGG ELEGANTE
Serve hearty eaters two portions!

Yield: 4 servings

4 Pepperidge Farm pastry   1 (4-ounce) can sliced
  shells, baked   mushrooms, drained
1 stick butter   1/4 cup parsley, minced
3 medium tomatoes, diced   4 poached eggs
4 green onions, sliced   1 cup Hollandaise sauce

Bake the pastry shells according to package directions. While they are baking, prepare the tomato mixture. In skillet, melt butter and sauté the tomatoes, green onions, and mushrooms. Add the parsley, stir well, and remove from heat. Place pastry shells on serving plate. Fill each pastry shell with the tomato mixture and top with a poached egg. Spoon Hollandaise sauce generously over the top. Sprinkle with paprika and garnish with parsley.

NOTE: Delicious for a special Sunday breakfast, followed by chickory coffee and Bananas Foster.

Mrs. Robert L. Lee (Pam)

221

HUMPTY DUMPTY EGGS

Kids have fun with these!

Yield: 1 serving

3 to 4 teaspoons butter
1 slice white bread
Whipped margarine

1 egg
Salt and pepper to taste

Melt butter in small skillet. Cut out center of bread and spread edges with soft margarine. (Set center aside for another use.) Put bread in pan, break egg into center, and fry, turning for desired firmness.

Mrs. J. Littleton Glover, Jr. (Kathryn)

★ ## CHEESE LOAF

Delightful served for a luncheon or buffet supper

Yield: 8 to 10 servings

4 cups medium sharp cheese
1/2 cup thick cream
1 cup mayonnaise
Red pepper to taste

1 cup pecans, finely chopped
Strawberry preserves

Grate and cream the cheese. Add cream, mayonnaise, pepper, and mix well. Add chopped pecans. Mold with hands into any shape desired and refrigerate. When ready to serve, pour strawberry preserves over the cheese loaf.

Mrs. William F. Lee (Parky)

❋❋❋❋❋❋❋❋❋❋❋❋❋

Which size egg is the best buy? Generally speaking, if there is less than 7¢ difference per dozen between one size and the next smaller size, the larger size is the better buy. If there is more than 7¢ difference per dozen, the smaller size is a better buy for the money.

JOHN WAYNE CASSEROLE

*One-dish meal when served with tossed salad
and crusty French bread*

Oven: 325° 1 hour   Yield: 6 servings

2 (4-ounce) cans green chiles, diced	2/3 cup evaporated milk
1 pound Monterey Jack cheese, grated	1 tablespoon flour
	1/2 teaspoon salt
1 pound sharp Cheddar cheese, grated	1/8 teaspoon pepper
	12 to 15 cherry tomatoes, cut in half
4 egg whites	
4 egg yolks	

Combine green chiles and all the cheeses in a large bowl. Turn into a well-buttered shallow 2-quart casserole. Beat 4 egg whites just until stiff peaks form. Beat 4 egg yolks, evaporated milk, flour, salt, and pepper together. Gently fold whites into yolk mixture. Pour egg mixture into casserole, and, using a fork, try to "ooze" it through the cheese. Bake 30 minutes at 325°, remove from oven, and add sliced tomatoes around edge. Return to oven and bake 30 minutes longer, or until knife inserted in center comes out clean.

NOTE: This recipe is an adaptation from an original recipe of actor John Wayne.

Mrs. Emily Miller Wilbert
Selfridge, Michigan

✳✳✳✳✳✳✳✳✳✳✳✳✳

Egg whites may be frozen for future use. Freeze them in an ice tray, 1 egg white per compartment. When frozen, remove from tray and store the blocks in a plastic bag. Take out the number needed each time and thaw them in the refrigerator — never at room temperature or they won't beat.

CHEESE TIMBALE

Oven: 350° 45 to 50 minutes   Yield: 4 servings

1 cup grated nippy cheese   Pepper
1 cup milk   Salt
4 eggs   Small amount onion juice

Beat together all ingredients with rotary egg beater and pour into buttered baking dish. Place in pan of hot water and cook until brown and firm at 350° for 45 to 50 minutes. Add an egg per person to increase.

Mrs. Charles J. Smith (Martha)

QUICHE LORRAINE
One of the puffiest and best ever!

Oven: 425° 15 minutes   Yield: 6 servings
        300° 35 minutes

1 cup Bisquick   4 eggs
1/4 cup light cream   2 cups light cream
1/2 pound bacon, crisply   3/4 teaspoon salt
  fried and crumbled   1/4 teaspoon sugar
1 cup shredded Swiss cheese   1/8 teaspoon red pepper
1/3 cup minced onion

Heat oven to 425°. Stir Bisquick with 1/4 cup light cream to make soft dough. Smooth dough into ball on floured board, knead 5 times. Roll out and put into pie pan. Sprinkle bacon, cheese, and onion into crust. Beat remaining ingredients until blended and pour over bacon mixture. Cover edge with foil to prevent browning. Bake 15 minutes. Reduce oven temperature to 300° and bake 35 minutes longer; remove foil for the last 15 minutes. Let stand 10 minutes before slicing.

Mrs. William E. Anderson (Dell)

MOCK CHEESE SOUFFLÉ
Make the night before

Oven: 350° 1 hour 15 minutes   Yield: 4 servings

5 slices white bread, crusts removed	1 teaspoon dry mustard
1/2 pound sharp Cheddar cheese, grated	Dash garlic powder
	Dash worcestershire sauce
1 teaspoon salt	4 eggs
	2 1/2 cups milk

Butter one side of bread and line a greased 9x13-inch casserole with slices. Add grated cheese, seasoned with salt, mustard, garlic powder, and worcestershire sauce to casserole. Beat milk and eggs and pour over cheese. Let stand 8 hours in refrigerator. It is better if done the night before using. Take out 1 hour before baking and bake in pan of water 1 hour and 15 minutes at 350°.

Mrs. John G. Chisolm (Martha)
Lookout Mountain, Tennessee

MUSHROOM RICE

Oven: 350° 20 to 30 minutes   Yield: 4 to 6 servings

1 1/2 cups cooked rice
1 (10 3/4-ounce) can cream of mushroom soup
1 cup New York State sharp cheese, grated
1 (2-ounce) jar pimiento, chopped
1/2 cup blanched almonds, chopped
1 egg, slightly beaten
Salt and pepper to taste

Mix all together. Bake in 1-quart casserole at 350° for 20 to 30 minutes.

Mrs. E. E. Gasque, Jr. (Jeane)
Elloree, South Carolina

CHINESE FRIED RICE

Yield: 4 to 6 serving

3 to 4 cups cooked rice at room temperature
2 to 3 tablespoons oil
1 small round onion, diced into 1/4-inch pieces
1 stalk celery, diced into 1/4-inch pieces (optional)
1/2 cup cooked ham or roast pork, diced into 3/8-inch pieces
2 stalks green onions, cut into 1/4-inch pieces
2 eggs, slightly beaten
1 tablespoon soy sauce
1/2 teaspoon salt
1/4 teaspoon pepper
Oyster sauce and Chinese parsley, if desired

Have 3 to 4 cups cooked rice cooled to room temperature Rich should be in separate grains rather than soft and sticky for best results.

Heat oil in heavy skillet or shallow saucepan. Stir fry onions and celery for 2 to 3 minutes before adding ham or pork. Add meat and continue to fry over lowered heat. Immediately add 3 to 4 cups cooked rice. When rice is well mixed and heated through, add green onions. Mix together the beaten eggs, soy sauce, salt, and pepper; stir into rice mixture Continue mixing until egg is cooked. Serve hot with oyster sauce and Chinese parsley for added flavor, if desired.

Mrs. Ray Grimshaw (Jane)
Tulsa, Oklahoma

꙾꙾꙾꙾꙾꙾꙾꙾꙾꙾꙾꙾꙾꙾

To save left-over egg yolks for later use, put them in a small bowl and add 2 tablespoons of salad oil. Cover and store in the refrigerator. The yolks will stay fresh and soft, but should be used within a day or two.

GARLIC RICE

Oven: 325° 1 hour   Yield: 4 to 6 servings

1 cup raw rice
1 (10 1/2-ounce) can of beef consommé
1 (10 3/4-ounce) can cream of chicken soup
1 teaspoon garlic salt
1/2 to 3/4 stick butter

Mix all of the ingredients except butter. Pour into a 1 1/2-quart casserole. Cut butter in slices on top of the rice mixture. Cook at 325° until all liquid has been absorbed, approximately 1 hour.

Mrs. Bryan B. Sargent (Ellen)

★   **RED RICE**
Delicious with ham

Yield: 8 servings

4 strips bacon   **2 teaspoons salt**
2 onions, finely chopped   **2 to 3 teaspoons sugar**
1 (6-ounce) can tomato paste   **Good dash of pepper**
1 1/2 to 2 cans water   **1 1/2 cups raw rice**
** (tomato paste cans)**   **4 tablespoons bacon grease**

Fry bacon; remove from pan. Sauté onions in grease. Add tomato paste, water, salt, sugar, and pepper. Cook uncovered slowly, about 10 minutes, until mixture measures 2 cups; then add to rice in the top of a double boiler. Add the additional grease and steam over simmering water for 1/2 hour. Add crumbled bacon and stir in with a fork. Cook 30 to 45 minutes longer.

Mrs. Ellis Arnall (Mildred)

Mrs. Arnall is a former First Lady of Georgia.

227

EASY RICE
Exceptional to be so easy and inexpensive

Oven: 350° 1 hour   Yield: 4 to 5 servings

1 cup raw rice
1 (10 1/2-ounce) can beef consommé
1 (10 1/2-ounce) can onion soup, not cream soup

Combine all ingredients and place in a buttered 1-quart casserole. Bake at 350° for one hour.

NOTE: Good with ham; needs no gravy.

Mrs. J. P. Lott (Douglass)

RICE AND CHEESE CASSEROLE
Can be made a day ahead

Oven: 350° 1 hour   Yield: 6 to 8 servings

1 cup bread crumbs
2 cups warm milk
1/2 cup butter or margarine,
  melted
3 cups cooked rice
3 cups cheese, grated

1 teaspoon salt
1 teaspoon onion, chopped
1 teaspoon parsley, chopped
1/2 teaspoon bell pepper,
  finely chopped
6 eggs, slightly beaten

Soak bread crumbs in warm milk and melted butter. Add rice, grated cheese, salt, onion, parsley, and bell pepper. Stir in slightly beaten eggs. Place in a greased 2-quart casserole. Bake 1 hour at 350°.

Mrs. William F. Lee (Parky)

✸✸✸✸✸✸✸✸✸✸✸✸✸

Egg whites whip best at room temperature, but cream whips best when cold.

228

RICE PARISIAN

Yield: 4 servings

1/2 cup uncooked rice
1/3 cup cooked mushrooms, or
  1 (4-ounce) can sliced mushrooms, drained
2 tablespoons butter or margarine
1 (10 1/2-ounce) can onion soup
1/2 soup can water

In skillet, brown lightly the rice and mushrooms in butter. Stir in soup and water. Cover; cook over low heat about 25 minutes or until rice is tender.

Mrs. Welborn Davis (Mary)

ST. PAUL'S RICE
Delicious with ham

Oven: 350° 30 to 40 minutes

Yield: 6 servings

1 pound pork sausage
2 packages Lipton Noodle
  Soup
1/2 cup raw rice
4 1/2 cups water

1 green pepper, diced
1 stalk celery, chopped
1 onion, chopped
1/2 to 1 cup almonds

Brown scrambled sausage and drain off fat. Boil rice with soup 7 minutes in 4 1/2 cups water. Add remaining ingredients. Pour into a 2-quart casserole. Cook at 350° for 30 to 40 minutes.

Mrs. Robert H. Shell (Mary)

❉❉❉❉❉❉❉❉❉❉❉❉

Cooking eggs in boiling water will produce tough, leathery eggs. To hard-cook eggs, bring the eggs to a boil, cover, remove from heat, and let eggs sit for 15 minutes.

RICE CASSEROLE

Oven: 300° 1 to 1 1/2 hours   Yield: 6 to 8 servings

1 cup uncooked rice
1 (10 1/2-ounce) can onion soup
1 soup can water
1 stick margarine

1 (4-ounce) can mushrooms
1 (8-ounce) can water chestnuts, sliced (optional)
Salt and pepper, to taste

Mix all ingredients in a 2-quart casserole. Bake 1 to 1 1/2 hours at 300°.

Mrs. Paul R. McKnight, Jr. (Totsie)
Senoia, Georgia

CHEESE-PASTA CASSEROLE

Oven: 350° 30 minutes   Yield: 6 to 8 servings

1 (8-ounce) package elbow macaroni or
  1 (8-ounce) package spaghetti
1 pound sharp cheese, grated
1 (10 3/4-ounce) can cream of mushroom soup
1/2 to 1 cup mayonnaise
1 medium onion, grated
1 (2-ounce) jar pimiento, chopped

Cook macaroni or spaghetti according to package directions. Mix with remaining ingredients. Bake at 350° for 30 minutes.

Mrs. Rhodes H. Shell (Kathy)

Mrs. Lester Morgan (Vora)
Senoia, Georgia

Mrs. James Sullivan (Vonice)
Jesup, Georgia

SAMRENY'S PILAFF

Yield: 6 servings

1 cup regular rice	Pinch of salt
2 tablespoons butter	1/4 cup piñola (pine nuts)
1/2 cup vermicelli	2 tablespoons butter

Brown rice in butter in heavy saucepan. Break vermicelli into bite-size lengths and add with the salt. Add water to cover plus 2 inches. Cover. Simmer over low heat until all water is absorbed. Sauté 1/4 cup piñola in another pan. Add before serving. Toss.

NOTE: This is based on a specialty of a fantastic Armenian restaurant in Pittsburgh. Piñola are hard to find but add **much** to this recipe.

Mrs. J. Littleton Glover, Jr., (Kathryn)

★ GRITS

Yield: 8 servings

1 cup enriched grits (not quick)
1 teaspoon salt
1/2 cup water
Milk

Combine grits, salt, and water in a saucepan. Cook. As water is absorbed, add milk and stir. Turn heat to low. Continue to cook, adding milk as necessary to thin. It is delicious if allowed to cook slowly up to 5 hours, but good cooked from 20 minutes to 1 hour.

NOTE: Allow 2 tablespoons of dry grits per person when preparing a small amount.

Mrs. Lawrence Keith, Jr. (Jane)

CHEESE-SPAGHETTI CASSEROLE
Freezes well

Oven: 350° 20 to 25 minutes   Yield: 15 to 18 servings

Meat Sauce:

1 1/2 pounds ground beef
3 (8-ounce) cans tomato sauce
5 1/2 cups water, divided
3 (1 1/2-ounce) packages spaghetti sauce mix
2 1/4 teaspoons salt, divided

Cheese Sauce:

1/3 cup all-purpose flour
1/4 cup margarine, melted
2 cups evaporated milk
1/2 cup grated Parmesan cheese
2 cups shredded Velveeta cheese, divided

1 1/2 pounds spaghetti, cooked

MEAT SAUCE: Brown meat in large saucepan; drain off excess oil. Add tomato sauce, 4 1/2 cups water, spaghetti sauce mix, and 3/4 teaspoon salt. Simmer uncovered for 30 minutes, stirring often.

CHEESE SAUCE: Combine flour and margarine. Cook over low heat until smooth. Combine milk and remaining 1 cup water. Gradually add to flour mixture, stirring constantly. Cook until smooth and thick. Season with 1 1/2 teaspoons salt. Add Parmesan cheese and 1 1/2 cups Velveeta cheese. Stir until melted.

Divide cooked spaghetti, meat sauce, and cheese sauce in half. Layer ingredients as follows in 2 lightly greased 9x13x2-inch dishes: spaghetti, meat sauce, cheese sauce. Top each with 1/4 cup Velveeta cheese. Bake at 350° for 20 to 25 minutes or until bubbly.

Mrs. Enman Sheppard (Vivian)

★ ## GRITS AND EGGS CASSEROLE

Oven: 325° 45 minutes   Yield: 6 servings

1 cup grits   2 teaspoons baking powder
4 cups water   1/2 cup sharp cheese, grated
2 egg yolks   Salt and pepper to taste
2 egg whites, stiffly beaten

Cook grits in water with dash of salt and let cool slightly. Add all remaining ingredients, blend well with grits, and turn into baking dish. Bake 45 minutes at 325°.

Mrs. Billy Carter (Sybil)
Plains, Georgia

★ ## GRITS CASSEROLE
Freezes well — before or after baking

Oven: 350° to 375° 1 hour   Yield: 6 to 8 servings

5 cups water   2 teaspoons salt
1 1/2 cups grits   1 teaspoon paprika
1 pound sharp cheese   2 dashes Tabasco sauce
3 eggs   Garlic powder to taste
1 1/2 sticks margarine   (optional)
3 teaspoons savory salt

Bring water to a boil and add grits. Stir in the cheese which has been cut into pieces. Beat eggs and add to grits. Add margarine and all the remaining ingredients, mixing well. Pour grits into a greased 3-quart casserole. Bake for 1 hour at 350° to 375°. Grits may be divided into two smaller casseroles for baking or freezing.

Mrs. Mary Ruth George
Metropolis, Illinois

233

LASAGNE
Freezes well

Oven: 350° 30 minutes   Yield: 4 to 6 servings

1 pound hot sausage
2 tablespoons olive oil
1/4 teaspoon garlic salt
1 (28-ounce) can Italian
   tomatoes
1/2 can (6-ounce) tomato
   paste
Salt and pepper

1/2 pound egg noodles,
   cooked and drained
1 pound Ricotta cheese or
   small curd cottage cheese
1 cup sliced Mozzarella cheese
2/3 cup grated Parmesan chees

Brown sausage and garlic salt in oil. Add tomatoes, tomato paste, and seasonings; simmer for 20 minutes. Layer in a 2-quart casserole: sauce, noodles, Ricotta cheese, Mozzarella, and Parmesan. Repeat layers until all ingredients are used. Top with Parmesan. Bake at 350° for 30 minutes.

Mrs. Thomas Barron (Margaret)

****

Scrambled egg additions: bread crumbs added to scrambled eggs will improve the flavor and make larger servings possible. A pinch of baking powder will also help stretch the servings. For onion scramble, sauté 1 small chopped onion in a few tablespoons of butter until soft but not brown. Add the onions to the eggs and scramble.

Press left-over grits into a tall glass. Store in the refrigerator overnight. For breakfast the next day, slide the grits from the glass, cut into 1/2-inch round slices, and fry in bacon grease. Serve with bacon and eggs. Delicious!

MACARONI MOUSSE

Oven: 325° 50 minutes   Yield: 8 servings

1 cup macaroni
1 1/2 cups milk
1 cup soft bread crumbs
1/4 cup butter, melted
1 pimiento, chopped
1 tablespoon chopped parsley
1 tablespoon chopped onion

1 1/2 cups processed cheese,
  grated
3/8 teaspoon salt
1/8 teaspoon pepper
Dash paprika
3 eggs, well beaten

Mushroom Sauce (optional):

1 (10 3/4-ounce) can cream of
  mushroom soup
1/2 soup can milk
1 (4-ounce) can mushrooms

Salt, pepper, and worcestershire
  sauce to taste
Slivered almonds, (optional)

Cook the macaroni in boiling, salted water; blanch in cold water and drain. Heat milk almost to boiling and pour over bread crumbs; add the butter, pimiento, parsley, onion, grated cheese, and seasonings. Mix well and add well beaten eggs. Put macaroni in a heavily buttered 8-1/2x3-5/8x2-5/8 inch loaf pan and pour the milk and cheese mixture over it. Bake about 50 minutes at 325°, or until the loaf is firm and will hold its shape when turned out onto a platter. Serve warm with mushroom sauce.

MUSHROOM SAUCE: Combine all ingredients in a saucepan and heat.

Mary Parks
Mrs. Welborn Davis (Mary)

※※※※※※※※※※※※※

Cheese is a good calcium source. A 1-ounce piece of Cheddar cheese has the same amount of calcium as 2/3 cup of milk.

MACARONI CASSEROLE
Can be made a day ahead

Oven: 350° 30 minutes   Yield: 8 servings

8 ounces small shell macaroni
1 (10 3/4-ounce) can cream of celery soup
1 (10 3/4-ounce) can cream of mushroom soup
1/4 cup chopped bell pepper
1 small onion, chopped
1 (2-ounce) jar pimiento, chopped
1 (4-ounce) can mushrooms, stems and pieces and juice
1/2 cup mayonnaise
1 1/2 cups grated mellow cheese, divided

Cook macaroni for a few minutes, but not until done. Add soups, other ingredients, and 3/4 cup cheese. Mix all ingredients well and place in a greased 2 1/2-quart casserole. Top with remaining 3/4 cup cheese. Bake at 350° for 30 minutes.

Mrs. John Goodrum (Marsha)

****

When cooking grits, follow package directions but let them cook down. Then add milk —makes them creamy and delicious.

A tablespoon of oil in the boiling water will keep spaghetti and other pasta from sticking together and from boiling over.

Remember 1-2-3 for rice: 1 cup of raw rice cooked in 2 cups of water with 1 teaspoon salt equals 3 cups of cooked rice.

To make rice whiter and fluffier, add 1 teaspoon lemon juice to each quart of cooking water.

Cooked rice freezes quite well for as long as 3 months. In the refrigerator, it stays fresh for a week.

Fish & Shellfish

FISH AND SHELLFISH

Fish and Shellfish Chapter Design: Columbia Family Scale (1910), Stoneware Mortar and Pestle (1779)

BAKED FLOUNDER

Oven: 400° to 425° 1 hour   Yield: 6 to 8 servings

1 whole flounder   Salt and pepper to taste
  (medium to large)   1 large onion
3 to 4 slices salt pork   2 to 3 large potatoes
2 tablespoons flour

Score, salt, and pepper flounder and place in 9x13-inch baking pan. Fry salt pork slices in a skillet. Extra oil may be needed. Add flour to drippings and brown. Add water to make a medium gravy. Add salt and pepper to taste. Pare and slice onions and potatoes. Place over fish. Pour gravy over fish, onions, and potatoes. Bake at 400° to 425° for one hour. Baste occasionally.

NOTE: This is a coastal North Carolina dish.

Mrs. Donald L. Hansen (Karen)

★   CRAB AND SHRIMP NEWBURG

Yield: 4 or 6 servings

2 tablespoons flour   3 tablespoons butter, melted
4 egg yolks   1/4 cup sherry
2 drops Tabasco sauce   3/4 pound crabmeat
1/4 tablespoon salt   1 1/2 pounds shrimp,
1/8 teaspoon pepper   cooked and peeled
2 cups milk

Blend flour and egg yolks. Add seasonings to milk and add to egg mixture; add melted butter. Blend until smooth. Stir while cooking over low heat until thickened. Add sherry and seafood, pour into casserole and brown quickly under broiler.

The Pirates' House
Savannah, Georgia

★   **BROILED SPANISH MACKEREL**

Oven: 350°   Yield: 4 servings

1 whole Spanish mackerel (2 1/2 to 3 pounds)
Salt, approximately 1/2 teaspoon to 1 pound of fish
5 tablespoons butter
1 cup catsup
2 tablespoons worcestershire sauce
Juice of 1 lemon
Dash of red pepper and cayenne (optional)

Melt 3 tablespoons butter in roasting pan on top of stove while rubbing salt on and in cavity of fish. Place fish in roasting pan and cook at medium heat until slightly browned on bottom. While fish is browning, combine the catsup, worcestershire, and lemon juice. Pour over top of fish and place in 350° oven; cook until fish is tender. Garnish with lemon slices and parsley sprigs.

Rachel S. Jenkins

★   **CRAB CASSEROLE**

Oven: 325° 30 to 35 minutes   Yield: 6 to 8 servings

1/2 stick margarine	2 teaspoons mustard
1 pound crabmeat	2 tablespoons catsup
4 slices toast	1 cup milk
1/4 cup chopped green pepper	1 teaspoon celery seed
1/4 cup chopped onion	Salt and pepper to taste
1/2 cup mayonnaise	Buttered toast, cubed

Melt margarine in a 2-quart casserole dish. Set aside. Mix crabmeat, crumbled toast, pepper, onion, mayonnaise, mustard, catsup, milk, celery seed, salt, and pepper. Pour half of melted margarine over mixture and mix well. Pour mixture into casserole dish. Top with 1 to 2 slices of cubed, buttered toast. Bake 30 to 35 minutes at 325°.

Mrs. Donald L. Hansen (Karen)

★
CRAB-MUSHROOM CASSEROLE
Freezes well. Very versatile!

Oven: 350° 45 minutes

Yield: 8 to 10 servings
10 to 12 when served on ham

1/4 cup butter or margarine
1/4 cup all-purpose flour
2 tablespoons parsley, finely chopped
2 tablespoons onion, finely chopped
1/4 cup celery, finely chopped
1/4 cup bell pepper, finely chopped
1 pound fresh mushrooms
1 1/2 cups chicken bouillon, or
   2 bouillon cubes, dissolved in 1 1/2 cups water
2 egg yolks, slightly beaten
3/4 teaspoon salt
1 pound fresh or frozen lump crabmeat
1/4 cup sherry
1/4 cup sharp cheese, grated
Buttered bread crumbs

Melt butter in saucepan; blend in flour, parsley, onion, celery, and bell pepper. Cook until golden. Clean mushrooms; slice and add to mixture. Cook 10 minutes. Slowly stir in bouillon and cook over low heat until mixture thickens. Remove from heat. Stir cooked mixture into egg yolks, a little at a time. Add salt, crabmeat, and sherry. Pour into a 1 1/2-quart baking dish. Sprinkle cheese and bread crumbs on top. Bake in preheated oven 350° for 45 minutes or until top is browned and bubbly.

NOTE: Omit cheese and bread crumbs until ready to bake if dish is prepared to be frozen. This is **extra** good on slices of baked country ham, or omit cheese-crumb topping and serve in tart shells.

Mrs. John P. Woods, Jr. (Elizabeth)

★ **BROILED CRAB SANDWICHES**

Oven: 350° 15 minutes   Yield: 6 servings

1 (8-ounce) package cream
  cheese, room temperature
1 tablespoon minced chives
1 teaspoon lemon juice
1 teaspoon worcestershire sauce
1/2 teaspoon salt
1 (7 1/2-ounce) can king
  crabmeat, drained, picked,
  and flaked

6 Holland Rusks
6 tomato slices
1/2 cup mayonnaise
1/2 cup sharp Cheddar
  cheese, grated

Beat cream cheese with chives, lemon juice, worcestershire, and salt until well blended and fluffy. Mix in crabmeat. Spread mixture on Holland Rusks and put on cookie sheet. Top each with slice of tomato. Spread each with mixture of mayonnaise and cheese. Bake at 350° for 15 minutes or until heated through and bubbly.

Mrs. Dyer Butterfield, Jr. (Ginny)
Lookout Mountain, Tennessee

❋ ❋ ❋ ❋ ❋ ❋ ❋ ❋ ❋ ❋ ❋ ❋ ❋

Hint when buying fresh fish: If fish eyes are clear, fish is fresh; if eyes are cloudy, fish is getting old.

Rule of thumb for cooking fish: cook 10 minutes per inch of thickness.

To keep raw fish fillets fresh and odorless, rinse them with fresh lemon juice and water, dry thoroughly, wrap, and refrigerate.

When using green shrimp with 21-25 count per pound, buy 1/3 pound per person.

★   **CRAB AND CHEESE CASSEROLE**

Oven: 325° 15 to 20 minutes   Yield: 6 servings

1/3 cup butter
1/4 cup chopped onion
1/4 cup diced green pepper
1/2 cup flour
1 teaspoon salt
1/8 teaspoon pepper
Dash of cayenne (optional)
1 teaspoon dry mustard
1 1/2 cups milk

1 tablespoon lemon juice
1 teaspoon worcestershire
    sauce
2 (6-ounce) cans crabmeat,
    flaked
2/3 cup shredded American
    cheese
1/2 cup buttered bread
    crumbs

   Melt butter in saucepan over low heat. Add onions and green
pepper and cook slowly until tender. Remove onions and pepper.
Blend flour, salt, pepper, cayenne, and mustard together; stir
into butter. Add milk, stirring constantly. Cook until sauce is
smooth and thickened. Fold in lemon juice, worcestershire,
crabmeat, 1/2 cup of cheese, and the sautéed vegetables. Spoon
mixture into 6 individual casserole dishes or shells, or 2-quart
casserole. Blend remaining cheese with bread crumbs; spread
around edge of dishes. Heat at 325° for 15 to 20 minutes.

Mrs. Everett Bryant (Mary)

＊＊＊＊＊＊＊＊＊＊＊＊＊

Salmon tips: the redder the salmon the higher the price, so
buy correctly. Pink salmon breaks into flakes, so it is good
for patties and loaves. The deeper reds break into large chunks,
so they are ideal for casseroles and salads.

If fish is to be dipped in egg before frying, add a little sherry
to the egg.

For a delicate crust when frying fish or seafood, add 1/2 to 1
teaspoon baking powder to the batter.

★ ## CRABMEAT IMPERIAL
Can be prepared ahead of time

Oven: 350° 20 minutes   Yield: 6 servings

1 tablespoon chopped green
  pepper and/or celery
1/4 cup chopped onion
4 tablespoons margarine
1/2 cup all-purpose flour
1/2 teaspoon salt
1/2 teaspoon dry mustard
1 1/2 cups milk
2 teaspoons lemon juice
1/2 teaspoon worcestershire
  sauce

2 eggs, beaten
2 (7 1/2-ounce) cans crabme
  flaked and boned
2 teaspoons minced parsley
1/2 cup white wine (optiona
1/4 to 1/2 cup bread
  crumbs (optional)
Parmesan cheese
Paprika

Cook green pepper, onion, and celery in margarine until
tender but not brown. Blend in flour, salt, and mustard. Add
milk; cook quickly, stirring constantly until thickened. Remove
from heat; add lemon juice and worcestershire sauce. Stir in
beaten eggs, then fold in crabmeat and parsley. Also add wine
and bread crumbs, if desired. Spoon into 1-quart casserole or
6 large baking shells. Sprinkle each with a little Parmesan cheese
and paprika. Bake at 350° for 20 minutes or until heated
through. Serve each topped with a lemon twist.

Mrs. Robert L. Lee (Pam)

✳✳✳✳✳✳✳✳✳✳✳✳✳✳

1 cup cooked shrimp equals 1 (5-ounce) can shrimp, 1/2 pound
frozen shelled shrimp, or 3/4 pound raw shrimp in the shell.

Improve canned shrimp by soaking them in ice water for an
hour.

For fresh-caught flavor, thaw frozen fish in milk. Drain well
before cooking.

★

CRAB-SHRIMP BAKE
Easy and delicious luncheon dish

Oven: 350° 20 to 25 minutes   Yield: 6 servings

1 medium green pepper,   1/2 teaspoon salt
  chopped   Dash pepper
1 medium onion, chopped   1 teaspoon worcestershire
1 cup celery, finely chopped   sauce
1 (6 1/2 or 7 1/2-ounce)   1/2 cup mayonnaise
  can crabmeat, flaked   1/2 cup salad dressing
1 cup cooked cleaned shrimp   1 cup buttered bread crumbs

Drain all ingredients well. Then combine ingredients, except crumbs; place in individual seashells, in pastry shells, or in a 2-quart casserole. Sprinkle with buttered crumbs. Bake in 350° oven about 20 to 25 minutes or longer if in one dish.

Mrs. Harvell Slaton (Inez)
Mrs. Ellis Crook (Patricia)

★

DEVILED CRAB CASSEROLE

Oven: 350° 40 minutes   Yield: 4 servings

1 onion   1 1/2 teaspoons horseradish
1 bell pepper   1 tablespoon sherry
3/4 stick butter   1 teaspoon prepared mustard
2 eggs   1 pound crabmeat, drained
1 teaspoon worcestershire   and cleaned
  sauce   1 cup fine bread crumbs
1 (10 3/4-ounce) can cream   Juice of 1 lemon
  of mushroom soup

Chop onion and bell pepper and sauté in 1/2 stick butter until tender. Beat eggs and add them to all other ingredients including sautéed onions and pepper. Pour mixture into a buttered 1 1/2-quart casserole. Top with bread crumbs and with 1/4 stick butter. Bake at 350° for 40 minutes.

Mrs. Walker Moody (Sally)

245

★ ## LINGUINE WITH CLAM SAUCE

Yield: 6 servings

1/4 cup olive oil
2 tablespoons butter
2 cloves garlic, crushed
1/4 cup finely chopped onion
1/2 teaspoon salt
1/4 teaspoon pepper
Pinch oregano
2 tablespoons chopped parsley
4 to 5 medium tomatoes, peeled, seeded, and chopped
3 (7 1/2-ounce) cans chopped clams
Juice from clams plus red wine to equal 2 cups
Flour or cornstarch plus water (optional)
1 pound linguine, cooked

Sauté garlic and onion in oil and butter. Add salt, pepper, oregano, parsley, and tomatoes. Simmer 10 minutes. Add clams and juice to sauce. Sauce may be thickened slightly with a flour and water or cornstarch and water paste. Reheat. Serve over hot linguine.

Mrs. Wallace Mitchell (Jeri)

****

Try cooking shrimp in beer. Serve hot with loads of butter. Good as appetizer or entrée.

Delicious borders for seafood or fish dishes:
1) Lemon cups filled with tartar sauce.
2) Scored, broiled mushroom caps.
3) Lemons cut in half with notched edges, sprinkled with chopped parsley or paprika.

CHARCOALED SOUTH AFRICAN ROCK LOBSTER TAILS
Serve with lots of napkins

Yield: 4 servings (1 1/2 tails per serving)

6 (6 to 8 ounces each) lobster tails,
  split through the shell
1 stick margarine, melted
Lemon juice to taste
Salt

Thaw lobster tails, if frozen. Mix margarine, lemon juice, and salt; brush on lobster tails. Place lobster tails, meat down, on grill rack. Cook 5 minutes. Turn and baste generously several times, cooking 10 minutes more. Lobster tails are done when meat loses its transparency and is firm to the touch. Serve hot with remaining butter mixture.

John P. Woods, Jr.

★ OYSTER CASSEROLE
Very easy

Oven: 350° 30 minutes   Yield: 4 servings

1 pint of stewing oysters
1/2 stick margarine
Salt and pepper to taste
Cracker crumbs
1 egg, beaten

Butter a 2-quart casserole. Layer the casserole with half the oysters. Dot the oysters with margarine. Salt and pepper the oysters to taste. Cover with cracker crumbs. Repeat layers. Pour egg over top. Bake at 350° for 30 minutes.

Mrs. W. Y. Ellis (Ida)

★ **OYSTER PIE**

Oven: 400°   Yield: 8 servings

2 pints oysters
3 cups thick white sauce
Tabasco sauce
Worcestershire sauce
Salt and pepper
2 packages saltines, crushed

1/2 pound Cheddar cheese,
  grated
2 (2-ounce) jars pimiento
  peppers
Buttered cracker crumbs

Heat oysters. Drain off liquid and reserve. Keep oysters warm over very low temperature. Make 3 cups thick white sauce using butter and any oyster liquid in milk measurement. Season with Tabasco sauce, worcestershire sauce, salt, and pepper. In a greased casserole layer cracker crumbs, grated cheese, pimientos, oysters, and white sauce. Repeat layers and top with buttered cracker crumbs. Put in 400° oven until thoroughly heated and the cheese is melted.

Mrs. G. J. S. Cappelmann (Sara)
Jesup, Georgia

★ **FRIED OYSTERS**

Yield: 4 servings

1 pint oysters
1 to 2 cups all-purpose flour
1 egg

1/2 cup milk
3 to 4 cups cracker meal
2 pounds vegetable shortening

Drain oysters. Place each oyster in the flour, then in the egg which has been beaten with the milk, and then in the cracker meal. Place oysters on a cookie sheet in a single layer and refrigerate for 1 hour. Bring shortening to boiling point in a deep fryer. Place oysters in a single layer in fryer basket. Cook 3 to 4 minutes. Drain on a paper towel and serve hot.

Mrs. R. A. Baxter (Margaret)
Gulf Shores, Alabama

OYSTERS AND WILD RICE CASSEROLE
Excellent with turkey and dressing

Oven: 350° 45 minutes   Yield: 8 servings

cups hot wild rice, drained	1/2 teaspoon salt
(may substitute wild and	1/4 teaspoon sage
long grain rice mixture)	1/4 teaspoon thyme
/2 cup chopped onions	1/8 teaspoon black pepper
cups chopped celery	2 (8-ounce) cans fresh oysters,
/2 stick butter or margarine	drained
/2 cup milk	1 stick butter, melted
tablespoons flour	Ritz cracker crumbs

While rice is cooking according to package directions, brown onions and celery in butter. Remove from heat and add milk, our, salt, sage, thyme, and black pepper. Add well-drained ice to mixture. Pour into 2-quart casserole. Drain oysters and et soak in lukewarm, melted butter for 5 to 10 minutes. Pour ysters and butter over rice mixture and spread the oysters venly. Top with Ritz cracker crumbs. Bake at 350° for 45 ninutes or until the oysters curl.

Mrs. Walker Moody (Sally)

❊❊❊❊❊❊❊❊❊❊❊❊❊

Combine 1 cup mayonnaise, 1/4 cup lemon juice, and 3 ablespoons chopped fresh chives, dill, or fennel. Delicious vith broiled, baked, or poached fish, salmon, or tuna.

Tuna tips: tuna is priced by type (white is more expensive han light) and by pack (depending on the size of the pieces). olid or fancy-pack is the most expensive and makes a pretty alad. Chunk tuna pieces hold their shape, so it is good for asseroles. Flaked tuna is ideal for sandwich spreads. All tuna s nutritionally equal, so choose the type that best suits the ecipe.

249

★ **BAKED OYSTERS BEACH HOUSE**
Bon Appetit!

Oven 350° 3 to 4 minutes   Yield: 6 servings

1/4 stick butter
1/4 cup chopped green onions
1/8 cup chopped white onions
1/2 cup sliced fresh mushrooms
1/8 cup diced peeled tomatoes
1/2 cup flour
2 cups milk
1 cup fish stock
1 cup white wine

1 teaspoon worcestershire
  sauce
1 touch Tabasco sauce
1 touch finely chopped garlic
Salt and white pepper
2 bay leaves
2 egg yolks, beaten
1/2 cup cream
36 Long Island oysters
  on the half shell

Topping:

Hollandaise sauce
Parmesan cheese

Bread crumbs

Melt butter in casserole, add chopped green and white onions, sliced mushrooms, and sauté for about 3 minutes. Add tomatoes and mix well. Mix in flour while heating the milk on the side. Add heated milk, fish stock, and white wine. Bring to a boil, then stir until thick and creamy. Add the other seasonings. Mix the egg yolks and cream together and stir into the sauce, bringing it to another boil. Remove from heat and cool.

Remove oysters from the shells. Dip the sauce into the empty shells and place the oysters on top of the sauce. Bake at 350° for approximately 3 to 4 minutes. Remove from the oven. Cover oysters with Hollandaise sauce, then sprinkle with Parmesan cheese and bread crumbs. Broil until browned to perfection. Serve with lemon wedge and worcestershire sauce.

The Abbey
Atlanta, Georgia

SEAFOOD AU GRATIN
Can't be beat!

Yield: 24 servings

1/2 pounds lobster	1/2 teaspoon red pepper
1/2 pounds shrimp	1 1/2 teaspoons paprika
1/2 pounds crabmeat	1 clove garlic, pressed
/2 pound butter	2 tablespoons monosodium
cup flour	glutamate
cups milk	5 ounces Gruyere cheese,
cup tomato purée	cut into small pieces
teaspoon salt	1 tablespoon sherry

Cook and clean lobster and shrimp. Pick crabmeat. To make sauce, melt 1/2 pound of butter in double boiler. Add 1 up flour. Cook 1 minute stirring constantly with a wire wisk. Add 7 cups of milk and continue to stir. After sauce thickens, add purée, salt, red pepper, paprika, pressed garlic, monosodium glutamate, and cheese. Stir until sauce becomes thick and bubbly. Add sherry. If it gets too thick, add more milk. Mix with seafood just before ready to use. Serve over 5 cups cooked rice.

Mrs. Jeanne Benson
Athens, Georgia

※※※※※※※※※※※※※

How to tell a hard-cooked egg from a raw one? A hard-cooked egg spins beautifully; a raw one wobbles as it spins.

tablespoon of vinegar added to the water when poaching eggs will help set the whites so they will not spread. Be sure to dip them in plain water to "rinse" before serving.

o keep egg yolks from crumbling when slicing hard-cooked eggs, dip the knife into water before each cut.

★ SEAFOOD CASSEROLE

Oven: 350° 20 minutes   Yield: 6 serving

1 cup small, cooked shrimp   6 hard-boiled eggs, sieved
1 cup crabmeat   1 tablespoon chopped parsle;
1 cup bread crumbs softened   1/4 teaspoon red pepper
  with 1 cup light cream   1 teaspoon grated onion
3/4 to 1 cup mayonnaise   Extra bread crumbs for
1/2 teaspoon salt   topping
1/2 teaspoon pepper

Cook shrimp, preferably in water seasoned with McCormick shrimp boil. Drain well. Mix together all ingredients and pou into a 2-quart casserole. Top with bread crumbs and paprik dot with butter. Bake at 350° for 20 minutes or until tho oughly heated.

NOTE: This is a treasured recipe of the late Mrs. Rut Cole Blackburn.

Mrs. Bryan B. Sargent (Eller

Mrs. Frank S. Wilkinson (Eleano Haralson, Georg

****

Poached eggs will not stick to the pan if the pan is grease before the milk or water is put in.

When eggs are not refrigerated, they lose more quality in o day than in one week under refrigeration. Help maintain e quality by refrigerating them with the larger end up.

When a small piece of eggshell falls into the mixing bowl, l it out using half an eggshell as a scoop. It will attract t other piece.

★   **SEAFOOD QUICHE**

Oven: 400° 40 minutes   Yield: 6 to 8 servings

1/2 cup crabmeat   1/2 cup cream
1/2 cup shrimp pieces   1/2 cup sour cream
1/2 cup lobster pieces   Dash Tabasco sauce
1 tablespoon butter   Salt and pepper
   or margarine   1 (9-inch) pie shell baked 5
1 teaspoon paprika   minutes at 400°
2 tablespoons sherry   1 cup Mozzarella cheese,
2 eggs, beaten   shredded

Sauté crab, shrimp, and lobster in butter. Add remaining ingredients. Pour into pie shell. Top with shredded cheese. Bake for 40 minutes at 400°.

NOTE: If lobster is not available, double the amount of shrimp.

Mrs. William Parks Cole (Judy)

★   **SEAFOOD SUPREME**
Perfect for luncheon, dinner, or cocktail party

Yield: 25 dinner servings, 75 to 100 cocktail servings

1 pint flour   Juice of 1 large lemon
1 cup chicken fat   2 1/2 pounds lump crabmeat
1 pint concentrated chicken   2 1/2 pounds lobster meat
   stock   2 1/2 pounds shrimp, cleaned
Salt and pepper to taste   9 hard-boiled eggs, chopped
1/4 cup sherry

Brown slowly 1 pint flour in 1 cup chicken fat. Add 1 pint concentrated chicken stock. Season the sauce with salt, pepper, 1/4 cup sherry, and juice of 1 large lemon. Add crab, lobster, and shrimp. Next add chopped eggs. Mix lightly, heat in oven. Serve in timbales. Use large timbales for dinner or bite-size timbales for cocktail party.

Mrs. Lawrence Keith, Jr. (Jane)

★ **SEAFOOD DISH**

Delicious and easy. The sauce can be made the day before.

Yield: 12 servings

Seafood:

3 cups shrimp, cooked
2 cooked lobster tails
  (optional)

2 small cans crab meat
  (more if lobster omitted)

Cream Sauce:

1 small onion, chopped
1 stick margarine
1/2 cup flour
3 (13-ounce) cans evaporated
  milk

1 tablespoon worcestershire
  sauce
1/2 cup sherry
1 tablespoon lemon juice
Salt and pepper to taste

Sauté onion in margarine and gradually add flour. Add 3 cans milk and cook until thick and creamy. Add worcestershire sauce, sherry, lemon juice, salt, and pepper. Add seafood. Serve over toast.

Mrs. Otis Jones (Ann)

✳ ✳ ✳ ✳ ✳ ✳ ✳ ✳ ✳ ✳ ✳ ✳ ✳

To make deviled eggs lie flat, slice a very thin slice of the white off the bottom side.

Peel hard-cooked eggs perfectly and easily: as soon as the eggs are cooked, place them in ice water for exactly 1 minute. Then return eggs to the boiling water for exactly 10 seconds. Remove eggs, crack shells all over, and begin peeling at the large end. The cold water shrinks the egg body away from the shell, and the hot water causes the shell to expand away from the egg.

★ **BARBECUED SHRIMP**

Oven: 350° 30 minutes   Yield: 8 to 10 servings

5 pounds shrimp in shells
1/2 of 5 ounce bottle worcestershire sauce
1/2 of 5 ounce bottle Kikkoman soy sauce
1 pound diet margarine
2 tablespoons cracked pepper
1/4 cup lemon juice
4 tablespoons catsup
1 tablespoon dried parsley, crumbled
2 tablespoons garlic salt
1 teaspoon oregano

If Kikkoman soy sauce is not available, use 5 ounce bottle worcestershire sauce. Diet margarine makes a less greasy sauce. Regular margarine works just the same.

Wash the shrimp in several changes of water. Remove the feet (and heads if necessary). Drain and dry as thoroughly as possible. Combine all remaining ingredients, and heat until butter has melted. Bake at 350° for 30 minutes, stirring occasionally. Let sit aside for about an hour to marinate before serving. Serve in individual bowls, pouring some sauce over each serving. Hard French bread is good for dunking in sauce.

Mrs. Robert K. Mayo (Betty)
Shreveport, Louisiana

NICKEL OMELET PAN (1898)

★ ## CREOLE SHRIMP

Yield: 4 to 6 servings

4 slices bacon
1/2 cup chopped onions
1/2 cup chopped celery
1/2 cup chopped bell pepper
2 cups tomatoes
1/2 cup chili sauce

1 teaspoon worcestershire
  sauce
1/4 teaspoon black pepper
4 shakes Tabasco sauce
1 teaspoon salt

Fry bacon and remove from pan. Put onion, celery, and bell pepper in the bacon fat and brown lightly. Add tomatoes, chili sauce, worcestershire sauce, black pepper, Tabasco, and salt. Cook slowly until thick, stirring occasionally. Add shrimp 30 minutes before serving. Break the fried bacon in small pieces and add last. Add more seasoning if needed.

Wesa Rice
Atlanta, Georgia

SHRIMP ALOHA

Yield: 6 to 8 servings

2 pounds shrimp
2 (10 3/4-ounce) cans cream
  of mushroom soup
1 pint sour cream

1 (8-ounce) can mushrooms
1/2 cup Parmesan cheese
1/8 cup sherry

Boil shrimp, shell, and devein. Mix remaining ingredients and heat. Add cooked shrimp. Do not boil. Serve over fluffy white rice.

Mrs. James Sullivan (Vonice)
Jesup, Georgia

SHRIMP AND CHEESE CASSEROLE
Easy to prepare!

Oven: 350° 1 hour   Yield: 6 servings

slices white bread, edges   3 eggs, beaten
  removed   1/2 teaspoon dry mustard
/2 pound Old English cheese   1/2 teaspoon salt
pound shrimp, cooked   1 1/2 cups milk
  and cleaned
/4 cup margarine or
  butter, melted

Break bread into pieces the size of a quarter, and break cheese into bite-size pieces. Arrange shrimp, bread, and cheese in layers in a greased casserole and pour melted butter over all. Beat eggs, add mustard and salt, then add milk. Pour over casserole. Let stand a minimum of 3 hours or preferably overnight, covered. Bake 1 hour at 350°. To double, use 3 pounds shrimp.

Mrs. Thomas Barron (Margaret)
Mrs. Hendree Harrison (Carol)

STEAMED SHRIMP

Yield: 8 to 10 servings

to 6 pounds of fresh shrimp,   2 tablespoons celery seed
  in shell   1/2 cup salt
quart white vinegar   2 tablespoons black pepper
cans of beer   1 teaspoon cayenne pepper

Bring unshelled shrimp to boil in mixture of remaining ingredients and steam 15 to 20 minutes. Each person can shell his shrimp at table and dip in butter.

Mrs. Larry Strickland (Mary)

★ **SHRIMP AND WILD RICE CASSEROLE**

Oven: 375° 35 minutes   Yield: 6 to 8 serving

1 (7-ounce) box long grain   2 tablespoons lemon juice
  and wild rice   1 1/2 teaspoons worcestershire
1 pound raw shrimp, cleaned   sauce
1 cup cream of mushroom soup   1/2 teaspoon dry mustard
2 tablespoons minced onion   1/4 teaspoon pepper
2 tablespoons butter   1 cup grated Cheddar cheese

Cook rice according to package directions. Mix all in
gredients with half the cheese and spread in a 2 1/2-quar
baking dish. If mixture seems too thick, add a little milk
Sprinkle the remaining 1/2 cup cheese over the top. Bake a
375° for 35 minutes.

Mrs. Benny Grant (Diane

★ **SHRIMP MULL**
Easy, a meal in one dish

Yield: 4 to 5 large serving

2 slices bacon, fried   1 teaspoon chili powder
1 medium onion, diced   1 tablespoon worcestershire
1 medium green pepper, diced   sauce
1 cup celery, diced   1 1/4 cups catsup
2 (4 1/2-ounce) cans
  small shrimp

After frying bacon, remove and save. Slightly brown onion
in bacon drippings. Add pepper and celery and cook unt
soft. Add undrained shrimp, chili powder, worcestershire sauce
crumbled bacon, and catsup. Cook until thickened. Serve ho
over cooked rice.

Mrs. Leonard N. Hunter (Sue
Senoia, Georgia

★ **SHRIMP THERMIDOR CREPES**
A luncheon specialty!

Yield: 4 or 8 servings

1/4 cup butter	1/2 cup sliced mushrooms
1/4 cup flour	1 pound shrimp, cooked
1 cup light cream or milk	and cleaned
1/4 teaspoon salt	8 cooked crêpes
1/8 teaspoon pepper	2 tablespoons butter, melted
1/4 cup dry white wine	1/4 cup grated Parmesan
	cheese

In a saucepan melt 1/4 cup butter and blend in flour. Stir in cream or milk, salt, pepper, wine, and mushrooms. Cook, stirring constantly, until thickened. Add cooked shrimp. Fill crêpes with shrimp mixture. Fold over and place in broiler pan. Brush crêpes with melted butter and top with cheese. Broil until brown.

Mrs. Dan B. Umbach (Marie)

★ **SOUTHERN FRIED SHRIMP**
Always a favorite

2 cups flour	1 1/2 cups milk
3 teaspoons baking powder	1 to 3 pounds of shrimp
1 teaspoon salt	Oil for frying
2 tablespoons shortening	

Shell and devein shrimp. Combine all ingredients except shrimp. Mix well. This makes a thick batter. Add 3 or 4 shrimp at a time, making sure each shrimp is coated well. Drop shrimp into hot cooking oil and cook until golden brown on both sides.

Mrs. B. M. Enger (Imogene)
Mobile, Alabama

★ **SHRIMP NEWBURG**
Good luncheon dish

Oven: 350° 25 minutes   Yield: 12 servings

1 (10 3/4-ounce) can frozen   1/3 cup mayonnaise
  cream of shrimp soup, thawed   1/4 cup dry sherry
2/3 cup evaporated milk   4 ounces noodles, cooked
2 ounces Cheddar cheese,   5 ounces boiled shrimp
  shredded

Mix cream of shrimp soup and evaporated milk; heat to boiling. Remove from heat and add cheese and mayonnaise. Stir until cheese melts. Blend in sherry, noodles, and shrimp. Bake in lightly greased 1 1/2-quart casserole dish about 25 minutes at 350°.

Mrs. Jim C. Luckie (Sandra)

★ **SHRIMP PILAU**

Oven: 350° 45 minutes   Yield: 4 to 6 servings

4 slices bacon   1/8 teaspoon Tabasco sauce
1/2 cup chopped onions   2 cups uncooked rice
2 cups canned tomatoes   1 1/2 cups raw shrimp, peeled
1/2 teaspoon salt   and deveined
1/4 teaspoon black pepper

Fry bacon. Remove from skillet and save. In the remaining bacon fat, fry onions over low heat until transparent. Add tomatoes and cook for a few minutes. Add seasonings, rice, shrimp, and crumbled bacon. Place in a 1-quart casserole and cover. Bake at 350° for 45 minutes. Stir with fork 2 or 3 times while baking.

The Pirates' House
Savannah, Georgia

★   SHRIMP PIE

Oven: 425° 20 minutes   Yield: 4 servings

1 (4-ounce) can chopped   1 teaspoon salt
  mushrooms, drained   1/4 teaspoon pepper
1 small onion, minced   2 cups milk
5 tablespoons butter   1 tablespoon chopped parsley
  or margarine   1 cup cooked, diced potatoes
1 pound shrimp, cooked,   1/2 cup cooked green peas
  cleaned, and shelled   Pastry for topping
3 tablespoons flour

Cook mushrooms and onions in 2 tablespoons of butter or margarine for 5 minutes; add shrimp. Prepare white sauce with 3 tablespoons butter, flour, salt, pepper, and milk. Pour over shrimp mixture and add remaining ingredients except pastry. Turn into a 1-quart casserole and top with the pastry, rolled 1/4-inch thick. Bake at 425° about 20 minutes.

NOTE: May reduce milk to 1 3/4 cups and add 1/4 cup sherry to sauce.

Mrs. William E. Anderson (Dell)

'EL-AN-GE' ENAMELED
COLANDER
(1910)

261

★ SHRIMP, CRAB, AND WILD RICE SUPREME
Elegant but easy

Yield: 6 servings

1 1/2 sticks butter
  or margarine
4 cloves garlic, minced
1 pound fresh mushrooms
1 pound fresh shrimp,
  peeled and deveined

1 pound fresh crabmeat
1 (6-ounce) package long grain
  and wild rice, cooked
Lemon juice, to taste
1/2 cup sour cream (optional)

Melt butter and sauté garlic and mushrooms. Add shrimp and cook until pink. Add crab, cooked wild rice, and lemon juice. Stir and cook until all ingredients are heated through. Add sour cream, if desired, and mix well.

Mrs. Henry L. Camp, Jr. (Susan)

★ SHRIMP IN CHEESE SAUCE
Good for appetizer or luncheon

Yield: 8 servings

2 (6-ounce) rolls garlic cheese
2 (10 3/4-ounce) cans cream
  of shrimp soup
2 (4-ounce) cans mushrooms
  (reserve liquid)
1 teaspoon onion juice
2 teaspoons worcestershire sauce

2 tablespoons lemon juice
Dash Tabasco
2 tablespoons dry sherry
2 (4-ounce) cans small shrimp
Salt to taste

Combine all ingredients, except canned shrimp and salt, in top of double boiler. Cook until thick, about 1 hour, stirring occasionally. If too thick, thin with mushroom liquid. Season with salt to taste. Add shrimp. Serve in chafing dish as an appetizer on Melba toast rounds or over Melba toast or patty shells for lunch.

Mrs. Jeanne Benson
Athens, Georgia

★

SHRIMP CURRY
Good one-dish meal

Yield: 4 to 5 servings

1 large onion	1/4 teaspoon salt
2 tablespoons margarine	Dash of pepper
1 (10 3/4-ounce) can cream of mushroom soup	4 tablespoons sour cream
	2 teaspoons lemon juice
1 (10 3/4-ounce) can cream of celery soup	1 pound fresh shrimp or 2 cups cooked shrimp
1/2 teaspoon curry powder	2 cups cooked rice
1 (8 1/2-ounce) can seedless grapes	

Chop onion; sauté in margarine. When onions turn yellow, add undiluted soups; then add other ingredients except sour cream, lemon juice, and shrimp. Add these just before serving. If uncooked shrimp are used, follow package directions for cooking. Have cooked rice ready to serve. Add shrimp, lemon juice, and sour cream to soup mixture. Heat thoroughly. Serve over rice.

Mrs. B. R. Miller, Jr. (Caroline)
Atlanta, Georgia

ROASTER AND BAKING PAN (1897)

263

★ **SHRIMP CASSEROLE**
Good buffet dish. Make ahead.

Oven: 350° 35 minutes   Yield: 6 to 8 servings

2 pounds medium shrimp
1 tablespoon lemon juice
3 tablespoons salad oil
3/4 cup quick-cooking rice
1/4 cup minced green pepper
1/4 cup minced onion
2 tablespoons butter
1 teaspoon salt
1/8 teaspoon pepper

1/8 teaspoon mace
Dash cayenne
1 (10 3/4-ounce) can tomato
   soup, undiluted
1 cup half and half cream
1/2 cup sherry
1/2 cup slivered almonds
Paprika

Clean and cook shrimp 5 minutes; drain and put into 2-quart casserole. Sprinkle shrimp with lemon juice and oil. Cook rice. Sauté pepper and onion in butter and add to rice. Add all additional ingredients except almonds and paprika and add to shrimp in casserole. Top with almonds and paprika. Bake at 350° for 35 minutes or until of serving consistency.

Mrs. Nathan G. Knight (Ann)

ROUND CHEESE BOX (1896)

Game

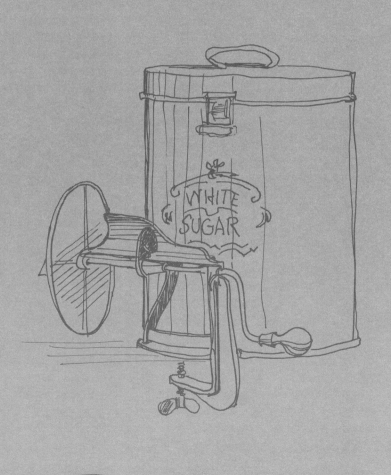

GAME

Game Chapter Design: Universal Kitchen Slicer (1889), Flat Top Sugar Box (1883)

★ **BAKED DOVE IN WINE SAUCE**
Great dish for the proud hunter!

Oven 350° 1 hour   Yield: 4 servings

1 cup flour   2 garlic cloves
10 dove   1/2 cup water
1 stick butter   1/2 cup sherry

Flour dove and brown them in butter with garlic. Put dove in deep baking dish. Add 1/2 cup water and 1/2 cup of sherry. Bake in 350° oven for 1 hour. Delicious served over white rice.

Mrs. Dan B. Umbach (Marie)

★ **DOVE, QUAIL, OR WOOD DUCK**
Has a fried taste, yet dove are very moist

Oven: 350° 30 minutes   Yield: Any number of servings

Salt, pepper, flour
2 to 3 dove per person
Butter, about 1 to 2 tablespoons per dove
Wine, to taste

Salt, pepper, and lightly flour dove. Melt butter in a black iron skillet. Sauté dove in the butter over medium heat for approximately 15 minutes. Remove dove and place them in an oven-proof casserole. Pour any favorite wine into butter while it is still hot and heat thoroughly. Pour butter mixture over dove to moisten well and to a depth of about ¼ inch of liquid. Bake at 350° for 30 minutes uncovered. If dove appear to be drying out, cover loosely with foil.

NOTE: Delicious served with wild rice, French blanched green beans, lady peas, or baby limas, and a good Pouilly-Fuisse wine.

Joe Lawson

267

★ MISSISSIPPI DUCK

Oven: 350° 15 minutes

Yield: 6 to 8 servings

2 to 3 wild ducks
1 package of crab and shrimp boil
2 cups garlic butter

Boil ducks in large pot with crab and shrimp boil. Boil for one hour, sticking fork into the meat to allow the shrimp boil to penetrate ducks. After boiling, put ducks into oven at 350° for 15 minutes. Baste with garlic butter while cooking.

Mrs. H. Brantley Kemp (Brenda)

★ SMOKED WILD DUCK

Wild ducks (Allow 1 duck
  per person for hearty eaters)
Milk
Salt

Pepper
Butter
Red Wine
Apples
Onions

Soak ducks in milk for 4 to 5 hours. Take ducks out of milk. Salt and pepper inside and out. Cut up apples and onions; stuff ducks with unpeeled apples and onions. Use a pit that cooks with smoke only. Put ducks on pit and cook slowly with smoke from fire until ducks are tender. Add hickory chips to fire for flavor. Make a marinating sauce of melted butter, red wine, salt, and pepper. Baste ducks often while cooking. Cooking time should take 2 to 4 hours depending on size of ducks and temperature of fire.

NOTE: Duck may be sliced and served cold as an appetizer. It can also be ground and used for making a meat dip.

Benny N. Grant

★ ## 'POSSUM AND 'TATERS
Roast beef may be substituted for the opossum

Oven: 375°   Yield: 6 to 8 servings

1 opossum, cut into serving   1/8 teaspoon black pepper
   pieces   4 baking-size sweet potatoes,
Water to cover   pared and quartered
2 teaspoons salt   1 cup sugar
                                     1 stick margarine, chopped

Skin and dress opossum. Put in Dutch oven and cover with water. Add salt and pepper. Cover and cook over medium heat until very tender. Place opossum pieces in center of large baking pan and arrange sweet potatoes around them. Sprinkle sugar and margarine over potatoes. Pour 2 cups of broth from cooked opossum over all. Place in preheated 375° oven and bake until potatoes are fork tender, slightly browned, and broth has evaporated.

Mrs. Bill Duncan (Ozella)

★ ## FRIED PHEASANT
A never-to-be-forgotten treat!

Yield: 2 servings

Pheasant   1 teaspoon paprika
Milk   1/2 teaspoon onion salt
1 teaspoon salt   1/4 teaspoon cayenne pepper
2 cups all-purpose flour   Vegetable oil
1 teaspoon black pepper

Remove skin from pheasant. Cut into 4 quarters. Soak in milk for at least 6 hours and then thoroughly coat with flour and seasonings. Fry in hot vegetable oil (1 inch deep) until brown on one side; turn only once. Total frying time should be about 20 minutes. Make brown gravy from drippings in pan. Serve over rice.

John C. Dunn

269

PHEASANT CALVADOS
Elegant!

Yield: 4 to 6 servings

2 pheasants	1/3 cup dry white wine
1/2 cup flour	1 cup half and half
8 to 10 tablespoons butter	3 egg yolks, beaten
1/3 cup Calvados	6 green apples, thinly sliced
1 teaspoon salt	1/4 cup sugar
1/2 teaspoon pepper	

Bone the breasts and thighs of the pheasants. Discard rest of bird. Shake the pheasant pieces in flour. Melt 8 tablespoons butter over medium heat in a large skillet and saute the pheasant pieces gently until meat is ivory-colored — not golden. This will take about 3 to 4 minutes. Pour the Calvados over the pheasant and flame. As the flame subsides, turn the pheasant pieces over once or twice. Add salt, pepper, and wine. Bring this mixture to a boil over medium heat. Lower heat and simmer partially covered 6 to 8 minutes. Do not overcook!

Remove pheasant to a serving platter and keep warm. Meanwhile add a few more drops of Calvados to the skillet. Mix the half and half and eggs together; slowly stir the egg mixture into the pan pieces, stirring constantly over medium heat. Do not allow sauce to boil, but cook it long enough for sauce to thicken. Pour sauce into a sauceboat to be passed separately.

In another skillet, sauté the apple slices over medium to high heat in 2 tablespoons butter until they are golden-about 5 minutes. Sprinkle the sugar over apples to glaze them. Surround the pheasant with the apple slices.

Delicious served with wild rice!

Christy King
Atlanta, Georgia

★   SMOTHERED QUAIL

Oven: 350° 1 hour   Yield: 12 servings

12 quail   2 1/2 cups chicken broth
12 tablespoons butter   1/2 cup sherry
3 tablespoons all-purpose flour   Salt and pepper to taste
                                     Cooked rice

Prepare quail; brown in heavy skillet in 12 tablespoons butter. Remove quail to baking dish (or crock pot). Add flour to butter in skillet and stir well. Slowly add chicken broth, sherry, salt, and pepper. Blend well and pour over quail. Cover baking dish and bake at 350° for about 1 hour (or 5 hours in crock pot). Serve with rice.

Mrs. Arthur G. Estes, III (Martha Ann)
Gay, Georgia

★   FRIED RABBIT

Yield: 4 to 5 servings

1 frying-size rabbit, cut into   1/2 teaspoon pepper
   serving pieces   1 cup cooking oil
1 cup flour
1 teaspoon salt

Coat rabbit with mixture of flour, salt, and pepper. Heat oil in heavy skillet. Place meat in skillet and brown well on both sides. Lower heat and cook, turning once again.

GRAVY: Drain all oil from skillet except 3 tablespoons. Add and brown 1/4 to 1/2 cup flour, stirring to scrape brown bits from skillet bottom.. When mixture is brown and smooth, add 1 1/2 cups water slowly. Cook over low heat until gravy thickens to consistency desired.

Mrs. Oliver P. Reason (Annette)

271

★ SOUTHERN FRIED QUAIL

Yield: Depends on appetite!

10 to 12 quail	1/2 teaspoon pepper
1 teaspoon salt	1/4 to 1/2 cup flour

Dry, pick quail. Clean and wipe thoroughly. Salt, pepper, and dredge with flour. Have a deep (heavy) frying pan with close-fitting lid half full of hot fat. Put in quail. Cook for a few minutes over a hot fire, then cover skillet and reduce heat. Cook slowly until tender, turning the quail when golden brown. Serve on hot platter garnished with slices of lemon and sprigs of parsley.

Mrs. John Goodrum (Marsha)

★ FRIED TURTLE

Yield: 4 to 6 servings

1 turtle, approximately 12 inches in diameter	1 (6-ounce) can evaporated milk
Salt and pepper to taste	Flour to coat

Kill turtle by removing head and dress as follows. Dip in boiling water. Remove immediately. Straighten legs, tail, and neck, one at a time, and scrape off excess skin with sharp knife. Remove lower shell with knife and cut off legs, neck, and tail, and reserve. Discard the rest of the turtle. Chill overnight. Dip turtle pieces in milk and sprinkle with salt and pepper. Coat with flour. Add enough cooking oil to 3/4 cover turtle pieces. Add turtle and cook over medium heat until well browned. Turn and reduce to low heat; cover and cook for 2 hours or until tender.

NOTE: Make gravy from pan drippings, if desired.

Mrs. Bill Duncan (Ozella)

★ **BRAISED VENISON**

Oven: 300° 2 hours   Yield: Any number of servings

Venison steaks   **1/2 cup chopped apple**
Flour, shortening   **1/2 cup chopped carrot**
1 tablespoon vinegar   **1/4 cup chopped onion**
1/2 cup chopped celery

Dredge steaks in flour and sear on all sides in shortening. Place steaks in oven-proof dish. Add enough water to cover the bottom of dish; add 1 tablespoon vinegar. Cover tightly and cook very slowly in 300° oven for about 2 hours, adding a little more liquid as necessary. About 30 minutes before meat is tender, add celery, apple, carrot, and onion. This mixture will flavor the gravy and add flavor to the meat.

Mrs. Arthur G. Estes, III (Martha Ann)
Gay, Georgia

MARINATED VENISON

Yield: Approximately 2 cups marinade

3/4 cup vinegar   **2 bay leaves**
3/4 cup cooking oil   **1 teaspoon garlic salt**
1/4 cup worcestershire sauce   **1/4 teaspoon thyme**
1 bell pepper, cut into strips   **Venison**

Combine all ingredients. Add enough water to make enough sauce to cover venison completely. Bring to boil and let simmer about 5 minutes. Cool and pour over venison. Cover tightly and let marinate in refrigerator at least 24 hours. Broil venison, basting occasionally with sauce. If preparing roast, wrap in foil, then bake in oven as usual, making sure the roast has enough fat.

Mrs. Joe Norman (Frances)

273

LAPIN A LA COCOTTE
(French Rabbit Stew)
Delicious! Poultry may be substituted for rabbit.

Yield: 4 servings

1 stick butter
6 shallots, sliced
1 rabbit, cut up
3 tablespoons flour
1 cup cold water
Bouquet garni (3 sprigs parsley, pinch thyme, 2 large garlic cloves)
Several baby carrots, cooked
3 tablespoons red wine, preferably port or madeira (optional)

Put into heavy skillet 2 round tablespoons butter (butter won't burn if it is clarified) and melt over low flame. Add 3 or 4 shallots and the pieces of rabbit. Do not flour rabbit. Cook rabbit until it is a golden color, about 5 minutes. Remove from skillet and set aside along with juice. Add 1 to 3 more rounded tablespoons butter; melt, then add 3 tablespoons flour. Make a paste, add 1 cup cold water; stir until well blended and thick. Add 3 small sprigs parsley, a pinch of thyme, and 2 cloves of garlic or to taste. Add pieces of rabbit with juice. Taste and season. Add more shallots, if desired, salt and pepper. Add cooked baby carrots. Add enough tepid water to cover and 3 tablespoons red wine. Bring to a boil. Cover and simmer about 1 hour.

NOTE: This recipe is from a French friend in Paris.

Mrs. R. Clark Williams, Jr. (Love)

Jams, Jellies, Pickles, Relishes

Blizzard Freezer

JAMS, JELLIES

PICKLES

RELISHES

Jams, Jellies, Pickles, Relishes Chapter Design: "Blizzard" Ice Cream Freezer (1910), Geneva Hand Fluter (1883)

APPLE JELLY

Yield: 8 to 10 jelly glasses

Approximately 2 gallons apples Sugar
Cold water   Paraffin
2 slices of lemon

Wash apples. Remove core, stems, and blossom ends. Cut into quarters, then smaller chunks. Put into preserving kettle or large boiling pan. Add enough cold water to cover apples. Add 2 slices of lemon. Cover and cook until apples are soft and clear. Remove from stove. Strain through 2 thicknesses of cheese cloth, reserving liquid. Return to preserving kettle by measuring one cup juice to one cup sugar less 2 tablespoons. Let juice boil rapidly. Test by placing 1/2 teaspoon juice into cold water. Let tested amount cool until it jells. Remove from heat. Pour immediately into sterilized glasses. Cover at once with lid or paraffin.

Mrs. T. K. Barron

APRICOT CONSERVE
Great Christmas present!

Yield: 2 1/2 pints

2 1/2 cups dried apricots   2/3 cup raisins
Water   2 tablespoons lemon juice
4 cups sugar   1/2 cup chopped pecans
1 (20-ounce) can crushed   1/2 bottle Certo
** pineapple with juice**

Soak apricots overnight in water to cover. Next morning, drain and chop. Combine apricots, sugar, pineapple, raisins, and lemon juice in heavy saucepan; bring to a boil one minute, stirring constantly. Remove from heat, stir in pecans and Certo. Pour into jars and process in hot water bath for 20 minutes. Makes about 2 1/2 pints.

Mrs. John Stuckey (Sandy)

277

★ ## FIG PRESERVES I

Figs are available in Georgia in August and September

Yield: 4 pints

2 quarts peeled figs
(approximately 3 quarts
unpeeled figs)
2 quarts sugar, granulated

1 lemon, thinly sliced
Sterilized jars

When peeling figs it is very important to protect hands by wearing gloves. Pick and prepare figs immediately. Cover figs and lemon with sugar. Place over very low heat until sugar completely dissolves. Stir carefully to avoid breaking figs. Turn heat high enough to bring mixture to a rolling boil. Let boil until the froth on top turns from a pink to a golden color, approximately 30 minutes. Place in jars to seal. There will be an extra amount of syrup in relation to figs. Several jars will be of just syrup, which is grand on waffles, etc.

NOTE: This makes a great Christmas gift. It also is delicious added to homemade fruit cake!

Mrs. John W. Anderson (Nancy)
Florence, South Carolina

★ ## FIG PRESERVES II
Delicious!

Yield: 2 to 4 pints

2 pounds peeled figs
2 3/4 pounds sugar

1 lemon, sliced
2 cups water

Prepare figs. Mix sugar, lemon, and water. Bring to a rolling boil. Drop figs in and cook 40 to 60 minutes until figs are clear and juice is thick. Put into jars and seal. Preserves are better when cooked in the 2-pound quantity.

Mrs. R.B. Hubbard, Jr. (Eleanor)

★ ## FIG PRESERVES III

Yield: 6 quarts

6 quarts figs   5 pounds sugar
1 cup soda

Wash figs. Leave small stem cap on figs to retain shape. Sprinkle soda over figs. Cover with 6 quarts boiling water. Soak for 15 minutes. Drain. Rinse in cold water. Mix sugar and four quarts water. Boil 10 minutes and skim. Add drained figs. Cook rapidly until figs are clear and tender, and syrup is consistency of honey (approximately 1 1/2 to 2 1/2 hours).

Mrs. Oliver P. Reason (Annette)

GRAPE JUICE JELLY

Good with turkey instead of cranberries

Yield: Approximately 2 pints

1 pint grape juice   1 whole clove
2/3 cup vinegar   1 box Sure Jell
1/2 teaspoon cinnamon   3 cups sugar

Mix first five ingredients and bring to a rolling boil. Remove from heat, add sugar, return to heat, and cook 5 minutes. Pour into clean jars. This will keep for months.

Mrs. Walter Sanders (Clara Berry)

WILD STRAWBERRY JAM

Good on biscuits with lots of butter

Yield: 2 to 3 jars

1 cup wild strawberries
1 cup sugar

Combine the berries and sugar and mix well. Stir in a pot over medium heat for 10 to 15 minutes. Place in one or one-half sterilized pint jars. Seal.

Mary Crowder Stephens

★ ## PEPPER JELLY I

Yield: 6 to 8 (6-ounce) jars

1 cup chopped hot peppers
2 bell peppers, chopped
6 cups sugar
2 cups vinegar

2 bottles Certo
1/2 teaspoon salt
Green food coloring (optional)

Boil chopped peppers, vinegar, sugar, and salt for five minutes. Remove from stove and strain into saucepan. Add Certo and food coloring, if desired. Pour into jars. This does not have to be sealed.

NOTE: Good served with meats, especially lamb, and fresh vegetables. A typically Southern appetizer is cream cheese covered with pepper jelly served with crackers.

Mrs. John Goodrum (Marsha)

★ ## PEPPER JELLY II

Yield: 6 to 8 half pints

3/4 cup red or green peppers, drained and ground
1/4 cup Jalapeño peppers or other hot peppers, ground
6 1/2 cups sugar
1 1/2 cups white vinegar
1 teaspoon salt
1 bottle Certo

Boil hard for 1 minute the following ingredients: all peppers, sugar, vinegar, and salt. Remove from heat and add Certo. Stir until partially cool so that the mix of peppers and jelly will be even. Ladle into hot, sterilized jars and seal with 1/8 inch paraffin. Delicious appetizer when spooned over a block of cream cheese and served with crackers.

Mrs. J. B. Kopp (Lynne)
Corbin, Kentucky

NECTARINE AND PINEAPPLE CONSERVE

Yield: 9 medium glasses

3 cups nectarines
(about 2 1/2 pounds), fully ripe
1/2 cup maraschino cherries,
finely chopped
1/4 cup lemon juice (2 lemons)
1 (8-ounce) can crushed pineapple

1 cup chopped nuts
7 1/2 cups sugar
1 (6-ounce) bottle liquid
fruit pectin
Paraffin

Peel and pit nectarines. Grind or finely chop them. Measure 3 cups into a large saucepan; add chopped cherries, lemon juice, and pineapple. Thoroughly mix nuts and sugar into fruit. Place over high heat, bring to a rolling boil, and boil hard 1 minute, stirring constantly. Remove from heat and immediately stir in fruit pectin. Skim off foam with a metal spoon. Then stir and skim for 5 minutes to cool slightly and prevent floating fruit. Ladle quickly into sterile glasses. Cover with 1/8 inch hot paraffin.

Mrs. James Hardy (Fay)

JALAPEÑO JELLY

Great with cream cheese and crackers or with meat

Yield: 5 (8-ounce) jars

3/4 cup diced green bell
pepper
1/4 to 3/4 cup diced fresh
Jalapeños

1 cup cider vinegar
5 cups sugar
1 bottle Certo

Chop bell peppers and Jalapeños. If done by hand, use gloves. Do not get near eyes, for Jalapeños will give intense burns. Place bell pepper, Jalapeños, vinegar, and sugar in large saucepan; bring to a boil. Boil for 4 to 5 minutes. Remove from heat. Add Certo. Cool. Pour into sterilized jars and seal.

Mrs. J. Littleton Glover, Jr. (Kathryn)

281

★ ## PEACH MARMALADE
A different blend of sweet and bitter

Yield: Depends on size of jars used

2 dozen medium Georgia
  peaches, peeled and chopped
1 small jar maraschino cherries

2 medium oranges
4 teaspoons Sure-Jell
Sugar

Grate orange rind and cut remaining orange into sections with seeds removed. Put peaches, cherries, and orange sections through food grinder. Then put into large Dutch-oven type container. Add grated rind. Add 1 cup sugar to each cup of the fruit mixture. Mix well. Add 4 teaspoons Sure-Jell. Cook over low heat until thick, about 30 minutes. Put into clean, hot jars. Seal while hot.

NOTE: Good for Christmas presents. Baby food jars make great containers.

Mrs. Billy Arnall, Jr. (Linda)

★ ## JAN'S RED PEPPER JAM

Yield: 3 pints

6 large red bell peppers
6 large green bell peppers
5 to 6 hot peppers

1 tablespoon salt
3 cups sugar
2 cups vinegar

Take out centers and all seed from bell peppers and hot peppers. Grind the cleaned peppers and add salt. Let stand 2 hours. Drain well. Put in saucepan and add sugar and vinegar. Cook over low heat 1 hour or until jam consistency. Pour into hot sterilized jars and seal. Process for 5 minutes in a boiling bath of 1/2 inch water.

NOTE: Delicious on cream cheese served with crackers!

Mrs. William Parks Cole (Judy)

MINT JULEP JELLY

Yield: 4 to 5 (8-ounce) glasses

1 1/2 cups bourbon
1/2 cup water
3 cups sugar

6 tablespoons Certo
Fresh mint

Combine bourbon, water, and sugar in top of double boiler. Place over boiling water. Stir until sugar is dissolved. Remove from heat. Add Certo. Pour into glasses. Add fresh mint sprig to each glass. Seal.

Mrs. J. Littleton Glover, Jr. (Kathryn)

PORT WINE JELLY

Yield: Approximately 5 half-pint jars

1 cup port wine
1 cup cranberry juice

3 1/2 cups sugar
Bottle of Certo

Stir all ingredients except Certo in a double boiler until sugar is dissolved. Remove from heat and add 1/2 bottle of Certo. Pour into sterilized jars immediately and seal or pour 1/8 inch paraffin on top.

Mrs. James Gould (Bea)
Mobile, Alabama

STRAWBERRY FIG PRESERVES

Yield: 3 or 4 pints

3 cups mashed, ripe figs
3 cups sugar
2 (3-ounce) packages strawberry-flavored gelatin or
1 (6-ounce) package strawberry-flavored gelatin

Mix all ingredients well. Bring to a boil. Cook 4 minutes at a rolling boil. Stir frequently. Skim and pour into sterilized jars. Seal.

NOTE: Do not double recipe.

Mrs. Hope Shirey (Frances)

283

GRANNA'S LIME PICKLES

Yield: Approximately 14 pints

Pickling lime
7 pounds cucumbers, sliced
2 quarts vinegar

4 1/2 pounds sugar
1 tablespoon salt
Pickling spice

Mix 2 cups pickling lime to 2 gallons water. Soak cucumber slices 24 hours in lime water, then rinse 3 times in cold water. Soak 3 hours in ice and water, then remove and drain well. Make a syrup by combining the vinegar, sugar, and salt. Pour syrup over cucumbers. Leave overnight. Add pickling spice to taste. Boil mixture for 35 minutes and place in sterilized jars. Seal.

Mrs. Carl A. Jones
Johnson City, Tennessee

LIME PICKLES
Good for large cucumbers (chunk-style)

Yield: 6 to 8 quarts

7 pounds cucumbers
1 cup lime per 1 gallon
   water
2 quarts vinegar
4 1/2 pounds sugar

1 teaspoon whole cloves
1 teaspoon pickling spice
1 teaspoon turmeric
1 teaspoon salt, non-iodized

Cut cucumbers into slices or 1/2-inch chunks. Cover with 1 cup lime to 1 gallon water and let stand 24 hours. Rinse several times and let stand in cold water 3 hours. Let stand overnight in 2 quarts vinegar, 4 1/2 pounds sugar, and the remaining spices. Boil 35 minutes and can in sterilized jars.

NOTE: Do not use an aluminum container.

Mrs. Leon Bauer (Florence)
Metropolis, Illinois

★   ## CRISP PICKLE
Delicious!

Yield: 8 pints

4 quarts cucumbers, unpeeled and thinly sliced	1/3 cup coarse salt
2 green bell peppers, thinly sliced	5 cups sugar
	3 cups cider vinegar
	2 tablespoons mustard seed
3 cloves of garlic	1 1/2 teaspoons turmeric
6 large onions, thinly sliced	1 1/2 teaspoons celery seed

Combine first five ingredients. Cover with cracked ice and mix thoroughly. Keep mixing 4 or 5 times. Let stand for 3 hours. Drain and remove garlic.

Combine rest of ingredients and pour over the cucumber mixture. Heat to boiling. Fill hot sterilized jars to within 1/2 inch of top; adjust lids. Process in boiling water bath for 5 minutes. Start timing when water begins to boil.

Mrs. Pat Yancey, Jr. (Jeane)

★   ## ZUCCHINI SQUASH PICKLES
No cooking!

Yield: 6 pints

2 pounds zucchini squash	2 cups sugar
2 small onions	1 teaspoon celery seed
1/4 cup salt	1 teaspoon mustard seed
2 cups white vinegar	1 teaspoon turmeric

Wash squash, slice thinly. Wash onions, peel, and slice thinly. Cover with water and salt and let stand 2 hours. Drain and place in jars and cover with mixture of other ingredients. Refrigerate.

NOTE: These keep for weeks in the refrigerator.

Mrs. C. W. Whetstone
Cameron, South Carolina

★ **PICKLED OKRA**

Delicious served with cold cuts

Yield: 8 pints

5 pounds okra
8 cups vinegar
1 cup water

1/2 cup salt
8 to 10 cloves garlic
8 to 10 hot, green peppers

Wash okra, leaving top cap and removing excess stem. Combine vinegar, water, and salt. Bring to a boil. Drop the okra into the boiling mixture. Bring to a rolling boil. Place in hot, sterilized jars. Add 1 clove garlic and hot pepper to each pint. Seal while hot. Let stand 8 to 10 weeks before serving.

Mrs. Oliver P. Reason (Annette)

★ **CRISP SWEET PICKLES I**

Yield: 8 to 10 quarts

8 to 10 pounds of cucumbers
2 cups household lime
5 pounds sugar
2 1/2 quarts white vinegar
1 tablespoon salt

2 teaspoons whole cloves
2 tablespoons pickling spice
1 tablespoon celery seed
1 tablespoon green food
  coloring

Wash and slice cucumbers and put them in a large ceramic container. Add lime to enough water to cover the cucumbers and let stand 24 hours. Stir several times with wooden spoon.

Take cucumbers out of lime water and rinse well. Let soak for 2 hours in clean water, drain, and let stand while pickle solution is being prepared.

Mix sugar, vinegar, salt, cloves, pickling spice, celery seed, and food coloring. Bring to a boil. Let cool, then add cucumbers. Let stand overnight. The next morning, simmer about 30 minutes. Put into hot, sterilized jars and seal.

Mrs. H. C. Tysinger (Judy)

★   **CRISP SWEET PICKLES II**

Yield: 6 to 8 quarts

7 pounds cucumbers, sliced	2 quarts vinegar
3 cups household lime, available	9 cups sugar
in grocery canning section	2 tablespoons pickling spice
2 gallons water for each soak	1 teaspoon salt

Wash cucumbers thoroughly. Do not peel. Soak sliced cucumbers in lime water for 24 hours. Rinse 3 times and soak in 2 gallons clear water 3 hours. Rinse twice again. Mix vinegar, sugar, spices, and salt. Soak cucumbers in this overnight. Bring to a boil and simmer for 30 minutes. Pack in hot jars and seal.

VARIATION: Onions and pepper rings may be added for variety and color change. Do not go over 7 pounds total.

NOTE: Hint for working homemaker. If recipe is begun on Thursday evening, canning will be done on Saturday morning.

Mrs. Oliver P. Reason (Annette)

DILL PICKLES

For each 1-quart jar:

Cucumbers, washed	1 green pepper, cut into fourths
1 bud of garlic	1 teaspoon mustard seed
1 stalk celery	1 hot pepper
Brine:	
1 cup salt	1 quart vinegar
2 quarts water	1 tablespoon dill seed

Put whole cucumbers into clean jars. Add to each 1-quart jar: bud of garlic, celery, and 1 green pepper, cut into fourths. Make brine of salt, water, and vinegar, and boil with dill for 5 minutes. Add 1 teaspoon mustard seed and 1 hot pepper to each jar. Pour hot brine over pickles in jars and seal immediately. Ready to enjoy in 6 weeks.

Mrs. Joe Norman (Frances)

CHOW CHOW RELISH
A marvelous gift

Yield: 4 quarts

4 cups chopped purple cabbage (may use green)
2 cups chopped onion
2 cups chopped green sweet peppers
2 cups chopped green tomatoes
1/2 cup salt
8 cups water
3/4 cup sugar
3 tablespoons mustard seed
4 cups vinegar

Wash all vegetables thoroughly. Peel onions and remove pepper seeds. Chop all vegetables and measure. Dissolve salt in 8 cups water. Pour over vegetables. Let stand one hour. Drain and taste. If too salty, rinse again. Mix vegetables with sugar, mustard seed, and vinegar. Simmer 20 minutes, then bring to a full boil. Pack, boiling hot, into hot jars and seal at once.

Mrs. Oliver P. Reason (Annette)

COLE SLAW RELISH
Hurrah, no cooking!

Yield: Approximately 6 quarts

2 medium heads cabbage
 (about 6 pounds)
3 red bell peppers
3 green bell peppers
6 small carrots
6 large onions

1/2 cup salt
3 pints vinegar
6 cups sugar
1 teaspoon celery seed
1 teaspoon mustard seed
2 teaspoons turmeric

Cut the vegetables as for cole slaw. Add salt and let stand for 2 hours. Squeeze out liquid. Mix vegetables with the remaining ingredients. Seal in sterile jars.

Mrs. Leon Bauer (Florence)
Metropolis, Illinois

288

GREEN TOMATO RELISH

12 large onions, chopped
8 cups chopped green
  tomatoes
1/2 cup salt
6 red peppers, chopped

6 green peppers, chopped
6 cups sugar
3 cups vinegar
1 heaping tablespoon celery
  seed

Put onions, tomatoes, and salt in saucepan. Cover with boiling water. Cook 5 minutes. Drain for 1/2 hour. Combine vegetables with remaining ingredients in saucepan. Bring to a boil and cook 10 minutes. Seal in jars.

Mrs. Joe Bohannon (Mary)

RELISH

Yield: Approximately 7 to 8 pints

1 quart green tomatoes, finely chopped
1 quart cabbage, finely chopped
1 pint chopped white onion
1 pint chopped red mango peppers
1 pint chopped green mango peppers
2 pints sugar
2 to 3 pints vinegar
4 teaspoons mustard
Salt to taste

Mix the chopped tomatoes and cabbage together and let stand 2 hours. Drain well. Add the onions and red and green peppers. In a large pan combine the sugar, vinegar, mustard, and salt. Bring to a boil. Add all the vegetables to this liquid and boil 15 minutes. Can while hot in sterilized jars.

Mrs. Leon Bauer (Florence)
Metropolis, Illinois

PERKY PEAR RELISH

Yield: 8 pints

1 peck pears (8 quarts)
6 onions
6 bell peppers, 3 red
and 3 green
5 cups vinegar

3 teaspoons salt
1 teaspoon pickling spices
1 teaspoon turmeric
3 cups sugar
8 pint canning jars

Peel and core pears. Grind pears, then onions and peppers. Place in large boiler. Add vinegar, salt, and spices. Bring to a boil and boil for 30 minutes, or until thickened. Seal in pint jars.

Mrs. Thomas A. Luckie (Pollye)

★ SPICED PEACHES

Yield: 2 quarts

4 cups sugar
2 cups cider vinegar
1 cup water
1 tablespoon whole allspice

1 tablespoon whole cloves
4 (3-inch) sticks cinnamon
4 pounds (16 medium) peaches

Mix sugar, vinegar, and water in 5-quart pan. Tie allspice and cloves in cheesecloth. Put this and cinnamon into mixture. Cover and boil 5 minutes. Peel peaches; drop into boiling syrup a few at a time. Simmer until tender, about 5 minutes. Pack in sterile jars. Cover with syrup. Seal.

Mrs. John W. Anderson (Nancy)
Florence, South Carolina

JO'S PEAR CHUTNEY

Yield: 3 pints

4 1/2 pounds ripe pears
1 large green pepper,
    seeded
1/2 pound seeded raisins
    (1 1/2 cups)
4 cups sugar
1 cup chopped,
    crystallized ginger
3 cups vinegar

1/2 teaspoon salt
1 cup water
6 bay leaves
1/4 teaspoon powdered cloves
1/4 teaspoon allspice
1/4 teaspoon nutmeg
1/2 teaspoon cinnamon
1/2 cup bottled liquid pectin

Pare, core, and slice pears. Chop pepper. In a saucepan, mix all ingredients but spices and pectin. Tie spices in bag and add to pear mixture. Simmer until pears are tender and mixture is thick, about 2 hours. Remove spice bag and add pectin. Boil 1 minute. Pour into jars and seal.

Mrs. Hugh Farmer (Charlsie)

PEPPER RELISH

Great over any vegetable, especially peas or green beans

Yield: 6 or 7 pints

12 red peppers, halved
12 green peppers, halved
12 onions, peeled
1 quart mild vinegar

2 cups sugar
3 tablespoons salt
1 tablespoon mustard seed or
    celery seed

Remove the seeds from peppers. Put vegetables through a food chopper. Put vegetables in a saucepan, cover with boiling water, then drain. Cover with cold water and bring to the boiling point; drain again. Add vinegar, sugar, salt, and mustard or celery seed. Cook 10 minutes. Taste and add more sugar or salt if desired. Ladle into pint jars and seal.

Mrs. Walker Connally (Guilford)

MAGNIFICENT MUSTARD

Great Christmas idea for gift-giving
A man's delight-really hot!

Yield: Approximately 2 cups

1 cup white vinegar
1 cup dry mustard
2 eggs, well beaten
1 cup sugar
1/8 teaspoon salt

Mix vinegar and dry mustard and let it stand overnight. Next morning, stir in well beaten eggs, sugar, and salt. Bring to a slow boil and cook until the mixture coats the spoon, stirring constantly. Cool and refrigerate. Great on ham or beef sandwiches.

Mrs. Richard L. Day (Gayle)

VARIATION: Use Coleman's brand of dry mustard — comes in a can; omit salt.

Mrs. Harry C. Mitchell (Judy)
Houston, Texas

ONYX ENAMELED
TEA KETTLE
(1910)

Meats

MEATS

Meats Chapter Design: Left to right: Swirled Glass Sugar Container (1883), German Meissen onion pattern Barley Canister (1883), Ribbed Glass Coffee Canister (1883)

BEEF TENDERLOIN

Oven: 450° 30 to 40 minutes rare   Yield: 6 to 8 servings
45 to 60 minutes medium

1 (4 to 6 pound) beef   **Mild steak sauce (optional)**
  tenderloin   **Mushrooms (optional)**
Dry mustard
Salt and pepper

Trim tenderloin closely. Generously sprinkle with dry mustard and rub surface **well**. Salt and pepper to taste. Place in shallow roasting pan. Brush steak sauce over tenderloin. Roast in preheated very hot oven (450°) for 30 to 40 minutes (rare) or 45 to 60 minutes (medium) being careful not to over-bake. Slice 1 to 1 1/2 inches thick or as desired. Serve hot. Serve plain or with mushrooms.

John P. Woods, Jr.

MARINATED ROAST

Oven: 350° and 275° 6 1/2 hours   Yield: 18 to 20 servings

15 to 17 pound roast   **1 teaspoon dry mustard**
1 cup sherry   **2 teaspoons soy sauce**
1/2 cup wine vinegar   **2 teaspoons rosemary**
1/2 cup olive oil   **2 teaspoons salt**
8 cloves garlic, crushed

Mix all ingredients and marinate the roast at room temperature for 1 to 24 hours, turning several times. Bake at 350° for 30 minutes, then at 275° for about 6 hours. Adjust baking time for rare or well-done roast.

NOTE: Perfect for before or after the ball game parties, picnics, or buffet suppers.

Mrs. Homer Wright (Wanda)
Auburn, Alabama

BEEF WELLINGTON, PERIGUEUX SAUCE

Oven: 400° 30 minutes   Yield: 8 servings

1 1/2 pounds mushrooms, minced

6 green onions or shallots, very finely minced

4 ounces butter or margarine

4 tablespoons minced parsley

1 1/2 cups beef consommé

1 1/2 tablespoons butter or margarine

1 tablespoon cornstarch

1 1/2 cups Madeira

3 chopped truffles

Salt and pepper

6 cups all-purpose flour

2 1/2 cups soft butter or margarine

1 beef filet, approximately 3 pounds and trimmed of all fat

1 small can pâté de foie gras

1 egg

First, cook the mushrooms and onions in 4 ounces butter until all moisture has cooked away. Add the minced parsley toward the end. Cool, cover, and refrigerate.

Next make a Perigueux sauce by heating the consommé with 1 1/2 tablespoons of butter, adding the cornstarch dissolved in 1/3 cup Madeira and stirring over low heat until thick. Add the truffles. Add salt and pepper. Refrigerate.

To make the pastry, blend the flour and 2 1/2 cups soft butter with the fingers until a sandy mass has been obtained. Add 1 cup cold water gradually, mix slowly, and work dough into a ball, the less water used, the better. (If you have a Cuisinart, use their recipe.) Wrap in waxed paper and refrigerate.

The day of serving, remove the duxelles (mushroom mixture) and the meat. Let come to room temperature. Tie tips beef if this is needed. Season with salt and pepper. Melt 4 ounces butter in a shallow pan which is long enough to hold the filet, but is as narrow as possible. Braise the meat on top of the range for approximately 30 minutes, turning it often with spoons. Moisten with Madeira, using about 2/3 cup from time to time. Allow the meat to cool at room temperature.

Add the pâté de foie gras to the duxelles, mix well, and add 1 teaspoon of the Perigueux sauce. Taste for seasoning.

296   (Continued)

Roll out the pastry in a rectangular shape, about 14 inches by 9 inches and about 1/4-inch thick—large enough to cover the filet. Spread the duxelles over the pastry, leaving a border uncovered. Place the meat in the center with the side down which will eventually be up. Fold the pastry over the meat and seal the seam and ends with water. Place, seam-side down, on a sheet to go into the oven. Brush the top and sides with the egg, well-beaten and mixed with a little water. Prick thoroughly with a fork in a crisscross design or cut designs such as leaves from any extra pastry left over and apply these to the top of the pastry case. Bake in a preheated 400° oven for about 30 minutes. Serve, thinly sliced, with the Périgueux sauce, hot, on the side.

Some of the preparations can be done ahead, even the day before serving.

Mrs. J. Littleton Glover, Jr. (Kathryn)

BEA'S BARBECUE BEEF ROAST

Oven: 325° 4 hours   Yield: 6 servings

4 to 5 pound pot roast
3 medium onions, chopped
1 clove garlic, diced

1 cup water
1 (8-ounce) can tomato sauce
Salt and pepper to taste

Sauce:

2 tablespoons brown sugar
1/2 teaspoon dry mustard
1/4 cup lemon juice

1/2 cup vinegar
1/2 cup catsup

Brown roast on both sides. Add next 5 ingredients and cook at 325° for 2 hours. Combine sauce ingredients. Pour over roast and cook an additional 2 hours at 325°.

Mrs. Earl Hilley (Bea)
Macon, Georgia

WINE BEEF ROAST
Extra good when carrots are cooked around meat

Yield: 6 to 8 servings

3 to 4 pounds rump roast
2 cloves of garlic
Salt
Pepper
Flour
1 small onion, minced

1/4 cup oil plus 2 tablespoons butter
Allspice
Ground cloves
Cinnamon
2 cups dry red wine

Cut 4 slits in roast. Place 1/2 clove of garlic in each slit. Flour the roast after salting and peppering it. Brown in Dutch oven or heavy pot. Brown minced onion in small amount of oil in small pan. Put onion on top of browned roast. Sprinkle with dash of allspice, cloves, and cinnamon. (Go easy on the spices!) Pour wine over roast, cover tightly, and simmer on top of stove until tender (about 2 to 3 hours for 4-pound roast). Add more wine or water as needed.

NOTE: This is also good for cooking venison.

Mrs. Gene Ankrom (Barbara)

****

Use greased muffin tins as molds when baking stuffed green peppers.

To prevent the gravy from soaking into the bottom crust of a meat pie, brush the crust with the white of an egg.

It is best to freeze meat pies and turnovers unbaked.

Quantity of meat to buy per serving:
Boneless meat-   1/4 pound per serving
Medium amount of bone-1/3 to 1/2 pound per serving
Large amount of bone-   3/4 to 1 pound per serving

BEEF BURGUNDY I

Oven: 325° 2 hours 20 minutes   Yield: 6 servings

1 1/2 pounds lean beef, cubed
2 teaspoons salt
Freshly ground black pepper
2 tablespoons fat
1 onion, chopped
1 cup sour cream
1 cup American cheese, grated

1/2 cup Burgundy or red wine
1 clove garlic, minced
1/4 teaspoon each: thyme, marjoram, and basil
1 (10 3/4-ounce) can cream of mushroom soup

Cut beef in 1-inch cubes; season with salt and pepper. Brown on all sides in hot fat. Add onion near end of browning time and cook until soft. Transfer to large casserole or Dutch oven and add sour cream, cheese, wine, garlic, and herbs. Cover and bake at 325° for 2 hours or until meat is almost tender. Add undiluted soup. Mix well and bake 20 minutes longer. Add a little water if necessary during cooking time. Serve over rice.

Mrs. George Busbee (Mary Beth)
Governor's Mansion
Atlanta, Georgia

Mrs. Busbee is the wife of the Governor of Georgia.

❋❋❋❋❋❋❋❋❋❋❋❋

Make small holes all over an eye of round roast. Fill the holes with small slices of peeled garlic cloves. Season with Lawry's Seasoned Salt and lemon-pepper seasoning and bake.

When a recipe calls for meatballs, place the prepared meatballs on a cookie sheet. Bake at 350° for about 30 minutes.

To prevent meat loaf from sticking, put strips of bacon on the bottom of the pan.

BEEF BURGUNDY II

Oven: 325° 3 hours   Yield: 6 servings

3 pounds round steak or 3
  pounds top sirloin, cut into
  cubes
1/2 cup margarine, melted
6 tablespoons all-purpose flour
1 teaspoon salt
1/4 teaspoon pepper

3/4 teaspoon thyme
2 cups Burgundy
1 (10 1/2-ounce) can beef broth
  (bouillon)
1 onion, chopped
1 (4 or 8-ounce) can sliced
  mushrooms
Cooked rice

Brown meat in melted margarine and put into a 2-quart baking dish. Blend flour and seasonings. Mix flour with wine and beef bouillon. Pour over meat. Cover and bake at 325° for 2 hours. Add onions and mushrooms. Cover and continue cooking 1 hour more. Serve over hot rice.

Mrs. Keith Brady (Katie)

✳✳✳✳✳✳✳✳✳✳✳✳✳

Make meatballs uniform in size by patting the meat mixture into a rectangle; then cut the meat into equal-size squares and roll each square into a ball.

Substitute beer for stock or water when cooking beef stew or pot roast. Mix 1/2 can beer with tomato paste for a super gravy.

Cook tougher cuts of meat in strong tea instead of water. The tannin in tea is a tenderizer.

For freezing bacon, arrange slices, strip by strip on waxed paper, then roll them up and freeze in a plastic bag. When ready to use, unroll and peel off the strips.

CHOP SUEY

Yield: 8 servings

1 pound round steak
1 pound pork ham
Cooking oil
1 stalk celery, chopped
3 medium onions, chipped
1 (5-ounce) bottle soy sauce

2 (16-ounce) cans bean sprouts
2 tablespoons molasses
  (Chinese)
Flour

Cut steak and ham in bite-size pieces. Salt and pepper, dip in flour, and brown in cooking oil. Add chopped celery, chipped onions, soy sauce, and juice from drained bean sprouts. Cook slowly and stir from time to time for about 1 hour. Add bean sprouts, cook about 20 minutes. Mix molasses with flour, using enough flour to make a thick consistency. Stir into chop suey and cook until thickened. Serve on rice.

Mrs. Wilkes Boarding House
Savannah, Georgia

ORIENTAL PEPPER STEAK
Great crock pot dish for working mothers
Crockpot: Low setting 8 to 10 hours   Yield: 4 servings

1 pound round steak
1 large onion, diced
1 green pepper, diced
Salt and pepper

2/3 cup soy sauce
2/3 cup water
4 cups cooked rice

Cut round steak into small pieces; dice onion and green pepper. Place meat, onion, green pepper, and dash of salt and pepper into crockpot. Add soy sauce and water. Cook on low setting for 8 to 10 hours.

Serve over cooked rice.

Mrs. Dan B. Umbach (Marie)

301

SKILLET STEAK
Oriental accent!

Yield: 4 servings

1 to 1 1/2 pounds round
  steak, trimmed and cut
  into thin slices
1/2 cup oil and 2 tablespoons
  butter
2 to 3 stalks celery, thinly
  sliced
1 medium onion, chopped
2 cups water
Salt and pepper
1 cup fresh mushrooms, or 1
  (3-ounce) jar button mushrooms, drained

1/4 cup soy sauce
1 (2-ounce) jar chopped
  pimiento
1 green pepper, seeded and cut
  into strips
2 to 3 tablespoons cornstarch
1/2 cup cold water
Cooked rice for 4 people

Brown steak strips in mixture of oil and butter; add celery and onion. Cook 2 to 3 minutes; drain off excess oil. Add 2 cups water and salt and pepper to taste. Cover and cook over low heat 30 minutes. Slice mushrooms and add along with soy sauce and pimiento. Continue cooking over low heat up to 2 hours, stirring occasionally and maintaining liquid level by adding water as needed. Add green pepper 15 minutes before serving. Five minutes before serving, mix cornstarch with water and add to meat to thicken. Serve over hot, cooked rice.

NOTE: This is delicious served with a salad of lettuce and mandarin oranges, tossed with oil and vinegar, and hot rolls.

Mrs. Charles M. Smith (Lynn)

✳✳✳✳✳✳✳✳✳✳✳✳

To marinate meat, put it into a plastic bag and add only half the amount of marinade called for. Tie securely and turn the bag several times.

CHINESE BEEF
Vegetables can be prepared early

Yield: 4 to 6 servings

2 pounds flank steak	1/4 teaspoon ground ginger
2 tomatoes	(optional)
2 green peppers	1/2 to 3/4 cup soy sauce
2 stalks celery	1/2 teaspoon sugar
2 tablespoons salad oil	1 (1-pound) can bean sprouts
1 clove garlic	1 (4-ounce) can sliced mush-
1 teaspoon salt	rooms (optional)
1/2 teaspoon pepper	1/4 to 1/2 cup water

. Cut flank steak into thin strips across the grain of the meat. Cut tomatoes into quarters; trim away seeds and ribs from green peppers and cut peppers into big chunks; slice celery diagonally. Set aside. Heat oil in large skillet. Add strips of beef, crushed garlic, salt, pepper, and ginger. Fry over high heat until brown on all sides. Season with soy sauce and sugar. Cover tightly and cook slowly for 5 minutes. At this point, toss in tomatoes, peppers, celery, drained bean sprouts, and mushrooms. Bring to a boil, cover, and cook briskly for 5 minutes. Make a smooth paste of cornstarch and water. Add to beef mixture and cook until sauce thickens slightly. Stir occasionally. May be served over rice or Chinese noodles.

Mrs. Thomas G. Kerley (Florence)
Paducah, Kentucky

❈ ❈ ❈ ❈ ❈ ❈ ❈ ❈ ❈ ❈ ❈ ❈ ❈

Breaded meats tend to stick to the pan and lose their coating if they are fried. To prevent this, bread the meat ahead of time and let it stand on waxed paper at least 20 minutes before frying.

CHINESE PEPPER STEAK

Delicious!

Yield: 6 servings

2 pounds round steak,
   1 1/2 inches thick
1/4 cup vegetable oil
1/2 teaspoon garlic salt
3 medium green peppers,
   seeded and thinly sliced

2 large onions, thinly sliced
1/4 cup soy sauce
1 (8-ounce) can tomato sauce
1/4 teaspoon sugar

Trim all fat from steak. Slice into 1/8-inch thick slices. Heat oil in large skillet. Sprinkle meat with garlic salt and add meat slices to oil. Cook rapidly for 1 minute or until meat is light brown, stirring once or twice. Remove meat with slotted spoon. Add green peppers and onions to remaining oil in pan. Cook 2 minutes, stirring often. Add soy sauce, tomato sauce, and sugar. Simmer 3 to 4 minutes. Return meat. Cook 1 minute or until heated. Serve over rice.

Mrs. Sidney Pope Jones, Jr. (Sue)

* * * * * * * * * * * * * *

Turn roasts with 2 wooden spoons to prevent piercing the meat and losing the juices.

Add about 1/4 cup cold water for every 2 pounds of ground beef for juicy, grilled hamburgers.

Sprinkle halves of fresh nectarines with brown sugar mixed with dry mustard and ground cloves. Broil until bubbly and heated through. Serve warm with baked ham or ham sandwiches.

Brown a pork roast on top of the stove before roasting it covered in the oven for a tender, juicer roast.

BEEF SUKIYAKI

Yield: 4 to 5 servings

1 pound sirloin
2 tablespoons salad oil
1 beef bouillon cube
1/2 cup water
1/2 green pepper, thinly sliced
1/2 medium onion, thinly sliced
1 cup celery, cut in 1 1/2-
  inch diagonal pieces

1/2 cup soy sauce
2 tablespoons sugar
1 (16-ounce) can mixed Chinese
  vegetables, drained
1 (3-ounce) can sliced mushrooms with liquid
Hot, cooked rice

Trim sirloin, cut into 1x2 inch strips. Heat oil in a large skillet or wok; then add sirloin and cook, stirring constantly, until meat turns gray. Remove meat and set aside. In same pan, add bouillon cube and water; then add pepper, onion, and celery. Cook about 10 minutes. Add soy sauce, sugar, Chinese vegetables, and mushrooms, stirring to mix thoroughly. Add steak and cook about 5 minutes or until heated through. Serve immediately over cooked rice. The vegetables should be a little crisp.

Mrs. B. R. Miller, Jr. (Caroline)
Atlanta, Georgia

****

A large roast can be carved more easily after it stands for about 30 minutes.

Before cooking link sausage, pierce each piece with a fork; this keeps them from bursting open.

Bake ham in a heavy brown bag. Bake in a moderate oven for the same length of time as usual. Good!

Use left-over peach pickle juice when baking a ham.

305

BEEF KABOBS

Yield: 4 servings

Juice of 1 1/2 lemons
3 tablespoons oil
1 onion, grated
1 teaspoon salt
1/2 teaspoon mustard
1/2 teaspoon ginger
2 teaspoons worcestershire
  sauce
1 bay leaf

1 garlic clove
2 pounds sirloin steak, cut in
  cubes
Mushroom caps
2 green peppers, cut in large
  cubes
Cherry tomatoes
Onion cubes

Combine the first 9 ingredients and add sirloin. Refrigerate overnight. Alternate sirloin, mushrooms, green peppers, cherry tomatoes, and onion cubes on skewers. Grill over glowing coals about 20 minutes.

Mrs. William E. Anderson (Dell)

VERY EASY MEAT LOAF

Oven: 375° 30 minutes

Yield: 4 servings

1 (13-ounce) can evaporated skim milk
1 package dry onion soup mix
1 pound ground beef

Mix skim milk and soup mix. Let it marinate 10 minutes. Add ground beef. Mix together and bake in small casserole dish or loaf pan for 30 minutes at 375° until lightly browned. Add strips of bacon to the top the last 10 minutes of baking time. This gives added flavor.

Mrs. Hope Shirey (Frances)

MEAT LOAF I

Freezes well

Oven: 350° 1 hour 45 minutes   Yield: 3 loaves

3 pounds ground beef
2 pounds cured ham, ground
2 cups bread crumbs
3 eggs
1 medium onion, chopped
2 stalks celery, chopped

3/4 cup milk
2 tablespoons chili sauce
1/4 teaspoon worcestershire
    sauce
1/2 teaspoon salt
1/4 teaspoon black pepper
Dry mustard and catsup (optional)

Mix ground meats and bread crumbs thoroughly. Break eggs into blender. Add chopped onion, celery, and remaining ingredients. Blend. Pour mixture over the meat and bread crumbs. Knead until mixed. Shape into 3 loaves and cook 1 hour and 45 minutes at 350°. During cooking, the loaves may be covered with a thin paste of dry mustard and catsup to add additional flavor.

NOTE: Meat loaf slices make excellent sandwiches combined with sliced dill pickles and lettuce.

Mrs. Billy Murphey (Frances)

※※※※※※※※※※※※※

When carving meat, cut across the grain. If cut with the grain, long meat fibers give a stringy texture to the slice. Steaks are the exception.

Before opening a package of bacon, roll it into a long tube. This loosens the slices, keeping them from sticking together.

When planning for a crowd, fry bacon the day before. Wrap in aluminum foil and freeze. When ready to serve, place bacon on cookie sheet and bake in oven at 300°-325° until heated through.

MEAT LOAF II

Oven: 350° 60 minutes   Yield: 4 to 6 servings

1 1/2 pounds ground beef   1/2 cup brown sugar
1 green pepper, chopped   1 tablespoon worcestershire
1 onion, chopped   sauce
3/4 cup cracker crumbs   Salt and pepper to taste
2 carrots, finely grated   1 (8-ounce) can tomato sauce
2 eggs, beaten   1 (6-ounce) can tomato paste

Combine all ingredients, except tomato paste. Put into loaf pan. Spread tomato paste evenly over top. Bake at 350° for 60 minutes.

Mrs. Norman Douglas McGowen (Sandy)
Atlanta, Georgia

MOCK COUNTRY FRIED STEAK

Cheaper way to serve country fried steak than when using round steak

Yield: 4 servings

1 egg, beaten   1 teaspoon chili powder
1/4 cup milk   1/4 teaspoon salt
1 cup coarsely crushed   1/4 teaspoon worcestershire
   saltines   sauce
2 tablespoons finely chopped   1 pound lean ground beef
   onions   Cooking oil

Mix egg, milk, 1/2 cup crushed saltines, onions, chili powder, salt, and worcestershire sauce well. Add beef. Again, mix well. Shape into 6 patties about 1/2-inch thick. Coat each with remaining cracker crumbs. In heavy skillet, cook the patties in about 1/2-inch hot oil over medium heat about 8 minutes on each side. Drain on absorbent paper before serving.

Mrs. Billy Arnall, Jr. (Linda)

SWEDISH MEAT BALLS

Yield: 6 servings

2 tablespoons minced onion
2 teaspoons margarine
1 pound ground chuck or
  round
1/2 cup uncooked quick
  rolled oats
1 egg, slightly beaten

1 teaspoon salt
1/8 teaspoon pepper
1/4 teaspoon caraway seed
3 tablespoons margarine or
  more
1 (10 3/4-ounce) can cream of
  celery soup
1/2 cup water

Brown the onion lightly in the margarine in a small pan over low heat. Combine the meat, oats, egg, seasonings, and cooked onion until thoroughly mixed. With floured hands shape the meat into 45 small balls (1 inch in diameter). Fry them slowly in margarine in a heavy skillet until brown, turning on all sides. As browned, remove. When all are browned, add the soup and water to the skillet drippings and stir until smooth and bubbly. Return meat balls, cover tightly, simmer over low heat for 20 minutes or until done. Serve at once or cool, chill, and reheat next day or later. They may also be frozen for later use.

Mrs. Jack Slavin (Ruth)
New York, New York

꜄꜄꜄꜄꜄꜄꜄꜄꜄꜄꜄꜄꜄

Stuff 2-inch cucumber boxes or tiny pickled beets with cottage cheese to make tasty garnishes for sliced cold meats.

Try smoked sausage biscuits instead of ham biscuits. Bake the sausage and slice it in thin rings.

Add zip to hamburgers or meatballs by lightly tossing grated cheese with the ground meat before shaping and cooking.

CASSEROLE SPAGHETTI

Ideal to do the night before and slip into oven on a busy day!

Oven: 350° 15 to 20 minutes   Yield: 6 serving

1 1/2 pounds ground chuck
1 bell pepper, chopped
1 large onion, chopped
1/2 cup chopped celery
2 cloves garlic (may use garlic
  salt)
1 (10 3/4-ounce) can cream
  of mushroom soup
1/2 can water

1 (16-ounce) can tomatoes
2 tablespoons chili powder
Salt and pepper to taste
1 (6 to 8-ounce) package spaghetti noodles
1/2 cup sharp cheese, in chunk
1 (4-ounce) jar olives
3/4 cup grated cheese

Brown ground chuck. Add next nine ingredients and simmer 2 hours. Cook spaghetti according to package directions. Combine meat sauce, spaghetti, chunks of cheese, and olives in 3-quart casserole dish. Sprinkle grated cheese on top. Bake in 325° oven for 15 to 20 minutes or until bubbly.

Mrs. A. Anderson (Maxine
Macon, Georgia

❊ ❊ ❊ ❊ ❊ ❊ ❊ ❊ ❊ ❊ ❊ ❊ ❊

For extra tender cooked shrimp, pour salted, boiling water over raw, shelled shrimp. Cover and let stand 5 minutes.

Here's a quick and tasty supper sandwich. Top buttered rye toast with hard-cooked egg slices, add just a bit of finely chopped onion, then cap with a slice of tomato and brick cheese. Broil until cheese starts to melt.

When making hamburgers for a crowd, season the meat and smooth it into a rectangle of desired thickness. Cut into squares with a moistened knife, or for smaller hamburgers, cut with a biscuit cutter.

MRS. RICK'S COMPANY SPAGHETTI

Oven: 325° 25 to 30 minutes   Yield: 10 to 12 servings

pound butter or margarine
1/2 pounds round steak,
cubed
(20-ounce) can tomatoes
large onion, chopped
cloves garlic
(6-ounce) can tomato
paste
Red and black pepper

1 1/2 pounds Italian spaghetti,
cooked and drained
1 1/2 pounds sharp hoop
cheese, grated
3/4 pound Swiss cheese, grated
1 (4-ounce) can mushrooms
1 (16-ounce) can English peas

Melt butter in large saucepan; add cubed steak and cook until tender over medium heat. Add next 4 ingredients; add seasonings to taste. Continue cooking until steak shreds easily. In buttered 2-quart casserole, layer cooked spaghetti, meat sauce, and grated cheeses. Repeat layers until casserole is filled. Top with the peas and mushrooms. Bake at 325° for 25 to 30 minutes or until bubbly.

The Ricks Family
Macon, Georgia

****

A paper towel can be the secret to keeping lettuce and other salad greens fresh and crisp longer in the refrigerator. Clean, wash, and dry greens, then store them in the refrigerator crisper drawer on a sheet or two of paper toweling.

For a pretty summer salad, half fill a chilled salad bowl with shredded lettuce and top with slices of fresh nectarines, then strips of chicken or ham and cheese. Serve with well-seasoned oil and vinegar dressing zipped up with chopped canned green chiles.

SPAGHETTI MEAT DISH
Make ahead!

Oven: 350°   Yield: 10 servings

2 tablespoons shortening
1 medium onion, chopped
1 medium green pepper,
  chopped
1 clove garlic, chopped
2 pounds ground beef
1 (16-ounce) can tomatoes
1/2 cup stuffed olives, diced

1 teaspoon seasoned salt
1/2 teaspoon salt
1 cup grated cheese
2 tablespoons worcestershire
  sauce
1 (4-ounce) can mushrooms
1 (10 3/4-ounce) can tomato
  soup
1/2 pound cooked spaghetti

Sauté onions, pepper, and garlic. Add beef and cook 30 minutes or until done. Add tomatoes, olives, salts, and cheese. Cook covered over slow fire 30 minutes. Add worcestershire sauce, mushrooms, and soup. Mix well with cooked spaghetti, put in covered dish, and leave in refrigerator for 2 days. When ready to serve, heat again.

Mrs. Otis Jones (Ann)

****

Good brunch or lunch dish: Make a thick cream sauce and add lots of sharp Cheddar cheese. Grease a flat casserole. Place thick slices of ham on bottom, next a layer of broccoli spears, and cover with the cheese sauce. Top with bread crumbs. Bake at 350° until heated through.

Beat 1/4 cup butter until creamy. Add 1 tablespoon finely chopped parsley, salt, pepper, and a few drops of lemon juice. Refrigerate to firm. Cut into small chunks and serve on broiled steak. Delicious!

ITALIAN MEAT SAUCE
The secret of good meat sauce is to simmer it for several hours

Yield: 6 servings

2 tablespoons olive or salad
  oil
1/2 cup chopped onion
1/2 cup green pepper, chopped
2 pounds groud beef
2 cloves garlic, minced
2 (1-pound) cans tomatoes
  (4 cups)
1 (8-ounce) can tomato sauce

1 1/2 teaspoons sage
1 teaspoon salt
1/4 teaspoon thyme
1/2 teaspoon monosodium glutamate
1 bay leaf
1 cup water

In large skillet cook onion and green pepper in hot oil until almost tender. Add meat and garlic and brown lightly. Add remaining ingredients. Simmer uncovered 2 1/2 to 3 hours or until sauce is thick. Stir occasionally. Remove bay leaf. Serve over hot spaghetti. Freezes well.

Mrs. Sidney Pope Jones, Jr. (Sue)

※ ※ ※ ※ ※ ※ ※ ※ ※ ※ ※ ※ ※

For a wine-tasting party, plan on 1/4 to 1/2 pound of cheese per person and 1/2 bottle of wine per person.

What to do with mushroom stems and pieces after stuffing the caps? Make duxelles: Finely chop mushrooms (about 1/2 pound) and 2 to 3 shallots, sauté in butter **slowly** until all moisture has evaporated and mixture is dark and dry. Add salt and pepper to taste. This freezes well and is great in omelettes, puff pastry filling, etc.

313

CABBAGE ROLLS

Yield: 6 servings

1 (3-pound) head white
  cabbage
2 cups ground beef
1 cup regular rice, uncooked
1 (16-ounce) can tomatoes,
  chopped

2 tablespoons salt
1 teaspoon pepper
2 cloves garlic, minced
Juice of 1 lemon

Remove hard center core of the cabbage; cut cabbage leaves off one at a time. Put leaves in hot water and cook 3 minutes. Remove from the water. Mix rice, ground beef, half of the tomatoes, salt, pepper, garlic, and lemon juice. Place 1 tablespoon of mixture into each cabbage leaf; roll and squeeze as much liquid out as possible. Place cabbage rolls in Dutch oven. Add remaining tomatoes and tomato juice. Cover cabbage with water. Cook slowly 35 minutes.

Mrs. Paul R. McKnight, Jr. (Totsie)
Senoia, Georgia

****

For a different hamburger bun, spread each half with margarine, then sprinkle with a tiny bit of seasoned salt and oregano. Toast and place meat on bun.

Delicious borders for meat dishes:
1) Scored, broiled mushroom caps.
2) Cranberry jelly cut-outs placed on orange slices. Slice canned cranberry jelly and cut with small cookie cutters.
3) Mincemeat baked in orange cups.
4) Lemons cut in half with notched edges, sprinkled with parsley or paprika (to garnish veal dishes).

STUFFED CABBAGE LEAVES

Yield: 8 to 10 servings

1 large cabbage
2 cloves garlic
1 (2-pound) can whole tomatoes, drained and reserved
1 1/2 cups water

Stuffing:

1 cup long-grain rice,
  uncooked
1 1/2 pounds ground round
  or lamb shoulder
1 teaspoon pepper
1 1/4 teaspoons salt

1 teaspoon cinnamon
1 teaspoon dried mint
  (optional)
Juice of 2 lemons
Juice of canned tomatoes

STUFFING: Thoroughly mix all ingredients.

CABBAGE: Core out cabbage and drop into large vessel of boiling water. As leaves soften, separate them without tearing. Cut away stem and lay leaf flat on board or plate. Fill with one tablespoon stuffing (or more, depending on size of leaf). Roll tightly, rolling from larger end into a cigar shape. Place rolls in vessel, packing close together in layers, placing garlic cloves between layers. Add water, salt, and tomatoes. Weigh down with inverted heat-resistant saucer or plate. Cook over medium heat approximately 20 minutes. Serve hot. Remove each roll with care, without breaking. Makes about 50 rolls.

NOTE: This recipe is of Lebanese origin.

Mayme B. Mansour

****

It saves time when preparing bacon for a large family or crowd to place it in a pan and bake it in the oven about 10 minutes. It will be evenly crisp and delicious.

BAKED KIBBEE
A Lebanese specialty

Oven: 400° 40 minutes

2 cups cracked wheat
(borgul)
2 pounds lean round steak,
ground
2 teaspoons salt (or season to
taste)
1/2 teaspoon pepper

1 teaspoon cinnamon
(optional)
2 medium onions, peeled and
quartered
1/2 cup ice water
1/2 cup butter

Filling:

1/2 cup pine nuts or 1/2
cup chopped pecans

Rinse and soak wheat in bowl of water until soft (about 5 minutes). Squeeze out all moisture and add to ground meat, salt, pepper, and cinnamon. Put twice through grinder along with onions. Sprinkle lightly with ice water. Mix and knead meat several times after each grinding.

Grease a 10x14-inch baking pan with butter or oil. Wet hands with ice water and pat portion of kibbee into bottom of pan, about 1/4 inch thick. Smooth over lightly to remove ridges. Spread nuts over this layer. Spread another layer of meat over nuts and smooth over, sprinkling with iced water. Loosen edge of layers away from pan with flat edge of knife. With wet knife, cut straight strips one inch apart across meat. Then starting in one corner, cut one inch strips diagonally across pan to form diamond shaped pieces. Score each diamond to allow butter to penetrate. Dot top layer with 1/2 cup butter.

Place in 400° degree oven and bake for 40 minutes or until well done and brown.

NOTE: Cracked wheat can be bought at health food stores. If meat grinder is unavailable, have butcher grind meat twice. Grate onion finely, and knead meat mixture until soft, sprinkling with ice water to soften.

Mayme B. Mansour

316

BEEF RAGOUT

Yield: 6 servings

3 tablespoons flour
1/2 teaspoon salt
1/4 teaspoon pepper
3 pounds chuck, cut into
　1-inch cubes
3 tablespoons shortening
1 clove garlic, crushed
1 envelope Lipton beef
　flavor mushroom mix
1 cup water

1 cup dry red wine
1/4 cup chopped parsley
2 bay leaves
1/2 teaspoon thyme
3/4 pound (about 16) small
　white onions, peeled
8 medium carrots, pared and
　cut into 1 to 1 1/2-inch
　pieces

Combine flour, salt, and pepper; dredge beef cubes. In Dutch oven melt shortening and brown beef. Add garlic and cook 2 minutes. Add mushroom mix, water, wine, parsley, bay leaves, and thyme. Stir, cover, and simmer for 1 1/2 hours or more. Add onions and carrots. Simmer an additional 30 to 40 minutes or until vegetables are tender. Remove bay leaves before serving.

Mrs. Jack Slavin (Ruth)
New York, New York

✳✳✳✳✳✳✳✳✳✳✳✳✳

If making a casserole the night before and the recipe calls for sherry, add the sherry the day the casserole is to be served because sherry loses its flavor.

To thicken a sauce, knead together flour and butter and add small balls of this mixture to the sauce. This is called beurre manié.

BEEF ITALIANO

Oven: 350° 20 minutes   Yield: 6 servings

1 pound ground beef
1 onion, chopped
1 teaspoon garlic powder
1/2 teaspoon salt
1/2 teaspoon black pepper
1/2 to 1 teaspoon oregano

1 (10 3/4-ounce) can tomato
   soup
1/3 cup water
2 cups cooked egg noodles
1 cup shredded cheese

Brown beef, onions, and seasonings. Add soup and water. Pour over noodles in a 2-quart casserole. Top with cheese; bake 20 minutes at 350°.

Victoria P. Hanson

HAMBURGER SUPREME
Freezes well

Oven: 350° 20 minutes   Yield: 6 to 8 servings

1 pound ground beef
1/2 cup chopped onion
1 (10 3/4-ounce) can cream of
   mushroom soup
1/2 cup milk
1/2 teaspoon salt
1/4 teaspoon pepper

1/4 teaspoon thyme
1 (4-ounce) can mushrooms
   (optional)
4 ounces (2 cups) noodles or
   macaroni, cooked
8 ounces sharp Cheddar cheese,
   grated

Brown meat. Add onion; cook until tender. Stir in soup, milk, seasonings, and mushrooms. Layer half of noodles, meat sauce, and cheese in 2-quart casserole. Repeat layers of noodles and meat sauce. Reserve last half of cheese. Bake at 350° for 20 minutes. Sprinkle with remaining cheese. Return to oven until cheese melts.

Mrs. Thomas G. Kerley (Florence)
Paducah, Kentucky

TAGLARINA
(TI-GER-REE-NY)
A one-dish meal that freezes well

Oven: 350° 60 minutes   Yield: 12 servings

1 large onion, chopped
1 bell pepper, chopped
3 cloves of garlic, chopped
Small amount of oil
2 pounds lean ground beef
2 teaspoons chili powder
Dash worcestershire sauce
Salt and pepper
1 (16-ounce) can of tomatoes

1 (16-ounce) can cream style corn
1 (8-ounce) can tomato sauce
1 (3 1/2-ounce) can ripe olives and juice
6 to 8 ounces shell macaroni, cooked
1/4 teaspoon oregano
Cheddar cheese

Sauté chopped onion, bell pepper, and garlic in small amount of oil until clear. Remove from pan, sauté ground beef and add chili powder, worcestershire sauce, salt, and pepper. Add sautéed seasonings, tomatoes, corn, and tomato sauce. Add olives cut from seeds and olive juice. Taste to adjust salt. Add macaroni which has been cooked in salt water as directed on package. Add oregano. Place in 9x13-inch casserole. Refrigerate 6 to 8 hours to allow flavors to blend. One hour before serving, slice cheese on top. Bake at 350° for 1 hour. If glass baking dish is used, remove from refrigeration sooner and bake at 325°.

NOTE: Mrs. Royal states that this recipe was brought back from North Africa by a friend whose Arab-Italian cook adapted it from a native dish to American tastes and used foods available to her.

Mrs. Howard Royal (Mary)

★ ## COUNTRY CURED HAM
This is not a salty, salty ham; it's sugar cured.

Oven: 300° to 325° 20 minutes per pound

Country Ham:

Have butcher cut hock end off. Cut hock into small pieces and freeze to use in cooking vegetables. Check for ham weight. Scrub ham. Leave skin on. Place on rack in roasting pan with fat side up. Cover and seal with foil. Bake 300° to 325° 20 minutes per pound. About 3/4 hour before time is up, uncover, remove skin and score fat in diamond pattern. Leave uncovered and finish baking. Remove ham. There will be natural ham juices approximately 1 1/2" to 2" deep in roasting pan. Let this congeal and remove and discard most of fat. Save stock to cook with vegetables. This stock is almost as great as the ham. Freeze until used. It will cook many vegetables, but be sure to reduce salt and use no other seasonings.

John P. Woods, Jr.

★ ## HAM IN MILK
Delicious with creamed asparagus on toast

Oven: 350° 1 1/2 to 2 hours   Yield: 6 servings

Center cut of ham (2 to 3 inches thick)
Brown sugar
Mustard
Milk

Rub ham slice with paste made of brown sugar and mustard. Put in covered roaster and cover with milk. Start cooking on top of stove, then put in 350° oven and cook until tender, about 1 1/2 to 2 hours.

Mrs. Emmett Sewell (Bessie)

★ TALMADGE COUNTRY CURED HAM

Oven Baking Method:

Wash ham thoroughly. Place in large container, filled with warm water and soak overnight. Drain. Place in roaster. Pour 2 pints of coke or fruit juice and an equal amount of water over ham. Cover with lid or foil. Bake in 350° oven 20 minutes to pound (approximately 4 hours). Remove outer skin and cut off excess fat. Score remaining fat, insert cloves. Cover with brown sugar or a fruit glaze. Bake in hot oven, 450°, for 20 minutes or until glazed or brown.

Top of Stove Method:

Wash ham thoroughly, soak overnight, drain. Place ham in roasting pan over burner in water containing 6 onions, 2 cups brown sugar, 1 pint vinegar, 2 bay leaves, and 24 cloves. Cover and simmer (do not boil) 20 minutes to pound. The ham is done when the small bone at the hock end can be twisted out. Let ham cool in liquid. Then remove skin and cut off excess fat, score, and insert whole cloves. Glaze with mixture of 1 cup brown sugar and 2 teaspoons dry mustard. Bake 20 minutes at 450° to glaze. To serve, slice thinner than commercial type ham.

Country Frying Method:

Cut slices 1/4" thick (very important). Fry on each side and remove from pan immediately. To hot grease, add 1/4 teaspoon sugar and 4 tablespoons water (or coffee). Cover pan and simmer a few more minutes to make red-eye gravy. Add paprika to make gravy redder.

Mrs. Betty Talmadge
Lovejoy, Georgia

FAVORITE HAM LOAF
Can be increased easily for larger groups. Freezes well.

Oven: 350° 1 1/2 hours   Yield: 8 to 10 servings

Ham Loaf:

1 1/4 pounds smoked ham   3/4 cup milk
3/4 pound pork   2 eggs, beaten
1/2 cup dry bread crumbs   1/4 cup chili sauce

Sauce:

6 tablespoons brown sugar   6 tablespoons water
2 tablespoons vinegar   1/4 teaspoon dry mustard

LOAF: Have smoked ham and fresh pork ground together twice. Combine with all remaining ingredients and shape into loaf. Cover with sauce.

SAUCE: Combine all ingredients for sauce in a saucepan and bring to a boil. Use to baste loaf gradually until all has been used. Then dip from around pan until loaf is done. Bake loaf in uncovered roaster at 350° for 1 1/2 hours. Brown last 20 to 25 minutes at higher temperature. Serves 8 to 10.

Mrs. Paul H. Johnson (Mary)

****

Brown peeled chestnuts lightly in hot butter; toss with hot cooked Brussels sprouts, broccoli, carrots, lima beans, or green beans.

Adding a small amount of salt to water will make the water boil faster.

HAM AND CHEESE PIE
Super for lunch, brunch, or Sunday night supper

Oven: 425° 30 minutes   Yield: 6 servings

1 small onion, chopped
4 ounces Swiss cheese, cut
 into strips
1/2 pound ham, thinly sliced

2 eggs
1 (8-ounce) carton sour cream
1 frozen 9-inch pie shell

Sauté onion. Beginning with cheese, alternate layers of cheese and ham in pie shell. Beat the 2 eggs with the sour cream, add onion, and pour over pie. Bake for 30 minutes at 425°. Cool in oven 15 minutes before cutting.

Mrs. Thomas Maybank (Bee)

* * * * * * * * * * * * *

1/4 pound Cheddar cheese = 1 cup shredded
1 pound hard cheese=5 1/2 cups grated

Use cracked eggs only in dishes that will be thoroughly cooked.

Salt toughens dried beans and prolongs cooking time.

To prevent breaking the tips of canned asparagus, open the can from the bottom.

When preparing low acid vegetables that have been home-canned under pressure, boil them at least 20 minutes before serving. This applies to peas and beans.

Red cabbage stays bright if 1 tablespoon vinegar or lemon juice or 1/4 cup wine is added to the cooking water.

LUSCIOUS LEFTOVERS

Oven: 350° 1 hour   Yield: 6 servings

2 cups cooked, cubed ham
3 potatoes, peeled and sliced 1/4-inch thick
2 to 3 onions, peeled and sliced into rings

Sauce:

4 tablespoons margarine	**White pepper, to taste**
4 tablespoons all-purpose	**1 teaspoon dry mustard**
flour	**1 teaspoon worcestershire**
2 1/2 cups milk	**sauce**
1 teaspoon salt	

Grease 2-quart casserole dish with high sides. Layer ham, potato slices, and onion rings until all are used. Make cream sauce and cook until thickened. Pour over ingredients in casserole and dust with paprika. Bake about 1 hour at 350° or until bubbly.

NOTE: Amounts don't have to be exact. They can be stretched according to number to be fed. More potatoes and onions could be used and whatever ham is left over.

Mrs. Dennis Simpson (Jan)

****

Refrigeration alters the taste of sweet potatoes. Temperatures below 50° cause starch changes, so store sweet potatoes in a cool, dark place.

Do not wash fresh fruit and mushrooms before storing; wash before eating. Moisture encourages spoilage. Store in crisper container or moisture-proof bags in the refrigerator.

CROWN ON LAMB "ARMENONVILLE"

Oven: 350° 30 minutes   Yield: 5 to 6 servings

2 (2-pound) French racks of
  lamb and bone trimmings
Salt
Pepper
2 garlic cloves, finely mashed
1 to 2 carrots
1 celery stalk
1 medium onion

2 bay leaves
1 tablespoon tomato paste
1 tablespoon flour or arrowroot
1 quart brown stock (if not
  available, use water)
1 1/2 cups bread crumbs
1/2 stick melted butter

Take two racks of lamb and turn them so that the bones turn outward; tie two ends together to form the crown. Cover rib bones with aluminum foil. Rub crown with salt, pepper, and very finely mashed garlic cloves. Place crown in roasting pan with chunks of carrots, celery, onion, and bone trimmings. Add salt, pepper, bay leaves, and a touch of garlic. Place in oven and roast at 350° for approximately 30 minutes. When roast is done, take crown out of pan and set aside to keep warm.

To Make Gravy: (To be served on the side)

Add 1 tablespoon of tomato paste and braise for about 10 minutes. Add approximately 1 tablespoon flour and fill pan with 1 quart of good brown stock (or water). Boil approximately 30 minutes. Thicken gravy, if necessary, with a little arrowroot. Then strain through a fine strainer.

Sprinkle Crown of Lamb with bread crumbs, then sprinkle with melted butter. Put Crown back in oven and turn to broil. Let bread crumbs turn lightly brown and crisp.

Serve with stuffed tomatoes: Peel 5 tomatoes, scoop out insides, and fill with stew from eggplant and zucchini. Crown of Lamb is generally served with a variety of vegetables, such as Peas a la Francaise, Whole Green Beans Panache, Cauliflower Mornay, Broccoli Millanaise, and Pommes Anna.

The Abbey
Atlanta, Georgia

LAMB PILAF

Oven: 400° 60 minutes   Yield: 6 to 8 servings

4 tablespoons margarine
3 pounds boned lamb, cut
  into 1-inch cubes
1 large onion, sliced into thin
  rings and separated
1/4 teaspoon ground cinnamon
1/2 teaspoon ground black
  pepper
2 cups uncooked rice
  (not instant)

1 cup white raisins
2 teaspoons salt
1 (10 1/2-ounce) can consommé
2 cups water
1/4 cup lemon juice
1 (3-ounce) package sliced
  almonds, toasted
3 tablespoons chopped parsley

Sauté half the lamb in 2 tablespoons margarine over high heat until just browned. Remove lamb and drain on paper towel. Repeat process with last half of lamb and margarine. Lower heat. In same skillet, sauté onion, cinnamon, and pepper until onion is tender, about 3 to 5 minutes. Butter 2 1/2-quart casserole. Sprinkle 1/2 cup rice over bottom of casserole. Layer rice, raisins, meat, and onions in casserole. Repeat layers. Sprinkle salt on top. Combine consommé and water and pour over casserole. Cover and bake for 50 minutes at 400°. Remove cover and sprinkle with lemon juice and almonds. Bake 10 minutes longer. Sprinkle with parsley to serve.

Christy King
Atlanta, Georgia

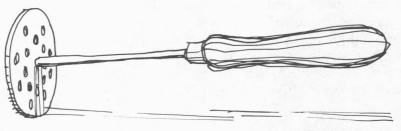

TINPLATED POTATO MASHER (1892)

SAUCED LAMB
Elegant!

Oven: 325° 25 to 35 minutes per pound   Yield: 10 to 12
                                                                                      servings

5 to 6 pounds leg of American lamb
Salt and pepper

Cumberland Sauce:

3 to 4 tablespoons currant jelly	1/2 teaspoon dry mustard
	3/4 teaspoon ginger
3 tablespoons Port wine	1/2 teaspoon paprika
3 tablespoons orange juice	4 tablespoons grated orange rind
2 tablespoons lemon juice	

Mint Gravy:

Pan juices	Flour for thickening
1 (8-ounce) jar mint jelly	

LAMB: Rub lamb with salt and pepper. Pour water in bottom of roasting pan to depth of 1/2 inch. Roast at 325° 25 to 35 minutes per pound (170° for pink; 175° for medium; 180° for done). Cover loosely with foil for the first 2 hours, then remove foil. When lamb is done, skim off grease from pan liquid and pour Cumberland Sauce over, slice thinly, and keep warm.

CUMBERLAND SAUCE: Melt jelly over low heat; add other ingredients and pour over lamb.

MINT GRAVY: Measure pan juices and add water to equal 2 cups liquid. Mix in 2 tablespoons flour and thicken slightly. Add 1/2 jar of mint jelly and stir to dissolve. Mint flavor should be subtle; adjust jelly according to amount of gravy. Pour gravy over lamb; keep warm. Serve in chafing dish.

NOTE: Good served with baked potatoes (stuffed with cream cheese and spinach), molded fruit salad, and a tart dessert.

Mrs. R. Clark Williams, Jr. (Love)

★ ## CHITTERLINGS
"Chitlins"

Yield: 8 to 10 servings

1 (5-pound) bucket chitterlings
1 to 2 tablespoons salt
1/4 teaspoon ground red
   pepper

2 eggs, slightly beaten
2 tablespoons flour
1 (5 1/4-ounce) can evaporated
   milk

Place chitterlings in Dutch oven and add enough water to cover. Add salt and red pepper and mix. Cover and cook over medium heat for 1 hour or until fork tender. Drain well. Mix together the eggs, flour, and evaporated milk to make batter. Dip chitterlings in batter to coat and fry in hot oil in large skillet to brown, turning once. Serve hot.

NOTE: A true "soul food", chitterlings are the lining of a pig's stomach.

Mrs. Bill Duncan (Ozella)

✳✳✳✳✳✳✳✳✳✳✳✳✳

1/2 pound onions=2 to 2 1/2 cups sliced or chopped
1/2 pound fresh mushrooms=1 to 1 1/2 cups sliced or
   2 cups coarsely chopped
1 pound fresh limas in pods=1 1/4 cups shelled beans
1 pound fresh peas in pods=1 cup shelled peas
1 cup small dried beans=2 1/2 cups cooked beans
1 cup large dried beans=2 cups cooked beans
1 pound cabbage=3 1/2 to 4 1/2 cups shredded or
   2 cups cooked cabbage

STUFFED PORK CHOPS (Kotletts)

Yield: 4 servings

8 ounces mushrooms, fresh
  or canned
1/2 cup water
3 1/2 ounces American or
  Monterey Jack cheese
2 small onions

1/2 teaspoon thyme
4 pork chops (let butcher slice
  a pocket in each pork chop
Salt and pepper
1 ounce shortening

If mushrooms are fresh, clean, wash, and slice them. Boil them in water for 10 minutes. Drain. Cut cheese into small squares. Peel and dice onions. Mix half of onions with thyme; add 2/3 of mushrooms and the cheese. Salt and pepper the inside of pork chops. Fill the pork chops with the onions, thyme, mushrooms, and cheese filling. Close the pocket with a toothpick. Fry both sides of pork chops for about 10 minutes in hot shortening. Put the rest of onions and mushrooms into the frying pan until onions are slightly brown.

Mrs. Thomas C. Jones (Carmen)

****

Leftover baked potatoes can be rebaked. Dip them in water and bake at 350° for about 20 minutes.

When cooking fresh lima beans, put a peeled, whole onion in the pan. The only other seasonings needed will be salt and butter.

★ SIDE MEAT WITH SAWMILL GRAVY

Yield: 4 to 6 servings

1 pound salt pork, 1/4-inch slices	1/4 teaspoon black pepper
	Dash of salt
2 tablespoons drippings	4 ounces milk
2 tablespoons Pillsbury Gravy and Sauce Flour	4 ounces water

Wash salt pork with hot water. Place in cold iron skillet. Cover with water; bring to a boil. Drain water and rinse meat until all salt residue is removed. Put salt pork in iron skillet again and cook slowly until golden brown. Drain on absorbent paper.

Remove all grease from pan except 2 tablespoons. Turn to medium heat, add flour, and brown. Add black pepper and salt. (Continuous stirring is important until finished.) Combine water and milk and add slowly to frying pan. Bring to a boil at medium heat. Remove and serve over hot biscuits or steamed rice.

Bruce R. Williams
Haralson, Georgia

※※※※※※※※※※※※※

Try baking beets like potatoes rather than boiling them.

Sauté green beans in a little oil before adding liquid to them. This greatly improves their flavor and reduces cooking time.

STUFFED PORK CHOPS

Oven: 325° 60 minutes

Yield: 4 servings

1 medium onion, chopped
1 small bell pepper, chopped
Butter or margarine
2 cups herb-seasoned stuffing
2/3 cup water
1/3 cup butter or margarine

1/8 teaspoon salt
1/8 teaspoon pepper
1/8 teaspoon thyme
4 (1-inch) thick pork chops

Sauté onions and pepper in small amount butter or margarine. In small bowl, mix sautéed onions and peppers with stuffing, 2/3 cup water, butter, salt, pepper, and thyme until well blended. For moist stuffing, add a little more water. Split chops to prepare for stuffing. Insert stuffing in chops and place them in lightly buttered baking pan. Bake for 30 minutes covered and 30 minutes more uncovered at 325°, or cook on charcoal grill for 1 hour.

Dan Umbach

ICE CREAM MOLD (1886)

BAKED PORK CHOPS

Oven: 350°   Yield: 4 servings

6 shoulder pork chops
Seasoned flour
1 (27-ounce) can spinach

3 egg yolks
2 cups medium white sauce
Grated American cheese

White Sauce:

4 tablespoons butter
4 tablespoons flour
1/2 teaspoon salt

1/2 teaspoon pepper
2 cups milk

Cover pork chops with seasoned flour and sear on both sides over high heat until well browned. Reduce heat. Cover the pan and cook about 30 minutes, turning pork chops frequently. While pork chops are cooking, cook spinach in separate pan until hot. Next, put hot spinach in a shallow, buttered baking dish and lay chops on it, side by side. Beat egg yolks well, stir into white sauce, and pour over the chops. Sprinkle with grated cheese and place in 350° oven until cheese bubbles. Serve from baking dish.

WHITE SAUCE: Melt butter in saucepan. Add flour, salt, and pepper, and stir until well blended. Slowly add milk and cook, stirring constantly, until sauce thickens.

Mrs. John M. Stuckey (Sandy)

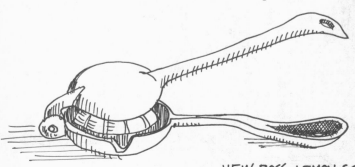

NEW BOSS LEMON SQUEEZER (1910)

BARBECUED FRANKS

Oven: 350° 20 minutes   Yield: 6 servings

1 tablespoon butter	1 teaspoon pepper
1/2 cup chopped onion	1 teaspoon mustard
1 teaspoon paprika	4 teaspoons sugar
4 teaspoons worcestershire	3 tablespoons vinegar
sauce	6 franks and buns
1/4 teaspoon Tabasco	Fresh green onions
1/4 cup catsup	

Melt butter. Add onions and cook until clear. Add all seasonings, sugar, and vinegar. Cut a 3-inch slit in each frank and place in flat baking pan slit side up. Add sauce mixture. Bake in 350° oven for 20 minutes. Baste frequently. Place franks in buns, garnish with fresh green onions. Serve extra sauce separately.

NOTE: Franks can be cut in 1-inch pieces and served heated in sauce as appetizers.

Mrs. James W. Roberts (Sue)

❊ ❊ ❊ ❊ ❊ ❊ ❊ ❊ ❊ ❊ ❊ ❊ ❊

Slice tomatoes lengthwise rather than crosswise for firmer slices.

Remove corn silk from fresh corn more easily by using a dry vegetable brush or a dampened paper towel.

★
FRIED STREAK O' LEAN
Talk about Southern!

Yield: Allow 2 slices per person

Sliced streak o' lean
Milk
Flour
Cooking oil

Select the number of slices needed. Soak several hours in milk. Drain. Coat with flour. Fry over medium heat in small amount of oil until crisp. (Be sure it is done.) Drain on absorbent paper.

NOTE: A Southern dish that is as good with vegetables as with breakfast food.

Mrs. Billy Arnall, Jr. (Linda)

WILD RICE AND SAUSAGE CASSEROLE
Men love this

Oven: 350°   Yield: 6 to 8 servings

1 (6-ounce) box Uncle Ben's long grain and wild rice
2 (10 3/4-ounce) cans consommé
1 pound lean ground beef

1 pound mild or hot bulk sausage
1 (4-ounce) can mushrooms
1/4 cup almonds (optional)

Put rice and consommé in casserole and bake at 350° for 1 hour or until consommé is absorbed. Brown ground beef and put aside. Brown sausage; drain off fat. Toss ground beef with sausage and mushrooms. Add meat and mushroom mixture to rice. Top with almonds. Heat in 350° oven until warm.

Mrs. Boyce Thomas (Melissa)

BRUNCH CASSEROLE
Sure to be a favorite

Oven: 325° 1 hour | Yield: 6 servings

2 pounds link sausage
8 slices bread, trimmed and cubed
3/4 pound Cheddar cheese, grated
6 eggs
2 1/4 cups milk

3/4 tablespoon dry mustard
1 (8-ounce) can sliced mushrooms, drained
1 (10 3/4-ounce) can cream of mushroom soup
1/2 soup can milk
2 tablespoons butter

Fry sausage and cut into bite-size pieces. Arrange bread in greased 9x13-inch pan. Cover with cheese. Scatter sausage over cheese. Beat eggs with milk and mustard and add mushrooms. Pour over top. Cover and refrigerate overnight. Let stand at room temperature for 1 hour. Dilute soup with milk and pour over top. Dot with butter. Bake at 325° for 1 hour. (Place a cookie sheet on lower oven shelf to catch spills.)

Mrs. Harry E. Chapman (Angela)
Nashville, Tennessee

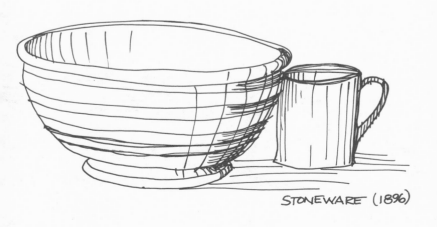

STONEWARE (1896)

SWEET AND SOUR SAUSAGE

Yield: 6 to 8 serving

2 pounds link sausage
2 (13 1/2-ounce) cans pineapple chunks
1/4 cup flour
1/2 cup vinegar
1/2 cup soy sauce
1 tablespoon worcestershire
sauce
3/4 cup sugar

1 tablespoon salt
3/4 teaspoon pepper
2 small green peppers, cut i
strips
2 (5-ounce) cans water chest
nuts, drained and thinly
sliced
Cooked rice

Cook sausage in boiling water until done; drain and se
aside. Drain syrup from pineapple chunks and add enough wate
to measure 1 3/4 cups liquid. Gradually stir in flour, then ad
vinegar, soy sauce, and worcestershire sauce. Heat to boiling
stirring constantly. Boil 1 minute. Stir in sugar, salt, pepper
and sausage. Reduce heat, cover, and simmer 1 hour, stirrin
occasionally. Add pineapple chunks, green pepper, and wate
chestnuts; cook 5 minutes longer. Serve over hot, cooked rice

Mrs. Arnold J. Bowers (Julia

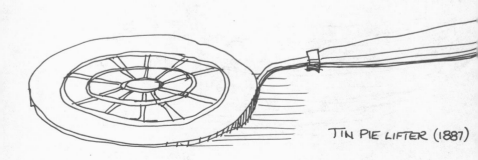

TIN PIE LIFTER (1887)

RICE AND SAUSAGE CASSEROLE

Oven: 375° 30 minutes   Yield: 6 to 8 servings

3/4 pound link sausage
2 tablespoons hot water
1 1/2 cups cracker crumbs
1 1/2 cups hot cooked rice
1 1/2 cups canned tomatoes
1/4 cup chopped green pepper
3 tablespoons chopped celery
 leaves

1 1/2 tablespoons chopped
 onion
1 1/2 teaspoons salt
1/4 teaspoon pepper
2 tablespoons butter or
 margarine

Cut sausage into small pieces and fry until brown. Add hot water. Combine other ingredients and mix with sausage. Turn into 2-quart casserole, dot with butter, and bake at 375° for 30 minutes.

Ruby L. White

PEPPER STEAK

Yield: 4 servings

4 green bell peppers, seeded
 and cut in strips
1 red bell pepper, seeded
 and cut in strips
2 tablespoons margarine
Salt, pepper, paprika

1/2 cup beef broth
Parsley, chopped
4 veal filets
Freshly ground black pepper
2 tablespoons oil

Sauté peppers in margarine; season with salt, pepper, and paprika. Add the beef broth; simmer for 15 minutes. Add chopped parsley. Sprinkle veal with ground black pepper and press into the meat. Fry the veal filets in hot oil two to three minutes on each side. Combine sautéed peppers and meat.

Mrs. Thomas C. Jones (Carmen)

CITY CHICKEN

Yield: 4 servings

1 1/2 pounds boneless veal
   and pork, cut in 1-inch
   pieces
1 cup cracker crumbs
1 egg, beaten

2 tablespoons water
Oil for frying
1 teaspoon salt
1 teaspoon paprika

Thread veal and pork alternately on wood or metal skewers. Dip meat in crumbs, then in egg mixed with 2 tablespoons water, then again in crumbs. Shake on salt and paprika. Fry on both sides in hot oil until brown. Place skewers upright in a pan with 2 inches of water. Cover and cook until tender, about 40 to 50 minutes.

NOTE: Cubed beef may also be used.

Mrs. S. L. Horvat (Teresa)
Fairburn, Georgia

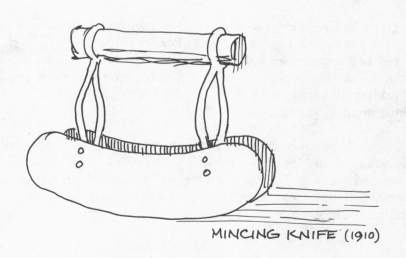

MINCING KNIFE (1910)

VEAL MARSALA (SCALLOPINI)
Simply delicious!

Yield: 4 to 6 servings

2 pounds thin veal (1/4-inch
  cutlets)
4 tablespoons butter
Flour
1/2 cup Marsala (sweet sherry)

1/2 cup beef stock
Salt and pepper to taste
Egg noodles, cooked
Parsley, chopped

Flatten veal. Cut to 4 inches square. Brown quickly in hot butter. Add broth a little at a time. Add salt and pepper. Sift a little flour over meat. When flour is browned, turn veal and repeat process. Add Marsala. Cover and simmer about 5 minutes. Sprinkle with parsley and serve hot over egg noodles.

Rosemary Slavin
New York, New York

BUTTER SLICER (1901)

VEAL BIRDS
Elegant and a real taste treat

Oven: 325° 30 to 45 minutes   Yield: 6 servings

6 veal cutlets, well trimmed and thinly pounded between wax paper	Pinch powdered thyme
	1/4 cup cream
	3/4 cup flour
2 cups onions, finely diced	1 pound fresh mushrooms, quartered
1 cup butter or margarine	
2 cups bread crumbs	8 artichoke bottoms, quartered
1/2 cup seedless raisins	1/4 cup parsley
Salt and pepper, to taste	1 cup dry sherry
	2 cups beef bouillon

Pound cutlets until thin and cut in half. Sauté onions in 1/2 cup butter; add crumbs, raisins, salt, pepper, and thyme. Remove from heat and add cream. Put 2 tablespoons filling in each cutlet and roll up and secure with toothpick. Salt and pepper the meat and roll in flour. Brown rolls in other 1/2 cup butter. Arrange rolls in baking dish and cover with mushrooms, artichokes, and parsley.

Add a little more flour to the drippings in the pan; stir in bouillon and sherry. Stir until thick. Pour gravy over rolls and bake in 325° oven for 30 to 45 minutes.

Mrs. W. Parks Cole (Judy)

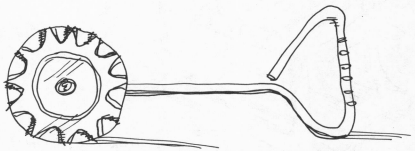

NICKEL PLATED PIE CRIMPER (TWENTIETH CENTURY)

Pies & Pastries

SCOOP SIFTER

PIES

PASTRIES

Pies & Pastries Chapter Design: National Flour Sifter (1910), Meissen onion patte
Rolling Pin (1898), Betty Taplin Eggbeater (1899)

APPLE PIE DELIGHT
Simple and delicious!

Oven: 350° 25 to 30 minutes   Yield: 1 (8 or 9-inch) pie

large apples, peeled, cored, and thinly sliced	1/2 stick margarine, divided in half
1/4 cups sugar	1 teaspoon sugar
tablespoons water	2 frozen pie shells, thawed

Put the apple slices in a bowl and sprinkle the sugar and water over them. Mix well and let stand for 10 minutes. Pour mixture into pie shell and dot with half the margarine. Add op pie shell. Seal the edges with a fork and prick the top everal times. Dot with remaining margarine and sprinkle with he 1 teaspoon sugar. Bake in a preheated 350° oven for 25 o 30 minutes or until golden brown.

Mrs. Bill Duncan (Ozella)

BROWNIE PIE

Oven: 375° 35 minutes   Yield: 1 (9-inch) pie

/3 cup evaporated milk	2 tablespoons flour
tablespoons butter	1/2 teaspoon salt
(6-ounce) package semi-sweet chocolate bits	1 cup chopped pecans
	1 teaspoon vanilla extract
eggs	1 pie shell, unbaked
cup sugar	

Mix milk, butter, and chocolate in double boiler. Beat until chocolate melts. Stir in remaining ingredients, adding anilla last. Pour into uncooked pie shell. Bake 35 minutes at 75°. Serve with ice cream or whipped topping.

Mrs. John Goodrum (Marsha)

★   **BLACK-BOTTOM PIE**

Yield: 1 (9-inch) pie

1/2 cup sugar	1 tablespoon (1 envelope)
1 tablespoon cornstarch	unflavored gelatin
2 cups milk, scalded	1/4 cup cold water
4 egg yolks, beaten	4 egg whites
1 (6-ounce) package semi-sweet	1/2 cup sugar
chocolate pieces	1 cup whipping cream,
1 teaspoon vanilla extract	whipped
1 (9-inch) deep pie shell, baked	

Combine sugar and cornstarch. Slowly add scalded milk to beaten egg yolks. Stir into sugar-cornstarch mixture. Cook in top of double boiler until custard coats a spoon. To 1 cup of the custard, add chocolate pieces. Stir until chocolate is melted. Add vanilla extract. Pour into cooled pie shell and chill. Soften gelatin in cold water and add to remaining hot custard. Stir until dissolved. Chill until slightly thick. Beat egg whites, adding sugar gradually, until mixture stands in stiff peaks. Fold in custard-gelatin mixture. Pour over chocolate layer and chill until set. Top with whipped cream and chocolate curls or shavings.

Mrs. Thomas G. Kerley (Florence)
Paducah, Kentucky

✳✳✳✳✳✳✳✳✳✳✳✳✳✳

To make a bought pie crust taste more "homemade," brush the bottom with milk and sugar before baking.

Handle pastry dough as little as possible; unlike bread dough, pastry dough that's over-handled will become tough. As soon as the dough holds together, form a ball, flatten the ball, then roll the dough out to the size specified.

BRANDY ALEXANDER PIE

Yield: 1 (9-inch) pie

1 envelope unflavored gelatin	1/3 cup creme de cacao
1/2 cup cold water	2 cups whipping cream,
2/3 cup sugar	whipped and divided
Pinch salt	1 (9-inch) graham cracker
3 eggs, separated	crust
1/3 cup cognac	Chocolate curls for garnish

In saucepan sprinkle gelatin over water. Add 1/3 cup sugar, salt, and egg yolks. Stir. Heat and continue stirring until thick. Do not boil. Remove from heat and add cognac and creme de cacao. Chill until the mixture mounds slightly when dropped from a spoon. Beat egg whites until stiff. Add remaining sugar and fold into mixture. Fold in one cup whipped cream. Turn into crust. Chill. Garnish with remaining whipped cream and chocolate curls.

Mrs. J. Littleton Glover, Jr. (Kathryn)

VARIATION: Instead of 1/3 cup each cognac and creme de cacao, use 1/4 cup brandy and 1/4 cup creme de cacao.

Mrs. Everett Bryant (Mary)

❊ ❊ ❊ ❊ ❊ ❊ ❊ ❊ ❊ ❊ ❊ ❊

Add a dash of cinnamon to graham cracker crust mixture. Delicious!

To keep the juices in a fruit pie from penetrating the bottom crust, mix 2 tablespoons sugar and 2 tablespoons flour together and sprinkle over the bottom crust before adding the filling.

Cut drinking straws into short lengths (or use uncooked macaroni!) and insert through slits in pie crusts to prevent juice from running over in the oven and to permit steam to escape.

BLUEBERRY PIE

Yield: 2 (9-inch) pies

2 deep (9-inch) pie shells
1 cup chopped pecans
3 bananas, sliced
1 cup sugar
1 (8-ounce) package
   cream cheese

1 (13 1/2-ounce) container
   frozen whipped dessert
   topping, thawed
1 (21-ounce) can blueberry
   pie filling

Bake pie shells. Line each with pecans and bananas. Cream sugar and cream cheese. Fold in dessert topping and spoon into pie shells. Top with blueberry pie filling. Chill.

Mrs. Arthur Estes, III (Martha Ann)
Gay, Georgia

HERSHEY PIE
No one can resist this!

Yield: 1 (9-inch) pie

6 (1.35-ounce) Hershey bars with almonds
16 marshmallows
1/2 cup milk
1 cup whipping cream
1 graham cracker pie shell or
   shell made with chocolate wafers

Melt Hersheys and marshmallows in milk in top of double boiler. Cool thoroughly. Beat whipping cream until stiff. Fold whipped cream into chocolate. Pour into crust. Place in refrigerator until serving time, or for at least 3 hours. Can be frozen.

Mrs. Boyce Thomas (Melissa)

BRENDA'S FROZEN CHOCOLATE VELVET PIE

Oven: 400° 12 minutes   Yield: 2 (8-inch) pies

3 egg whites
1/4 teaspoon salt
6 tablespoons sugar
3 cups chopped pecans
6 tablespoons corn syrup
4 teaspoons water
6 teaspoons vanilla extract

1 1/2 cups semi-sweet
   chocolate pieces
1 cup chilled, canned, sweetened, condensed milk
2 cups heavy cream

While oven heats to 400°, beat egg whites with salt to soft peaks; gradually add sugar and beat until stiff; add nuts. Spread this over bottom and sides of 2 (8-inch) greased pie plates. Bake pie shells 12 minutes and cool.

Meanwhile, bring corn syrup and water just to boiling point, stirring; remove from heat and stir in vanilla extract and chocolate until melted. Cool. Reserve 2 tablespoons of this mixture; pour rest of mixture into large bowl with milk and cream. With electric mixer at low speed, blend it well, then beat it at medium speed until it stands in soft peaks when beater is raised.

Next, pour this chocolate filling into cooled pie shells. Place in freezer until frozen. When frozen, remove and decorate with the reserved chocolate; use a pastry bag with plain writing tip and pipe a chocolate lattice design on top — or any design preferred. Wrap and freeze up to 30 days.

About 25 minutes before serving, remove pie to rack to soften slightly. Then serve with an assortment of favorite fruits cut in wedges or slices, such as apples, pears, grapes, or any other fruit in season.

Mrs. James C. Elrod (Brenda)

CHOCOLATE PIE
Rich

Oven: 400° 5 minutes
      350° 25 minutes

Yield: 1 (9-inch) pie

Margarine
Graham cracker crumbs
6 large eggs, separated and
   at room temperature
1 (12-ounce) package semi-
   sweet chocolate morsels
2 tablespoons instant coffee

3/4 cup sugar
1 1/2 cups boiling milk
1/8 teaspoon salt
1 envelope unflavored gelatin
1/4 cup rum
1 pint whipping cream

Grease 1 (9-inch) pie plate with margarine. Sprinkle moderately with cracker crumbs. Preheat oven to 400°. Put egg yolks, chocolate morsels, coffee, sugar, and milk into blender. Cover and blend until smooth, scraping sides occasionally. Beat egg whites with salt until stiff, but not dry. Blend 1 1/2 cups of chocolate mixture with one-quarter of beaten egg whites. Fold in remaining whites gently until mixed. Put into pie plate. Bake at 400° for 5 minutes. Reduce heat to 350° and bake 25 more minutes. Cool completely on wire rack. The center will sink and form a shell. As shell is cooking, heat gelatin and rum in saucepan until gelatin is dissolved. Add this to remaining chocolate mixture. Leave at room temperature while shell is cooling. In a large bowl, blend chocolate mixture and whipping cream. Beat with electric mixer at high speed until it has doubled in volume. Put into pie shell. Garnish with chocolate curls. Chill until firm.

Mrs. Keith Brady (Katie)

****

Substitute crushed corn flakes for pecans in pecan pie. They will rise to the top and be crisp.

★   ## BUTTERMILK PIE I

Oven: 350° 45 to 50 minutes   Yield: 1 (9-inch) pie

2 cups sugar	1 cup buttermilk
1/2 cup butter, softened	1 teaspoon vanilla extract
3 rounded tablespoons all- purpose flour	Dash nutmeg
	1 (9-inch) unbaked pie shell
3 eggs, beaten	

Cream together sugar and butter. Add flour and eggs; beat well. Add buttermilk and flavorings. Pour into an unbaked 9-inch pie shell. Bake at 350° for 45 to 50 minutes, or until top is lightly browned.

Mrs. John Dunn (Teresa)

★   ## BUTTERMILK PIE II

Oven: 325° 1 hour   Yield: 2 (9-inch) pies

2 1/2 cups sugar	1 stick butter, melted
1/2 cup all-purpose flour	1 tablespoon lemon extract
2 cups buttermilk	2 uncooked pie shells
2 eggs	

Mix sugar and flour. Add buttermilk and eggs; beat with electric mixer. Add melted butter and lemon extract, mixing thoroughly. Pour into uncooked pie shells. Bake at 325° for 1 hour or longer until set.

Mrs. John G. Chisolm (Martha)
Lookout Mountain, Tennessee

****

Bake a frozen apple pie as package directs. When pie is removed from oven, top with shredded Cheddar cheese. The cheese melts and forms a delicious topping.

★　　　　ROSE MARIE'S BUTTERMILK PIE

Oven: 350° 50 to 60 minutes　　　　Yield: 2 (9-inch) pies

2 2/3 cups sugar
6 tablespoons flour
3 eggs, beaten
1 1/2 sticks butter, melted

1 1/2 tablespoons lemon extrac
1 1/2 cups buttermilk
2 unbaked (9-inch) pie shells

　　Blend sugar and flour. Add to eggs, then add butter, lemon extract, and buttermilk. Stir well to mix. Pour into 2 unbaked pie shells. Bake at 350° until custard sets and tops are brown, approximately 50 to 60 minutes.

Mrs. Sid Villines, Jr. (Rose Marie)
Brooks, Georgia

BUTTERNUT SQUASH PIE

Oven: 425° 15 minutes
　　　350° 30 minutes

Yield: 2 (8 or 9-inch) pies

3 cups mashed, cooked squash
1 cup sugar
3 eggs, beaten
1 (14-ounce) can sweetened
　　condensed milk
1/2 (5.33-ounce) can
　　evaporated milk

1 teaspoon vanilla extract
1/2 teaspoon salt
1 teaspoon cinnamon
2 tablespoons butter, melted
2 unbaked pie shells

　　Mix all ingredients well. Pour into 2 unbaked pie shells. Bake at 425° for 15 minutes, then at 350° for 30 minutes or until a knife inserted comes out clean. Cool and serve with whipped cream.

Mrs. Mike Spitler (Rita)

★ ## CHESS PIE

Oven: 400° 5 minutes Yield: 1 (9-inch) pie
     325° 40 to 50 minutes

1/2 cup margarine	1/2 cup milk
or butter, softened	3 large eggs
2 cups sugar	1 tablespoon vanilla extract
1 tablespoon flour	1 (9-inch) pie shell, unbaked

Cream butter, sugar, and flour. Add milk. Add eggs, one at a time, beating well after each addition. Add vanilla extract. Pour into uncooked pie shell. Bake 5 minutes at 400°; then reduce heat to 325° and cook until middle of pie remains firm when shaken (about 40 to 50 minutes). Cool.

Mrs. Carl E. Williams (Eddy)

★ ## COCONUT CHESS PIE
Rich, but delicious and easy

Oven: 350° 45 minutes Yield: 1 (8 or 9-inch) pie

3 large eggs	1 teaspoon vanilla extract
1 1/2 cups sugar	1/3 cup coconut
1 tablespoon vinegar or	Shake of salt
lemon juice	Unbaked 8 or 9-inch
1 stick margarine, melted	pie shell

Beat eggs. Stir in other ingredients. Mix well. Pour into pie shell and bake at 350° to 375° for 45 minutes or until well set.

Mrs. John P. Woods, Jr. (Elizabeth)

❋ ❋ ❋ ❋ ❋ ❋ ❋ ❋ ❋ ❋ ❋ ❋ ❋

For a quick lemon pie with a soft and tasty filling, use lemon pie or pudding mix and follow package directions. Increase from 2 to 3 eggs and add the juice from a fresh lemon and grated lemon peel.

351

★ **EMORY CHESS PIE**

Oven: 400° 45 minutes   Yield: 1 (8 or 9-inch) pie

1 1/2 cups sugar   3 egg yolks
7 tablespoons margarine   2 egg whites
2 3/4 tablespoons corn meal   1 1/4 cups milk
3 1/2 tablespoons cake flour   1 tablespoon vanilla extract
1/3 teaspoon nutmeg   1 unbaked pie shell

Cream sugar, margarine, and meal in mixer until consistency of meal. Do not overmix. Add flour and nutmeg; cream well. Add egg yolks, egg whites, milk, and vanilla extract; mix well. Let stand one hour. Stir with spoon to mix meal in well. Pour into unbaked pie shell. Bake 45 minutes at 400°.

Mrs. Wright Lipford (Faye)
Peachtree City, Georgia

★ **LEMON CHESS PIE I**

Oven: 350° 45 minutes   Yield: 1 (8 or 9-inch) pie

2 cups sugar   Juice and rind of 2 lemons
4 eggs   1 pie shell, unbaked
1 stick butter
2 tablespoons cornstarch

Combine ingredients and mix well. Pour into unbaked pie shell and bake at 350° for 45 minutes or until done.

New Perry Hotel
Perry, Georgia

❋❋❋❋❋❋❋❋❋❋❋❋❋

Put a layer of marshmallows in the bottom of a pumpkin pie, then add the filling. The marshmallows will come to the top and make a very nice topping.

★ ## LEMON CHESS PIE II

Oven: 350° 45 to 50 minutes   Yield: 1 (8 or 9-inch) pie

2 cups sugar   1/4 cup mayonnaise
4 teaspoons corn meal   2 lemons (juice of two and
3 teaspoons flour   rind of one)
4 eggs   1 unbaked pie crust
1/4 cup milk

   Mix ingredients as listed and beat by hand until lemon in color and fluffy. Pour into an unbaked pie shell. Bake at 350° for 45 to 50 minutes or until firm. (It should have the texture of baked custard.)

                                   Mrs. B. R. Miller, Jr. (Caroline)
                                         Atlanta, Georgia

STRAWBERRY CHEESECAKE

                                   Yield: 2 (9-inch) pies

2 (9-inch) frozen pie crusts, baked
1/4 cup chopped nuts
1 (8-ounce) package cream cheese
1 (3-ounce) package cream cheese
1 cup sugar
1 pint whipping cream, whipped
1 (16-ounce) package frozen strawberries, or
   1 pint fresh strawberries

   Sprinkle chopped nuts over baked, cooled pie crusts. Blend cream cheese and sugar; fold in whipped cream. Spread mixture in pie shells. Sweeten fresh strawberries to taste; arrange over cream cheese and chill at least 1 hour. If using frozen strawberries, thaw; then spread over pies and chill.

                                   Mrs. Steven Fanning (Diane)

                                                             353

CHEESECAKE

Oven: 375° 20 minutes   Yield: 2 (9-inch) pies
       500° 5 minutes

2 (9-inch) graham cracker pie shells

Filling:

1 1/2 pounds cream cheese
1 cup sugar
3 eggs
1/2 teaspoon vanilla extract

Topping:

1 pint sour cream
3 tablespoons sugar
1/2 teaspoon vanilla extract

FILLING: Whip cream cheese, gradually adding sugar. Rebeat until smooth. Add eggs, one at a time, while beating. Add vanilla extract. Carefully pour into pie shells. Bake at 375° for 20 minutes.

TOPPING: Whip sour cream. Mix in sugar and vanilla extract. Pour over baked pies. Bake for 5 minutes at 500°. Cool and refrigerate.

NOTE: Top this with canned pie filling. Cherry is great!

Mrs. Gene Ankrom (Barbara)

****

To make a fruit pie more decorative, cut holes in the top crust with a thimble. Place crust on pie. The holes will stretch and become larger. Place the little round circles back in place and bake. This makes a prettier pie and serves for steam and juice openings.

★ RUN FOR THE ROSES PIE

Oven: 350° 45 minutes   Yield: 2 (8 or 9-inch) pies

1 cup chopped English   1 stick butter, melted
  walnuts   1 cup chocolate chips
3 tablespoons bourbon   1 teaspoon vanilla extract
1 cup sugar   2 (8 or 9-inch) unbaked
1 cup white corn syrup   pie shells
4 eggs

Pour bourbon over nuts and set aside. Beat sugar, syrup, and eggs together. Add butter, chocolate chips, and vanilla extract. Add bourbon and nuts. Pour into unbaked pie shells. Bake 45 minutes at 350°.

Mrs. John Goodrum (Marsha)

★ EASY COCONUT PIE I
Quick and economical

Oven: 325° 40 to 45 minutes   Yield: 3 (8 or 9-inch) pies

6 eggs   1 teaspoon vanilla extract
1 1/3 cups buttermilk   1/4 teaspoon salt
3 cups sugar   3 (8 or 9-inch)unbaked pie
1 1/2 sticks margarine, melted   shells
1 (14-ounce) package   Whipping cream, whipped
  angel flake coconut   and sweetened

Beat eggs very well. Add remaining ingredients one at a time and blend well after each addition. Pour into three unbaked pie shells. Bake at 325° for 40 to 45 minutes. Cool and serve topped with a dollop of sweetened whipped cream.

NOTE: Pies freeze well after baking.

Mrs. John N. White (Martha)

355

★   **EASY COCONUT PIE II**

Oven: 350° 1 hour   Yield: 1 (9-inch) pie

1 1/2 cups sugar   1 tablespoon vanilla extract
1 stick margarine   1/2 cup angel flake coconut
3 eggs   1 (9-inch) unbaked pie shell
1 tablespoon vinegar

Cream together sugar and margarine. Add eggs, one at a time, and mix well. Add vinegar, vanilla extract, and coconut. Blend together and pour into unbaked pie shell. Bake at 350° for 1 hour.

NOTE: 1 cup pecans may be substituted for coconut to make pecan pie.

Mrs. S. T. Hammond
East Point, Georgia

★   **FRENCH COCONUT PIE**

Oven: 375° 10 minutes   Yield: 1 (9-inch) pie
      300° 35 to 40 minutes

1 1/4 cups sugar   1 3/4 cups angel flake coconut
6 tablespoons butter   1 teaspoon vanilla extract
1/4 cup buttermilk   1 unbaked pie shell
3 eggs

Cream sugar and butter. Add buttermilk to sugar and butter. Beat eggs lightly and add to sugar and butter, stirring lightly. Add coconut and vanilla. Pour into an unbaked pie shell. Cook 10 minutes at 375°. Lower heat to 300° and cook until done, approximately 35 to 40 minutes.

Mrs. Ellis Arnall (Mildred)

Mrs. Arnall is a former First Lady of Georgia.

EASY FRENCH SILK PIE
Can be frozen and taken out to thaw just before serving

Yield: 1 (10-inch) pie

Crust:

1 1/2 cups Famous Chocolate Wafer crumbs
1 stick margarine, melted
1/4 cup sugar

Filling:

1 cup sugar
1 stick margarine, softened
4 squares unsweetened chocolate
2 teaspoons vanilla extract
3 large eggs
1 (10-ounce) carton whipped topping

Combine crust ingredients and press into 10-inch pie plate. Refrigerate. Add sugar to soft margarine, creaming well. Melt chocolate and cool, then blend chocolate and vanilla into margarine mixture. Add eggs, one at a time, beating 5 minutes after each is added, 15 minutes in all. Fold in carton of whipped topping and turn into cold pie shell. Chill about 4 hours or overnight. Garnish with shaved chocolate, chocolate crumbs, almonds, or whipped cream.

NOTE: This is a modified version of the original French Silk that makes an elegant dessert.

Mrs. William Donald Tomlinson (Jane)

❊❊❊❊❊❊❊❊❊❊❊❊❊

For extremely flaky pie pastry, measure the flour and shortening into a bowl and chill at least an hour before mixing.

357

EGG CUSTARD PIE

Oven: 350° 15 minutes
     325° until done

Yield: 1 (8 or 9-inch) pie

1/2 cup margarine, melted	1 teaspoon vanilla extract,
1 1/4 cups sugar	or a combination of vanilla
3 eggs	and lemon extracts
1 tablespoon flour	1 unbaked (8 or 9-inch)
1/4 cup buttermilk	pie shell

Mix all ingredients and pour into unbaked pie shell. Bake at 350° for 15 minutes, then lower the temperature to 325° and cook until firm. Delicious served warm.

NOTE: Coconut and coconut extract may be used instead of the vanilla extract for variety.

Mrs. Ray Sewell (Edith)

PECAN PIE I

Oven: 350° 50 minutes

Yield: 1 (8-inch) pie

2/3 cup sugar	1/3 cup melted butter
1 cup light corn syrup	1 cup pecans
3 eggs, beaten	Unbaked pie shell
1/4 teaspoon salt	

Mix ingredients. Pour into unbaked pie shell. Bake at 350° for 50 minutes.

Mrs. Hugh Carter (Ruth)
Plains, Georgia

★   **PECAN PIE II**

Oven: 450° 10 minutes   Yield: 1 (9-inch) pie
      350° 50 minutes

3 eggs, slightly beaten   1 cup sugar
1 cup light corn syrup   1 tablespoon flour
1/8 teaspoon salt   2/3 cup pecans
1 teaspoon vanilla extract   1 unbaked pie shell

Mix together all ingredients, adding nuts last. Pour into a deep 9-inch pie shell. Place pie in a **cold** oven. Bake at 450° for 10 minutes. Then reduce heat to 350° or lower and continue baking for approximately 50 minutes or until done. Test pie for doneness by shaking it; if it doesn't move, it's done.

Mrs. Ronald Wassenberg (Betty)

★   **PECAN PIE III**
The pecan taste is fantastic!

Oven: 325° 45 minutes   Yield: 1 (9-inch) pie

1 cup brown sugar   1/4 teaspoon salt
2 tablespoons flour   1 teaspoon vanilla extract
1 1/2 tablespoons butter   1 1/2 to 2 cups pecans
1 cup light corn syrup   1 (9-inch) unbaked pie shell
3 eggs, beaten

Allow butter to soften at room temperature. Mix sugar and flour. Cream butter with sugar and flour mixture. Add corn syrup and eggs. Beat with mixer until frothy. Add salt, vanilla, and pecans. Pour into unbaked pie shell. Bake 45 minutes at 325°.

Mrs. Joe P. MacNabb (Patty)

★

PECAN PIE IV

Oven: 350° 1 hour   Yield: 1 (8 or 9-inch) pie

1 cup sugar
1/2 cup dark corn syrup
1/4 cup melted margarine
3 eggs, slightly beaten

1 cup broken pecans
1 teaspoon vanilla extract
1 unbaked pie shell

Combine all ingredients in order given. Pour into unbaked pie shell. Bake 1 hour at 350°.

Winnie Cook

★

PECAN PIE V

Oven: 350° 30 minutes   Yield: 1 (9-inch) pie

1 tablespoon butter
1 cup sugar
2 eggs
1/2 cup white corn syrup

1 tablespoon flour
1/2 teaspoon vanilla extract
3/4 cup chopped pecans
1 unbaked (9-inch) pie shell

Melt butter and cream with sugar. Add eggs and mix well; then add all other ingredients. Pour into pie shell and bake at 350° for 30 minutes or until browned.

Mrs. Otis Jones (Ann)

****

To cut down the richness of packaged mincemeat, add up to 1 cup of cooked and chopped apples, peaches, prunes, or raisins.

★ **FABULOUS PECAN PIE**
Easy to prepare!

Oven: 400° 15 minutes   Yield: 1 (9-inch) pie
       350° 30 to 35 minutes

3 eggs   1 teaspoon vanilla extract
1 cup dark corn syrup   1/8 teaspoon salt
1 cup sugar   1 cup pecans
2 tablespoons melted butter   1 (9-inch) pastry shell,
   or margarine   unbaked

Beat eggs slightly. Mix in corn syrup, sugar, butter or margarine, vanilla, and salt. Add nuts. Pour into unbaked shell. Bake at 400° for 15 minutes; then at 350° for 30 to 35 minutes. Filling should be slightly less set in center than around edge.

Mrs. Phil S. Vincent (Mary Anna)

★ **SOUTHERN PECAN PIE**
Orange flavor makes the difference

Oven: 350° 45 minutes   Yield: 1 (8 or 9-inch) pie

3 large eggs   2 tablespoons butter, melted
1 cup white corn syrup   1 cup pecans, coarsely chopped
3/4 cup sugar   1 pie shell, unbaked
1 tablespoon orange juice   Whipped cream, optional
2 tablespoons grated orange rind

Beat eggs slightly. Add syrup, sugar, juice, and rind. Stir in butter. Spread pecans over unbaked pie crust and pour filling over. Bake approximately 45 minutes at 350°. Serve topped with whipped cream, if desired.

New Perry Hotel
Perry, Georgia

361

★ **OLD-FASHIONED PECAN PIE**

Oven: 375° 40 to 45 minutes   Yield: 1 (8 or 9-inch) pie

1 1/2 cups (12-ounce bottle) Log Cabin syrup
1 cup coarsely chopped pecans
1 unbaked pie shell, 8 or 9-inch
3 tablespoons butter or margarine
1/4 cup sugar
2 tablespoons self-rising flour
3 eggs, well beaten
1 teaspoon vanilla extract

Bring syrup to a gentle boil and boil for 8 minutes. Cool 15 minutes. Sprinkle nuts in pie shell. Cream butter and blend in sugar and flour. Add eggs, syrup, and vanilla extract. Mix well. Pour into shell. Bake at 375° for 40 to 45 minutes, or until pie is completely puffed across top and brown.

Mrs. Jack Connally (Sandra)
Smyrna, Georgia

****

Meringue hints:
. . . beat a little cornstarch into egg white along with the sugar to keep meringue from falling.
. . . the secret to good meringue is having as much sugar dissolved as possible. For best results, add sugar only after egg whites are foamy white.
. . . meringue weeps? Be sure to spread meringue over pie filling that is hot.
. . . meringue shrinks? When spreading meringue, make sure it touches the crust all the way around.
. . . use a greased knife when cutting meringue — it will not pull.

★
CHOCOLATE PECAN PIE I
Absolutely divine!

Oven: Crust: 325° 10 to 12 minutes
      Pie: 350° 45 minutes   Yield: 1 (9-inch) pie

Cream Cheese Crust:

1 stick butter (not margarine)   1 cup flour
3 ounces cream cheese

Pie Filling:

1 cup sugar   1 teaspoon vanilla extract
1/2 cup all-purpose flour   1 cup pecans, chopped
1/2 cup melted butter   6 ounces semi-sweet
2 eggs, beaten   chocolate mini-chips

CREAM CHEESE CRUST: Allow butter and cream cheese to soften in a bowl. Cream together and gradually add the flour. Wrap in wax paper and refrigerate approximately 1 hour. Roll out a 9-inch crust on a floured board. Place in an oiled pie plate. Prebake at 325° for 10 to 12 minutes before filling.
PIE FILLING: Combine sugar and flour, mixing well. Stir in melted butter, beaten eggs, and vanilla extract. Fold in chopped pecans and mini-chips. Pour into crust and bake at 350° for 45 minutes. Let cool before serving.

NOTE: Top this scrumptious pie with vanilla ice cream and hot fudge sauce for an extra treat.

Mrs. John Dunn (Teresa)

★ **CHOCOLATE PECAN PIE II**

Oven: 375° 40 minutes   Yield: 1 (9-inch) pie

1 cup chocolate bits
2/3 cup evaporated milk
2 tablespoons butter or
  margarine
1 cup sugar

2 tablespoons flour
1/4 teaspoon salt
1/2 teaspoon vanilla extract
1 cup chopped pecans
1 unbaked (9-inch) pie shell

Combine chocolate bits, evaporated milk, and butter in a small saucepan. Cook over low heat until mixture is smooth and creamy. Combine other ingredients and gradually stir into chocolate mixture. Pour into unbaked pie shell. Bake in moderate oven (375°) for 40 minutes or until firm. Cool pie completely before covering.

Mrs. Emmett Caldwell (Lilly)
Senoia, Georgia

LIME PIE

Yield: 2 (8-inch) pies

1 (3-ounce) package lime-flavored gelatin
1 cup hot water
Juice of 2 lemons
1 (13-ounce) can evaporated milk, chilled
3/4 cup sugar
2 graham cracker crusts

Dissolve gelatin in water, add lemon juice, and put aside to cool — not congeal. Beat milk until stiff in large, chilled mixing bowl. Add sugar gradually while beating. Turn off mixer, add gelatin mixture, and fold together. Pour into graham cracker crusts. Refrigerate.

Mrs. Larry Strickland (Mary)

STRAWBERRY PIE I

Yield: 1 (9-inch) pie

1 pint fresh strawberries	1 teaspoon lemon juice
3/4 cup water	1 (9-inch) baked pie shell
3 tablespoons cornstarch	1/2 pint whipping cream,
1 cup sugar	whipped

Line the bottom of baked pie shell with half the strawberries, sliced in half. In a saucepan, bring to a boil the remainder of the whole berries and 3/4 cup water. Simmer for 3 to 4 minutes. Combine cornstarch and sugar and add to berries. Cook until mixture is clear, stirring constantly. Add lemon juice. Cool slightly and pour over berries in pie shell. Chill several hours. Top with whipped cream.

NOTE: This recipe is from Humboldt, Tennessee, home of the Strawberry Festival.

Mrs. Carl E. Williams (Eddy)

※※※※※※※※※※※※※

For a more nutritious pie, add 1/2 cup wheat germ to a basic graham cracker pie crust.

Impress company or the family with this easy pie idea. Beat 2 egg whites and 1/4 teaspoon cream of tartar until foamy; beat in 1/2 cup sugar, 1 tablespoon at a time, until meringue forms stiff peaks. Spread meringue over bottom and sides of a buttered 9-inch pie plate; leave a small hollow in the center. Place in a 400° oven, turn off oven immediately, and leave in oven for 5 hours or overnight. To serve, fill with fresh fruit and whipped cream.

STRAWBERRY PIE II

Yield: 1 (9-inch) pie

1 (9-inch) pie crust
3/4 to 1 cup sugar
1 cup water
3 tablespoons cornstarch
3 tablespoons strawberry-flavored gelatin
1 pint strawberries, cleaned and hulled
1 (9-ounce) container non-dairy whipped topping or
   1/2 pint whipping cream, whipped

Bake pie crust. In saucepan, mix sugar, water, cornstarch, and gelatin thoroughly; cook until thickened. Place strawberries in pie crust. Pour thickened mixture over strawberries and chill 4 to 5 hours. Top with whipped topping or whipped cream before serving.

Mrs. Walker Connally (Guilford)

Mrs. Warren C. Budd (Courtenay)

****

Always hull strawberries **after** washing them.

A great way to start the day: slice a fresh nectarine into a serving bowl. Pour on a little orange juice and sprinkle with crisp granola.

Wrap adhesive tape around the first finger to prevent cuts and stains when paring large quantities of vegetables or fruits.

When cooking fruits, add the sugar when the fruit is almost done. Less sugar is needed this way.

FRESH STRAWBERRY PIE
7-UP gives a unique flavor

Yield: 1 (9-inch) pie

(9-inch) baked pie shell
cup sugar
tablespoons cornstarch
cup 7-UP
Red food coloring

Fresh strawberries to fill
pie shell
1/2 pint whipping cream,
whipped and sweetened

Bake pie shell and cool. In a medium saucepan, mix together the sugar and cornstarch; add the 7-UP and the red food coloring. Cook until thick. Cool. Fill the pie shell with whole strawberries. Pour the cooled filling over the strawberries and chill. Top with whipped cream.

NOTE: This should be served the day it is made because the crust will become soggy.

Mrs. Ellis Crook (Patricia)

❊ ❊ ❊ ❊ ❊ ❊ ❊ ❊ ❊ ❊ ❊ ❊ ❊

Cut a cantaloupe in half. Fill each half with sliced, sugared strawberries and blueberries, then top with a sprinkling of white or port wine.

Always have a whipped cream garnish on hand for pies, puddings, or shortcake. Whip cream, spoon into little mounds on a cookie sheet, then freeze. When frozen, store mounds in a plastic bag in the freezer. Defrost them for 20 minutes before using.

★ **FRIED PIES**
A Southern specialty!

1 teaspoon salt
1 teaspoon baking powder
2 cups all-purpose flour, sifted
2 tablespoons solid shortening

1 egg yolk
4 tablespoons sugar
1/2 cup milk
Dried fruit, cooked and
sweetened

Sift salt and baking powder with sifted and measure
flour. Blend in shortening. Combine egg yolk, sugar, and mil
Stir into flour mixture.

Roll out on a floured board to 1/4-inch thickness. Cut in
circles 4 or 5 inches in diameter. Spread a small amount (
cooked and sweetened dried fruit on half of each round. Fo
the other half of crust over filling. Seal edges with a fork dippe
in flour. Fry in deep fat at 360° until browned. Drain on a
sorbent paper and sprinkle with powdered sugar.

Mrs. Gene C. Threlkeld (Freddi

****

To get orange sections without the white membrane clingin
to them, cover the unpeeled oranges with boiling water fc
5 minutes before peeling.

Freeze cranberries before grinding or chopping them; ther
will be less mess.

1 pound dried apricots=3 cups dried or 5 cups cooked
1 pound dried prunes=2 1/2 cups dried or
4 1/2 cups cooked

FUDGE SUNDAE PIE

Yield: 1 (9-inch) pie

Graham cracker crust
1 cup evaporated milk
1 (6-ounce) package semi-sweet
   chocolate chips
1/4 teaspoon salt

1 cup miniature marshmallows
About 1/2 gallon vanilla ice
   cream (do not soften)
Pecan pieces

If making graham cracker crust, add 1/2 teaspoon cinnamon to mixture. If using a bought crust, sprinkle lightly with cinnamon before filling.

Stir evaporated milk, chocolate chips, and salt into a heavy saucepan over low heat until melted and thickened. Stir in marshmallows until melted. Cool. Spoon half the ice cream into crust, taking care not to let it soften. Cover with half the chocolate sauce. Repeat layers. Place pecan pieces on top and freeze.

NOTE: Could use salted peanuts rather than pecans for a touch of Southern politics!

Mrs. Billy Arnall, Jr. (Linda)

❄ ❄ ❄ ❄ ❄ ❄ ❄ ❄ ❄ ❄ ❄ ❄ ❄

Grate lemon and orange zest and keep on hand in the freezer.

Fresh pineapple freezes beautifully. Cut the fruit away from the shell and wrap in airtight, heavyduty bags. No need to add ascorbic acid or sugar syrup.

ICE CREAM PIE

Oven: 400° 10 minutes   Yield: 1 (9-inch) pie

Pie:

2 egg whites
1/4 teaspoon salt
1/3 cup sugar

1 cup pecans, finely chopped
Vanilla ice cream, slightly
   softened

Sauce:

3 tablespoons butter
1 cup light brown sugar

1/2 cup evaporated milk
1 teaspoon vanilla extract

PIE: Butter bottom and sides of 9-inch pie plate. Beat egg whites until stiff, gradually adding salt and sugar. Fold in nuts and spread on bottom and sides of pie plate. Prick with a fork. Bake 10 minutes, or until brown, at 400°. Refrigerate to cool. Fill with ice cream and freeze.

SAUCE: Melt butter in saucepan and add sugar. Cook over low heat until smooth, stirring constantly. Remove from heat, add milk, stirring until blended. Return to heat for one minute. Stir in vanilla extract. Spoon over each slice of pie before serving.

Mrs. Norman D. McGowen (Sandy)
Atlanta, Georgia

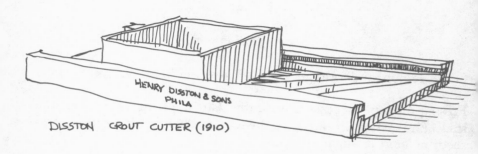

HENRY DISSTON & SONS
PHILA

DISSTON CROUT CUTTER (1910)

GRASSHOPPER PIE

Oven: 375° 8 minutes   Yield: 1 (9-inch) pie

Crust:
1 1/2 cups chocolate wafers, crushed
1/4 cup butter, melted
1/4 cup sugar

Filling:
32 large marshmallows, or
  3 cups miniature marshmallows
1/2 cup milk
1/4 cup creme de menthe
3 tablespoons white creme de cacao
1 1/2 cups whipping cream, chilled
Few drops green food coloring
Grated chocolate (optional)

CRUST: Blend all ingredients; spread in 9-inch pie pan and bake 8 minutes at 375°. Cool.

FILLING: In saucepan over medium heat, cook marshmallows and milk, stirring constantly, just until marshmallows melt. Chill until thickened; blend in liqueurs. In chilled bowl, beat cream until stiff. Fold marshmallow mixture into whipped cream; fold in food coloring. Pour into cooled crust. If desired, sprinkle with grated chocolate. Chill at least 3 hours.

Mrs. Maurice Sponcler, Jr. (Betty)
Dalton, Georgia

HARVEY WALLBANGER PIE

Yield: 1 (9-inch) pie

1 envelope unflavored gelatin	1/3 cup Galliano
1/2 cup sugar	3 tablespoons vodka
1/4 teaspoon salt	3 egg whites
1/2 cup orange juice	1/4 cup sugar
1/4 cup water	1 cup whipping cream
2 teaspoons lemon juice	1 (9-inch) pastry shell, baked
3 egg yolks, slightly beaten	and cooled

In medium saucepan, combine gelatin, sugar, and salt. Add orange juice, water, lemon juice, and egg yolks. Mix well. Cook and stir until gelatin dissolves and mixture is slightly thickened. Cool and add Galliano and vodka. Chill until partially set. Beat whites and gradually add sugar. Beat until stiff peaks form. Fold into gelatin mixture. Whip the cream until stiff, and fold into mixture. Chill until mounds form when dropped from spoon. Pour into pie shell and chill until firm, 4 to 5 hours.

Mrs. Pat Yancey, Jr. (Jeane)

****

Use bananas as placecards for children's birthday parties. With a felt tip pen, print each child's name on the skin. Place these at each guest's place and tell the children they can eat their name cards.

Banana arithmetic:
Sliced: 1 medium banana makes 2/3 cups
Diced: 2 medium bananas make 1 cup
Mashed: 3 medium bananas make 1 cup

LEMON PARFAIT PIE
Good for bridge club dessert

Oven: 450° 3 minutes   Yield: 1 (9-inch) pie

/4 cup butter or margarine
cup sugar
tablespoons cornstarch
/4 teaspoon salt
tablespoon grated lemon
  peel
/3 cup lemon juice

3 egg yolks
2 pints vanilla ice cream
1 graham cracker crumb
  pie crust (9-inch)
3 egg whites
1/4 teaspoon cream of tartar
1/3 cup sugar

Melt butter in top of double boiler; stir in sugar, cornstarch, and salt. Blend thoroughly. Add lemon peel and lemon juice. Add egg yolks, stir until smooth. Cook over simmering water, stirring constantly, 8 to 10 minutes or until mixture is thick. Cool. Soften 1 pint ice cream to room temperature; smooth into pie shell; freeze until firm. Spread half the lemon sauce over frozen ice cream. Return to freezer until firm. Repeat with remaining ice cream and sauce. Freeze until firm.

Beat egg whites and cream of tartar until soft peaks form. Beat in 1/3 cup sugar gradually; continue beating until sugar is dissolved and meringue is stiff. Cover pie with this. Place pie on board and bake at 450° for 3 minutes or until meringue is browned. Return to freezer. Before serving, let pie stand at room temperature several minutes.

Mrs. Otis Jones (Ann)

OLIVE & PICKLE FORK (1914)

KEY LIME PIE

Yield: 2 (10-inch) pie

2 (10-inch) pie shells, baked
3 (14-ounce) cans sweetened
    condensed milk
10 egg yolks

12 large limes
Green food coloring
Whipping cream, whipped
Extra lime slices to garnish

Bake pie shells and cool. Whip egg yolks. Add condensed milk. Squeeze the juice from the limes; finely grate one lime skin and reserve. Add the lime juice to the egg mixture and blend thoroughly. Add the grated lime peel. Stir in a few drops of green food coloring. Pour into pie shells and smooth. Place in freezer for 3 hours. When serving, cover top of pie with whipped cream and decorate with twisted slices of lime.

Crowley's Brandy House & Tavern
Atlanta, Georgia

MILLIONAIRE PIE

Yield: 2 (8-inch) pies

1 (8-ounce) can crushed pineapple
1 (29-ounce) can sliced peaches
Juice of 2 lemons
1 (14-ounce) can sweetened condensed milk
1 (9-ounce) container whipped topping
2 graham cracker pie shells

Drain pineapple and peaches well. Mix lemon juice and condensed milk. Add fruit. Fold in whipped topping. Pour into graham cracker crusts and chill.

Mrs. Ray Sewell (Edith)

MILLION DOLLAR PIE
May be frozen. Make a pretty pie!

Yield: 2 (8 or 9-inch) pies

1 cup sweetened condensed milk
1/2 cup lemon juice
1 (9-ounce) container non-
   dairy whipped topping
1/2 cup chopped nuts

1 (20-ounce) can crushed
   pineapple, drained
Maraschino cherries, chopped
2 graham cracker pie crusts

Combine condensed milk and lemon juice. Add whipped topping and the remaining ingredients. Pour into 2 graham cracker crusts. Must be refrigerated. Garnish with a few extra chopped cherries and nuts if desired.

NOTE: Serve after a light meal. Delicious but rich.

Mrs. Ben. C. Wetherington (Denise)
Valdosta, Georgia

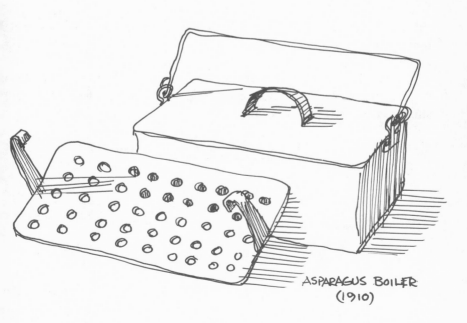

ASPARAGUS BOILER
(1910)

★ **PEACH PIE**

Crust may be made a day ahead

Oven: 300° 40 minutes   Yield: 1 (9-inch) pie

Crust:

2 egg whites, room temperature   1/2 cup sugar
Pinch salt   1/2 cup pecans, chopped
1/8 teaspoon cream of tartar   1/2 teaspoon vanilla extract

Filling:

1 (3-ounce) package cream   1 (9-ounce) container non-dairy
  cheese   whipped topping
1/2 cup powdered sugar   1 (16-ounce) can peach slices,
1/2 teaspoon almond extract   drained

CRUST: Beat egg whites slightly. Add salt and cream of tartar. Beat until soft peaks form, gradually adding sugar, 2 tablespoons at a time. Fold in nuts and vanilla extract. Pour into buttered 9-inch pie pan, spreading evenly over bottom and sides. Place in cold oven. Bake 40 minutes at 300°, or until lightly browned. This may be made the day before serving. Refrigerate.

FILLING: In bowl of electric mixer, blend cream cheese, sugar, and almond extract; add whipped topping. Fold in peach slices. Pour into pie shell and chill.

Mrs. Parnell Odom (Pat)

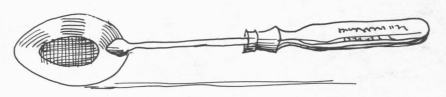

MRS HUTCHINS' STRAINER SPOON   (191

★ **PEACH CREAM PIE**
Delicious made with Georgia peaches, fresh or from the freezer

Yield: 1 (9-inch) pie

2 cups vanilla wafer crumbs
1 stick margarine, melted
1 (14-ounce) can sweetened condensed milk
1/2 cup lemon juice
1 pint carton frozen peaches (or 2 cups)
1 (9-ounce) carton frozen whipped dessert topping, thawed

Make crust of 2 cups vanilla wafer crumbs and 1 stick melted margarine. Press into 9-inch pie plate and chill.

Blend condensed milk and lemon juice until thick. Partially thaw frozen peaches; put them into blender and blend for a few seconds until smooth. Pour peaches into milk mixture and blend well. Fold in dessert topping with spoon and pile into crumb crust.

Mrs. William Donald Tomlinson (Jane)

★ **SWEET POTATO PIE**

Oven: 350° 1 hour

Yield: 1 (9-inch) pie

1 1/2 cups sugar
3 eggs
1 1/2 cup mashed sweet
   potatoes
1 teaspoon vanilla extract

1 stick butter, melted
1/2 cup milk
1 deep 9-inch pie shell,
   unbaked

Beat together sugar and eggs. Add potatoes, vanilla extract, and melted butter. Mix, then add milk. Cook in unbaked pie shell for 1 hour at 350°.

Mrs. Robert Sewell (Ethel)

377

★ **OLD-FASHIONED SWEET POTATO PIE**

Oven: 300° to 350°   Yield: 1 (9-inch) pie
     25 to 30 minutes

2 cups mashed sweet potatoes   1/2 cup orange juice
1 stick butter or margarine   Grated orange rind to flavor
2 eggs   1 pie shell, unbaked
1 cup sugar

Skin, boil, and mash sweet potatoes. Cream butter, eggs, and sugar. Mix the potatoes with the creamed ingredients; add the orange juice and rind. Pour in unbaked pie shell and bake at 300° to 350° for 25 to 30 minutes until crust is brown.

Polly Crowder Lyle

RHUBARB PIE

Oven: 400°   Yield: 1 (9-inch) pie

3 tablespoons flour   2 cups rhubarb, diced
1 cup sugar   1/2 cup evaporated milk
2 eggs, beaten   1 (9-inch) pie shell, unbaked

Mix all ingredients well. Pour into an unbaked pie shell and bake at 400° until done.

Variation: **Rhubarb-Pineapple Pie**

2 cups rhubarb, diced   Scant 2 tablespoons tapioca
1/2 cup crushed, drained   1 1/2 cups sugar
   pineapple

Mix all ingredients together and bake as for Rhubarb Pie.

Mrs. David Woodworth (Mary)

RITZ CRACKER PIE

May be prepared in advance

Oven: 350° 25 minutes   Yield: 1 (8 or 9-inch) pie

3 egg whites
1 cup sugar
24 Ritz crackers, finely crushed
1 cup pecans, chopped

Topping:

1/2 pint whipping cream
2 tablespoons instant chocolate

Beat egg whites until stiff, gradually adding sugar. Mix finely crushed crackers with chopped nuts and fold egg whites into cracker and nut mixture. Pour into well-buttered pie pan. Bake in a 350° oven for 25 minutes and cool.

Beat whipping cream with chocolate until stiff and place on top of first layer. Top with pecans or chocolate. Best when refrigerated.

Mrs. Lloyd L. Reynolds (Marie)

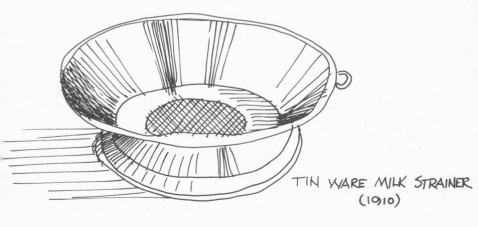

TIN WARE MILK STRAINER
(1910)

SUNNY SILVER PIE

Yield: 1 (9-inch) pie

1 1/2 teaspoons gelatin	Few grains of salt
1/3 cup cold water	1 cup sugar, divided
4 eggs, separated	1 cup whipping cream
3 tablespoons lemon juice	1 (9-inch) pie shell, baked
Grated rind of 1 lemon	

Soak gelatin in 1/3 cup water. Place egg yolks, lemon juice, rind, salt, and 1/2 cup sugar in a round bottom enamel bowl. Set bowl in a larger pan of boiling water. As the water is boiling, whip the egg yolk mixture until thickened, then whip in the gelatin. Remove from heat. Beat the egg whites very stiff, then add the remaining sugar. Combine the two mixtures. Pour into a baked pie shell and chill for two hours or more. Whip the cream until stiff and spread on top before serving.

Mrs. Welborn Davis (Mary)

Mrs. J. F. Herbst (Dora)
Kansas City, Missouri

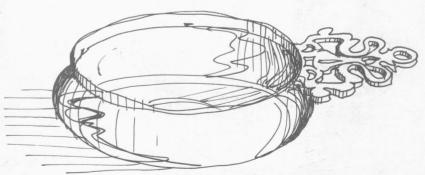

NINETEENTH CENTURY PEWTER PORRINGER

FLAKY PIE CRUST
An extra special pie crust

Yield: 3 (9-inch) single crusts

3 cups all-purpose flour
1 teaspoon salt
1 1/4 cups shortening

5 tablespoons water
1 tablespoon vinegar
1 egg, beaten

Mix flour and salt together. Cut in shortening until shortening particles are the size of small peas. Mix water, vinegar,
and beaten egg. Add to flour mixture and stir ingredients
together with a fork. Turn onto floured board or pastry cloth
and knead several times. Divide into three portions. Roll out
portions into a circle one inch larger than the greased pie pan.
If baked pie shell is needed, prick bottom and sides with fork
and bake at 425° for 12 to 15 minutes.

Mrs. John N. White (Martha)

PASTRY
No rolling pin necessary!

Yield: 1 single pie crust

1 1/3 cups all-purpose flour
Dash of salt
1/3 cup oil
3 tablespoons milk

Put flour in pie plate. Make a well; add salt, oil, and
milk. Mix with a fork until dough forms a ball. Press out
evenly over pie plate with hands.

Mrs. Arthur Thornton (Catherine)

PATE A CHOUX (PUFF SHELLS)

Oven: 400° 30 to 45 minutes   Yield: 40 to 50 small shells or
                                          10 large shells

1 cup water   4 eggs
1/4 pound butter   Optional: 3 ounces Gruyere,
1/2 teaspoon salt   Swiss, or Cheddar cheese,
Dash of pepper (optional)   thinly grated
1 cup sifted flour

In a heavy pan boil 1 cup water, butter, salt, and pepper (optional). Reduce temperature to low heat; add flour all at once. Stir briskly until mixture leaves the side of the pan and forms a ball. Remove from heat. Cool slightly. Add eggs, one at a time, beating after each addition until mixture is smooth and glossy. (Optional: add cheese to mixture; reserve 2 tablespoons.) Drop onto greased cookie sheet by teaspoon or tablespoon, depending on size desired. Bake 30 minutes for small puffs, 45 minutes for larger ones. When done, remove from cookie sheet and cool on racks. When cooled, freeze, or cut off tops and fill. To serve, if frozen, it is not necessary to defrost shells; place in oven at 400° for 15 to 20 minutes.

CUISINART DIRECTIONS: Follow puff shell directions until dough forms a ball and pulls away from side of pan. Place the dough in the Cuisinart with the steel blade, blending for about 15 seconds. Add eggs, while motor is running, one at a time until 4 eggs have been added. Process until dough is glossy. Directions now continue same as before.

FILLING SUGGESTIONS:
APPETIZER: Prepare basic puff shell recipe with Cheddar cheese added. Mix together 6-ounces cream cheese and 1 (3-ounce) can ham; moisten with milk and enough Poupon mustard to flavor. Add salt and pepper to taste. Fill pastry shells.
MAIN DISH: Fill with favorite recipe of meat or fish salad, for example; shrimp, tuna, salmon, crab, chicken, ham.

(Continued)

DESSERT: Chocolate eclairs (short cut method) — make vanilla pudding and fill shells with pudding. Top with hot chocolate sauce made from 6-ounce package of real chocolate morsels melted with 2 tablespoons butter and 1/4 cup light corn syrup.

ICE CREAM: Fill shells with favorite ice cream and top with favorite topping and chopped nuts.

Mrs. Charles M. Smith (Lynn)

PIE CRUST I
Delicious

Yield: 2 single pie crusts

2 1/4 cups flour
1 teaspoon salt

2/3 cup Crisco shortening
1/3 cup water

Mix flour, salt, and shortening to a mealy state. Add water. Roll between 2 pieces plastic. Put into pie plates.

Mrs. Mary Clary
Blowing Rock, North Carolina

PIE CRUST II
Does better if prepared ahead of time

Yield: 2 single pie crusts

2 cups flour
1 teaspoon salt
1 stick butter, room temperature

1/2 cup Crisco
6 tablespoons ice cold water

Put flour, salt, butter, and Crisco into a bowl and mix with pastry mixer. Add ice water and mix to pastry consistency. This recipe does better if prepared ahead of time; let sit in refrigerator, then roll out for pie shell.

Mrs. G. L. Kerley (Eula)
Topeka, Kansas

CHOCOLATE ECLAIRS

Oven: 400° 30 minutes

Yield: 12 large eclairs or
60 - 70 miniature eclairs

Pastry:

1 cup water
1 stick margarine

1 cup sifted flour
4 eggs

Filling:

3 cups rich milk
3/4 cup sugar
1/2 teaspoon salt

6 tablespoons flour
3 whole eggs, beaten
2 teaspoons vanilla extract

Icing:

2 (1-ounce) squares chocolate
2 cups sugar

1 cup whipping cream

Heat water and margarine to boiling point. Add flour and stir constantly until mixture forms a ball. Remove from heat and let cool. Beat in eggs, one at a time. Drop dough from teaspoon to form small eclairs on ungreased cookie sheet. Cook at 400° for 30 minutes or until lightly browned. Cool slowly away from draft.

Combine milk, sugar, salt, and flour. Cook slowly until thick. Add beaten eggs and cook until even thicker. When cool, add vanilla. Cut off the tops of puffs and fill with the custard mixture. Replace tops.

Melt chocolate; add sugar and cream. Cook over medium heat until soft ball stage is reached. Cool, then beat. Ice tops of the eclairs.

Mrs. Arthur Klugh (Gloria)
Anderson, South Carolina

Poultry

POULTRY

Poultry Chapter Design: Left to right: Apple Corer (1890), "Onyx" Enameled Basting Spoon (1910), Oval Ham Boiler (1898)

CHICKEN BREASTS IN DRUNKARD'S GRAVY

Yield: 4 servings

4 chicken breasts split into halves
1/2 cup vegetable oil
1 quart milk
1 quart water
1/2 cup catsup
3 tablespoons Heinz 57 Steak Sauce
4 tablespoons worcestershire sauce
Salt and pepper
2 teaspoons Accent
3 tablespoons flour for thickening
1/2 cup water

Brown the breasts of chicken in oil.

Mix 1 quart milk and 1 quart **cold** water. Add catsup, worcestershire sauce, Heinz 57 Sauce, salt, and pepper. Put in a large saucepan on medium heat. When hot add 2 teaspoons Accent.

Place the browned chicken in the saucepan with above ingredients. Let slowly come to boil and cook until breasts are well done and will separate easily from bone.

Take breasts out of liquid and separate from bone.

Thicken the gravy with thickening made from 3 tablespoons flour and 1/2 cup water.

Place breasts back in thickened gravy and allow to remain on low heat until ready to serve over noodles or rice.

Can add 1/2 pint raw oysters to gravy for 3 minutes as final step if desired.

Clifford A. Cranford

****

Heat chopped pecans or almonds with drained mincemeat or chutney and serve with roast meats or poultry.

ELEGANT BREAST OF CHICKEN

Yield: 8 servings

4 whole chicken breasts, split
1/4 cup butter or margarine
2 cups sliced mushrooms
2 (10 3/4-ounce) cans cream
of chicken soup

1 large clove garlic, minced
1/8 teaspoon rosemary, crushed
Generous dash crushed thyme
2/3 cup light cream (optional)
Toasted almond slivers

In a very large skillet, brown chicken in butter or margarine; remove. Brown mushrooms. Stir in soup, garlic, and seasonings; add chicken. Cover and cook over low heat 45 minutes. Stir now and then. Blend cream; heat slowly. Serve on wild rice. Garnish with toasted, slivered almonds.

Mrs. James Hardy (Fay)

BAKED CHICKEN
For "no-fret" elegance

Oven: 350° 1 hour

Yield: 4 to 6 servings

1 carrot, chopped
1 stalk celery, chopped
1 onion, chopped
6 chicken breasts
1/2 cup white wine

Juice of 1 lemon
Salt, pepper, and paprika
6 tablespoons butter
Minced parsley

Make a bed of chopped vegetables. Lay chicken breasts on top. Pour wine and lemon juice over the chicken. Shake salt, pepper, and paprika over breasts. Dot butter over the top. Place in covered 2 1/2-quart casserole or clay cooker. Bake at 350° for one hour. Baste once or twice. Sprinkle with parsley and serve. Delicious served with rice; spoon lemon-butter sauce over chicken and rice.

Mrs. Charles B. Woodroof, Jr. (Amelia)

CHICKEN BREASTS ELAINE
Good company dish

Oven: 450° 20 minutes   Yield: 4 servings
      300° 45 minutes

4 large chicken breasts   1/4 cup orange marmalade
Salt and pepper to taste   1/4 cup dry white wine
1/4 cup margarine

Wash chicken, pat dry, and salt and pepper to taste. Place in baking dish, skin side up. Bake in preheated 450° oven for 20 minutes.

Melt margarine in small saucepan. Add marmalade and heat until bubbling. Remove from heat and add wine.

Pour sauce over chicken breasts. Reduce heat to 300° and bake about 45 minutes or until tender and well-browned. Baste chicken twice during baking.

NOTE: Yellow rice makes a good side dish.

Mrs. C. W. Jackson (Jeanine)

CHICKEN PACIFIC

Oven: 350° 1 hour   Yield: 6 servings

1 1/2 cups sour cream   1 teaspoon garlic salt
2 teaspoons salt   4 chicken breasts, split
1 teaspoon thyme   1 1/2 cups cornflake crumbs
1 teaspoon paprika

Combine sour cream and seasonings. Dip chicken in mixture. Roll in crumbs. Bake in well-buttered pan at 350° for 1 hour or until tender.

Mrs. T. Leigh Sanders, Jr. (Martha)

389

CHICKEN BREASTS IN SOUR CREAM
WITH MUSHROOMS

Oven: 325° 45 minutes   Yield: 8 servings
       400° 15 minutes

8 slices dried beef
8 pieces (halves) boneless
   chicken breasts
8 half strips bacon

1 (8-ounce) carton sour cream
1 (10 3/4-ounce) can cream
   of mushroom soup

In 9x13-inch Pyrex dish arrange dried beef slices on bottom. Put one piece of chicken breast on each slice of beef and top with the half strip of bacon.

Bake at 325° degrees for 45 minutes. Remove from oven and do not drain bacon grease. Mix together sour cream and soup. About 15 minutes before serving, pour mixture over meat. Return to oven and bake at 400° until bubbly and golden. Serve with wild rice and a green salad for a great buffet dish.

Mrs. Sid Villines, Jr. (Rose Marie)
Brooks, Georgia

* * * * * * * * * * * * * *

For delicious oven-fried chicken, whirl 1 1/2 cups poultry stuffing mix in blender with 2 tablespoons grated Parmesan cheese. In a saucepan, melt 4 tablespoons butter and add a dash of garlic powder or half a crushed garlic clove. Dip 4 to 6 pieces of chicken in butter, then in crumbs. Bake at 350° for 1 hour.

Before roasting chicken, rub it well with some good brandy, then season as usual.

CHICKEN BREASTS PARMESAN
Can be prepared in advance and cooked in time to serve

Oven: 350° 1 hour   Yield: 10 servings

2 cups bread crumbs
3/4 cup Parmesan cheese
1 cup parsley, chopped
1/4 teaspoon garlic powder

2 teaspoons salt
10 chicken breast halves,
  boned and skinned
1/2 cup butter, melted

Mix first 5 ingredients. Dip chicken breasts in 1/2 cup melted butter, coating well. Dip in bread crumb mixture. Pack heavily on breasts. Place flat in roasting pan lined with foil. Do not overlap. Drizzle rest of butter over breasts. Bake 1 hour at 350° uncovered. Make sure pan is not too close to bottom heat.

Mrs. Lawrence W. Keith, Jr. (Jane)

CHICKEN CRUNCH

Oven: 325° to 350° 1 hour   Yield: 4 servings

1 (10 3/4-ounce) can cream
  of mushroom soup
1/3 cup milk
1 tablespoon chopped onion
1 tablespoon chopped parsley

1 package Pepperidge Farm
  Cornbread Stuffing Mix
2 tablespoons margarine,
  melted
1 to 2 pound fryer or breasts

Mix first 4 ingredients. Crush stuffing. Add 2 tablespoons melted margarine. Dip chicken into soup mixture, then dredge in stuffing. Place in greased baking pan. Drizzle melted margarine over top. Cook slowly at 325° to 350° for 1 hour or until done. May have to add a little water.

Mrs. A. L. Fuller (Kate)

CHICKEN CUTLETS WITH CHEESE SAUCE

Oven: 350° 35 to 40 minutes   Yield: 4 to 8 servings

Cutlets:

6 to 8 chicken breasts, boned   Salt and pepper
1/3 cup mayonnaise   3/4 cup bread crumbs

Sauce:

1/2 cup milk   1/2 cup shredded sharp cheese
1 cup mayonnaise   1 teaspoon dried thyme leaves

CUTLETS: Brush chicken with 1/3 cup mayonnaise. Add salt and pepper to crumbs and coat chicken. Place in greased baking pan and bake for 35 to 40 minutes at 350° (longer for large pieces).

SAUCE: Stir milk into 1 cup mayonnaise; add cheese and thyme. Cook over medium heat, stirring constantly, for 10 minutes. Serve sauce with cutlets.

NOTE: Cheese sauce is also good over green vegetables and potatoes.

Mrs. Dan Rainey (Lynn)

❋❋❋❋❋❋❋❋❋❋❋❋❋❋

For a delightful flavor, soak chicken in buttermilk for at least an hour or more before frying. This process also makes the chicken more tender.

Before frying chicken, squeeze lemon juice on it to enhance the flavor and make the meat clearer.

CHICKEN SUPREME
A favorite of President Jimmy Carter's mother

Oven: 350° until tender   Yield: 4 servings

4 boned chicken breasts   Fine bread crumbs
Cardamon   Butter or margarine
Chervil   2 ounces brandy
Salt and pepper   4 tablespoons Burgundy
1 egg   1 pint chicken stock
1/4 cup milk

Season chicken breasts with cardamon, chervil, salt and pepper. Beat egg and milk together. Dip chicken breasts into egg mixture, then into bread crumbs. Brown chicken on both sides in butter until tender. Place chicken in baking dish large enough to hold it in one layer. Pour the following over chicken: brandy, Burgundy, and chicken stock. Bake at 350, until tender and done.

Mrs. Lillian Carter
Plains, Georgia

※ ※ ※ ※ ※ ※ ※ ※ ※ ※ ※ ※ ※

For a crisp, brown crust on roast or broiled chicken, rub mayonnaise over the skin before cooking.

Fill an atomizer that has a glass or plastic rod with vegetable oil. Use it to spray roasting poultry or fish. It's much handier and not as messy as using a pastry brush.

Dark meat takes longer to cook than white meat. So, when preparing chicken, cook thighs and legs about 5 to 10 minutes longer than the other pieces.

ROLLED CHICKEN BREASTS
Freezes well

Oven: 300° 2 hours   Yield: 9 to 10 servings

9 to 10 boned chicken   9 to 10 slices Swiss Cheese
  breasts   9 to 10 slices dried chipped
Garlic salt to taste   beef or shaved ham
9 to 10 small onion slices

Sauce:

1 (8-ounce) carton sour cream   Juice of one lemon
1 (10 3/4-ounce) can mushroom   1/4 teaspoon paprika
  soup

Flatten chicken breasts between waxed paper. Sprinkle with garlic salt. On each breast place a slice of onion, cheese, and beef or ham. Roll up and fasten with toothpicks. Combine 4 sauce ingredients. Pour over chicken. Bake covered for 1 1/2 hours at 300°. Uncover and cook for 30 minutes more.

Mrs. Joe Wall
Macon, Georgia

❋❋❋❋❋❋❋❋❋❋❋❋❋

Poultry, fish, or ground meat should not be stored more than 2 days in the refrigerator. Other raw meats should not be stored longer than 5 days.

Always remove stuffing from cooked poultry and refrigerate separately.

CASEROLE CHICKEN

Oven: 325° 1 1/2 hours   Yield: 4 to 6 servings

1 whole chicken
1 (8-ounce) carton sour
  cream
1 (10 3/4-ounce) can mushroom soup

1 package dry onion soup mix
1 (3-ounce) can chow mein
  noodles

Cut chicken into servings pieces and place in a casserole large enough to hold chicken comfortably. Combine the sour cream, mushroom soup, and onion soup mix. Spread the soup mixture over the chicken. Cover with chow mein noodles and bake for 1 1/2 hours at 325°.

Mrs. Ellis Arnall (Mildred)
Mrs. Arnall is a former First Lady of Georgia.

CHICKEN AND DRESSING CASSEROLE
Good and easy

Oven: 425° 25 minutes   Yield: 6 to 8 servings

2 pounds boiled chicken
1/2 stick margarine
1/2 (10 3/4-ounce) can cream
  of celery soup
1/2 (10 3/4-ounce) can cream
  of chicken soup

1/2 (13-ounce) can evaporated
  or whole milk
1 box cornbread stuffing mix
1 1/2 cups chicken broth

Take chicken off the bone and place in 2-quart casserole. Melt margarine and add soups and milk. Pour over chicken in casserole. Mix stuffing with broth and spoon over mixture in casserole dish. Do not stir layers together. Bake at 425° for 25 minutes or until brown.

Mrs. Eddie Lovett (Teresa)

CHICKEN CASSEROLE I

Freezes well. Delicious and different from the usual chicken casserole

Oven: 325° 1 1/2 hours   Yield: 10 servings

2 to 2 1/2 cups cooked chicken,
    cut into bite-size pieces
2/3 cup chopped onion
2/3 cup chopped celery
2/3 cup chopped bell pepper
2/3 cup mayonnaise
1/3 cup chicken broth
Salt and pepper to taste

8 slices bread, cubed
2 eggs
1 1/2 cups milk
1 (10 3/4-ounce) can cream of
    mushroom soup
1/2 can milk (mushroom soup
    can)
1/2 cup cheese, grated

Combine chicken, onion, pepper, celery mayonnaise, broth, salt, and pepper. Place 4 slices of cubed bread in bottom of 3-quart casserole and spread chicken mixture over. Beat eggs into 1 1/2 cups milk and pour over chicken mixture. Put other 4 pieces of bread cubes over and refrigerate overnight (or freeze) until ready to serve. When ready, mix 1 can mushroom soup with 1/2 can milk and heat until lumps are gone. Pour over the casserole. Cover with grated cheese and bake at 325° for 1 1/2 hours.

Mrs. John Goodrum (Marsha)

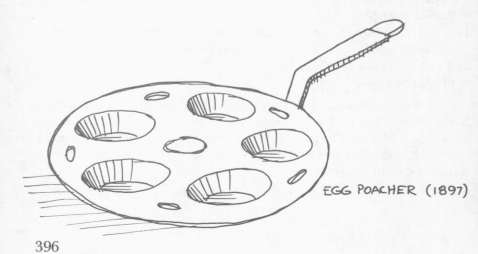

EGG POACHER (1897)

CHICKEN CASSEROLE II
Must be prepared ahead of time; can be frozen

Oven: 350° 60 minutes   Yield: 8 to 10 servings

2 large fryers
1 cup water
2 cups sherry
1 teaspoon salt
3/4 teaspoon curry powder
1 medium onion, sliced
1 pound fresh mushrooms

1/2 cup butter
2 (6-ounce) packages long
  grain and wild rice
1 cup sour cream
1 (10 3/4-ounce) can cream of
  mushroom soup

Place chickens in kettle; add water, sherry, salt, curry, and onion. Cover and bring to a boil; reduce heat and simmer for 1 hour. Remove from heat; strain broth. Refrigerate chicken and broth without cooling.

When chicken is cool, remove from bones; discard skin. Cut meat into bite-size pieces. Rinse mushrooms and pat dry; slice and saute in butter 5 minutes, stirring constantly.

Measure broth; use as part of liquid for cooking rice, following directions for firm rice on package. Combine chicken, mushrooms, and rice in 3 1/2 to 4-quart casserole. Blend in sour cream and mushroom soup and toss with chicken mixture. Cover and refrigerate overnight. Bake covered 1 hour in 350° oven.

Mrs. Parnell Odom (Pat)

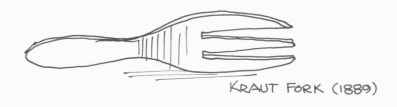

KRAUT FORK (1889)

397

BROCCOLI, CHICKEN, AND RICE CASSEROLE
Good company dish

Oven: 350° 15 to 20 minutes   Yield: 6 servings

2 (10-ounce) packages frozen chopped broccoli
2 (13-ounce) cans diced, boned chicken
2 cups cooked rice
1 (10 3/4-ounce) can cream of chicken soup
1 (10 3/4-ounce) can cream of mushroom soup
1/2 cup chopped onion
1/2 cup chopped celery
1 (11-ounce) can Cheddar cheese soup

Cook broccoli as directed on package. Drain. Mix with other ingredients but use only 1/2 can cheese soup. Pour into 1 to 2-quart casserole. Top with rest of Cheddar cheese soup. Cook at 350° for 15 or 20 minutes until bubbly.

Mrs. Phil S. Vincent (Mary Anna)

EVERYONE'S FAVORITE CHICKEN CASSEROLE

Oven: 275° 30 minutes   Yield: 8 servings

1/2 soup can chicken broth or milk
1 (10 1/2-ounce) can cream of mushroom soup
1 (10 1/2-ounce) can cream of chicken soup
1 1/4 teaspoons onion powder
4 cups cooked rice
3 cups cooked, boned chicken cut into large bite-size pieces
1 1/2 cups grated sharp cheese
2 tablespoons pimiento, chopped

Mix broth and soups. Heat, stirring until smooth and hot. Add remaining ingredients. Bake 30 minutes at 275° in a 3-quart casserole.

Mrs. Charles Connally (Rosa)

CHICKEN RICE CASSEROLE
Good and easy family dish or for informal company

Oven: 325° 2 hours and 15 minutes   Yield: 4 to 6 servings

(7-ounce) box instant or
quick rice, uncooked
(10 3/4-ounce) can cream of
mushroom soup
(10 3/4-ounce) can cream of
celery soup

1/2 cup milk
1 frying chicken, cut into pieces
or preferred chicken parts
1 envelope onion soup mix
1 (4-ounce) can mushrooms

Grease a 9x13-inch casserole. Put rice in casserole. Mix the two soups and milk and heat until all are well blended (do not boil). Pour soup mixture over the rice. Stir slightly so that the rice on the very bottom is moistened, too. Place chicken pieces on top of rice. Sprinkle chicken with the onion soup mix, then with mushrooms. Cover with foil and bake at 325° for 2 hours and 15 minutes.

Mrs. Thomas G. Kerley (Florence)
Paducah, Kentucky

❋❋❋❋❋❋❋❋❋❋❋❋❋

For the finest onion rings, fish, shrimp. It's virtually impossible to find a more delicious, yet simple-to-make batter than the classic beer batter. Two simple rules . . . use exactly the same proportions of plain flour and beer (one can of beer and the same amount of flour is a good start), blend well, and allow the batter to stand at room temperature no less than three hours.

The result is a delicately flavored batter that cannot be topped for deep fat frying. The alcohol in the beer quickly disappears when the batter is first heated. What is left is a delightfully flavored combination of wheat, malt, barley, and hopps.

399

1st PLACE CHICKEN CASSEROLE

Oven: 350° 35 to 40 minutes

Yield: 12 to 15 serving

3 cups chicken, cooked and diced
4 hard-cooked eggs, chopped
2 cups cooked rice
1 1/2 cups celery, chopped
1 small onion, chopped
1 cup mayonnaise

2 (10 3/4-ounce) cans mush-room soup
1 (3-ounce) package slivered almonds
1 teaspoon salt
2 tablespoons lemon juice
1 cup bread crumbs
2 tablespoons margarine, melt

Combine all ingredients except bread crumbs and margarine mixing well. Pour into one 3-quart oblong casserole, two 1 1/2 quart casseroles, or three 1-quart casseroles. Combine melted margarine and bread crumbs and sprinkle over top. Bake a 350° for 35 to 40 minutes or until bubbly and hot.

NOTE: Terrific for a covered-dish meal, or divide int 2 or 3 small casseroles — eat one and take extras to friends

Mrs. William Donald Tomlinson (Jane

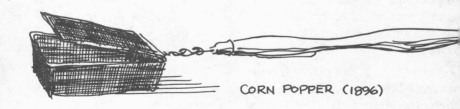

CORN POPPER (1896)

BAKED CHICKEN SOUFFLE
Great because it must be done the night before serving

Oven: 350° 1 1/2 hours   Yield: 8 to 10 servings

9 slices of white bread
4 cups cooked chicken, cut
   into pieces
1/2 pound fresh mushrooms or
   1 large can of B&B mushrooms
1 (8-ounce) can water chestnuts, drained and sliced
1/2 cup mayonnaise
9 slices Cheddar cheese
4 eggs, well-beaten

2 cups milk
1 1/2 teaspoons salt
1 (10 3/4-ounce) can cream of
   mushroom soup
1 (10 3/4-ounce) can cream of
   celery soup
1 (2-ounce) jar pimientos, sliced
2 cups buttered bread crumbs,
   using 1/4 cup butter

Remove crusts from bread and line one large or 2 small buttered casseroles with single layer of bread. If using fresh mushrooms, cook them in 1/2 cup water for 5 minutes. Top bread with chicken, mushrooms, and sliced chestnuts. Dot with mayonnaise and top with cheese. Combine eggs, milk, and salt, and pour over all. Mix soups and pimientos and spoon over all. Cover with foil and store overnight in refrigerator. Just before baking, sprinkle with buttered bread crumbs. Bake at 350° for 1 1/2 hours until center is set.

Mrs. Thomas Maybank (Bee)

TIN DINNER HORN (1897)

COQ AU VIN I
The longer it sits, the better it is!

Oven: 350° 1 1/2 hours Yield: 4 servings

1/4 pound diced salt pork
1 (10-ounce) box pearl onions
3 tablespoons butter
1 large fryer or fryer parts
   (2 pieces per person)
1 clove garlic
2 tablespoons flour
2 tablespoons brandy

1 1/2 cups red wine
2 tablespoons fresh, minced
   parsley
1 bay leaf
1 teaspoon salt
Generous pinch thyme
Pinch of marjoram
1/2 pound sliced mushrooms

Fry out salt pork. Brown onions slowly, about 10 to 15 minutes or until tender. Remove. Add butter and brown chicken. Put chicken aside. Add garlic and cook until soft. Add flour and make a roux. Add brandy and wine. Cook until smooth. Add other seasonings. Place chicken in 2-quart casserole. Pour sauce over chicken. (May be prepared in advance to this point.) Cook 1 1/2 hours at 350°. Last 10 minutes add mushrooms and onions. Serve with rice or boiled potatoes.

Mrs. Charles B. Woodroof, Jr. (Amelia)

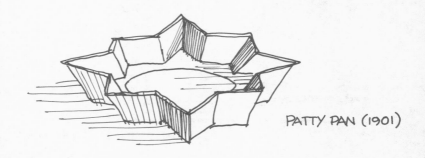

PATTY PAN (1901)

COQ AU VIN II
Great "make-ahead" for a dinner party

Oven: 375° 2 hours   Yield: 8 servings

1/2 pound bacon, diced
2 tablespoons butter
2 fryers, quartered
16 whole mushrooms
16 small white onions
2 cloves garlic, crushed
3 tablespoons flour
1 teaspoon salt
2 tablespoons chives, chopped

1/2 teaspoon thyme (1/4 dried)
1/4 cup parsley, chopped
1/8 teaspoon pepper
2 cups Burgundy
1 cup chicken stock
16 small new potatoes

In Dutch oven sauté bacon until crisp. Remove. Add butter to drippings and brown chicken well. Remove. Add mushrooms and onions. Cook until nicely browned, then remove. Pour off all but 3 tablespoons fat. Add garlic. Sauté 2 minutes. Stir in flour, salt, chives, thyme, parsley, and pepper. Cook until flour is browned, about 3 minutes. Gradually stir in Burgundy and chicken stock. Bring to a boil, stirring. Remove from heat. Stir in bacon, chicken, onions, and mushrooms. Cover and refrigerate overnight. Next day add scrubbed new potatoes to the chicken mixture. Bake covered at 375° about 2 hours or until chicken and potatoes are tender. Serve with noodles or brown rice.

Mrs. T. Leigh Sanders, Jr. (Martha)

COQ AU VIN III

Oven: 375° 90 minutes   Yield: 6 servings

3/4 cup rosé wine
1/4 cup soy sauce
1/4 cup salad oil
2 tablespoons water
1 clove garlic, crushed
1 teaspoon ginger (optional)
1/4 teaspoon oregano
1 tablespoon vinegar

6 chicken breasts (or equivalent
   amount of thighs)
Flour or cornstarch
1 medium green pepper,
   chopped or sliced
1 medium onion, chopped
1 (6-ounce) can sliced mushrooms
4 tablespoons margarine
Cooked rice

Mix first 8 ingredients and pour over chicken. Marinate several hours or overnight. Bake at 375° for 1 1/2 hours. Remove from oven and thicken pan liquid with flour or cornstarch. Saute pepper, onion, and mushrooms in margarine until tender; add to chicken. Serve over rice with pineapple slices.

Mrs. Susan Milam

CHICKEN—ITALIAN STYLE
Good and easy

Oven: 350° 60 minutes   Yield: 8 servings

2 chickens, cut-up
1 (8-ounce) bottle
   Italian dressing

1 stick margarine
Salt and pepper, to taste

Place chicken in Pyrex dish. Pour dressing over chicken. Dot with margarine, salt, and pepper. Bake in oven for 1 hour at 350°.

Mrs. Paul R. McKnight, Jr. (Totsie)
Senoia, Georgia

MOCK COQ AU VIN

Oven: 325° 1 to 1½ hours   Yield: 4 to 6 servings

1 frying chicken, cut up
Flour
Salt
Pepper
1 bunch green onions, sliced
1 cup sliced fresh mushrooms
    or 1 (4-ounce) can sliced
    mushrooms

2 tablespoons chopped parsley
1/8 teaspoon thyme
1/8 teaspoon marjoram
Dash of worcestershire sauce
1 bay leaf, crumbled
1/2 to 1 cup dry white wine
1 (10 3/4-ounce) can cream
    of chicken soup, undiluted

Shake chicken pieces in paper bag with seasoned flour. Brown chicken in butter. Remove the chicken and place in a casserole large enough to hold chicken pieces in a single layer. In butter in fry pan, put sliced onions and mushrooms. When lightly browned, add parsley, thyme, marjoram, worcestershire sauce, bay leaf, and wine. Salt and pepper to taste. Simmer gently for a few minutes to blend flavors. Pour over chicken in casserole. Cover and bake at 325° for 1 to 1 1/2 hours or until chicken is tender. For a delicious gravy, remove chicken from casserole; add cream of chicken soup to juice, blend, and simmer on stove until bubbly. Pour over chicken or pass in gravy boat. Good with rice.

Mrs. Robert L. Lee (Pam)

COCOBOLO HANDLE BREAD KNIFE
(1897)

★ **COUNTRY CAPTAIN**
Excellent served with chutney

Oven: 350° 2 hours   Yield: 4 servings

3 pounds chicken, cut up
4 tablespoons butter
1 green pepper, chopped
1 clove garlic, chopped
1 onion, chopped
1 cup water (more, if
    necessary)
1 1/2 teaspoons curry powder

6 fresh tomatoes, peeled
1 tablespoon chopped parsley
1/4 teaspoon thyme
1/4 pound blanched almonds
3 tablespoons dried currants or
    raisins
4 slices crisp bacon, chopped

Cut up and flour chicken; there should be about 10 pieces. Heat butter and brown the chicken pieces. When browned, place chicken in casserole. In the same frying pan, sauté pepper, garlic, and onion 5 minutes, stirring constantly. Add water mixed with curry powder, tomatoes, parsley, and thyme. Pour mixture over chicken in casserole. Cover and bake at 350° until chicken is very tender (about 2 hours). Add almonds which have been sautéed in butter or margarine until golden brown. Add the currants. Place chicken pieces on serving dish and pour the gravy over it. Garnish with chopped bacon.

Mrs. William Griffin (Florence)
Atlanta, Georgia

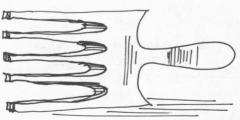

BUTTER FORK (1890)

CHICKEN LOAF

Oven: 350° 45 minutes   Yield: 16 servings

Loaf:

hen, cooked and diced   3 cups broth
cups bread crumbs   4 eggs, well-beaten
cups cooked rice   1 cup diced celery
1/2 teaspoons salt   1 small grated onion
/2 cup chopped pimientoes

Sauce:

tablespoons butter   1 1/2 cups broth
tablespoons flour   1 (8-ounce) can mushrooms
tablespoons grated onion   Salt and pepper to taste

Mix all ingredients for the loaf and bake at 350° for 45 minutes. While the loaf is cooking, make the sauce in the following manner: cook butter, flour, and onion until lightly browned, add broth and mushrooms, cook until slightly thickened, and add salt and pepper to taste. Serve with the chicken loaf.

Mrs. T. L. Lang

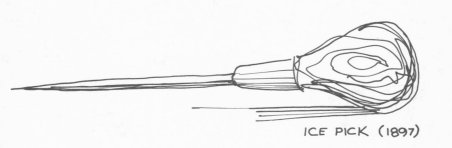

ICE PICK (1897)

PAPERBAG CHICKEN
Delicious and different!

Oven: 350° 30 minutes per pound   Yield: 4 serving

Margarine
Salt
Pepper
1 whole fryer
Chopped celery, bell pepper, onion, and garlic, varying
amounts according to taste

Rub margarine all over whole fryer, inside and out. Sal
and pepper fryer, inside and out. Stuff fryer with choppec
vegetables. Place fryer in a greased brown paper bag. Roll uị
the open end and bake at 350° for 30 minutes to the pound

Mrs. J. P. Lott (Douglass

SKILLET CHICKEN AND RICE

Yield: 6 serving

3 tablespoons butter
2/3 cup uncooked rice
1 (4-ounce) can mushroom
stems and pieces

1 envelope (1 1/2-ounce) dry
onion soup mix
2 cups cooked chicken
2 cups water

Melt butter; add rice and mushrooms with liquid. Add dr
onion soup and mix. Add chicken and water and mix. Turi
skillet to low and cook covered about 30 minutes or until ric
is tender.

Mrs. Parnell Odom (Pat

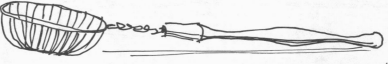

VEGETABLE STRAINER (1897)

CHICKEN DIVAN
This recipe will make the cook proud!

Oven: 300° 15 minutes

Yield: 6 to 8 servings

3 (10-ounce) packages
frozen broccoli
3 tablespoons butter
1/2 cup cheese, Romano
or Parmesan
1 1/2 cups sherry

6 large chicken breasts,
cooked, or several slices of
cooked turkey
Pepperidge Farm Stuffing
mix (optional)

Béchamel Sauce:

3 tablespoons butter
3 tablespoons flour
3 cups milk

4 egg yolks, beaten
4 tablespoons whipping cream
(optional)

CASSEROLE: Cook broccoli and drain. Place broccoli in bottom of shallow greased baking pan. Sprinkle with butter, 3 tablespoons cheese, and 3/4 cup sherry. Add layer of chicken or turkey. Sprinkle with half of remaining cheese and remaining sherry. Add cream sauce (recipe follows). Sprinkle with remainder of cheese. Bake at 300° about 15 minutes until bubbly. Top with stuffing if desired.

BECHAMEL SAUCE: Melt butter in saucepan. Remove from heat, add flour and blend well. Stir in milk and cook until thick. Add egg yolks and whipping cream.

Mrs. Bruce Deakin (Fran)

EASY CHICKEN DIVAN
Everyone goes back for more

Oven: 400° 25 to 30 minutes

Yield: 6 to 8 servings

2 (10-ounce) packages frozen
broccoli spears
1 fryer, cooked and sliced
2 (10 3/4-ounce) cans condensed cream of chicken soup
1 cup mayonnaise

1 1/2 teaspoons lemon juice
3/4 teaspoon curry powder
1/2 cup sharp Cheddar
cheese, grated
3/4 cup stuffing mix
2 tablespoons margarine

Cook broccoli; drain; arrange spears in baking dish. Place sliced chicken on top. Combine soup, mayonnaise, lemon juice, and curry powder, Pour over top. Sprinkle with grated cheese and put stuffing mix on top. Dot with margarine. Bake at 400° for 25 to 30 minutes.

Mrs. Parnell Odom (Pat)

TREASURE ISLAND CHICKEN

Oven: 400° 20 minutes

Yield: 6 to 8 servings

1 (5-pound) hen
6 tablespoons butter
1/2 cup flour
1 cup milk
2 cups chicken broth
1 cup mayonnaise
1/2 teaspoon curry powder

1 teaspoon lemon juice
2 (10-ounce) packages
frozen broccoli
1 teaspoon salt
Sliced almonds (optional)

Cook hen. Remove meat from bones and leave in large pieces. Melt butter. Blend in flour; add milk and chicken broth. Cook until thick and smooth. Remove from heat and add mayonnaise, curry powder, and lemon juice. Season with salt. Arrange broccoli in bottom of a large shallow casserole. Place chicken on top and pour sauce over it. Almonds may be added. Bake at 400° for 20 minutes.

Mrs. Maurice Sponcler, Jr. (Betty)
Dalton, Georgia

CHEESY CHICKEN AND BROCCOLI CREPES

Great for groups; delicious luncheon dish

Yield: 14 or 16 servings

1 (10-ounce) package
  chopped broccoli
1 (10 3/4-ounce) can cream
  of chicken soup
1/2 teaspoon worcestershire
  sauce

1/3 cup grated Parmesan
  cheese
2 cups cooked, slivered
  chicken
14 or 16 cooked crêpes

Topping:

1/3 cup mayonnaise
1 tablespoon milk

1/4 cup grated Parmesan
  cheese

Cook broccoli according to package directions and drain thoroughly. Combine broccoli with soup, worcestershire sauce, 1/3 cup cheese, and chicken. Fill crêpes with chicken mixture; roll up and place in baking dish. Combine mayonnaise with milk and spread over crêpes. Sprinkle with 1/4 cup cheese. Broil until bubbly.

Mrs. Dan B. Umbach (Marie)

GEM PAN (1897)

411

★ ## SOUTHERN FRIED CHICKEN
One of the many delicious ways Southerners fry chicken

1 fryer, cut into serving-size
  pieces
1 egg
Milk or buttermilk
Flour
Salt
Pepper
Cooking oil or solid shortening
Butter (optional)

Salt fryer pieces, cover well, and refrigerate overnight. Beat egg and add milk or buttermilk. Dip salted fryer pieces in the mixture, making sure they are completely covered. Dredge in a mixture of flour, salt, and pepper. Place in a skillet filled with hot cooking oil and fry, uncovered over medium heat, until chicken is tender and golden brown on both sides. Make sure chicken is not crowded while frying. Drain well and serve.

NOTE: The cooking oil (or shortening) should be very deep to properly fry the chicken. The addition of a small amount of butter to the oil adds special flavor and a golden color. Watch to be sure the butter does not burn, however.

SAUCE PAN (1897)

WORKING WOMAN'S CHICKEN PIE

Oven: 375°   Yield: 4 servings

Unbaked 10-inch pastry shell with top or
   2 deep-dish frozen pastry shells
1 (10 3/4-ounce) can cream of chicken soup
4 cooked chicken breasts, bones removed
1 (10 3/4-ounce) can chunky chicken soup
4 to 5 hard-boiled eggs, sliced

In a large baking dish, place lower pastry shell. Spread with cream of chicken soup right out of can. Arrange chicken on top of soup. Spread chunky soup over chicken. Layer sliced eggs on top of chunky soup. Cover all with upper pastry, sealing and crimping edges. Punch steam holes in top crust with fork. Bake at 375° until crust is brown. To serve 6 or 8, use 1 large chicken breast per person to be served.

Lavinia Barron Rosenzweig

ROYAL CHICKEN PIE

Leftovers and a microwave oven combine to create this easy dish.

Microwave Oven: 7½ minutes   Yield: 8 servings

3 tablespoons butter or
   margarine
5 tablespoons flour
1 teaspoon salt
1/8 teaspoon pepper
1 3/4 cups chicken stock

3 cups cooked chicken, chopped
1 (4-ounce) can mushrooms,
   drained
1 (8 1/2-ounce) can carrots
   and peas
8 puff pastry shells, baked

In 2-quart casserole melt butter or margarine in microwave oven for 30 seconds. Blend flour, salt, and pepper. Gradually stir in chicken stock. Heat uncovered in microwave oven for 4 minutes or until thickened and smooth. Stir occasionally. Add remaining ingredients, except shells, and heat uncovered for 3 minutes or until thoroughly heated. Fill pastry shells with chicken mixture.

Mrs. Dan B. Umbach (Marie)

413

HOT CHICKEN SALAD

Oven: 350° 30 minutes   Yield: 8 servings

4 cups diced, cooked chicken
1 1/2 cups celery, finely
  chopped
1 cup toasted slivered almonds
1 teaspoon salt
4 tablespoons grated onion
1 cup green pepper, chopped
1 cup mayonnaise
4 tablespoons chopped pimiento
4 tablespoons lemon juice

1 (10 3/4-ounce) can cream
  of chicken soup, undiluted
2 hard-boiled eggs, chopped
2 cups grated New York State
  cheese
Crushed potato chips for
  topping

Combine all ingredients except potato chips and cheese; blend well together. Spoon into a lightly greased 3-quart shallow casserole. Top with 2 cups cheese. Bake at 350° for 30 minutes. Put sprinkling of crushed potato chips over surface during last 10 minutes.

Mrs. Jack Keith (May)
West Point, Georgia

CHICKEN-WITH-A-DATE

Yield: 8 to 10 servings

3/4 cup sour cream
1 teaspoon salt
Black pepper to taste
1 tablespoon finely chopped
  onion
1 tablespoon lemon juice
2 tablespoons orange juice

1/2 cup chopped celery
1 (2-ounce) jar pimiento,
  chopped
1 cup chopped dates
1/4 cup chopped pecans
3 cups chicken, cut in large
  pieces

Blend first 6 ingredients. Gently toss with the next 5 ingredients. Mound on a platter and garnish with orange sections.

Mrs. William Dudley (Jakie)
Montgomery, Alabama

HOT TURKEY SALAD
Great for Thanksgiving or Christmas leftovers

Oven: 350° 20 minutes   Yield: 10 to 12 servings

3 cups cooked turkey, chopped
1 cup mayonnaise
1 (10 3/4-ounce) can cream of
  chicken soup
1 (10 3/4-ounce) can cream of
  mushroom soup
4 hard-boiled eggs, chopped

1 cup almonds, sliced and
  toasted
2 tablespoons onions, minced
1 (8-ounce) can water
  chestnuts, sliced
1/3 cup bread crumbs

Mix together all ingredients except bread crumbs. Place in a 9x13x2-inch greased pan. Top with bread crumbs. Bake at 350° until bubbly, about 20 minutes.

NOTE: Chicken may be substituted for turkey. One pound uncooked chicken = one cup cooked chicken.

Pamela Hough
Fort Lauderdale, Florida

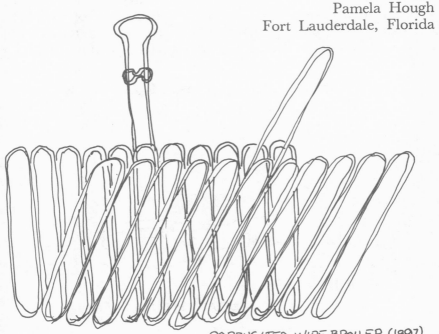

CORRUGATED WIRE BROILER (1897)

TURKEY TETRAZZINI

Oven: 400° 20 minutes

Yield: 6 to 8 servings

1/2 cup sliced, canned mushrooms, drained
1/2 cup thinly sliced onions
1/4 cup margarine
1/4 cup flour
2 cups chicken broth or bouillon
1 cup light cream
1 teàspoon salt

1/4 teaspoon pepper
1/2 teaspoon poultry seasoning
1 (8-ounce) package spaghetti, cooked and drained
3 cups diced, cooked turkey
1/2 cup shredded, aged cheese

Lightly brown the mushrooms and onions in margarine. Stir in flour. Cook until bubbly. Stir in the broth and cream. Add salt, pepper,. and poultry seasoning. Cook, stirring often, until mixture boils. Place a layer of cooked spaghetti in a buttered 2-quart casserole. Cover with a layer of diced turkey and a layer of sauce. Repeat. Finish with a layer of spaghetti. Sprinkle cheese on top. Bake at 400° for 20 minutes or until bubbly. This can be made ahead and refrigerated until baking time.

Mrs. Maurice Sponcler (Dot)

STEAK POUNDER (1894)

Salads &
Salad
Dressings

Salads

Salads & Salad Dressings Chapter Design: Egg and Cream Beater (1898), Mrs. Hutchins' Strainer Spoon (1910)

BLACKBERRY SALAD

Yield: 15 to 20 servings

2 (6-ounce) packages blackberry-flavored gelatin
3 1/4 cups hot water

1 (15-ounce) can blueberries
and juice
1 (8-ounce) can crushed
pineapple

Topping:
1 (8-ounce) package cream
cheese
1/2 cup sour cream

1/3 cup sugar
1 1/2 cups nuts, finely chopped

Mix gelatin and hot water until gelatin is dissolved. Add blueberries and pineapple including juices. Pour into a 9x13-inch dish. Chill until congealed. Mix topping and spread on mixture just before serving. Sprinkle with nuts.

Mrs. Gordon Brown (Ginny)
Atlanta, Georgia

ORANGE CHEESE SALAD

Yield: 8 servings

1 (8-ounce) can crushed
pineapple, undrained
1/2 cup sugar
1 cup water
1 (3-ounce) package orange-
flavored gelatin

1/2 cup sharp grated cheese
2/3 cup pecans, chopped
1 cup frozen whipped dessert
topping, thawed

Bring pineapple, sugar, and water to a boil. Dissolve gelatin in hot mixture. Cool in refrigerator until it is the consistency of egg whites. Add cheese and nuts. Fold in dessert topping. Pour into individual salad molds or one large mold. Refrigerate until set.

Mrs. Thomas W. Barron (Margaret)

WINE SALAD

Yield: 6 to 8 servings

1 (10-ounce) jar white cherries (Queen Anne), cut in halves
1 (3-ounce) package cherry-flavored gelatin
1 cup port wine
1/2 cup nuts
1 teaspoon unflavored gelatin (optional)

Add enough water to juice from cherries to make 1 cup liquid. Heat to boiling. Pour over gelatin. When cool, add the wine, cherries, and nuts. Add unflavored gelatin dissolved in 1 tablespoon water to assure a firm mold. Pour into a large mold or individual molds.

Mrs. Roy Wortham (Louise)

BLUEBERRY SALAD I

Yield: 8 to 10 servings

Gelatin:

2 (3-ounce) packages blackberry-flavored gelatin
2 cups boiling water
1 (20-ounce) can crushed pineapple with juice
1 (1-pound) can blueberry pie filling

Topping:

3 ounces cream cheese,
  softened
1/4 pint sour cream

1/4 cup sugar
1/2 teaspoon vanilla extract
1/2 cup chopped nuts

GELATIN: Mix ingredients thoroughly and congeal.
TOPPING: Mix all ingredients, except nuts, with mixer. Spread on congealed salad and sprinkle with nuts.

Mrs. Clark Hudson (Corille)

BLUEBERRY SALAD II

Yield: 10 to 12 servings

Salad

2 (3-ounce) packages blackberry-flavored gelatin
2 cups boiling water

1 (15-ounce) can blueberries
1 (8-ounce) can crushed
  pineapple

Topping:

1 (8-ounce) package cream
  cheese, softened
1/2 cup sugar

1/2 pint sour cream
1/2 teaspoon vanilla extract

1 cup chopped pecans

SALAD: Dissolve gelatin in boiling water. Drain blueberries and pineapple; measure liquid and add enough water to make 1 1/2 cups. Add to gelatin mixture. Stir in blueberries and pineapple. Put in shallow 2-quart dish and congeal.

TOPPING: Combine cream cheese, sugar, sour cream, and vanilla extract. Spread over congealed salad and sprinkle with chopped pecans.

Mrs. Ellis Crook (Pat)

✻ ✻ ✻ ✻ ✻ ✻ ✻ ✻ ✻ ✻ ✻ ✻ ✻

Add zip to gelatin salads by substituting a carbonated soft drink for part or all of the water. Use cola, gingerale, root beer, or any of the carbonated lemon and lime-flavored mixers.

In congealed cranberry salads, add a little extra gelatin for firm molds as the tartness of cranberry juice causes "weeping" after a short standing period.

BLUEBERRY SALAD III

Yield: 8 servings

1 (3-ounce) package lemon-
flavored gelatin
1 (3-ounce) package raspberry-
flavored gelatin
1 cup hot water

1 cup cold water
1 tablespoon lemon juice
1 (21-ounce) can blueberry
pie filling

Topping:

1 (3-ounce) package cream
cheese, softened

4 teaspoons mayonnaise or
pineapple juice

Dissolve gelatins in hot water. Add cold water and lemon juice. Stir in pie filling. Pour into 1 1/2 to 2-quart container and congeal. Blend cream cheese with mayonnaise or juice; the juice makes a sweeter topping. Spread this mixture on top. Chill and serve.

Mrs. L. E. Sport, Jr. (Melba)
Palmetto, Georgia

COTTAGE CHEESE SALAD

Yield: 8 servings

1 (3-ounce) package lime-
flavored gelatin
1 (3-ounce) package lemon-
flavored gelatin
1 cup hot water

1 cup evaporated milk
1 cup cottage cheese
1 (8-ounce) can crushed
pineapple, drained
3/4 cup homemade mayonnaise

Mix all ingredients together. Pour into 8 small individual molds and congeal.

Mrs. William C. Bowen, Jr. (Idawee)
Dalton, Georgia

CRANBERRY SALAD I
Next time try it as a dessert!

Yield: 16 servings

Salad:

2 (16-ounce) cans whole
  cranberry sauce
2 cups water
1 (6-ounce) package cherry-
  flavored gelatin

1 (20-ounce) can crushed
  pineapple
1 cup chopped pecans

Topping:

1 (8-ounce) package cream
  cheese, crumbled
1 (6 1/4-ounce) package
  miniature marshmallows

1 pint whipping cream

SALAD: In saucepan combine cranberry sauce and water, boiling until sauce is dissolved. Add gelatin, pineapple and juice, and nuts. Chill in a 9x13-inch pan for 15 hours.

TOPPING: Place in a large mixing bowl in layers: crumbled cream cheese, marshmallows, and whipping cream. Chill for 15 hours in refrigerator. When ready to serve, whip the topping mixture and spread on top of salad.

Mrs. Lynn B. Hooven (Melinda)

❋❋❋❋❋❋❋❋❋❋❋❋❋❋

To use unflavored gelatin properly, "season" it: dissolve 1 envelope gelatin in 1/4 cup cold water. Let gelatin sit until it gels. After it gels, place it in a pan of hot water to liquify. It's then ready to use — proceed with the recipe.

CRANBERRY SALAD II

Yield: 6 to 8 servings

2 cups fresh cranberries
1 orange, peeled
1 cup marshmallows
1 (8-ounce) can crushed
  pineapple
1/2 cup sugar

1 (3-ounce) package raspberry
  flavored gelatin
1 cup hot water
1 cup pecans, chopped

Process cranberries, peeled orange, and marshmallows in blender until smooth. Pour into mixing bowl. Add pineapple and sugar. Mix gelatin with hot water and stir until dissolved. Add gelatin along with pecans to mixture and chill until set.

Mrs. Wright Lipford (Faye)
Peachtree City, Georgia

CRANBERRY SALAD III
Refreshing

Yield: 6 to 8 servings

1 (3-ounce) box cherry-
  flavored gelatin
1 cup boiling water
1 (14-ounce) jar cranberry-
  orange relish

1 (8-ounce) can crushed
  pineapple
1 teaspoon lemon juice
1/2 cup walnuts
1/2 cup celery, chopped

Dissolve gelatin in boiling water. Add relish. Stir in remaining ingredients. Pour into 6-cup mold or individual molds. Refrigerate until congealed.

Mrs. Irwin H. Pike (Helen)

CRANBERRY SALAD IV
Freezes well

Yield: 20 servings

1 pound fresh cranberries
3 medium apples
30 large marshmallows or
　2 1/2 cups miniature
　marshmallows
1 1/2 cups sugar
1 (20-ounce) can crushed
　pineapple

1 1/2 cups chopped nuts
1/2 to 1 cup whipping cream,
　whipped
Lettuce leaves or sliced
　pineapple

Put cranberries and apples through a food chopper or chop finely. Cut large marshmallows into fourths and combine with cranberry mixture. Add pineapple and sugar. Let stand in refrigerator overnight.

At serving time add nuts and whipped cream. Serve over lettuce leaves or on slices of pineapple.

Mrs. Al Robertson (Carole)

CHRISTMAS SALAD

Yield: 20 servings

1 quart fresh cranberries
2 oranges
1/2 cup water
2 cups sugar
3 envelopes unflavored gelatin

1 cup chopped pecans
1 (8-ounce) can crushed
　pineapple
1 cup chopped celery
1/2 teaspoon salt

Grind cranberries and oranges. Simmer fruit with water and sugar until sugar is dissolved. Add gelatin and stir until dissolved. Add rest of ingredients and mix well. Pour into a mold or 9x13-inch pan and refrigerate to congeal.

Mrs. Marion Truitt (Pauline)

MANDARIN ORANGE SALAD

Yield: 10 servings

1 (6-ounce) package orange-flavored gelatin
1 cup very strong hot tea
1 cup juice from orange segments and crushed pineapple
1 (11-ounce) can mandarin oranges
1 (8-ounce) can crushed pineapple
1 (8 1/2-ounce) can water chestnuts, drained and thinly
   sliced
1/3 to 1/2 cup Sauterne
2 tablespoons fresh lemon juice
3/4 cup whipping cream, whipped
Mace

Dissolve gelatin in tea. Add 1 cup of juices. Chill until partially set. Add other ingredients, including all fruit juices. Pour into ten 1/2-cup molds. Congeal. Unmold and top with dollop of whipped cream. Sprinkle with mace.

Mrs. John P. Woods, Jr. (Elizabeth)

ORANGE DREAM

Yield: 10 to 12 servings

1 (8-ounce) can crushed
   pineapple
1 cup water
1/3 cup sugar
1 (3-ounce) package orange-
   flavored gelatin

1/2 cup grated Cheddar cheese
1/2 cup chopped pecans
1 (1 1/2-ounce) package
   whipped topping, prepared
   according to directions

In saucepan, bring to a boil crushed pineapple, water, and sugar. Remove from heat. Dissolve gelatin in hot mixture. Cool. Stir in remaining ingredients and pour into greased 6-cup mold. Chill.

Mrs. D. M. Worth (Judi)

ORANGE SALAD SUPREME
Also delightful as a dessert

Yield: 12 to 15 servings

1 (6-ounce) package orange-flavored gelatin
1 (20-ounce) can crushed pineapple, drained
1 (1 1/2-ounce) package Dream Whip

1 (8-ounce) package cream cheese, softened
1 cup pineapple juice
2 tablespoons lemon juice
3/4 cup sugar
2 teaspoons flour
2 eggs, beaten

Mix gelatin by directions, using 1/2 cup less water. Pour into a 9x12-inch dish. Chill until gelatin begins to thicken; add pineapple and let congeal completely.

Whip 1 package Dream Whip according to directions on box. Cream the cheese and combine with Dream Whip. Spread over congealed mixture and chill.

Combine remaining ingredients and cook over low heat until thick. Chill and spread over Dream Whip. Refrigerate two hours.

Mrs. Phil S. Vincent (Mary Anna)

LIME CHIFFON SALAD
Light

Yield: 16 to 20 servings

20 large marshmallows
1 (3-ounce) package cream cheese
1 (3-ounce) package lime-flavored gelatin

1 (13-ounce) can evaporated milk, chilled
1 (20-ounce) can crushed pineapple, drained

Melt marshmallows and cream cheese in top of double boiler until softened. Dissolve gelatin as directed on package. Add marshmallow mixture. Chill until slightly thick then beat until smooth. Whip evaporated milk until stiff. Fold in first mixture; add pineapple. Stir all together and pour into mold.

Mrs. Sam M. Banks (Mary Willie)

LIME SALAD

Yield: 6 to 9 servings

1 (3-ounce) package lime-
flavored gelatin
12 large marshmallows or
45 to 50 miniature
marshmallows
1 1/2 cups boiling water

1 (3-ounce) package cream
cheese, softened
1 cup crushed pineapple
1/2 cup pineapple juice
1 cup nuts, chopped

Dissolve gelatin and marshmallows in hot water. Refrigerate until slightly thickened. Cream the cheese and combine with pineapple and pineapple juice. Add nuts and mix with gelatin mixture. Refrigerate overnight, if possible.

Mrs. S. S. Vincent
Milledgeville, Georgia

STRAWBERRY CREAM CHEESE DELIGHT
Also delicious as dessert

Yield: 10 (1/2-cup) servings

2 (8-ounce) packages cream cheese, softened
1/2 cup sugar
1 (1-pound) package frozen, sliced strawberries, thawed and
drained
1 cup whipping cream, whipped

Beat cheese and sugar with mixer until light and fluffy. Fold in strawberries and whipped cream. Turn into 5-cup mold. Freeze at least 8 hours. Let stand at room temperature 30 minutes; unmold. Garnish with mint or strawberries. For Christmas, garnish with holly and berries.

Mrs. Robert L. Lee (Pam)

STRAWBERRY SALAD

Delicious holiday salad

Yield: 20 servings

2 (3-ounce) packages strawberry-
 flavored gelatin
1 cup boiling water
2 (10-ounce) packages frozen
 sliced strawberries, thawed
1 (16-ounce) can crushed
 pineapple, drained

3 bananas, mashed
1 cup chopped pecans
1 1/2 to 2 (8-ounce)
 cartons sour cream

Dissolve gelatin in 1 cup boiling water. Add next 4 ingredients and mix well. Put 1/2 of this mixture in a 9x13-inch pan. Let set until very firm. Spread with sour cream. Pour on remaining gelatin mixture and spread evenly. Chill until set. Cut into squares and serve on lettuce leaves.

Mrs. Thomas G. Kerley (Florence)
Paducah, Kentucky

GREEN GRAPE SALAD

A do-ahead that is elegant and easy

Yield: 6 servings

1 (8-ounce) carton sour cream
1/4 cup brown sugar
1 pound seedless green grapes

Mix sour cream and brown sugar. Add grapes. Mix until grapes are well covered with cream and sugar. Place in covered dish. Refrigerate about 24 hours before serving. Serve on lettuce leaf.

Mrs. Joe W. Wray (Sara)
Atlanta, Georgia

429

CHRISTMAS FRUIT SALAD

Red, white, and green layers make this perfect for holiday entertaining.

Yield: 10 to 12 servings

Bottom Layer:

1 (6-ounce) package lime-flavored gelatin
2 heaping cups vanilla ice cream
1 (16-ounce) can crushed pineapple, drained

Middle Layer:

16 ounces sour cream
1 cup mayonnaise
2 cups walnuts, chopped

Topping:

1 (6-ounce) package raspberry-flavored gelatin
1 (16-ounce) package frozen strawberries, sliced and thawed
2 1/2 cups miniature marshmallows

BOTTOM LAYER: Mix lime-flavored gelatin according to package instructions using 1 cup boiling water and 1 cup cold water. Add ice cream and pineapple, stirring until ice cream is dissolved. Pour in large mold or 9x13-inch dish. Refrigerate until completely set.

MIDDLE LAYER: Mix sour cream, mayonnaise, and walnuts. Spread on lime mixture and return to refrigerator.

TOPPING: Mix raspberry-flavored gelatin according to package directions using 1 1/2 cups boiling water and 1 1/2 cups cold water. Stir in strawberries and marshmallows. Allow to cool completely before adding to salad. Then gently pour over sour cream layer. Refrigerate until serving time, at least overnight.

Cut into squares or unmold and serve on lettuce.

Mrs. Bruce Deakin (Fran)

JANE FOSTER'S GRAPEFRUIT SALAD
Different and impressive

Yield: 12 servings

Salad:

grapefruit (3 1/4 cups grapefruit and juice)	2 (3-ounce) packages lemon-flavored gelatin 3/4 cup boiling water

Dressing:

heaping tablespoon flour	4 large marshmallows, cut up
heaping tablespoons sugar	1/3 cup chopped pecans
egg yolk, beaten	1/2 pint whipping cream, whipped
juice of 1 lemon	
1/3 cup pineapple juice	

SALAD: Cut each grapefruit in half; remove sections and chop, reserving juice. Scrape shells clean and reserve. Dissolve gelatin in boiling water; add grapefruit juice and sections. Pour into grapefruit cups and congeal. When firm, cut in half again. Top with dressing.

DRESSING: In saucepan, mix flour and sugar. Add egg yolk, lemon juice, and pineapple juice. Cook over medium heat until thick, stirring constantly. Remove from heat, cool slightly, and add chopped marshmallows and pecans. Cool completely. Fold in whipped cream and serve over wedges of salad.

Mrs. Gene C. Threlkeld (Freddie)

****

Add a small amount of beet vinegar to mayonnaise to give it a pretty color for salads.

When unmolding a congealed salad, always sprinkle a few drops of water on the serving plate. It will be easy to move the salad around to position it correctly.

431

COCONUT CONGEALED SALAD

Yield: 10 serving

1 stick margarine
1 (7-ounce) can coconut
1 cup vanilla wafer crumbs
1 (6-ounce) package lime-
  flavored gelatin
1 cup boiling water
1 (3-ounce) package cream
  cheese, softened
1 cup miniature marshmallows

1 (8-ounce) can crushed
  pineapple, undrained
1 cup chopped pecans
1 (6-ounce) bottle maraschino
  cherries, chopped
1 (5 3/4-ounce) can evaporate
  milk (chilled to whip)

Melt margarine, add coconut and brown lightly. Ad
vanilla wafer crumbs and mix thoroughly. Line 9x13-inc
casserole dish with 1/2 mixture, reserving other 1/2 for topping
and put dish in refrigerator to cool. Mix gelatin in boilin
water to dissolve. Add softened cream cheese and blend wit
fork. Add marshmallows, then undrained pineapple, pecans
and cherries. Chill until thick; then fold in whipped milk. Pou
into dish lined with crumbs. Cover the gelatin with remainin
coconut mixture. Chill until firm; cut into squares to serve.

Mrs. Bob Hammock (Glenn

****

For a different salad, soak dried figs in wine, then stuff with
a mixture of cream cheese and black walnuts. These are pretty
as a garnish, too.

Make garlic-flavored potato chips by placing a peeled clove o
garlic in a container with regular chips for several hours. Discard
garlic before serving chips.

CREAM CHEESE CONGEALED SALAD

Yield: 12 to 15 servings

1 cup hot water
1 (3-ounce) package orange-
flavored gelatin
1 (8-ounce) package cream
cheese, cut into pieces
and softened

2 teaspoons lemon juice
1/2 cup crushed pecans
1 (8-ounce) can crushed
pineapple, drained
1 cup miniature marshmallows

Pour hot water into a blender container. Add gelatin and mix. Add softened cream cheese, 1 piece at a time, and blend after each addition. Add lemon juice and blend. Pour into a mixing bowl and add pecans, drained pineapple, and marshmallows. Stir until marshmallows are coated with mixture. Pour into a 9x13-inch pan and refrigerate until congealed.

Mrs. Fred Gilbert (Ann)

PEAR SALAD

Yield: 6 servings

1 (3-ounce) package orange-flavored gelatin
1 (13 1/2-ounce) container non-dairy whipped topping
1 (8-ounce) package cream cheese, room temperature
1 (29-ounce) can pear halves, cubed

Drain juice from pears into saucepan and heat. Dissolve gelatin in hot juice. Chill until mixture is consistency of egg whites. In bowl of electric mixer, blend whipped topping and cream cheese; fold into gelatin along with cubed pears. Chill until firm.

Mrs. Larry Strickland (Mary)

433

SALAD WITH BANANA DRESSING

Yield: 8 to 12 servings

Salad:

2 (3-ounce) boxes orange or
lemon-flavored gelatin
2 cups boiling water
1 (28-ounce) can pineapple
chunks

1 (20-ounce) can Queen Anne
cherries
3 large or 4 small grapefruit,
sectioned
Juice from drained grapefruit

Dressing:

3 large bananas
1 (3-ounce) package cream
cheese, softened

Lemon juice to taste
1/2 pint whipping cream,
whipped

SALAD: Dissolve gelatin in 2 cups boiling water. Drain pineapple chunks and cherries, reserving liquid. Add grapefruit juice and water to measure 2 cups liquid. Stir into gelatin. Arrange fruit in mold or oblong 2-quart dish. Pour gelatin over; congeal.

DRESSING: Mash bananas and mix with cream cheese. Add lemon juice and whipped cream, mixing well.

To serve, cut salad into squares and pour dressing over.

Mrs. Clark Williams (Love)

FROZEN SALAD

Yield: 12 servings

1 (14-ounce) can sweetened condensed milk
1 (9-ounce) carton frozen whipped dessert topping, thawed
1 (20-ounce) can crushed pineapple, drained
1 (21-ounce) can cherry pie filling

Mix all ingredients. Place in a shallow container, preferably one with a top. Cover and freeze for several hours. Keeps for 2 weeks in the freezer.

Mrs. Harvell Slaton (Inez)

PEG'S PEACH SALAD

Yield: 10 servings

2 (3-ounce) packages peach-flavored gelatin
3 1/2 cups boiling water
4 cups chopped canned peaches
1 cup syrup from canned peaches
1/2 cup sugar
2 tablespoons flour
1 egg, slightly beaten

1 (3-ounce) package cream cheese, softened
1 cup whipping cream, whipped
1 cup chopped nuts
1/2 cup miniature marshmallows
1/2 cup shredded Cheddar cheese

Dissolve gelatin in water; chill until it begins to set. Fold in peaches; turn into a 3-quart mold. Chill until firm. In top of double boiler, combine peach syrup, sugar, flour, and egg. Cook over simmering water. Stir constantly until thickened. Cool. Fold in softened cream cheese and whipped cream. Add nuts and marshmallows. Spread on gelatin; sprinkle cheese on top. Chill several hours.

Mrs. Parnell Odom (Pat)

SEVEN CUP SALAD
Very easy!

Yield: 8 servings

1 cup grated coconut
1 cup cottage cheese
1 cup sour cream
1 cup chopped nuts

1 cup crushed pineapple
1 cup fruit cocktail, drained
1 cup miniature marshmallows

Combine all ingredients and refrigerate until ready to serve. Flavor improves in the refrigerator.

Mrs. Al Robertson (Carole)

435

RASPBERRY SALAD

Yield: 10 servings

2 (3-ounce) packages raspberry-
flavored gelatin
1 cup boiling water
Pinch salt

2 teaspoons lemon juice
2 1/2 cups applesauce
1 (10-ounce) package frozen
raspberries, partially thawed

Dissolve gelatin in boiling water. Add salt, lemon juice, and applesauce. Mash raspberries with fork or process them in blender. Add raspberries to the gelatin mixture. This will make 10 individual molds or a scant 6-cup ring mold.

NOTE: Also good with strawberries and strawberry-flavored gelatin.

Mrs. Hendree Harrison (Carol)

ROSY ROSÉ
A beautiful luncheon salad

Yield: 10 to 12 servings

2 envelopes unflavored gelatin
1/2 cup water
1/2 cup sugar
1 bottle rosé wine or pink
champagne

Rosebuds
2 cups seedless white grapes
Fresh mint

Sprinkle gelatin over 1/2 cup water in a saucepan. Place on low heat, stirring until dissolved. Add sugar. Stir until dissolved. Remove from heat. Add rosé wine (or pink champagne); refrigerate until it begins to slightly mound. Pour about 1/2 cup to 1 cup into mold and arrange washed rosebuds in inverted fashion so as to be attractive when unmolded. Chill until firm. Add grapes to gelatin mixture. Pour into mold, being careful not to disturb roses. Let set.

NOTE: Pretty unmolded with mint leaves and more grapes.

Mrs. J. Littleton Glover, Jr. (Kathryn)

FROZEN FRUIT SALAD
Good for ladies' luncheon

Yield: 8 servings

1 (8-ounce) package cream cheese
1 (3-ounce) package cream cheese
1 (15 1/2-ounce) can pineapple chunks
1 (15-ounce) can fruit cocktail

Soften cream cheese and mix well with juice from fruits. Add pineapple and fruit cocktail. Put in individual molds or 9x13-inch pan and freeze. Serve on lettuce and top with mayonnaise.

Mrs. James Wilkinson (Alice)

ASPARAGUS SALAD

Yield: 9 servings

3/4 cup sugar
1/2 cup vinegar
1 cup water
1 teaspoon salt
1 package unflavored gelatin
1/2 cup cold water
1 tablespoon minced onion
1 (8-ounce) can water chestnuts,
  drained and thinly sliced

2 tablespoons lemon juice
1 (4-ounce) jar pimiento, cut
  into strips
1 (16-ounce) can green
  asparagus, drained and cut
1 cup celery, chopped

Combine sugar, vinegar, 1 cup water, and salt. Bring to boil to dissolve sugar. Dissolve gelatin in cold water. Remove boiling mixture; add gelatin and onion and cool. Combine remaining ingredients and add to liquid. Put into greased molds and chill.

Mrs. Frank M. Arnall (Ruth)

437

QUICK AND EASY SALAD

Yield: 15 serving

1 (24-ounce) container small-curd cottage cheese
1 (9-ounce) container frozen, whipped dessert topping, thawed
1 (15 1/2-ounce) can crushed pineapple, drained

1 (11-ounce) can mandarin oranges, drained
1 (4-ounce) can coconut
1/2 cup nuts, shaved or chopped
1 (3-ounce) package orange-flavored gelatin

Mix all ingredients together. Don't add water for gelatin Store salad in refrigerator at least 4 hours before serving.

NOTE: Substitute strawberry or cherry-flavored gelatir for Christmas.

Mrs. George Neff (Ruth
Metropolis, Illinoi

YUMMY FRUIT SALAD

A pretty salad

Yield: 8 to 10 servings

2 eggs, beaten
4 tablespoons vinegar
4 tablespoons sugar
2 tablespoons butter
1 cup whipping cream, whipped

2 cups white cherries, halved (white grapes can be used)
2 cups pineapple chunks
2 fresh or canned oranges, cut up
2 cups miniature marshmallow

Put eggs in top of double boiler; add vinegar and sugar. Cooking over hot water on medium to low heat, beat constantly until thick and smooth. Remove from heat, add butter, and let cool. When cool, fold in whipped cream, fruit, and marshmallows. Refrigerate for 24 hours.

Mrs. James W. Roberts (Sue)

ASPIC SALAD
Easy!

Yield: 6 servings

(3-ounce) package lemon-
flavored gelatin
teaspoon salt
cup hot water
(8-ounce) can tomato sauce

1 1/2 tablespoons vinegar
2 tablespoons grated onion
1 cup celery, chopped
1/2 cup olives, sliced

Dissolve gelatin and salt in hot water. Add remaining ingredients. Blend. Pour into 3-cup mold or 6 individual salad
molds.

Mrs. Larry Strickland (Mary)

TOMATO ASPIC
Cayenne pepper adds zip

Yield: 12 to 14 servings

can (1 quart 14 ounces)
tomato juice
tablespoons vinegar
tablespoon grated onion
tablespoon lemon juice,
or to taste
tablespoon salt
1/4 teaspoon cayenne pepper

1 teaspoon brown sugar
3 envelopes unflavored gelatin
1/2 cup cold water
2 1/2 cups celery, finely
chopped
1 (3-ounce) bottle olives,
chopped

Season the tomato juice with vinegar, grated onion, lemon
juice, salt, pepper, and brown sugar. Soak gelatin in water for
5 minutes, then heat over boiling water. Add the melted gelatin
to the seasoned tomato juice. When mixture begins to thicken,
add celery and olives. Pour into molds.

Mrs. William F. Lee (Parky)

VEGETABLE SALAD

Yield: 16 to 20 serving

3 envelopes (2 1/2 tablespoons)
unflavored gelatin soaked
in 1/2 cup water
1 cup clear chicken broth
3/4 cup asparagus juice
1 (14 1/2-ounce) can cut
asparagus

1/2 cup stuffed olives, sliced
1 cup diced celery
1 1/2 cups tiny pickled onion
drained
1 teaspoon salt
Dash cayenne pepper

Soak gelatin in 1/2 cup water. Heat chicken broth to boil
ing. Pour hot broth over gelatin. Add all other ingredients
Pour into 1 1/2-quart mold or individual molds and refrigerat
until congealed.

Mrs. Everett Bryant (Mary

ARTICHOKE AND RICE SALAD

Yield: 6 to 8 serving

2 (7-ounce) packages paella rice
4 green onions, thinly sliced
1/2 green pepper, seeded and chopped
12 pimiento-stuffed olives, sliced
2 (6-ounce) jars marinated artichoke hearts
3/4 teaspoon curry powder
1/3 cup mayonnaise

Cook rice as directed, omitting butter. Cool in a large
bowl. Add onions, pepper, and olives. Drain artichoke hearts
reserving marinade, and cut in half. Combine the marinade
curry powder, and mayonnaise. Add the hearts to the ric
and toss with the dressing. Chill.

Mrs. B. DeWitt Storm (Kathy
Jacksonville, Florida

BACON SALAD

Lettuce
Diced onion
Salt and pepper

Cubed bacon
1/4 cup vinegar
3/4 cup water

The amounts of lettuce, onion, and bacon will vary depending on number of servings.

Cut lettuce up in a bowl, salt and pepper, and add diced onions. Fry cubed bacon until done. Mix vinegar and water and add to hot bacon grease. Pour over lettuce and onion. Serve at once.

NOTE: This is a Pennsylvania Dutch recipe of my grandmother's.

Mrs. W. E. Anderson (Dell)

CUCUMBERS IN SOUR CREAM

Yield: 5 to 6 servings

2 or 3 medium cucumbers,
    peeled and sliced
3/4 teaspoon salt
1/2 cup sour cream
2 teaspoons minced onion

1 tablespoon lemon juice
1/2 teaspoon dill weed
1/8 teaspoon salt
1/8 teaspoon pepper

Place cucumbers in a bowl. Sprinkle with salt, cover bowl, and chill for 1 hour or more. Drain and pat dry. Mix remaining ingredients together and stir into cucumber slices. Refrigerate at least another hour.

NOTE: Cucumbers can soak in salt on one day, drain on the next, and be combined with other ingredients several hours before serving to allow ample time for the flavors to mix.

Mrs. Joe W. Wray (Sara)
Atlanta, Georgia

CUCUMBERS AND ONIONS
Can be prepared a day or two in advance

Yield: 4 servings

2 cucumbers
1 onion
1/2 cup dark vinegar
1/2 cup water

Pepper to taste
1/4 teaspoon salt
1/4 cup sugar

Slice cucumbers and onion. Place in a bowl. Sprinkle a little salt over them and set aside.

Combine the remaining ingredients in a saucepan. Heat until just hot, not boiling. Pour over the cucumbers and onions. Let cool, then cover and refrigerate. If too sweet, add more vinegar; if too sour, add more water; sometimes more salt is needed.

NOTE: Delicious for a barbecue or cookout dinner. Tastes better the second or third day as the flavors blend. Will keep in the refrigerator for many days.

Mrs. Thomas G. Kerley (Florence)
Paducah, Kentucky

BEET MOLD

Yield: 6 servings

1 (16-ounce) can shoestring
  beets
1 (3-ounce) package lemon-
  flavored gelatin

3 tablespoons vinegar
1/2 teaspoon salt
1/2 cup grated cucumber
3 tablespoons grated onion

Drain beets; reserve juice. Heat juice with enough water to make 1 cup. Dissolve gelatin in hot liquid. Combine all ingredients. Pour into oiled mold and chill until firm.

Mrs. A. M. Bowen (Julia)

BEET AND NUT SALAD
For a change of pace

Yield: 8 to 10 servings

1 (20-ounce) can sliced beets, cut into strips
1 (20-ounce) can crushed pineapple
1/4 cup water
1/4 cup white vinegar

3 tablespoons lemon juice
1 tablespoon sugar
1 (3-ounce) package raspberry-flavored gelatin
1/2 cup chopped walnuts

Drain liquid from beets and pineapple. Heat with the rest of liquids and sugar. Dissolve gelatin in liquid. Stir in beets, pineapple, and walnuts. Pour into mold and chill.

Mrs. Lloyd Reynolds (Marie)

MARINATED BROCCOLI

Yield: 6 to 8 servings

1 bunch fresh broccoli or 2 (10-ounce) packages frozen broccoli
2/3 cup wine vinegar

1/3 cup salad oil
1/2 teaspoon sugar
1 to 2 teaspoons minced onion
Salt and pepper

Cook broccoli until tender but crisp and drain.

Mix rest of ingredients together in medium bowl. Add hot broccoli and stir to coat. Cover and refrigerate. Toss occasionally. Refrigerate all day or overnight. Serve chilled on fresh salad greens.

NOTE: For variation, add cooked, drained cauliflower.

Mrs. Edward Bannister (Margie)
Charleston, South Carolina

★

PEACH PICKLE SALAD
Sure to receive compliments!

Yield: 6 servings

1 (3-ounce) package orange-
  flavored gelatin
1 1/2 cups hot water
1 (29-ounce) jar peach pickles

1/2 cup peach pickle juice
1 (3-ounce) package cream
  cheese
Ground nuts

Dissolve gelatin in hot water and juice. Cool. Remove seeds from peaches. Roll cream cheese into tiny balls, then roll in nuts. Stuff whole peaches with cheese balls and place one in each individual mold. Pour gelatin mixture over each and congeal.

Mrs. Bryan B. Sargent (Ellen)

KIDNEY BEAN SALAD
For something different

Yield: 4 servings

1 (16-ounce) can kidney beans
1 small onion, finely chopped

3 to 4 sweet pickles, chopped
2 hard-boiled eggs, chopped

Mayonnaise Dressing:

2 1/2 tablespoons sugar
1 tablespoon flour
1 egg

1/3 cup vinegar
1/4 cup water

Drain and rinse kidney beans. Combine beans, onion, pickles, and eggs. Set aside.

DRESSING: Combine sugar and flour in a saucepan. Beat in one egg. Add vinegar and water. Cook over low heat until slightly thickened. Pour over bean mixture. Chill to serve.

Mrs. James W. Roberts (Sue)

CUCUMBER CREAM SALAD

Yield: 8 servings

1 (3-ounce) package
  lime-flavored gelatin
1 teaspoon salt
1 cup hot water
2 tablespoons vinegar

1 cup sour cream
1/2 cup mayonnaise
2 cups cucumbers, finely
  chopped and drained
1 teaspoon onion juice

Dissolve gelatin and salt in hot water. Add vinegar and chill until slightly thickened. Fold in sour cream, mayonnaise, cucumbers, and onion juice. Mix well and chill until firm in individual molds. Unmold on salad greens and top with ripe olives.

FIRE AND ICE

Yield: 6 servings

2 large purple onions, cut in
  1/4-inch slices
6 large, firm tomatoes, peeled
  and quartered
1 bell pepper, seeded and cut
  into strips
3/4 cup cider vinegar

1/4 cup water
1 1/2 teaspoons celery seed
1 1/2 tablespoons mustard seed
1/2 teaspoon salt
2 tablespoons sugar
1/2 teaspoon cracked black
  pepper

Place onions, tomatoes, and bell pepper in a bowl. In a saucepan, bring all other ingredients to a boil. Boil for 1 minute only. Pour over vegetables and chill. This is good with char-coaled steak.

Mrs. Walker Connally (Guilford)

ORIENTAL SALAD
A healthy salad

Yield: 6 servings

Salad:

1/2 (8 1/2-ounce) can
  water chestnuts
1/2 (16-ounce) can bean
  sprouts
1/2 (8 1/2-ounce) can
  bamboo shoots

1 bunch spinach
1 head butter lettuce
4 tablespoons sesame seeds

Dressing:

2 tablespoons soy sauce
1/2 cup oil

2 tablespoons vinegar

Slice water chestnuts. Combine with sprouts, shoots, spinach, and lettuce. Toast sesame seeds in oven. Add to salad. Add dressing. Toss.

Mrs. J. Littleton Glover, Jr. (Kathryn)

MARINATED VEGETABLE SALAD

Yield: 8 servings

1 (1-pound) can French or
  cut green beans
1 (1-pound) can English peas
1 cup vinegar
1 medium onion, diced or
  sliced
2 cups chopped celery

1/4 cup chopped, canned
  pimiento
1 bell pepper, chopped
1 1/2 cups sugar
1/2 cup low-calorie Italian
  dressing
Salt and pepper to taste

Drain beans and English peas, saving 1/2 cup English pea juice. Add juice to vinegar. Simmer beans and peas in 1/2 cup water until tender. Drain and combine with other ingredients. Refrigerate overnight.

Mrs. Ray Sewell (Edith)

TWENTY-FOUR HOUR SALAD

Yield: 12 to 15 servings

1 1/2 to 2 heads lettuce,
broken into bite-size pieces
1 1/2 cups celery, chopped
1 bell pepper, chopped or
sliced into rings
1 to 2 red onions, thinly sliced
1 (16-ounce) can English
peas, drained

1 pint mayonnaise
2 to 3 tablespoons sugar
1 (3-ounce) can grated
Parmesan cheese
Croutons
Small, cooked shrimp
(optional)

Arrange first five ingredients in a large bowl in layers. Coat
the top with mayonnaise; sprinkle on the sugar and cheese.
Cover tightly and refrigerate overnight. At serving time, toss
the salad and add croutons, shrimp, or other garnishes as
desired. This is pretty served untossed in a glass bowl.

Mrs. E. E. Gasque, Jr. (Jean)
Elloree, South Carolina

VARIATION: To salad layers, add 8 ounces grated, mild
Cheddar cheese and 13 strips bacon, fried and crumbled. Substitute 1 (10-ounce) package frozen peas, thawed and uncooked,
for the canned peas. Garnish with 1 hard-boiled egg, 1 quartered tomato, and parsley.

Mrs. Joe Snyder (Bud)
Oconomowoc, Wisconsin

VARIATION: Divide lettuce in half and use as bottom and
top layers of salad. Coat with mayonnaise and refrigerate. At
serving time, toss and add crisp, crumbled bacon and a dusting
of Parmesan cheese.

Mrs. John G. Chisolm (Martha)
Lookout Mountain, Tennessee

COLE SLAW I
Will keep for a week in the refrigerator

Yield: 12 servings

1 head of cabbage
2 onions
3/4 cup sugar
1 cup white vinegar

3/4 cup vegetable oil
2 teaspoons sugar
1 teaspoon dry mustard
1 teaspoon celery seed

Shred cabbage. Chop onions and add to cabbage. Top with 3/4 cup sugar. Boil vinegar, oil, 2 teaspoons sugar, mustard, and celery seed. Let cool. Pour this mixture over the cabbage and onions and mix. Refrigerate for at least 6 hours before serving.

Mrs. Otis Jones (Ann)

COLE SLAW II

Yield: 10 servings

2 medium cabbages, chopped
2 bell peppers, chopped
2/3 cup mayonnaise

1/4 cup vinegar
1/2 cup sugar
Salt

Mix all ingredients, adding salt to taste just before serving.

Jane Hutchinson

****

Whipping cream may be substituted for the oil in almost any vinaigrette dressing.

Half lemon juice and half lime juice substituted for vinegar in French dressing makes a tasty dressing for fruit or vegetable salads.

GARLIC SLAW
Men like this!

Yield: 12 servings

Slaw Mixture:

1 head cabbage, sliced
1/2 to 3/4 head lettuce, sliced
3 or more green onions, sliced
1 cucumber, chopped
1 small green pepper, chopped

Radishes, sliced
Celery, chopped
Tomatoes, quartered or cut smaller
1/4 to 1/2 teaspoon dehydrated garlic flakes

Dressing:

1/2 cup oil
1/4 cup dark vinegar
4 to 5 individual packets artificial sweetener or equal amount of sugar

Salt and pepper
1 teaspoon Hidden Valley Ranch dry dressing mixture

SLAW MIXTURE: Ingredients may be cut up ahead of time and put into a large bowl. The amounts may be adjusted to suit individual tastes. Cover and store in refrigerator.

DRESSING: Combine ingredients in saucepan. Heat until just hot, not boiling. Pour over slaw mixture 45 minutes before serving. Water may be added to the mixture if the vinegar taste is too strong.

Mrs. Thomas G. Kerley (Florence)
Paducah, Kentucky

❈ ❈ ❈ ❈ ❈ ❈ ❈ ❈ ❈ ❈ ❈ ❈ ❈

For crunchy cole slaw, cut cabbage in half and soak in salted ice water for an hour. Drain well then proceed with recipe.

For a quick and easy cole slaw, grate cabbage and carrots; sprinkle generously with celery salt and add enough green goddess dressing to moisten well.

"GOOD AS LONG AS IT LASTS" COLE SLAW

Yield: 6 to 8 servings

1 medium cabbage, finely
   chopped

Dressing:

2 teaspoons sugar
1 cup vinegar
1 tablespoon dry mustard

2 medium onions,
   finely chopped
7/8 cups sugar

1 tablespoon celery seed
1 tablespoon salt
2/3 cup cooking oil

Combine cabbage and onions. Sprinkle sugar over them and mix well. Combine all ingredients for dressing in a saucepan and bring to a boil. Cool 5 minutes. Pour over cabbage mixture and mix well. Refrigerate.

Mrs. Sidney Pope Jones, Sr. (Katherine)

MARINATED COLE SLAW

Yield: 6 servings

1 large cabbage
1 medium green pepper,
   finely chopped
1 small red pepper, finely
   chopped (optional)
1 medium sweet onion, finely
   chopped

1 cup sugar
1 teaspoon salt
1 teaspoon dry mustard
1 teaspoon celery seed
1 cup vinegar
2/3 cup vegetable oil

Shred cabbage. Add chopped peppers and onion and mix. Bring other ingredients to a boil and pour over cabbage. Cool to room temperature and refrigerate for 24 hours.

Mrs. John Dunn (Teresa)
Mrs. Thomas Maybank (Bee)

MOUNTAIN CABBAGE SLAW

Yield: 8 to 10 servings

3 pounds cabbage, finely
  chopped
1 bell pepper, finely chopped
2 onions, finely chopped
1 cup vinegar

1 cup vegetable oil
2 cups sugar
1 tablespoon salt
1 tablespoon celery seed

Mix vegetables in large bowl. Put remaining ingredients in saucepan. Bring to a boil. Pour over cabbage mixture. Mix well. Cool. Refrigerate.

NOTE: This will keep for 3 weeks. Best when 1 week old.

Delilia Marie Jeter
Grantville, Georgia

KRAUT SALAD
Excellent with seafood

Yield: 8 servings

1 (27-ounce) can kraut, drained
1 1/2 cups celery, finely
  chopped
3/4 cup sweet onion, finely
  chopped
1 carrot, grated

1/2 green pepper, chopped
1/2 red pepper, chopped
1 cup sugar
1/2 cup salad oil
1/2 cup white vinegar
1 teaspoon celery seed

Cut up kraut. Combine with celery, onion, carrot, and peppers. Dissolve sugar in oil and vinegar. Add celery seed. Pour over vegetables and toss. Cover and chill for several hours. Drain before serving and place on a bed of lettuce.

Mrs. Ronald Wassenberg (Betty)

CONGEALED CHICKEN SALAD
Perfect for a bridge luncheon

Yield: 12 servings

1 baking chicken
1 envelope unflavored gelatin
1/2 cup water
2 cups chopped celery
1 (8-ounce) can peas

1 pint chicken stock (or canned broth)
1 cup mayonnaise
3 hard-cooked eggs, chopped
1/2 cup pickles, chopped

Cook and cut up chicken. Dissolve gelatin in 1/2 cup water over low heat. Combine all ingredients and pour into 9x13-inch pan. Congeal. Cut into squares and serve on lettuce.

NOTE: Spiced crabapples and twice-baked potatoes are good served with this dish.

Mrs. John N. White (Martha)

CHICKEN SALAD
Colorful!

Yield: 6 servings

3 cups cooked chicken, cut into bite-size pieces
1 cup diced celery
1 1/2 cups diced, canned pineapple
1/4 cup shredded carrots
1 cup toasted almond halves

1/2 cup mayonnaise
1/4 cup sour cream
1 1/4 teaspoons curry powder
1 teaspoon lemon juice
1/2 teaspoon salt
Salad greens
Parsley

Combine chicken with celery, pineapple, carrots, and almonds. Blend mayonnaise with sour cream and seasonings; pour over chicken and toss lightly. Chill thoroughly. Arrange on salad greens and garnish with parsley.

Mrs. Parnell Odom (Pat)

CURRIED CHICKEN SALAD

chicken breasts, split
medium onion, sliced
stalk celery, cut into
  1-inch pieces
1/2 teaspoons salt
whole black peppers
bay leaf
cup mayonnaise

1/2 cup heavy cream
1/4 cup chutney
1 tablespoon curry
1 cup celery, chopped
1 small pineapple or 2 cups
  canned pineapple, drained

Boil chicken, onion, celery, salt, peppers, and bay leaf in cups water until tender. Cool chicken in broth for 1 hour. Remove from bone and refrigerate 1 to 2 hours or overnight. Mix mayonnaise, cream, chutney, curry, and celery, and add cubed chicken. Cover and refrigerate for at least 2 hours. Add pineapple. Arrange chicken salad in avocado halves and top with chutney, salted peanuts, coconut, and egg, if desired.

Mrs. Pat Yancey, Jr. (Jeane)

MEXICAN SALAD
Perfect light summer meal

Yield: 4 servings

1 pound ground beef
1 cup grated Cheddar cheese
1/2 cup chopped tomatoes
1 cup lettuce, torn into
  small pieces
1 avocado, peeled and chopped
1/2 cup chopped onion

1 (6-ounce) bag corn chips
Green pepper, chopped
  (optional)
Jalapeños (optional)
Salt and pepper to taste
Thousand Island dressing

Brown ground beef; drain well. Mix with remaining ingredients in large bowl. Toss with salad dressing.

Mrs. William Starnes (Carol)

453

DELUXE CHICKEN SALAD

Yield: 25 serving

3 (5-pound) chickens
4 onions, cut in half
2 tablespoons salt
12 eggs
2 cups pecans, chopped
2 tablespoons butter or
margarine
3 cups mayonnaise
1/2 cup wine vinegar

1 1/2 cups milk
2 teaspoons salt
1/2 teaspoon pepper
1 cup onions, chopped
2 to 6 cups sliced celery,
including tops
2 heads lettuce
Watercress

Place whole chickens in 2 inches of boiling water witl onions and 2 tablespoons salt. Cover and cook until tender 1 1/2 to 2 hours. Chill chickens in refrigerator. Meanwhile simmer eggs 20 minutes in water to cover; cool under runnin; water. Peel, chop, and refrigerate the eggs. Sauté nuts in butte until crisp; drain and cool. Remove chicken in large piece from bones, discarding skin. Mix mayonnaise, vinegar, milk salt, and pepper. Toss with chicken pieces, chopped eggs, nuts chopped onions, and celery. Chill 2 hours. Serve on a bed c lettuce; garnish with watercress.

Mrs. Joseph E. Williams, II (Nadine

❊❊❊❊❊❊❊❊❊❊❊❊❊

Mix together cottage cheese and diced tomatoes. Serve o lettuce leaves and sprinkle with paprika.

Cook and drain mixed vegetables. Marinate in bottled Italia dressing and refrigerate until ready to serve.

For an easy spring salad, combine avocado slices, orange sec tions, and a few red onion rings; toss with garlic dressing.

TACO SALAD
Good one-dish meal

Yield: 12 to 15 servings

pound ground beef
bell pepper, chopped
medium onion, chopped
teaspoon salt
head lettuce, chopped
tomatoes, diced
(1-pound) can red kidney
beans, drained

8 ounces grated Mozzarella
or Cheddar cheese
Dash of hot sauce
1 (8-ounce) bottle French
dressing
1 medium package taco chips,
crushed
Tortillas (optional)

Mix ground beef, bell pepper, onion, and salt, and cook in heavy skillet until done. Combine lettuce, tomatoes, kidney beans, cheese, hot sauce, and French dressing. Mix all ingredients except chips. Serve on tortillas and top with chips.

Helen Taylor
Michigan

SHRIMP SALAD
Good for summer luncheons

Yield: 8 to 10 servings

1/2 pounds fresh shrimp,
boiled and cut into
small pieces
(8-ounce) package macaroni
/2 pint sour cream
cup mayonnaise (not
salad dressing)
large green pepper, chopped

1 small onion, grated
3 to 4 tablespoons catsup,
or to taste
5 to 6 stalks celery, chopped
Juice of 1/2 lemon
2 to 3 teaspoons horseradish
Salt and pepper to taste

Have all ingredients prepared except macaroni. Cook and drain macaroni. Then add macaroni to rest of ingredients and mix. Refrigerate until serving.

Make day before, if possible, to allow flavors to blend.

Mrs. Donald L. Hansen (Karen)

455

BACON DRESSING

Yield: 4 serving

4 slices bacon, diced
1/2 to 1 teaspoon garlic salt
1 teaspoon oregano

1 teaspoon sesame seed
1 teaspoon worcestershire sau
Wine vinegar to taste

Put first four ingredients in small skillet. Cook over low hea
until bacon is done, stirring occasionally. Remove from heat an
cool. Add worcestershire sauce and vinegar, mixing well. Serv
over salad of lettuce, tomato, red onion rings, and kidney bean

Mrs. Wallace Mitchell (Jer

BUTTERMILK DRESSING
Keeps in refrigerator for weeks

1 quart mayonnaise
3 cups buttermilk
1 teaspoon salt
1 teaspoon coarsely ground
   black pepper

1 teaspoon Accent
1 teaspoon garlic powder
1 teaspoon onion powder

Mix ingredients well, but do not beat. Use as dip, sala
dressing, or on baked potato.

Mrs. A. J. Saraf (Beth
Palmetto, Georgi

****

French dressing concentrate: heat 1 cup vinegar and 1 peele
crushed clove of garlic to boiling. Strain, add salt, pepper, an
dry mustard; store in a corked bottle. Add this concentrate t
oil whenever dressing is needed.

CLOISTER DRESSING

Yield: Approximately 4 cups

8 eggs
1 onion
1 clove garlic
1 (2/3-ounce) can anchovies
2 cups cottonseed oil
1 teaspoon white pepper

1 teaspoon dry mustard
Salt to taste
1 cup cider vinegar
Juice of 1 lemon
1 soupspoon worcestershire
  sauce

Place the eggs in a mixing bowl and set them to warm in a sink filled with warm water. Peel and coarsely chop the onion, garlic, and anchovies. Set aside. When the eggs are warm, beat with an electric mixer at speed 1 for 5 to 6 minutes. Gradually add half the oil plus the chopped vegetables and dry seasonings. Blend well. Gradually add the remaining oil. Add vinegar, lemon juice, and worcestershire sauce. Blend, a little at a time, with the egg and oil mixture. Continue to mix at speed 1 for 10 minutes.

This dressing keeps for weeks in a sealed container in the refrigerator. Stir well before using.

Executive Chef John deBeus
The Cloister
Sea Island, Georgia

FRENCH DRESSING I
Easy and tasty

Yield: 4 cups

1 1/2 cups catsup
1 1/2 cups vinegar
1 1/2 cups sugar
1 1/2 cups cooking oil

1 medium onion, grated
1 1/2 teaspoons salt
1 1/2 tablespoons paprika

Mix ingredients; then beat 20 minutes by hand.

Miss Carrie May McElroy

457

FRENCH DRESSING II
Keeps well

Yield: 12 servings

1/3 cup red wine vinegar
1 clove garlic, halved
1 teaspoon paprika
1 teaspoon dry Di jon
mustard

Pinch sugar
1 teaspoon salt
Freshly ground pepper
Dash cayenne
2/3 cup safflower oil

Mix all ingredients together except oil. Using wire whisk, gradually beat in oil. Chill.

NOTE: Serve over mixed greens or avocado and grapefruit sections.

Mrs. Charles B. Woodroof (Amelia)

FRESH FRUIT DIP
Good even without the fruit!

Yield: 2 1/2 cups

1/2 cup sugar
1/2 teaspoon salt
Juice and grated rind of
1 orange
2 eggs, beaten
4 teaspoons cornstarch
Juice and grated rind of
1 lemon

1 cup pineapple juice
2 (3-ounce) packages
cream cheese or
1 (8-ounce) package at
room temperature

Combine all ingredients except cream cheese in the top of a double boiler. Stir and cook until thick. Cool. Whip cream cheese until fluffy and mix thoroughly with other ingredients. Chill. Use as a dip for fresh pineapple, strawberries, or melon balls.

Mrs. R. Clark Williams, Jr. (Love)

TANGY FRENCH DRESSING

Yield: Approximately 1 1/2 cups

1/2 cup sugar	1/4 cup vinegar
1/2 cup salad oil	1/2 teaspoon salt
1 tablespoon lemon juice	1/4 teaspoon pepper
1/4 cup catsup	

Shake well in jar or mix in blender. Store in refrigerator.

Mrs. Mike Spitler (Rita)

HONEY DRESSING

Versatile fruit dressing

Yield: 2 cups

2/3 cup sugar	5 tablespoons vinegar
1 teaspoon mustard	1 tablespoon lemon juice
1 teaspoon paprika	1 teaspoon grated onion
1/4 teaspoon salt	1 cup salad oil
1/3 cup strained honey	

Mix dry ingredients. Add honey, vinegar, lemon juice, and onion. Pour oil into mixture very slowly, beating constantly with electric beater. Keeps well in refrigerator.

SERVING SUGGESTIONS: Arrange slices of pineapple on lettuce; add a spoonful of cottage cheese to each and top with a peach half, rounded side up. Top with honey dressing. Or arrange pineapple on lettuce, then top with alternating slices of red apple and grapefruit sections. Top with honey dressing.

Mrs. Welborn Davis (Mary)

GLADY'S SECRET (NO LONGER) DRESSING

Yield: 4 cups

3/4 cup sugar
3 tablespoons water
1 onion, grated
1 cup vegetable oil
1/2 cup hot catsup
Juice of 1 lemon
1 teaspoon salt

1 teaspoon paprika
1 teaspoon celery salt
1 teaspoon celery, finely cut
1 teaspoon dry mustard
3 tablespoons vinegar
2 tablespoons tarragon
   vinegar

Bring 3/4 cup sugar and 3 tablespoons water to soft boil. Let cool. Mix remaining ingredients in blender or mixer. Add sugar water and mix well.

Mrs. Arthur G. Estes III (Martha Ann)
Gay, Georgia

DRESSING FOR GRAPEFRUIT
Delicious for luncheon salad

Yield: 4 cups sauce or 16 servings

1/2 cup Wesson oil
1/2 cup catsup
2 cups grated sharp cheese

1 cup chopped nuts
1/2 cup chopped green olives
1 teaspoon salt

Combine Wesson oil and catsup and beat well. Add remaining ingredients and mix thoroughly. Store in covered container in refrigerator.

NOTE: Instead of catsup, substitute chili sauce. For the nuts, use toasted pecans for a change.

Mrs. Lawrence Keith, Jr. (Jane)

Mrs. James Key (Alice)
Lakeland, Florida

MAGGIE'S MYSTERY DRESSING

Yield: 1 1/2 cups

cup salad oil
/3 cup vinegar
tablespoon sugar
1/2 teaspoons salt

1/2 teaspoon paprika
1/2 teaspoon dry mustard
1 clove garlic
1 egg white

Combine ingredients in blender and process until smooth.

BASIC MAYONNAISE
Must be refrigerated

Yield: 1 pint

egg yolks
pint Wesson oil
uice of 1 lemon

1 teaspoon salt
Dash of red pepper
1 tablespoon boiling water

Chill all ingredients, bowl, and beaters. Beat egg yolks at
iighest speed of mixer. Add chilled oil, a drop at a time, until
ipproximately 1/4 cup has been added. Alternately add a little
alt, a little lemon juice, and a little oil, until all ingredients
iave been added. Add red pepper. Add 1 tablespoon of boiling
water to keep mayonnaise from separating.

Mrs. Ella P. MacNabb

MY OWN SALAD DRESSING

Yield: 2 cups

cup mayonnaise
tablespoons cooking oil
tablespoons sweet pickle
vinegar

1/4 teaspoon prepared mustard
Dash of salt
Dash of garlic salt
3 tablespoons catsup

Mix all ingredients. Keep in refrigerator.

Mrs. Johnny Rainwater (Inez)

461

MAYONNAISE
Make in the blender!

Yield: 2 cup

2 eggs
1 1/2 teaspoons salt
1/4 teaspoon red pepper

1/2 teaspoon sugar
2 tablespoons lemon juice
1 pint cooking oil

Put all ingredients, except oil, into the blender and mix well. Slowly add the oil until thick. All the oil may not be needed.

Mrs. Otis Jones (Ann

BUTTERMILK ORANGE DRESSING
Very versatile

Yield: Approximately 2 cup

2 tablespoons flour
1 1/2 teaspoons salt
3/4 teaspoon dry mustard
2 tablespoons sugar
Few grains of cayenne pepper

1 2/3 cups buttermilk
1 egg
1/2 cup orange juice
1 tablespoon lemon juice

Combine flour, salt, dry mustard, sugar, and cayenne pepper in top of double boiler. Add 3 tablespoons of buttermilk and stir until smooth. Beat egg well and stir in remaining buttermilk and orange juice. Gradually stir into flour mixture. Cook in double boiler, stirring constantly until thickened. Remove from heat and stir in lemon juice, then chill. Serve on vegetables mixed greens, or fruit salads.

Bill Myers, Executive Che
Crowley's Brandy House & Taver
Atlanta, Georgia

RUSSIAN DRESSING
Delicious on salads or veal cutlets

Yield: 2 1/4 gallons

gallon catsup
/2 gallon honey
quart salad oil
(10-ounce) bottles
worcestershire sauce

6 onions, finely grated
1/2 cup mustard
1/8 teaspoon powdered cloves
Salt and pepper to taste

Mix all ingredients with mixer for 20 to 30 minutes.

NOTE: Nice to make and share with friends.

Mrs. Lawrence W. Keith, Jr. (Jane)

SWEET RED DRESSING
Light and zesty

Yield: 1 cup

/4 cup sugar
/4 teaspoon onion salt
/4 cup catsup
/4 cup vinegar

1/4 cup vegetable oil
1/8 teaspoon cayenne pepper
1 tablespoon chopped parsley

Combine all ingredients except parsley. Beat thoroughly. Chill. Add parsley just before serving.

Mrs. R. Daniel Freeman (Diane)
Senoia, Georgia

✳✳✳✳✳✳✳✳✳✳✳✳✳✳

'or tossed salad, sprinkle 1/2 to full amount of Good Seasons talian dressing packet over salad just before serving. Toss well nd add a little oil and vinegar mixture. Toss again and erve. Try this with other dressings, too.

UNBELIEVABLE SALAD DRESSING

Yield: Approximately 3 cup

1 cup whipping cream
1 cup sour cream
1/2 cup dry white wine
3 teaspoons sugar
3 teaspoons sweet basil

1 teaspoon liquid hot pepper
   sauce
3 teaspoons chopped parsley
1/2 cup paprika

Combine all ingredients in a large mixing bowl. Place in refrigerator overnight. Stir before serving. It is especially good with mixed salad greens.

Mrs. James Hardy (Fay

❊ ❊ ❊ ❊ ❊ ❊ ❊ ❊ ❊ ❊ ❊ ❊ ❊ ❊

Keep this seasoning mix on hand for making a quick dip Combine 1/4 cup grated Parmesan cheese, 2 tablespoons toastee sesame seeds, 2 teaspoons salt, 1 teaspoon celery seed, 1 teaspoon paprika, 1/4 teaspoon pepper, and 1/2 teaspoon garlic powder Store in a screw-top jar. For a delicious dip, combine 1 table spoon of dry mix with 1 cup of sour cream.

For a quick hors d' oeuvre, mix one 3-ounce package of crean cheese with 1 to 2 ounces bleu cheese and stir in about 1/4 cup chopped black olives. Spread on crackers and broil unti bubbly.

Mix 1 cup Parmesan cheese and 1 cup mayonnaise and keep covered in the refrigerator. Add 2 tablespoons frozen choppee onions to each cup of mix, spread on sliced French bread melba toast, or crackers, and broil until bubbly.

Sauces

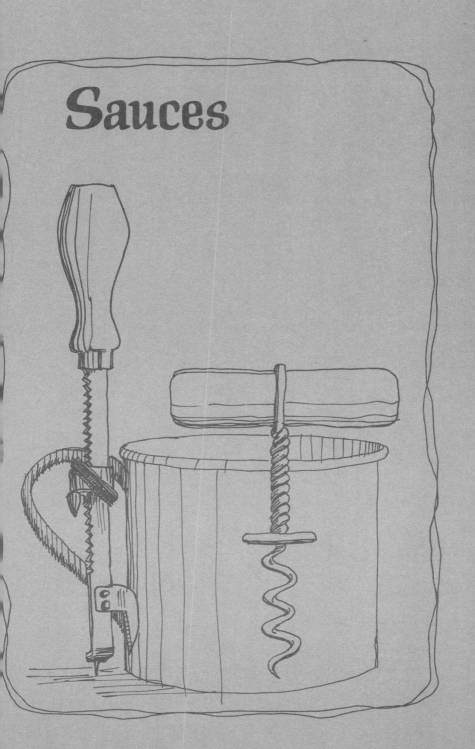

SAUCES

Sauces Chapter Design: "Perfect" Can Opener (1910), Seamless Straight Drinking Cup (1910), Cork Screw (1910)

★ **BARBECUE SAUCE I**
Great for pork chops

Yield: 2 cups

1/3 cup catsup
1/3 cup worcestershire
  sauce
1/3 cup vinegar
1 cup water
2 tablespoons butter or
  margarine

2 tablespoons lemon juice
1/2 teaspoon dry mustard
1/2 teaspoon cayenne pepper
1 teaspoon salt

Mix all ingredients in small saucepan and simmer for 30 minutes. This makes a thin sauce.

NOTE: Marinate pork chops for several hours in this sauce before grilling chops. Baste while cooking.

Mrs. Otis Jones (Ann)

★ **BARBECUE SAUCE II**
Keeps well in refrigerator

Yield: 1 quart

1/2 pound butter
1 cup vinegar
2 cups tomato catsup
4 tablespoons worcestershire
  sauce
1 tablespoon Tabasco sauce

1 tablespoon salt
3 tablespoons prepared
  mustard
Dash of red pepper
Juice of 1 lemon

Melt butter. Add vinegar, then other ingredients, and bring to a boil. Let simmer for a few minutes. Serve with cooked barbecue meat.

Mrs. James L. Fricks (Marjora)
Rising Fawn, Georgia

★   **BARBECUE SAUCE FOR CHICKEN**
May be prepared ahead of time. Freezes well.

Yield: Sauce for basting 2 to 5 chickens

For 2 chickens:

2/3 cup margarine
1/2 medium onion, finely
  chopped
2 tablespoons sugar
1 teaspoon salt
Few grains red pepper
2 tablespoons flour
2/3 cup water
2 tablespoons worcestershire
  sauce
1 1/2 tablespoons lemon juice
1/3 cup vinegar
1/2 teaspoon Tabasco sauce

For 5 chickens:

1 2/3 cups margarine
3/4 to 1 medium onion,
  finely chopped
5 tablespoons sugar
2 1/2 teaspoons salt
Few grains red pepper
5 tablespoons flour
1 2/3 cups water
5 tablespoons worcestershire
  sauce
3 1/2 tablespoons lemon juice,
  possibly more
3/4 cup vinegar
1 1/2 teaspoons Tabasco sauce

Melt margarine. Saute onions in margarine. Combine dry ingredients and add to margarine, stirring until well blended. Remove from heat. Combine remaining ingredients and gradually stir mixture. Return to heat and stir constantly until thick and smooth. Partially cook chickens on grill before beginning to baste chickens with this barbecue sauce. Cook chickens slowly and keep turning and basting.

Mrs. Thomas G. Kerley (Florence)
Paducah, Kentucky

❈ ❈ ❈ ❈ ❈ ❈ ❈ ❈ ❈ ❈ ❈ ❈ ❈

Make catsup with 1 cup tomato sauce plus 1/2 cup sugar and 2 tablespoons vinegar.

For a quick tartare sauce, combine 1 cup mayonnaise with 1 1/2 tablespoons each minced pickle, capers, parsley, and chopped onion.

ZESTY BARBECUE SAUCE

Yield: 1 quart

2 ounces chili sauce
6 ounces catsup
ounces worcestershire sauce
ounces steak sauce
small onion, chopped

1 teaspoon Tabasco sauce
Juice of 2 lemons
12 ounces water
Salt and pepper to taste

Mix all ingredients in a saucepan. Cook over medium heat bout 30 minutes or until onion is done. May be used hot as a lip, or for grilling as a brush-on sauce.

Roy G. Brady
Marietta, Georgia

BAR-B-QUE SAUCE
Great on chicken or pork

Yield: 3 1/4 cups

cups catsup
small Coca-Cola
bay leaf
tablespoon worcestershire
sauce
teaspoon mustard

2 teaspoons vinegar
1 package dry onion soup
1 teaspoon garlic powder
Salt and pepper

Mix all ingredients and simmer one hour, stirring occa-.onally. This makes a thick, delicious sauce.

Mrs. William E. Anderson (Dell)

※※※※※※※※※※※※※

Jse evaporated skim milk instead of heavy cream and cut alories by three-fourths.

469

STRAWBERRY BUTTER

Yield: 2 1/2 cups

**1 pint fresh or 1 (10-ounce) package frozen strawberries,
thawed and drained**
1/2 pound unsalted butter
**1 cup powdered sugar (if using frozen berries, use 1/2 cup
sugar)**

Put ingredients in blender in order given. Blend until smooth and creamy. If mixture appears to curdle, continue blending until smooth and creamy. Chill. Serve with toast, biscuits, muffins, pancakes, and waffles.

Mrs. Walker Connally (Guilford)

LEMON BUTTER
Serve on nut bread, banana bread, or crackers

Yield: 1/2 cup

3 egg yolks
3 tablespoons sugar
Juice of 2 lemons

1/2 stick butter
1 teaspoon all-purpose flour

In saucepan over medium heat, beat 3 egg yolks and slowly add 3 tablespoons of sugar, mixing well. Then add lemon juice and butter. Stir until butter melts. Sift flour into the mixture; mix well and cook slowly to thicken the sauce. Store in refrigerator.

Mrs. Charles Woodroof (Minerva)

****

When adding wine and milk to something (like a white sauce), add them separately and stir in between. Mixture will curdle if they are added together.

★
RED EYE GRAVY
Serve with country ham over grits or biscuits

Yield: 1/2 to 3/4 cup

Country ham drippings (after frying 2 pieces of ham)
1/2 cup water
1/2 teaspoon instant coffee or
  1 tablespoon strong perked coffee

After frying country ham, remove from skillet, leaving drippings. With heat still on, add water and stir a few minutes. Add coffee and boil a little longer. Serve hot. For more gravy, add more water and cook longer.

Mrs. Warren C. Budd (Courtenay)

★
TOMATO GRAVY
Good to serve on biscuits for breakfast

Yield: 2 to 2 1/2 cups

1/4 cup chopped onion (optional)
3 tablespoons bacon drippings
1 tablespoon flour
3 or 4 fresh tomatoes, peeled and chopped
1 cup water
Salt and pepper to taste

Saute onion in bacon fat. Add flour and brown. Add tomatoes and their juice; stir as gravy thickens. Add water, a little at a time, and cook longer until gravy is of desired consistency. Add salt and pepper to taste. This gravy is also good as a casserole sauce.

Mrs. Warren C. Budd (Courtenay)

471

GREAT GRAVY

Yield: 2 cups

1 teaspoon cornstarch
1/2 teaspoon salt
3/4 cup water to dissolve
2 beef bouillon cubes

1/4 cup brandy
1 (4-ounce) can mushrooms, drained
Juice from cooked meat

Mix all ingredients except mushrooms and meat juice in a saucepan. Cook until thick. Add mushrooms and pour in juice from roast or steaks.

Mrs. Donald L. Hansen (Karen)

CARAMEL SAUCE
A family treasure

Yield: 2 to 2 1/2 cups

1 cup sugar, browned
1/4 pound butter
1 pint milk, heated
1 1/2 cups sugar
2 heaping tablespoons all-purpose flour

1 teaspoon vanilla extract
Chopped pecans or almonds (optional)

Put sugar in a black iron skillet and stir constantly over medium-low heat until it turns a golden brown. Add butter to browned sugar and mix thoroughly. Add the hot milk and cook until the sugar is dissolved. Add 1 1/2 cups of sugar mixed with 2 heaping tablespoons flour. Add enough extra milk to make a smooth mixture. Add vanilla extract and cook until thick. May be served warm or cold. Chopped pecans or chopped almonds may be served on top of this sauce.

NOTE: This is delicious served with puddings, sponge cake, angel food cake, or ice cream, and keeps indefinitely in the refrigerator.

Mrs. Bryan Sargent (Ellen)

TANGY MEAT MARINADE

Yield: 3 1/2 cups

1/3 cup lemon juice
1 1/2 cups oil
3/4 cup soy sauce
1/4 cup worcestershire sauce
2 tablespoons dry mustard
2 1/2 teaspoons salt

1 tablespoon freshly ground
    black pepper
1/2 cup wine vinegar
2 cloves garlic, crushed
2 teaspoons fresh or dehydrated
    parsley flakes

Combine all ingredients except parsley in blender container or jar and mix thoroughly. Stir in parsley. Marinate meat overnight or several hours. The marinade saves up to 3 weeks in the refrigerator.

Mrs. James C. Elrod (Brenda)

TERIYAKI SAUCE FOR LONDON BROIL
A good marinade for almost any beef

Yield: 4 to 6 servings

1 cup soy sauce
1/2 cup salad oil
4 teaspoons ground ginger
4 teaspoons dry mustard

1/2 teaspoon dehydrated
    minced garlic or 1 garlic
    clove, minced
1 flank steak (approximately
    1 to 1 1/2 pounds)

Mix first 5 ingredients in screw-top jar and shake. Marinate meat in sauce in glass casserole dish for 4 to 6 hours. Remove from marinade and cook on grill over medium to hot coals about 4 minutes per side. Take off grill and let sit 5 minutes. Slice on the diagonal very thinly.

Leftover marinade keeps several weeks in refrigerator.

Mrs. Dennis Simpson (Jan)

BEEF MARINADE

Yield: Marinade for 4 pounds of meat

1 cup soy sauce
1/4 cup sherry
1 tablespoon powdered ginger

2 cloves garlic or equivalent
  in garlic powder
2 teaspoons sugar

Mix ingredients and pour over as much as 4 pounds of chuck roast cut into 2x4-inch strips. Marinate 3 hours at room temperature or overnight in refrigerator, turning meat occasionally. Grill meat over charcoal until pink in center.

Mrs. Carleton Jones (Julie)

BÉARNAISE SAUCE
Delicious with steak or chicken

Yield: Approximately 2 cups

4 egg yolks
Juice of 1 lemon
3 sticks butter or margarine,
  melted
Salt
Pepper
1/2 teaspoon dried tarragon
  (optional)

1 tablespoon finely chopped
  shallots
2 tablespoons capers
1/4 cup chopped parsley
1 tablespoon tarragon
  vinegar

Beat egg yolks and lemon juice in top of double boiler. Cook very slowly over low, low heat. Never allow water to boil. Add melted butter slowly, stirring constantly with a wooden spoon. Add salt and pepper to taste and dried tarragon (optional). Stir in shallots, capers, parsley, and vinegar. Keep warm in double boiler. Beat with wire whisk just before serving to re-blend all ingredients.

Mrs. Robert L. Lee (Pam)

CREAMY CHEESE SAUCE

Yield: 1 1/2 cups

4 tablespoons margarine
2 tablespoons flour
1 cup milk

1/4 teaspoon salt
1 cup mild Cheddar cheese,
chopped

Melt margarine in saucepan over medium heat. Add flour and mix with wire whisk or a fork until smooth. Add milk all at once and continue to cook, stirring constantly, until thickened. Stir in salt and cheese and continue mixing until cheese melts. Serve immediately over prepared vegetable.

Mrs. Cliff Smith (Martha)

ITALIAN SAUCE FOR MEAT
Makes a hamburger patty a gourmet treat!

Yield: 4 servings

2 tablespoons butter
2 tablespoons chopped onions
8 ounces fresh mushrooms,
sliced lengthwise
1/2 teaspoon lemon-pepper
seasoning
1/2 teaspoon salt

1/2 teaspoon minced garlic
1/2 teaspoon oregano
1/2 teaspoon Italian seasoning
1 (6-ounce) can tomato paste
3 tablespoons red wine
1/2 cup whipping cream

In butter, sauté onions until transparent, then add mushrooms and sauté. Add spices and tomato paste and blend. Add 3 tablespoons red wine and simmer 4 to 5 minutes over low heat. Right before serving, add 1/2 cup whipping cream. Serve immediately.

Mrs. Warren C. Budd (Courtenay)

NEWCOMB HOLLANDAISE
Very easy and good
Use only a wire whisk for making this recipe

Yield: About 1 cup

1 stick margarine
2/3 cup mayonnaise
2 teaspoons lemon juice

Salt
Paprika

Melt margarine over very low heat. Remove from heat. Add mayonnaise and whip with a wire whisk until well blended. Add more mayonnaise for a thicker sauce. Add lemon juice; use more than 2 teaspoons for a more tart sauce. Do not return to heat right after adding lemon juice or sauce will separate. Add salt and paprika to taste. Blend well. Serve warm or at room temperature. To reheat, warm very slowly in double boiler and beat with whisk. Delicious with artichokes, eggs benedict, etc.

NOTE: Make up a batch and keep in covered jar in refrigerator to have on hand. Will keep indefinitely.

Mrs. Robert L. Lee (Pam)

PIZZA SAUCE

Yield: Sauce for 4 pizzas

3/4 cup chopped onion
2 to 3 tablespoons cooking oil
1 (8-ounce) can tomato sauce
2 (6-ounce) cans tomato paste
1/2 cup water

1 1/2 teaspoons oregano
1 1/2 teaspoons salt
1/8 teaspoon garlic salt
3/4 teaspoon pepper

Sauté onions in oil until clear. Add all other ingredients and simmer 15 to 20 minutes.

Mrs. Russ Thomson (Pat)

WINE SAUCE
Good over meat, especially steak

Yield: Approximately 2 cups

1/2 quart beef stock
1 onion, peeled and quartered
1 bay leaf

1/4 teaspoon sage
1 tablespoon cornstarch
1/2 cup wine

Combine all ingredients except cornstarch and wine. Boil for 10 to 15 minutes. Add cornstarch, strain, and add wine.

NOTE: This recipe came from The Jamaica Inn in Ocho Rios, Jamaica.

Mrs. Thomas W. Barron (Margaret)

★ ## MUSCADINE SAUCE
Excellent with pork, fowl, or beef

Yield: 6 pints

10 pounds muscadines,
   hull and pulp
9 pounds sugar

1 pint vinegar
3 tablespoons cinnamon
1 1/2 tablespoons cloves

Wash and pulp the grapes, separating hulls and pulp. Cut hulls in half and cook until tender in water to cover, about 30 minutes. Heat pulp until seeds separate. Run through a colander to remove seeds. Mix hulls and pulp. Weigh. The mixture should weigh 10 pounds. Add other ingredients. Simmer until thick, 35 to 45 minutes. Seal in hot jars.

Mrs. Tom L. Sanders (Margaret Starr)

✻✻✻✻✻✻✻✻✻✻✻✻✻

Instant potatoes are great for thickening stews or gravies, and they won't lump.

REMOULADE SAUCE

Yield: 1 cup

1 cup mayonnaise
1 hard-boiled egg,
  finely chopped
1 teaspoon dry mustard
1 teaspoon anchovy paste

2 teaspoons capers (small size)
1 teaspoon chopped tarragon
  leaves
1 teaspoon minced garlic

Place mayonnaise in a mixing bowl and stir in hard-boiled chopped egg. Then stir in dry mustard, anchovy paste, capers tarragon leaves, and garlic. Stir until anchovy paste disappears This is used as one of the sauces served with beef fondue a Dante's Down the Hatch.

Dante's Down the Hatch
Underground Atlanta
Atlanta, Georgia

★ SAUCE FOR VENISON

Yield: 3 1/2 cups

1/2 teaspoon soy sauce
1 cup corn oil
1/2 cup vinegar
1/2 cup catsup
1/2 cup worcestershire sauce
1 teaspoon chili powder

1 cup brown sugar
Juice of 2 lemons
1 clove garlic
1 teaspoon each: salt, pepper,
  and cayenne pepper

Mix ingredients. Bring to boil and simmer 5 minutes. Use warm on meat. Refrigerate unused portion.

Mrs. Ben Wetherington (Denise)
Valdosta, Georgia

TARTARE SAUCE
Keeps well in refrigerator

Yield: Approximately 1 1/2 cups

1 cup salad dressing
3 tablespoons chopped
  sweet pickle
1 teaspoon pickle juice
1 tablespoon chopped parsley

1 tablespoon chopped capers
2 tablespoons chopped stuffed
  olives
1 teaspoon grated onion

Mix all ingredients. Chill.

Mrs. John P. Woods, Jr. (Elizabeth)

QUICK AND EASY LEMON-BUTTER SAUCE
Good with seafood

Yield: 3/4 cup

1/2 cup butter or margarine
Juice of 1 lemon

1/2 teaspoon salt
Dash Tabasco sauce

In small bowl, cook butter in microwave oven 45 seconds or until melted; stir in remaining ingredients. Serve hot.

Mrs. Dan B. Umbach (Marie)

WHIPPED BUTTER
Money-saver idea (good, too!)

Yield: 2 cups

1/2 pound butter
1/2 pound margarine
1/4 cup sour cream

Blend butter and margarine at medium speed with electric mixer. Beat in sour cream 1 tablespoon at a time until smooth and fluffy.

Mrs. James W. Roberts (Sue)

★ TOMATO TOPPER

A very sweet Southern condiment

Yield: Approximately 2 1/2 cups

1 (16-ounce) can whole
  tomatoes
1 small onion, chopped
1 hot or bell pepper, chopped

1 cup sugar (or less)
1/4 teaspoon salt
Corn starch (if needed)

In a saucepan over medium heat, cook the tomatoes, onion, and pepper until onion and pepper are tender. Add sugar; this makes a very sweet sauce, so add less sugar if preferred. Cook until thick. Corn starch may be added to thicken if sauce does not become thick enough. Delicious topping for black-eyed peas, butter beans, or roast beef.

Mrs. Henry Reese (Alice)

VEGETABLE SAUCE

Yield: 1 1/2 cups

1/2 cup sour cream
1/3 cup chopped parsley
2 1/2 tablespoons tarragon
  wine vinegar
2 tablespoons anchovy paste
1 teaspoon worcestershire sauce

1 teaspoon dry mustard
1 clove garlic, mashed
1/2 teaspoon salt
1 cup mayonnaise
3 tablespoons chopped chives

Mix all ingredients until well blended. Serve over favorite vegetables.

NOTE: Sauce can be used as a dip for raw vegetables.

Mrs. Mike Livingston (Barbara)
Paducah, Kentucky

Soups

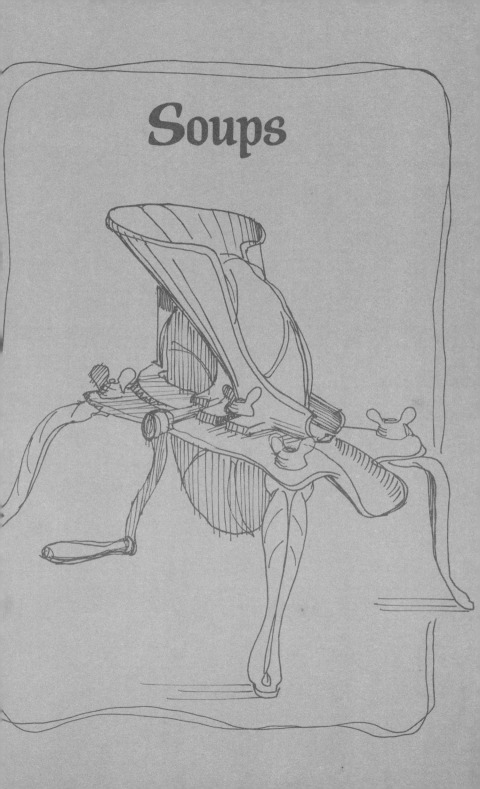

SOUPS

Soups Chapter Design: Cast-Iron Cherry Stoner (1863)

★   **BLACK BEAN SOUP**

4 cups black beans
5 quarts cold water
3 stalks celery, finely chopped
3 large onions, finely chopped
1/2 cup butter
2 1/2 tablespoons flour
1/2 cup parsley, finely chopped
Rind and bone of cooked, smoked ham
3 leeks, thinly sliced
4 bay leaves
1 tablespoon salt
1/2 teaspoon pepper, freshly ground
1 cup dry Madeira
2 hard-cooked eggs, finely chopped
Lemon slices to garnish

Pick over and wash beans (usually available at Latin groceries). Soak overnight in cold water to cover, then drain. Add 5 quarts cold water and cook the beans over low heat for 1 1/2 hours. In a soup kettle over low heat, sauté the celery and onions in butter for about 8 minutes, or until tender. Blend in flour and parsley and cook this mixture, stirring for 1 minute. Gradually stir in the beans and their liquid. Add the smoked ham rind and bone, leeks, bay leaves, salt, and pepper. Simmer the soup for 4 hours.

Remove and discard the ham bone, rind, and bay leaves. Force the beans through a sieve. Combine puréed beans and their broth and add Madeira. Heat the soup, remove from stove, and stir in the finely chopped eggs. Float a thin slice of lemon on each serving.

The Coach and Six Restaurant
Atlanta, Georgia

✳ ✳ ✳ ✳ ✳ ✳ ✳ ✳ ✳ ✳ ✳ ✳ ✳

Save the liquid from canned asparagus. Add an equal quantity of milk, butter, and flour (as required in white sauce) to make a delicious cream of asparagus soup.

Save the liquid from a pot of greens cooked with side meat to serve as a very Southern soup, "pot likker." Many Southerners add crumbled corn bread for a heartier dish.

GARBANZO BEAN SOUP

Yield: 8 servings

12 ounces garbanzo beans
2 small soup bones
1 ham bone
1/2 pound hot, large, link
  sausage, sliced
8 medium potatoes, diced
1 medium bell pepper, diced

2 medium onions, diced
1 tablespoon olive oil
1/3 cup tomato sauce
4 slices bacon
1/2 teaspoon salt
1/8 teaspoon pepper
1 garlic clove

Soak beans overnight. Rinse and drain. Heat 4 1/2 quarts of water in a large pot. Add all ingredients, cover, and cook for 3 hours. Check taste; add more salt or pepper if desired. Cook 1 additional hour. If necessary, uncover to thicken sauce. Remove bones before serving.

NOTE: Beans may be reduced to 8 ounces, if desired.

Mrs. Dan Umbach (Marie)

★ OKRA SOUP

Yield: 8 servings

2 pounds beef chuck, diced
1/4 pound margarine
2 (16-ounce) cans tomatoes
1 1/2 pounds fresh or
  frozen okra

2 cups lima beans, cooked
1 pound cured ham, cooked
  and diced
Salt and pepper
Toasted white bread

In deep kettle, brown beef chuck in margarine. Add tomatoes and okra. Cover with boiling water and simmer, covered, over medium heat for 1 hour. Then add an additional 4 cups boiling water. Bring to boil and simmer, stirring frequently. Skim soup as it boils. Cook until okra and tomatoes are done. Add cooked lima beans and ham. Salt and pepper to taste. Cut toasted bread into squares and float on top of each serving.

Mrs. Dan Umbach (Marie)

★
BRUNSWICK STEW I
A very thick meat stew that is delicious with barbecue; freezes well

Yield: 6 to 8 quarts

1 large hen	2 sticks butter
2 pounds boneless stew beef	Salt and red pepper to taste
1 small pork loin roast	1 cup worcestershire sauce
3 (16-ounce) cans of tomatoes	2 cups catsup
2 large onions, finely chopped	1 (28-ounce) can cream corn

Place hen, stew beef, and loin roast in 4-gallon container with salted water and boil slowly, covered, until meat is very tender. Remove all meat from bone and grind, keeping chicken separate. Place ground beef and pork in broth. Add tomatoes, chopped onions, about 2 sticks butter, salt, red pepper, approximately 1 cup worcestershire sauce, and about 2 cups catsup. This varies because of weight of meat. Cook until tomatoes disappear. Add chicken and corn and cook for 15 minutes more over low heat, stirring often.

NOTE: Flavor improves second day. Seasoning never seems right first day.

Mrs. Lawrence Keith, Jr. (Jane)

❈ ❈ ❈ ❈ ❈ ❈ ❈ ❈ ❈ ❈ ❈ ❈ ❈

For a elegant but easy first course, heat a can of consomme with a little sherry and some freshly ground pepper. Serve piping hot with a dollop of sour cream.

★ ## BRUNSWICK STEW II

Yield: 8 to 10 servings

2 pounds pork
1 pound beef
2 quarts water
1 (16-ounce) can corn
1 (16-ounce) can tomatoes
1 large onion
1 tablespoon worcestershire
sauce

2 tablespoons margarine
1/2 teaspoon red pepper
1/2 cup vinegar
1 (14-ounce) bottle catsup
2 small Irish potatoes,
chipped (optional)

Boil meats in 2 quarts of water until tender; cut up finely or grind. Add 1 quart of the water in which meats were cooked. Grind corn, onion, and tomatoes and add to meat. Add remaining ingredients and boil, covered, for 1 1/2 hours.

Mrs. Leroy Mann (Bertha)

★ ## BRUNSWICK STEW III
Freezes well

Yield: 3 gallons

3 pounds lean pork
1 hen
3 pounds ground beef
1 gallon tomatoes, fresh
or canned
1 gallon corn, fresh or canned
2 onions, chopped

1/2 (10-ounce) bottle
worcestershire sauce
Salt to taste
1/2 ounce Tabasco, or to taste
1/2 gallon catsup
3 cups chicken broth,
approximately

Cook pork and chicken; bone. Grind all meat and vegetables together. Combine all ingredients except seasonings and bring to a boil. Reduce heat and simmer stew to cook ground beef, about 30 to 45 minutes. Add seasonings. The amount of chicken broth may be adjusted to obtain the right consistency for a stew.

Mrs. Phillip Hammock (Bobbie)

★ ## CHICKEN CORN SOUP

Yield: 20 servings

1 (6-pound) hen	12 ears corn
Salt and pepper to taste	1/2 stick margarine
1 cup rice	Milk

Cook chicken in 2 to 3 quarts water with salt and pepper added. When tender, remove chicken from liquid, debone, and run through food chopper. Cook rice in chicken stock for ten minutes. Add ground chicken to rice and bring to boil. Add corn which has been prepared as follows: barely cut top off corn kernels and scrape the remainder from cob. Stir constantly over low heat until corn is tender, approximately 10 minutes. Add margarine and more water if needed.

If entire recipe is needed for one meal, add milk as desired for right consistency and serve with crackers or toast.

NOTE: Soup can be frozen in 2 1/2 cup containers and prepared for four people by adjusting milk.

Mrs. Fred R. Smyre (Martha)
Hickory, North Carolina

❊ ❊ ❊ ❊ ❊ ❊ ❊ ❊ ❊ ❊ ❊ ❊ ❊

Use leftover soup to make a delicious sauce or gravy for vegetables or meat. Simply remove any bones and process the soup in a blender for a few minutes.

Add a little instant coffee powder when making gravy to give it a rich brown color and a deeper flavor.

COOK'S CORNER APPLE SOUP
Very easy

Yield: 6 to 8 servings

2 (10 1/2-ounce) cans beef
   bouillon or consommé
1 onion, quartered

1 apple, quartered
2 tablespoons Scotch whiskey
1/2 pint light cream

Simmer bouillon with quartered onion and apple for 20 minutes. Strain and add other ingredients. Serve either very hot or well chilled.

Cook's Corner
Atlanta, Georgia

CHILI I
Good and easy

Yield: 6 servings

2 tablespoons bacon drippings
1 large onion
1 pound ground beef
2 cups tomatoes or tomato
   juice
1 (6-ounce) can tomato paste
1 teaspoon salt
1 teaspoon sugar
1/8 teaspoon red pepper

1/8 teaspoon paprika
1/8 teaspoon garlic salt
3/4 to 1 tablespoon chili
   powder (dissolved in a little
   cold water)
1 bay leaf
1 (16-ounce) can kidney
   beans, drained

Chop onion and brown slightly in bacon drippings. Add ground beef and cook until browned. Add other ingredients, except kidney beans, cover and simmer for one hour, stirring occasionally. Add a little water if mixture gets too thick. Add kidney beans and heat.

Mrs. Harvell Slaton (Inez)

CHILI II

Freezing will enhance the flavor!

Yield: 3 quarts

3 pounds ground beef
1/2 cup onions, diced
1 tablespoon olive oil
1/4 pound butter
1 teaspoon salt
1 tablespoon seasoned salt
1 tablespoon garlic salt or 1 clove garlic
2 (16-ounce) cans kidney beans
1/4 cup catsup
1 (8-ounce) can mushrooms, chopped
1 (8-ounce) can tomato sauce
1 (6-ounce) can tomato paste
1 (16-ounce) can tomatoes
1 (8-ounce) can tomato and herbs
3 large Jalapeno peppers, seeded and chopped
1 teaspoon chili powder
1 tablespoon Tabasco sauce

Brown meat and onions in olive oil. Drain. Add butter, salts, and garlic. Mix thoroughly. Add remaining ingredients. Simmer for 2 hours, covered, over low heat. Stir often.

Mrs. Gayle Golden
Valdosta, Georgia

****

When adding flour to a hot liquid for thickening purposes, first blend the flour with several tablespoons of cold water and mix to a thin paste. There will be no lumps.

Instant "bearnaise" sauce: combine 1 cup mayonnaise with 3 tablespoons butter, 2 tablespoons tarragon vinegar, and a good pinch of tarragon in a small saucepan. Heat, stirring constantly with a whisk, until smooth. Do not allow to boil or mixture will separate.

DEAN MERCER'S CHILI
Warms your insides!

Yield: 20 servings

4 tablespoons olive or
vegetable oil
2 large onions, chopped
3 bell peppers, chopped
1 pound ground beef
2 tablespoons chili powder,
or to taste
1 tablespoon crushed red pepper,
or to taste

1 tablespoon cayenne, or to
taste
1 tablespoon salt
1/2 teaspoon black pepper
1 (16-ounce) can tomatoes
2 (16-ounce) cans kidney
beans

Combine the oil, onions, and bell peppers in a deep pot. Cook slowly for 20 minutes, covered. Add the ground beef and brown slowly for 30 minutes. Add the rest of the ingredients and cook slowly for 12 to 24 hours. This chili is very spicy hot. Adjust seasonings if a milder chili is desired. The longer this is cooked, the better it will be!

NOTE: This recipe is from the Dean of Men at East Tennessee State University. It may also be used as a dip after the chili has cooked down.

Mrs. Brantley Kemp (Brenda)

✳✳✳✳✳✳✳✳✳✳✳✳✳

Use fine, dry bread crumbs to thicken cream sauces for casseroles or a la king dishes. Use them for a toasted flavor in a sauce.

For a tasty topper for broiled fish, hot vegetables, toasted bread, and baked potatoes: combine 3/4 pound shredded Gruyere cheese, 1/2 cup sour cream, and 1 tablespoon milk. Heat until cheese melts.

HOMEMADE CHILI CON CARNE WITH BEANS
Freezes well

Yield: 9 to 14 servings

5 tablespoons corn oil
1 cup onions, coarsely chopped
3 cloves garlic, finely chopped
1/2 cup green pepper, diced
2 pounds ground beef, lean
  and coarsely ground
4 cups fresh tomatoes, peeled
  and quartered
4 cups kidney beans,
  freshly cooked

1 teaspoon salt
4 tablespoons chili powder
1 cup boiling water
1 tablespoon wine vinegar
  (optional)
1 tablespoon brown sugar
  (optional)

Heat corn oil in Dutch oven or large cast iron frying pan. Sauté onions, garlic, and green pepper until onions become translucent. Add ground beef and brown. Add remaining ingredients except water. Cover and simmer for at least one hour. Add the water, plus additional water for a thinner consistency. For a more authentic Mexican taste, add a tablespoon each of wine vinegar and brown sugar. And, of course, vary the salt and spice to taste. Overnight storage and reheating will blend and ripen the flavor. Will yield nine 8-ounce servings or fourteen 5-ounce servings.

Mary Parks

JAR FUNNEL (1897)

★

CRAB BISQUE

Yield: 6 to 8 ample servings
10 to 12 small servings

2 (10 3/4-ounce) cans
  cream of asparagus soup
2 (10 3/4-ounce) cans
  cream of mushroom soup
3 cups milk
2 cups light cream

2 cups crabmeat
1/2 cup cooking sherry
1/2 pint whipping cream,
  whipped and salted lightly
  to taste (optional)
Minced chives for garnish

Combine soups, milk, and cream; stir in crabmeat. Cook over low heat until almost boiling, stirring often. Add sherry just before serving. Top with fluffs of salted whipped cream and sprinkle with minced chives.

Mrs. Jim Leverett (Mayme)
Greenville, Georgia

★

BUDD'S CATFISH STEW

Yield: 8 servings

5 large potatoes, peeled
  and sliced
1 large catfish (8 pounds or
  more), cleaned and
  cut in half

3 large onions, sliced
1 cup water
Salt and pepper
1 teaspoon Tabasco sauce

In a big iron pot, arrange all ingredients in layers beginning with potatoes. Combine water, salt, pepper, and Tabasco sauce; pour over all. Cook over low heat about 1 1/2 hours.

Warren C. Budd

CAPTAIN DAN'S FISH SOUP

Yield: 18 servings

boiled potatoes, diced	2 large onions, diced
(10 3/4-ounce) cans	2 1/2 pounds scallops
Manhattan-style clam	2 1/2 pounds fish fillets
chowder	2 1/2 pounds shrimp, boiled
(16-ounce) cans stewed	16 ounces lobster
tomatoes	2 teaspoons thyme
(24-ounce) package frozen	2 teaspoons black pepper
corn	2 teaspoons Tabasco sauce
(18-ounce) package frozen	2 teaspoons salt
okra	

In large pot, place cooked, diced potatoes, canned soup, and tomatoes. In separate pot cook corn and okra according to package directions. When okra and corn are cooked, drain and add to soup pot. Add remaining ingredients: onions, scallops, fish, shrimp, lobster, thyme, pepper, Tabasco sauce, and salt. Simmer for 2 to 3 hours. Do not let boil.

Dan B. Umbach

CREAM OF PEANUT SOUP

Yield: 4 cups

cup boiled peanuts, shelled	1/4 cup raw rice
cups chicken stock	1 tablespoon sherry

Purée peanuts with 1/2 cup stock. Cook rice until soft; purée with 1/2 cup stock. Combine peanuts and rice. Add remaining 2 cups of stock and sherry. Season to taste. Serve hot.

Mrs. Frank Conner (Vi)

NEW ENGLAND CLAM CHOWDER

Yield: 8 to 10 serving

1/4 pound salt pork or
   4 slices
6 cups diced potatoes
1 large bunch green onions,
   chopped
4 (6 1/2-ounce) cans
   minced clams
6 cups milk
4 tablespoons butter

1 teaspoon salt (optional)
1/4 teaspoon garlic powder
   or garlic salt
Dash pepper
Dash onion salt
6 tablespoons flour
1 1/2 cups milk

Fry salt pork strips until crisp. Remove salt pork and ad
potatoes and onions to fat. Add juice from clams to potato
and onions. Add 1/2 cup water or just enough to almos
cover potatoes. Cover and simmer 20 to 30 minutes, or unt
potatoes are cooked.

Add clams, 6 cups milk, butter, salt, garlic, pepper, an
onion salt. Mix thoroughly.

Mix 6 tablespoons flour and 1 1/2 cups milk. Blend int
chowder, and bring to a boil to thicken.

Mrs. Joe P. MacNabb (Patty

★   **OYSTER STEW**

Yield: 4 to 6 serving

1/4 stick butter or
   margarine
1 tablespoon flour

1 quart milk
1 pint oysters
Salt and pepper to taste

In saucepan over medium heat, melt margarine and ad
flour; cook until bubbly. Gradually add milk and stir unti
mixture thickens; add more milk if mixture becomes too thick
Add oysters and seasonings and simmer 10 minutes.

Mrs. H. C. Tysinger (Judy

SEAFOOD GUMBO I
Freezes well

Yield: 12 servings

crabs or 1 pound crabmeat or
1 pound crab fingers
pounds shrimp
large onions
pods garlic
stalks celery
pounds okra
large green pepper
heaping tablespoons
shortening
heaping tablespoon flour

1 (8-ounce) can tomato sauce
1 pound ham, chopped
1 pound veal, chopped
Salt, pepper, creole seasoning
to taste
1 teaspoon Accent
1/2 teaspoon thyme
1 pint oysters
1/2 pound picked crabmeat
(optional)

Shell and clean crabs and shrimp. Cut up onion, garlic, celery, okra, and pepper. Set aside. Melt shortening in large, heavy pot. Brown flour to a light brown. Add the cut up vegetables. Fry until tender and the okra is not slimy. Stir in tomato sauce. Cook for 15 minutes. Add 2 quarts water, then add crabs and shrimp. Also add ham and veal which have been browned. Add salt, pepper, seasonings, and simmer one hour. Add oysters about 20 minutes before serving. One half pound of picked crabmeat is a delicious addition to this gumbo — add when oysters are added. Serve over mounds of hot rice.

NOTE: Serve with garlic bread and green salad.

Mrs. Gerald Wessler (Margaret)
Gulfport, Mississippi

* * * * * * * * * * * * * *

Freezing Ease: Freeze liquids such as soup in coffee cans lined with plastic bags. When the liquid is frozen, remove the bag from the can. The liquid stores easily and the can is free for use.

★ **SEAFOOD GUMBO II**

Yield: 8 servings

Roux:

3 tablespoons cooking oil   3 tablespoons flour

Gumbo:

1 stick margarine
1 cup chopped onion
1/2 cup chopped celery
1/2 cup chopped green bell
  pepper
4 cloves garlic, minced
1 (14 1/2-ounce) can chopped
  okra, drained

3 quarts water
1 tablespoon worcestershire
  sauce
2 (6 1/2-ounce) cans crabmeat
1/2 pint oysters
1 (16-ounce) can whole
  tomatoes
1/2 cup green onion tops

ROUX: Heat oil in frying pan. Gradually add flour, stirring constantly. Reduce heat and cook until roux is dark brown being careful not to burn. Remove from heat and set aside

GUMBO: Melt margarine in large aluminum pot. Add onions, celery, green pepper, garlic and drained okra; sauté for 10 minutes. Add roux, water, and worcestershire sauce to mixture. Cook for one hour. Add other ingredients except onion tops and cook for another hour. Serve over cooked rice garnished with onion tops.

Mrs. John M. Stuckey (Sandy)

※ ※ ※ ※ ※ ※ ※ ※ ※ ※ ※ ※ ※ ※

Minced parsley and onion added to cream soups improve their flavor. Dried celery leaves may also be used to flavor soups.

To accent the flavor of navy bean soup, rub the bottom of the soup bowl with a sliced whole garlic clove.

★

$100.00 SHRIMP GUMBO

Freezes well if there's any left!

Yield: 8 servings

2 pounds fresh shrimp
1/2 teaspoon crab boil
2 teaspoons bacon drippings
Small amount of flour
1 large onion, chopped
1 cup cooked ham, chopped
2 pounds okra, steamed
  and chopped
3 stalks celery, chopped
1/8 teaspoon parsley

1 (1-pound) can tomatoes
1 large bell pepper, chopped
1 pound crabmeat
1 clove garlic
1 tablespoon salt
1/2 teaspoon pepper
1/4 teaspoon ground thyme
1/4 teaspoon ground oregano
2 bay leaves

Cover washed shrimp with water and crab boil. Cook until tender. Save water. Peel shrimp. Make a roux with bacon drippings and flour. Add onions and about 1/2 cup plain water. Cook until mixture is transparent. Add ham and okra and cook for 20 minutes over medium heat, stirring constantly. Add shrimp water (3 to 4 cups), celery, parsley, tomatoes, bell pepper, crabmeat, garlic, salt, and pepper. Simmer for one hour. Add thyme, oregano, bay leaves, and shrimp. Cook for 20 minutes. Serve over rice.

Mrs. J. P. Lott (Douglass)

❋ ❋ ❋ ❋ ❋ ❋ ❋ ❋ ❋ ❋ ❋ ❋ ❋

Keep a 2-4 cup container in the freezer. Accumulate any small portions of left-over meats, vegetables, rice, stock, etc. This makes a great base for soup. Add canned or fresh tomatoes and stew all together. If soup needs additional seasoning, use bouillon cubes. Add at least one fresh vegetable for a really good tasting soup.

FRUIT SOUP
Make ahead

Yield: 5 or 6 servings

2 tablespoons quick-cooking
tapioca
1 1/2 cups water
1 tablespoon sugar
Dash salt

1/2 cup frozen orange juice
concentrate
2 1/2 cups of any diced fresh
fruit (peaches, cherries,
bananas, apples, melon balls
or frozen fruit

Mix tapioca and water in saucepan; bring to boil, stirring constantly. Remove from heat. Add sugar, salt, and concentrated orange juice; blend. Cool, stirring once after 15 to 20 minutes. Cover and chill. Before serving, add fruits. If thinner soup is desired, add more juice or less fruit.

NOTE: For prettiest results, choose small, colorful fruits. Berries and melon balls are good.

Mrs. John F. Anderson, Jr. (Nancy)
Dallas, Texas

COLD WEATHER SOUP
Men love it!

Yield: 4 servings

1 (10-ounce) package frozen
mixed vegetables
1/2 pound ground beef
1 (1-pound) can tomatoes

1 medium potato, diced
1 onion, diced
Salt and pepper to taste
Water

Begin cooking vegetables according to package directions. Add meat and other ingredients immediately. Cook until potatoes are done and onions tender. Add salt and pepper to taste. Add water to desired thickness.

Mrs. Brad Sears (Carolyn)

★　　　　OKRA STEW WITH CHICKEN

Yield: 6 to 8 servings

2 pounds fresh okra,
　stemmed, or
2 (10-ounce) packages
　frozen whole okra
1 chicken, cut into serving
　pieces
3 tablespoons oil or
　margarine

1/2 teaspoon pepper
1 1/4 teaspoons salt
1 medium onion
1 (8-ounce) can tomato sauce
1 cup water (or more)
1 (1 pound) can
　whole tomatoes

Wash okra, drain, and dry in towel. Place in baking pan with a little oil and broil on each side until light, golden brown. Set aside.

Saute chicken with salt, pepper, and onion in oil or margarine until brown. Add tomato sauce, tomatoes, and water, and simmer until chicken is done. Add okra. Simmer about fifteen minutes longer. Serve with rice.

Mayme B. Mansour

POTATO ALMOND SOUP

Yield: 4 to 6 servings

1 (10 3/4-ounce) can cream of potato soup
1 1/2 soup cans half and half cream
1/2 cup toasted, slivered almonds
1 (10 3/4-ounce) can chicken broth
Dash of salt and pepper
Chives or parsley for garnish

Process first 3 ingredients in blender on high speed until smooth. Pour into saucepan. Add chicken broth, salt, and pepper. Cook over medium heat until soup is very hot, stirring occasionally. Garnish with chives or parsley.

Mrs. R. O. Jones (Evelyn)

499

MINESTRONE A LA MILANESE

A complete meal with hot crusty bread and a crisp green salad; freezes well

Yield: Approximately 6 quarts

1/4 cup dried kidney or
  navy beans
2 quarts soup stock or canned
  bouillon or consomme
1/4 pound salt pork or
  bacon, chopped
1 or 2 sticks celery, chopped
  or sliced
1 quart shredded cabbage
2 cups chopped carrots
1 cup turnips or rutabaga
1 (1-pound) can tomatoes

2 onions sliced
Parsnips—put in whole then
  removed, or cut up and
  left in
1/4 cup minced parsley
1 clove garlic
Dash of powdered sage
Salt and pepper to taste
Worcestershire sauce
  (optional)
1/4 cup uncooked elbow
  macaroni
2 cups fresh spinach

Soak dried beans in water overnight; drain. Put soup stock in large kettle and bring to boiling point. Add all of the ingredients except the macaroni and spinach. Cover and simmer until vegetables are tender but not overcooked. Cook macaroni. Add macaroni and spinach to soup for very short time. Serve with Parmesan cheese on top. The minestrone should be thick.

Dean Rusk
Athens, Georgia

Mr. Rusk is a former U.S. Secretary of State.

❄❄❄❄❄❄❄❄❄❄❄❄❄

To remove grease from top of soup, chili, etc., put a piece of ice in a small piece of cheese cloth. Run it around the top of the soup. Grease will cling to it.

Add a slice of lemon to each bowl of black bean soup. It will sharpen the soup's flavor and make a more tasty looking bowl of soup.

STEAK SOUP
This super special soup is not only elegant, but economical.

Yield: Approximately 4 quarts

pound round steak, finely
  chopped
medium onion, finely chopped
large carrot, finely chopped
sticks celery, finely chopped
/2 pound butter
cup flour

3 1/2 cups canned, diced
  tomatoes
3 quarts beef stock
Salt and pepper to taste
1 1/2 tablespoons Accent
1 tablespoon worcestershire
  sauce
1 1/2 cups half and half cream

Braise meat and onions in large pot. Add rest of vegetables, utter, and flour. Mix well and cook for 10 minutes. Add omatoes, beef stock, and all spices; simmer for about 1 hour, tirring frequently. Add cream the last 5 minutes before removing from heat. If mixture is too thick, add more beef stock and djust seasoning. This soup freezes well.

NOTE: This famous soup comes from the Pam Pam Resaurant in San Francisco.

Alice Fleming
Atlanta, Georgia

DESK TOP SPICE BOX (1883)

BEEF AND BARLEY SOUP
Excellent reheated

Yield: 6 serving

2 cups canned tomatoes
3/4 pound boneless chuck,
   cut into 1-inch cubes
1 1/2 to 2 teaspoons salt
1/4 teaspoon pepper
Celery tops from 1/2 bunch
   of celery
2 sprigs parsley
1/4 cup regular barley

1 cup tomato juice
1 (10-ounce) package frozen
   cut green beans
1/2 cup chopped rutabaga
1 1/2 cups coarsely chopped
   cabbage
1/2 cup sliced carrots
1/2 cup sliced celery
1/2 cup thinly sliced onion

Drain tomatoes and add enough water to liquid to make 2 quarts. Place liquid in large kettle with chuck, salt, pepper, celery tops, and parsley. Cover and cook slowly for 1 hour Add the barley; cook 1 hour longer. Remove and discard celery tops and parsley. Add remaining ingredients, including reserved tomatoes. Bring to a boil. Reduce heat and cook about 45 minutes.

NOTE: Soup can be frozen in individual portions and heated before putting into insulated container for school lunches

Ann G. Parrot

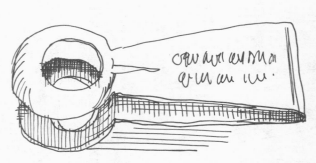

`BOSTON HULLER' STRAWBERRY HULLER (1894)

KNIFE AND FORK SOUP

(11 1/2-ounce) cans
condensed bean soup
(16-ounce) can tomatoes
package Southern-style hash
brown potatoes or
1 to 2 medium potatoes,
diced

2 cups water
1 cup sliced carrots
1 cup sliced celery
1/2 teaspoon chili powder
1/2 teaspoon salt
1 (12-ounce) smoked sausage,
cut into small slices

Stir together soups, tomatoes, potatoes, and water in Dutch
ven. Add carrots, celery, chili powder, and salt. Cover and
ring to a boil. Reduce heat and simmer 20 minutes stirring
ccasionally. Add sausage and continue cooking slowly for 40
ɔ 45 minutes, or until vegetables are tender. Stir occasionally.

Ann G. Parrott

STORM SOUP

Yield: 6 servings

cups chicken broth, or
bouillon cubes and water
/3 cup dried green split peas
medium onion, chopped
cups chopped, cooked ham

1/2 teaspoon salt
1/4 teaspoon freshly ground
pepper
3 medium Idaho potatoes, diced
3 medium carrots, sliced

Combine first six ingredients in heavy kettle. Place over
igh heat and boil 5 minutes. Cover and simmer for 1 hour,
tirring occasionally. Add potatoes and carrots and continue
ɔ simmer for 20 minutes or until vegetables are done.

Mrs. Wright Lipford (Faye)
Peachtree City, Georgia

503

VEGETABLE SOUP WITH BEEF
Perfect on a cold night

Yield: 8 to 12 serving

1 pound lean ground beef
4 cups water
1 (16-ounce) package frozen soup mix
1 (10-ounce) package frozen cut okra
1 medium potato, diced
2 small or 1 large yellow squash, thinly sliced
3 tablespoons dry onion soup mix
1 (28-ounce) can whole tomatoes, mashed
1 (15-ounce) can herb-seasoned tomato sauce
Salt and pepper to taste

Brown ground beef and drain (set aside). In a large soup
pot place 4 cups water, soup mix, cut okra, diced potatoes
sliced squash, and onion soup mix. Bring to a boil. Add ground
beef, mashed tomatoes, herb-seasoned tomato sauce, salt, and
pepper to taste. Return to boil and simmer over low heat fo
2 hours. Turn off 30 minutes before ready to serve to allow
soup to cool.

NOTE: This soup may be frozen in small quantities for
lunches.

Mrs. Fred Gilbert (

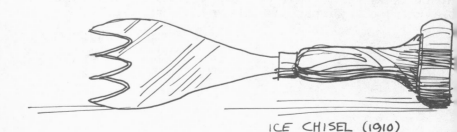

ICE CHISEL (1910)

Vegetables

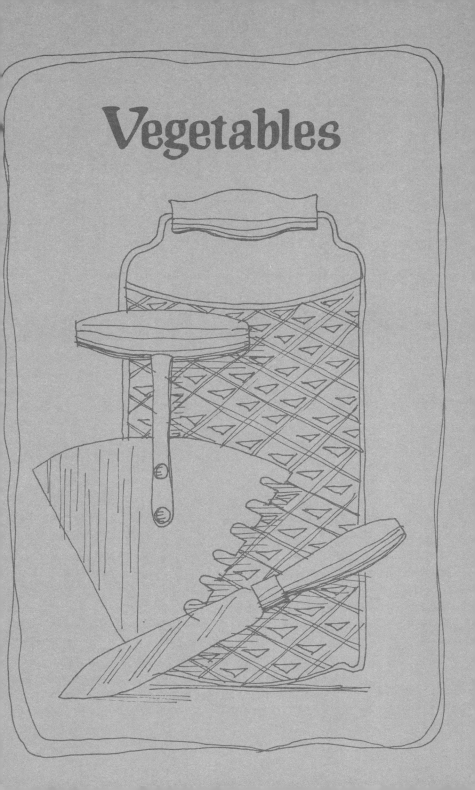

VEGETABLES

Vegetables Chapter Design: Bread or Radish Grater (1910), Triple-Edged Chopper (1890), Mincing Knife (1890)

ASPARAGUS CASSEROLE WITH MUSHROOM SAUCE

Oven: 375° 50 minutes   Yield: 8 servings

3 tablespoons chopped onions
2 tablespoons butter
4 cups asparagus, cut in
   1-inch pieces

1 cup skim milk
1 1/2 cups corn flakes
2 eggs, slightly beaten
1 teaspoon salt

Mushroom Sauce:

2 tablespoons butter
3 tablespoons flour
2 cups skim milk
1 teaspoon prepared mustard
1 3/4 teaspoons salt

2 teaspoons chopped chives
2 teaspoons chopped pimiento
14 tablespoons sliced
   mushrooms

Cook onions in butter until tender, stirring occasionally. Fold together cooked onions, asparagus, skim milk, corn flakes, eggs, and salt. Pour into 1 1/4-quart baking dish. Bake at 375° for 50 minutes or until set.

MUSHROOM SAUCE: Melt butter in heavy saucepan. Stir in flour gradually until well blended. Pour in skim milk and stir vigorously over moderate heat. Continue to cook until thickened, stirring constantly. Add mustard and salt; blend well. Fold in chives, pimiento, and mushrooms. Heat and serve over asparagus custard.

Bill Myers, Executive Chef
Crowley's Brandy House & Tavern
Atlanta, Georgia

✻ ✻ ✻ ✻ ✻ ✻ ✻ ✻ ✻ ✻ ✻ ✻ ✻

For quick and handy seasoning while cooking, keep on hand a large shaker containing 6 parts of salt and one part of pepper.

To keep fresh parsley, mint, and watercress, wash it thoroughly, shake off excess water, place in a glass jar, cover, and place in the refrigerator. It will stay green and fresh for a long time.

BAKED BEANS I

A Junior League picnic tradition

Oven: 325° 1 hour   Yield: 6 servings

1 pound lean ground meat
1 medium onion, chopped
Garlic salt and pepper to
  taste

1 (16-ounce) can of pork and
  beans
1/2 tablespoon prepared mustard
3 tablespoons heavy molasses

Brown meat and onion with garlic salt and pepper. Add this mixture to canned beans in oven-proof pot. Stir in mustard and molasses and mix well. Cover beans and cook at 325° for at least 1 hour; uncover the last 30 minutes.

Mrs. Ronald Wassenberg (Betty)

BAKED BEANS II

Oven: 450° 25 to 30 minutes   Yield: 8 servings

1 teaspoon margarine
1 clove garlic
1/2 pound ground beef
3 tablespoons catsup
1 teaspoon mustard
1 tablespoon brown sugar

2 teaspoons worcestershire sauce
1 dash hot sauce
2 (1-pound) cans pork and
  beans
Salt and pepper to taste
2 strips bacon

Melt margarine in saucepan. Crush clove of garlic and simmer in margarine for a few minutes. Add ground beef and cook until browned. Add remaining ingredients and pour into a 3-quart baking dish. Place strips of bacon on top and bake at 450° for 25 to 30 minutes.

Mrs. Alton Haynie (Helen)

※※※※※※※※※※※※※

For white cauliflower, add a little milk or a piece of lemon to the cooking water. Overcooked cauliflower tends to be dark.

BARBECUED BAKED BEANS
Good picnic dish

Oven: 325° 1 to 1 1/2 hours   Yield: 8 to 10 servings

2 (1-pound) cans pork
  and beans
1 medium onion, chopped
3/4 cup brown sugar
1 tablespoon mustard

1 teaspoon worcestershire
  sauce
6 slices bacon, cut into pieces
1/2 cup catsup

Empty one can of beans into bottom of greased casserole. Combine onion, sugar, mustard, and worcestershire sauce. Sprinkle over beans. Top with second can of beans. Spread catsup over beans and top with bacon pieces. Bake uncovered in slow oven (325°) for 1 to 1 1/2 hours or until bacon is done.

Mrs. Ellis A. Mansour (Melinda)

★   **FRESH BUTTER BEANS**

Yield: 6 servings

1 quart boiling water
Small piece of ham hock,
  preferably cured ham
1 quart butter beans,
  shelled and washed

6 to 7 pods okra
1 teaspoon butter
Salt and pepper to taste

Into boiling water, place ham hock and let boil 10 to 15 minutes. Add beans. Simmer, covered, for 30 minutes. Add okra, butter, salt, and pepper. Continue cooking 30 minutes longer, maintaining water level.

NOTE: Quantities of beans and okra may be adjusted to taste.

Mrs. John P. Woods, Jr. (Elizabeth)

GREEN BEAN DELIGHT

Especially good with ham

Oven: 325° to 350° 40 minutes   Yield: 6 to 8 servings

1 tablespoon margarine
2 (1-pound) cans sliced or French-style green beans
1 (10 3/4-ounce) cream of celery soup, undiluted
1 (3-ounce) can Chow Mein noodles
1 1/2 cups shredded sharp cheese

Butter 2-quart casserole. Combine well-drained beans and soup. Pour into casserole. Cover top with Chow Mein noodles. Top this with cheese, covering noodles well. Bake in 325° to 350° oven about 40 minutes or until cheese melts and begins to toast. If mixed before baking time, do not add noodles and cheese until ready to bake.

Rachel S. Jenkins

GREEN BEAN DIJON

An original family recipe from France

Yield: 4 servings

3 tablespoons Dijon mustard
4 tablespoons oil
1 1/2 tablespoons vinegar

Salt and pepper to taste
1 pound green beans
Tomato wedges, optional

Mix together all ingredients except green beans and tomato wedges with a fork or wire wisk. Cook green beans just until tender, approximately 15 to 20 minutes. Cool. Toss dressing with beans and serve cold. Tomato wedges may be added.

Mrs. Howard G. Boone (Nancy)

★ **LOUISIANA RED BEANS AND RICE**

Yield: 4 main-dish servings or
8 side-dish servings

2 cups dried red kidney beans	Salt and pepper to taste
1 large onion, chopped	1 bay leaf
1 celery stalk, chopped	1 pound ham with bone or
1 clove garlic, chopped	1 pound Polish sausage

Wash beans and soak overnight or at least 6 to 8 hours in fresh cold water. When ready to cook, drain off water and put beans into a large cooking pot. Cover with 5 cups of water. Bring beans to a boil, then reduce to simmer. Add the onion, celery, garlic, salt, pepper, and bay leaf. If adding ham, cut ham into chunks; if adding Polish sausage, cut into large pieces to fit into pot; add meat to beans. Simmer at least 2 hours, or until beans are soft enough that one may be easily mashed with a fork. Add more water during cooking if necessary. Serve beans and meat over mounds of hot fluffy rice. Good served with cornbread.

Mrs. Robert L. Lee (Pam)

✵ ✵ ✵ ✵ ✵ ✵ ✵ ✵ ✵ ✵ ✵ ✵ ✵

A tablespoon of vinegar in hot water will remove the onion odor from the pot in which the onions were cooked.

To get onion juice for a recipe, cut a slice from the root end of the onion and scrape juice from the center with the edge of a spoon.

To keep onion or cabbage odors from going through the house, boil a cup of vinegar in a saucepan at the same time.

Instead of boiling corn on the cob, try steaming it over boiling water for 20 minutes. What a difference!

★
NEW ORLEANS RED BEANS
Very economical, yet high in protein

Yield: 8 servings

1 pound of red kidney beans, dried
Salt to taste
1 clove of garlic, finely chopped
1 medium onion, finely chopped
3 or 4 stalks of celery, finely chopped

24 inches of link sausage, browned and cut into small sections
3 bay leaves
4 pieces of ham hock
6 or 7 cups of water

Wash one pound of red kidney beans and put into large pot with salt to taste. In separate skillet saute garlic, onion, and celery and add to beans. Add browned small portions of sausage, bay leaves, ham hock pieces, and 6 or 7 cups of water. Cover and cook over low heat for 2 to 2 1/2 hours.

This may be served with rice and can be a protein substitute for a main course of meat.

Mrs. C. M. Barron (Lavinia)

BAKED APRICOTS

Oven: 300° 35 to 45 minutes

Yield: 6 to 8 servings

2 (16-ounce) cans apricot halves, drained
2/3 cup brown sugar

1 stick butter, melted
1 cup buttery cracker crumbs

In greased 1 1/2-quart casserole, layer apricots, sugar, and crumbs until all ingredients are used. Pour melted butter over all; bake at 300° for 35 to 45 minutes.

NOTE: Serve with grits casserole and ham for an easy Sunday night supper.

Mrs. Parnell Odom (Pat)

BROCCOLI AND CHEESE CASSEROLE
Freezes well

Oven: 325° 1 hour   Yield: 12 servings

1 cup rice, cooked and drained
2 (10-ounce) packages frozen chopped broccoli, cooked and
   drained
1 (10 3/4-ounce) can cream of mushroom soup, or
   1 (10 3/4-ounce) can cream of chicken soup
1 (10 3/4-ounce) can cream of celery soup
1 stick margarine, melted
1 (8-ounce) jar Cheese Whiz
Chopped onion (optional)

Mix all ingredients, adding a little milk, if necessary.
Bake at 325° for 1 hour.

Mrs. Ray Sewell (Edith)

BROCCOLI AND CAULIFLOWER CASSEROLE

Oven: 350° 20 to 25 minutes   Yield: 6 servings

1 (10-ounce) package
   frozen cauliflower
1 (10-ounce) package
   frozen chopped broccoli
1 (10 3/4-ounce) can cream
   of asparagus soup
1 (10 3/4-ounce) can cream
   of celery soup
1 (8-ounce) carton sour
   cream
Sharp cheese, grated

Cook broccoli and cauliflower by package directions. Drain.
Mix all ingredients except cheese. Put in a 1 1/2-quart casserole dish. Grate cheese and sprinkle on top. Bake at 350°
for 20 to 25 minutes.

Mrs. Wright Lipford (Faye)
Peachtree City, Georgia

BROCCOLI CASSEROLE I

Perfect for company, bridge club, or church suppers

Oven: 350° 20 to 30 minutes   Yield: 10 servings

3 (10-ounce) packages   3 teaspoons grated onion
  frozen chopped broccoli   1/2 cup mayonnaise
1 (10 3/4-ounce) can cream   3 eggs, well beaten
  of mushroom soup   3/4 cup Ritz crackers, crushed

Cook broccoli 5 minutes. Drain and spread in bottom of 2 or 3-quart casserole. Mix soup, onion, mayonnaise, eggs, and pour over broccoli in the casserole. Sprinkle cracker crumbs on top. Bake 20 to 30 minutes at 350°. Casserole may be assembled ahead of time.

Mrs. William F. Lee (Parky)

BROCCOLI CASSEROLE II

Oven: 350°   Yield: 10 to 12 servings

2 (10-ounce) packages frozen   1 small onion, grated
  chopped broccoli   3 eggs
1 (10 3/4-ounce) can cream   Buttered bread crumbs
  of mushroom soup   Toasted almonds
1 cup sharp cheese, grated   Herb Stuffing Mix
1/4 cup mayonnaise   (optional)

Cook broccoli 7 minutes and drain. Add next 5 ingredients and mix. Place in a 2-quart buttered casserole. Top with buttered bread crumbs and toasted almonds or with herb stuffing. Bake at 350° until bubbling hot and crumbs have browned.

Mrs. Roy Wortham (Louise)

❋❋❋❋❋❋❋❋❋❋❋❋❋

Kumquats halved and served with peeled grapefruit sections make an attractive fruit cup. For color contrast, pour cranberry cocktail juice over the fruit.

BROCCOLI CASSEROLE III
Terrific for a women's luncheon. Do not freeze.

Oven: 350° 45 minutes   Yield: 8 servings

2 (10-ounce) boxes chopped   1 medium onion, chopped
  broccoli   Salt and pepper to taste
1 (10 3/4-ounce) can cream   1 cup sharp grated cheese
  of mushroom soup   1/2 stick margarine, melted
1 cup mayonnaise   1/2 package Pepperidge Farm
2 eggs, beaten   Stuffing Mix, herb seasoned

Cook broccoli according to package directions. Drain well. Combine soup, mayonnaise, eggs, onions, salt, and pepper. Add to broccoli. Pour into 1 1/2-quart casserole. Sprinkle cheese on top. Pour melted margarine over cheese. Spread stuffing on top. Bake uncovered for 45 minutes at 350°.

Barbara Valenz

BROCCOLI AND RICE
Easy and very good

Oven: 325° 20 minutes   Yield: 12 to 15 servings

2 (10-ounce) packages chopped broccoli, cooked and drained
1 cup uncooked white rice
1 (8-ounce) jar Cheese Whiz
1 (10 3/4-ounce) can cream of chicken soup or
  1 (10 3/4-ounce) can cream of mushroom soup
1 cup sliced water chesnuts (optional)
2 onions, chopped and sautéed in butter (optional)
Buttered cracker or bread crumbs

Cook broccoli according to package directions and drain. Cook rice. Mix all ingredients together. Put into 3-quart buttered casserole. Top with buttered cracker crumbs or bread crumbs. Bake uncovered at 325° for 20 minutes.

Mrs. Ellis Crook (Patricia)
Mrs. Otis Jones (Ann)

515

SWEET AND SOUR BRUSSELS SPROUTS
Different!

Yield: 18 servings

1 (8-ounce) package bacon,
  diced
6 (10-ounce) packages frozen
  Brussels sprouts, thawed
1 medium onion, minced

1/3 cup cider vinegar
3 tablespoons sugar
1 1/2 teaspoons salt
1/2 teaspoon dry mustard
1/8 teaspoon pepper

In 6-quart Dutch oven or saucepot over medium to low heat, cook bacon until browned. With slotted spoon, remove bacon to drain on paper towels. In same Dutch oven, in bacon drippings, cook Brussels sprouts with remaining ingredients until tender-crisp, about 10 minutes. Stir occasionally. Stir in bacon. Serve hot.

Mrs. Tom F. Farmer (Mary Anne)

BAKED CABBAGE
A little microwave magic goes into this dish

Microwave oven: 8 minutes   Yield: 6 servings

3 cups chopped cabbage   Salt and pepper
1/2 stick of butter

Place cabbage in a 2 1/2-quart covered casserole. Add butter, dash of salt, and pepper. Cook 4 minutes. Stir cabbage and cook an additional 4 minutes or until tender.

Mrs. Dan B. Umbach (Marie)

※※※※※※※※※※※※※

Pour curacao over fresh pear halves for a delicious dessert.

CABBAGE CASSEROLE
Great with turkey

Oven: 350° 30 minutes   Yield: 10 to 12 servings

1 small head of cabbage
4 tablespoons butter
4 tablespoons flour
1/2 teaspoon salt
1/4 teaspoon pepper

2 cups milk or evaporated
  milk
1/2 pound Cheddar cheese,
  grated
Butter or margarine

Cut cabbage into small pieces; cover with water and cook 10 minutes. Drain. Make a white sauce of the butter, flour, salt, pepper, and milk. Stir constantly until thickened. In a 10x10x2-inch casserole, layer the cabbage, sauce, and cheese. Repeat twice. Dot with butter. Bake at 350° for 30 minutes.

Mrs. R. A. Baxter (Margaret)
Gulf Shores, Alabama

★ ## HOT SLAW
A special Southern way to enjoy cabbage

Yield: 6 to 8 servings

4 cups shredded cabbage
3 tablespoons sugar
1 1/2 to 2 teaspoons salt
1/4 cup water
2 tablespoons margarine or
  cooking oil

1/3 cup sour cream
1 1/2 tablespoons vinegar
1/4 teaspoon white or
  black pepper

Combine shredded cabbage, sugar, and salt, and let stand a few minutes. In saucepan, place water and oil, then add cabbage mixture. Cook until cabbage is tender (8 to 10 minutes). Remove from heat. Mix together sour cream, vinegar, and pepper. Pour over hot cabbage and mix well. Serve immediately.

Mrs. Fred R. Smyre (Martha)
Hickory, North Carolina

517

DELIGHTFULLY DIFFERENT CARROTS
Prepare 24 hours in advance

Yield: 8 to 10 servings

2 pounds carrots, sliced
1 large green pepper, chopped
1 large onion, chopped
1 (10 3/4-ounce) can tomato soup, undiluted
1 tablespoon worcestershire sauce

1/4 cup vinegar
1/4 cup cooking oil
1/2 teaspoon pepper
1 teaspoon prepared mustard
1/4 cup sugar
1 teaspoon salt
1 teaspoon celery seed
1 teaspoon basil leaves

Slice carrots and cook in lightly salted water until done. Drain and cool. Combine the remaining ingredients, pour over carrots, and marinate 24 hours. Delicious served hot or cold. Will keep up to 2 weeks in the refrigerator.

Mrs. George Neff (Ruth)
Metropolis, Illinois

CREAMY CAULIFLOWER

Oven: 350° 20 minutes

Yield: 4 to 6 servings

2 (10-ounce) packages frozen cauliflower
1 (10 3/4-ounce) can cream of onion soup, undiluted
1 cup sour cream
1 cup herbed stuffing mix
Butter

Cook cauliflower according to package directions; drain. Add soup and sour cream. Mix well. Pour into buttered 1 1/2-quart baking dish. Top with paprika or stuffing mix dotted with butter. Bake in 350° oven about 20 minutes.

Mrs. Ray Moore (Marie)

CARROT RINGS

Keeps well in refrigerator for 2 weeks

Yield: 15 servings

2 pounds carrots,
  sliced into rounds
1 green pepper, diced
1 large onion, diced
1 (10 3/4-ounce) can
  tomato soup
1/2 cup salad oil

1 cup sugar
3/4 cup vinegar
1 teaspoon mustard
1 teaspoon worcestershire
  sauce
Salt and pepper to taste

Cook carrots until tender. Make layers of carrots, onions, and pepper in large bowl. Mix all other ingredients well with mixer. Pour over vegetables. Refrigerate 2 days for flavor. Serve chilled.

Mrs. Carl Robertson (Sarah)
Mrs. Carl E. Williams (Eddy)
Ruby L. White

★ CORN PUDDING

Oven: 350° 45 to 60 minutes

Yield: 8 servings

1 (16-ounce) can cream-
  style corn
3 tablespoons flour
1 cup milk, slightly
  heated

3 tablespoons butter
1 tablespoon sugar
1/2 teaspoon salt
Dash of pepper
2 eggs, lightly beaten

Combine corn and flour. Add remaining ingredients ending with beaten eggs. Mix well. Pour into a 2-quart casserole and bake in 350° oven about 45 to 60 minutes.

Mrs. Parnell Odom (Pat)

★
WHITE HOMINY CASSEROLE
Excellent with baked ham and curried fruit

Oven: 350° 40 minutes   Yield: 6 serving

1 (1-pound) can white hominy, drained
1 cup sharp cheese, grated
2 pimientos, chopped or
  1 small jar chopped pimientos
12 to 15 black olives, sliced or chopped
1 (10 3/4-ounce) can mushroom soup, blended with 1/3
  cup water
1/2 teaspoon worcestershire sauce
1/4 teaspoon prepared mustard
Bread crumbs

Butter an oven-proof pie dish or 1 1/2-quart casserole. In this, place a layer of hominy, then a layer of cheese, and over this sprinkle some pimientos and olives. Cover with a layer of soup which has been mixed with the worcestershire sauce and mustard. Repeat until all ingredients are used, ending with soup on top. Bake at 350° for 25 to 30 minutes until bubbly and hot, then sprinkle with bread crumbs and bake for an additional 10 minutes until slightly browned on top.

NOTE: Hominy is a uniquely Southern corn product made by boiling the dried corn kernels in a weak lye solution, then hulling, washing, and drying the kernels.

Mrs. Willis Edwards (Catharine)

✳✳✳✳✳✳✳✳✳✳✳✳✳

For an easy salad, stuff canned or fresh peach halves with mincemeat. Broil or serve as is.

Use canned peaches instead of fresh ones to make delicious spiced peaches. Add 1/2 cup vinegar, 1 cup brown sugar, 1-ounce stick cinnamon, and a few whole cloves to the peaches and the syrup they are canned in. Simmer 15 minutes.

★ ## FRIED CORN

Yield: 4 servings

8 ears tender corn
1/4 cup bacon drippings
1 cup milk

Salt and pepper to taste
1 teaspoon sugar
1 tablespoon butter

Cut corn close to outer edge, then scrape the ear to remove all the milk. Add corn to bacon drippings which have been heated. Add milk, salt, pepper, and sugar. Stir often as corn burns easily. Cook approximately 20 to 30 minutes, adding butter during the last few minutes of cooking.

Mrs. Bryan Sargent (Ellen)

EGGPLANT CASSEROLE I

Oven: 350° 1 hour

Yield: 6 servings

2 medium-size eggplants
1 large onion, chopped
1 teaspoon salt
1/2 teaspoon pepper
1 1/2 pounds ground beef
or lamb

2 (8-ounce) cans tomato
sauce
1/4 cup pine nuts
(optional)

Peel eggplant and cut into slices 1/2 inch thick. Soak in salted water for an hour. Drain on paper towels. Brown both sides of sliced eggplant in oil, or broil.

Brown onion and meat in fry pan and season with salt and pepper. Alternate layers of the eggplant and meat mixture in a shallow casserole. Pour tomato sauce over top layer of ingredients and add water to cover.

Bake for one hour at 350°. Serve over rice.

NOTE: This recipe is of Lebanese origin.

Mayme B. Mansour

EGGPLANT CASSEROLE II

Oven: 350°   Yield: 6 servings

1 medium-size eggplant, peeled and cubed
1 small onion, coarsely chopped
1 (10 3/4-ounce) can cream of mushroom soup
1/2 cup mayonnaise
1 cup grated American cheese
1/2 cup Pepperidge Farm dressing mix

Cook eggplant and onion in salted water until tender. Mash and mix with soup, mayonnaise, and 1/2 of the cheese. Put into 2-quart casserole and use remaining cheese and dressing mix as topping. Bake at 350° until bubbly.

NOTE: Mrs. Ira F. Hutchinson of Rock Hill, South Carolina, won a *Better Homes and Gardens* magazine cooking contest with this original recipe.

Mrs. Tom Wise (Dottie)

※※※※※※※※※※※※※

4 or 5 whole cloves and 1 teaspoon of sugar added to a quart of prunes while soaking give them a delicious flavor. For zip, add 2 or 3 thin lemon slices and simmer prunes in the same water for 30 minutes.

When baking apples, fill the centers with raisins, nuts, cranberry sauce, or mincemeat. Serve with whipped evaporated milk or cream.

Frosted grapes: Dip grapes in slightly beaten egg whites. Coat with granulated sugar, and place on waxed paper to dry.

Sugared grapes: Dip wet grapes in granulated sugar. Refrigerate until needed.

EGGPLANT CASSEROLE III

An interesting shrimp - eggplant combination

Oven: 325° 1 hour   Yield: 8 to 10 servings

1 eggplant, peeled and cubed
1 tablespoon sugar
1 large onion, chopped
1 bell pepper, chopped
1/4 cup margarine
1 (10 3/4-ounce) can
    mushroom soup
1 (4-ounce) can sliced
    mushrooms
1 pound raw shrimp

1 pound New York State
    cheese
Worcestershire sauce
Cayenne pepper
Tabasco
Black pepper
Garlic salt
1 cup cracker crumbs
Paprika

Cook eggplant with sugar until tender. Add onion and pepper that have been sautéed in butter until tender. Add soup and mushrooms. Clean raw shrimp. Add to above mixture. Add half of cheese. Add the next five seasonings to taste. Put into a 2-quart casserole. Cover with cracker crumbs and remaining cheese. Dust with paprika and cook 1 hour or more in slow oven or until almost dry.

Mrs. Lawrence K. Keith, Jr. (Jane)

※ ※ ※ ※ ※ ※ ※ ※ ※ ※ ※ ※ ※

To frost fresh fruit cups, first dip rims of glasses into grapefruit juice, then into granulated sugar. Let dry slightly, then fill glass with fruit.

Place peeled bananas in baking dish and brush with melted butter. Bake about 12 minutes at 450°. Add sherry, brandy, or almond extract to softened vanilla ice cream and serve over hot bananas.

Quick dessert: 1 can sliced pineapple topped with maraschino cherries and 1 jigger Kirschwasser.

EGGPLANT CASSEROLE IV
Tastes like oyster casserole

Oven: 375° 20 minutes   Yield: 8 servings

2 medium-size eggplants
1/2 teaspoon salt or to taste
1 medium onion, chopped
2 (10 3/4-ounce) cans cream
   of mushroom soup

Chopped pecans
1/2 stick margarine or butter
5 to 6 saltine crackers,
   crushed
1/2 cup grated cheese

Peel and cut eggplants in cubes. Add chopped onion and salt to taste. Cover with water in boiler and cook until tender, about 15 to 20 minutes. Drain. Put 1/2 of eggplant and onion mixture into a baking dish. Cover with 1 can of mushroom soup. Sprinkle with a few pecans and dot with margarine or butter. Repeat layers. Top with cracker crumbs mixed with grated cheese. Dot with butter. Bake at 375° until cheese is melted and top is brown.

Mrs. Babe Jenkins

MARY'S GARDEN VEGETABLE CASSEROLE
Delicious

Oven: 325° 1½ hours   Yield: 6 to 8 servings

1/3 cup uncooked rice
3 to 4 small summer squash,
   sliced
2 to 3 medium onions,
   sliced
1 bell pepper, sliced

3 to 4 medium tomatoes,
   sectioned
Salt and pepper to taste
2 tablespoons butter, thinly
   sliced

In greased 1 1/2-quart casserole arrange vegetables in layers (layer squash — layer onion . . . etc.) In between layers, make 2 layers of rice. Be sure not to have rice on top or bottom of caserole. Preferably have tomato layer on top. Salt and pepper to taste. Place butter slices on top. Bake covered at 325° for 1 1/2 hours.

Mrs. John P. Woods, Jr. (Elizabeth)

MRS. SWANSEN'S EGGPLANT OR ASPARAGUS CASSEROLE
Freezes well. Everyone's favorite!

Oven: 325° 50 minutes   Yield: 8 to 10 servings

3 eggs, beaten
1 cup milk
3 slices bread, cubed and
   crusts removed
1 medium eggplant or
   2 (16-ounce) cans cut
   asparagus, drained
1 teaspoon salt

Pepper to taste
1/4 pound sharp cheese,
   grated
1 (8-ounce) can sliced mushrooms, drained
1 (2-ounce) jar or 2 whole
   pimientos, chopped and
   drained
1/4 cup butter or margarine,
   melted
1 small onion, grated

Beat eggs; add milk and bread cubes to soften. If using eggplant, prepare by making cuts almost through the raw, unpeeled eggplant. Generously sprinkle with salt and stand up in cup to drain. This aids in removing bitterness and dark color from eggplant. After letting eggplant sit for about 30 minutes, peel, cube, and cook until slightly tender. (A microwave oven works well for this.) Drain eggplant well. Add all other ingredients, except eggplant, to the bread mixture and mix well. Fold eggplant or asparagus into bread mixture. Bake in a greased 1 1/2 to 2-quart casserole at 325° for 35 minutes, covered. Uncover and bake 15 minutes longer until casserole begins to brown.

NOTE: This recipe came originally from Mrs. Eula Swansen, formerly of Newnan, who now resides in Newburgh, Indiana.

Mrs. John P. Woods, Jr. (Elizabeth)

MUSHROOM PUFFS

Yield: 6 to 8 serving

1/4 cup chopped shallots
2 tablespoons butter or
   margarine
4 egg whites
2 cups fresh mushrooms,
   chopped
1/2 cup grated Parmesan cheese

2 tablespoons flour
1/2 teaspoon salt
1/4 teaspoon cayenne pepper
1/4 teaspoon black pepper
Vegetable oil
Parsley sprigs

Cook and stir shallots in butter in small skillet until tender
Cool. Beat egg whites stiff but not dry. Fold in shallots. Mi:
mushrooms, cheese, flour, salt, and peppers into egg white
until blended. Pour oil into heavy skillet to a depth of 3 to ‹
inches and heat to 375°. Measure mix by rounded tablespoon
and fry in hot oil. Garnish with parsley sprigs and fresh
mushrooms.

James Mann

★   **SOUTHERN FRIED OKRA**
A summer specialty in many Southern homes

Yield: 6 to 8 serving

2 pounds small okra
1 cup plain corn meal

1 cup all-purpose flour
1 1/2 quarts vegetable oil, for deep fryir

Wash okra and cut into fairly thin slices; do not use sten
or tip. Make sure okra is moist with water, and place in larg‹
plastic container with a lid. Add meal and flour. Place lid o1
container and shake several times. Remove lid and make sur‹
all okra slices are coated with meal-flour mixture. Fry coate‹
okra slices in deep vegetable oil until brown. Remove witl
slotted spoon and drain on paper towel. Salt to taste whil
hot.

Mrs. R. A. Baxter (Margaret
Gulf Shores, Alabam.
Mrs. Dan B. Umbach (Marie

SALLY'S MUSHROOM CASSEROLE
Must be prepared ahead

Oven: 325° 55 minutes   Yield: 6 to 8 servings

1 pound fresh mushrooms,
  sliced
1/2 stick margarine
8 slices bread, trimmed and
  cubed
1/2 cup chopped onions
1/2 cup chopped celery
1/2 cup mayonnaise

1 teaspoon salt
1/2 teaspoon pepper
2 eggs
1/2 cup milk
1 (10 3/4-ounce) can cream
  of mushroom soup
Grated cheese (optional)

Sauté mushrooms in 1/2 stick margarine. Cut 4 slices of bread into cubes and put on bottom of 2-quart casserole. Add the next 5 ingredients to the sautéed mushrooms and spread over cubes of bread. Top with remaining 4 slices of bread, cubed. Mix eggs and milk; pour over casserole. Refrigerate overnight. Spread the can of mushroom soup on top when ready to cook, and top with grated cheese, if desired. Cook at 325° for 55 minutes.

Mrs. Thompson Kurrie, Jr. (Sally)
Atlanta, Georgia

FRENCH FRIED ONION RINGS
A very special recipe!

Yield: One large onion will feed two people

Buttermilk
Vidalia onions, large

Flour
Cooking oil or shortening

Slice onions and separate into rings. Cover with buttermilk and allow to stand for 1 hour. Put flour in a plastic or paper bag. Add onion rings, inflate bag, and shake until rings are coated with flour. Fry in hot grease and drain on paper towels.

James Thomasson

527

GRILLED ONIONS
Great as a side dish or appetizer

Yield: 4 serving

4 Bermuda onions, unpeeled
4 tablespoons butter, melted
Dash salt, pepper

Place 4 onions on grill. When juice starts coming out c the top, cut top off onion and brush with butter. Season witl salt and pepper. Cook until tender, approximately 30 minutes

Dan B. Umbacl

★ **VIDALIA ONION CASSEROLE**

Oven: 375° 30 minutes

Yield: 6 servin₉

2 tablespoons butter or
  margarine
2 tablespoons flour
1 cup chicken broth, or
  1 chicken bouillon cube
  plus 1 cup water
1 (5 1/3-ounce) can
  evaporated milk

3 cups wedged Vidalia onion₅
  parboiled
1/2 cup slivered almonds
1/2 teaspoon salt
1/2 teaspoon pepper
1 cup bread crumbs
1/2 cup grated cheese

Melt butter; stir in flour, then all broth, and evaporate milk. Stir constantly until mixture begins to thicken and smooth. Add drained onions, almonds, and seasonings. Pou into buttered 1 1/2-quart casserole. Cover with crumbs an cheese. Bake at 375° for 30 minutes.

NOTE: Vidalia onions are very mild, sweet onions grow exclusively in sandy soil near Vidalia, Georgia. They are usual. available from late spring through mid-summer. Any simila type onion could be substituted in this recipe.

Mrs. Banks A. Moorman (Joyce

★

ONION CASSEROLE
Delicious with steak

Oven: 325° 30 minutes   Yield: 6 servings

5 large onions (Vidalia, if available)
1 stick margarine
Parmesan cheese
Crispy buttery crackers

Peel and slice onions into thin rings. Sauté in margarine until limp or opaque. Pour half of onions into 1 1/2-quart casserole, cover with Parmesan cheese, then crushed crackers. Repeat layers and bake uncovered in 325° oven until golden brown, about 30 minutes.

Mrs. Wright Lipford (Faye)
Peachtree City, Georgia

AU GRATIN POTATO CASSEROLE
So simple

Oven: 350° 35 minutes   Yield: 6 to 8 servings

1 quart of sliced potatoes
1 (10 3/4-ounce) can cream
of mushroom soup
1/2 cup milk
1/2 cup sharp Cheddar cheese,
grated

1 (3-ounce) can French fried
onion rings
Salt and pepper to taste
Paprika

Cook potatoes until partially done. Combine soup, milk, and cheese. Alternate layers of potatoes and soup mixture in a buttered baking dish, adding the salt and pepper as you go. Add a dash of paprika. Bake at 350° for 25 minutes. Remove from oven and top with partially crumbled onion rings. Return to oven and bake for 10 minutes longer.

Mrs. Edwin Brown (Mary)
Turin, Georgia

OVEN-ROASTED POTATOES
Especially good with roast pork or beef

Oven: 375° approximately 1 hour   Yield: 4 to 6 servings

4 large white potatoes   **Salt**
  or 8 small Idaho potatoes,   **Pepper**
  peeled   **Paprika**
1 stick butter

   Boil potatoes in water about 15 minutes; drain well and return to low burner for two minutes to slightly dry potatoes. Put potatoes in a buttered 2-quart casserole and top each with a pat of butter. About 1 hour before roast is done, put casserole in 375° oven. When butter has melted, turn potatoes and sprinkle on salt, pepper, and paprika. Repeat this process every 10 to 15 minutes. The potatoes should be crisp and golden.

Mrs. Charles M. Smith (Lynn)

★   ## BLACK-EYED PEAS AND HOG JOWL
A New Year's Day MUST!

Yield: 4 servings

1 cup dried black-eyed peas
2 cups water
1 teaspoon salt
About 1/4 pound of hog jowl, or streak o' lean boiling meat

   Soak peas overnight; drain and sort. Slice jowl or boiling meat to the skin, leaving it in one piece, but allowing slices to season well. Put into water and bring to a boil. Add peas. Return to a boil; simmer for about 1 1/2 hours or until peas are tender. Add more water, if necessary.

Mrs. V. J. Bruner (Ethel)

BAKED PINEAPPLE
Delicious side dish for meat

Oven: 350° 45 to 60 minutes   Yield: 6 servings

1 (16-ounce) can crushed   4 tablespoons cornstarch
   pineapple, drained   Butter
3 eggs, beaten   Cinnamon
3/4 cup sugar

Combine pineapple with 3 well-beaten eggs. Mix the sugar and cornstarch together and add to the egg and pineapple mixture. Mix well. Pour into 1-quart baking dish. Dot with butter and sprinkle with cinnamon. Bake at 350° for 45 to 60 minutes or until firm and brown.

Mrs. Edwin L. Wyrick (Lois)

POTATO CASSEROLE I
Freezes well

Oven: 350° 25 minutes   Yield: 8 servings

6 medium potatoes   1/3 cup chopped green onions
2 cups Cheddar cheese,   1/2 teaspoon salt
   shredded   1/4 teaspoon white pepper
1/2 cup butter or margarine   2 tablespoons butter or
2 cups sour cream   margarine

Cook potatoes in skins. Cool and peel. Coarsely shred on grater. Stir cheese and butter over low heat until almost melted. Remove from heat and add sour cream, onion, salt, and pepper. Toss lightly with potatoes. Put in buttered 2-quart casserole. Dot with butter. Bake at 350° for 25 minutes.

Mrs. Wesley Nunn (Cindy)
College Park, Georgia

POTATO CASSEROLE II
Easy and can be prepared ahead

Oven: 350° 25 minutes

Yield: 10 servings

9 baking potatoes
2/3 cup margarine
1 1/2 teaspoons salt
1/4 teaspoon pepper
2/3 cup warm milk

1 2/3 cups shredded Cheddar cheese
1 cup whipping cream, whipped

Peel and boil potatoes until tender; drain and beat in large bowl of electric mixer until fluffy. Add margarine, salt, pepper, and milk; mix well. Turn into buttered 2-quart shallow casserole. Fold cheese into whipped cream and spread over potatoes. Bake 350° for 25 minutes, only until golden brown. May be prepared ahead of time, adding the topping just before baking.

Mrs. Parnell Odom (Pat)

SCALLOPED POTATO CASSEROLE
Freezes beautifully after baking

Oven: 350° 45 minutes

Yield: 8 to 10 servings

1 (2-pound) sack frozen hash brown potatoes, thawed
1 teaspoon salt
1/4 teaspoon pepper
1/2 cup chopped onion
1 (10 3/4-ounce) can cream of chicken soup

1 pint sour cream
2 cups grated Cheddar cheese
1/4 to 1/2 cup melted butter or margarine
2 cups crushed corn flakes

Combine all ingredients except butter and corn flakes. Place in a 2-quart greased casserole. Pour butter over top. Sprinkle corn flakes over all. Bake at 350° for 45 minutes. For smaller servings, bake in two (1-quart) casseroles. Serve one and freeze the other for later.

Mrs. James W. Roberts (Sue)

SNOWY POTATO CASSEROLE

Oven: 350° 30 minutes   Yield: 6 to 8 servings

pounds potatoes (12 medium),   1 clove garlic, crushed
  peeled and sliced   1/4 cup chopped chives
(8-ounce) package cream   (optional)
  cheese, softened   1/2 teaspoon paprika
cup dairy sour cream   1 tablespoon butter or
teaspoons salt   margarine
/8 teaspoon pepper

Cook potatoes in boiling, salted water in a large kettle 15 minutes or until tender; drain. Mash potatoes in large bowl of electric mixer; add cream cheese, sour cream, salt, pepper, and garlic. Beat at high speed until smooth and light. Stir in chopped chives. Spoon into a lightly greased 10-cup baking dish. Sprinkle with paprika and dot with butter or margarine. Bake at 350° for 30 minutes or until lightly golden and heated through.

Mrs. William F. Lee, Jr. (Susan)
Mrs. James W. Roberts (Sue)

SPUDS Á LA ELEGANT

Oven: 350° 45 minutes   Yield: 6 to 8 servings

cups hot mashed potatoes   1/3 cup finely chopped onion
ounces cream cheese,   1/4 cup chopped pimiento
  softened   1 teaspoon salt
egg, beaten   Dash pepper

Mix all ingredients well. Bake in a greased 1 1/2-quart casserole for 45 minutes at 350°.

Mrs. Thomas R. Kerley (Lynda)
Lexington, Kentucky

STUFFED BAKED POTATOES

Oven: 400° 60 minutes
     350° 15 to 20 minutes

Yield: 2 serving

2 large Idaho potatoes
4 strips bacon, quartered
1/4 cup chopped green onion
1/2 cup chopped bell
   pepper (optional)
2 tablespoons grated
   Parmesan cheese

1/2 cup sour cream
1/2 teaspoon salt
1/2 teaspoon white pepper
Melted butter
Paprika

Bake potatoes at 400° for 1 hour. While potatoes are cooling, fry bacon pieces until crisp. Drain off all but 3 tablespoons oil. Add onion and bell pepper and sauté slowly. Remove from heat. Cut shallow lengthwise slice from each potato and carefully spoon out inside. Add potato to skillet. Add cheese, sour cream, and seasonings. Blend thoroughly. Return skillet to heat and cook until thoroughly heated. Stuff the mixture into potato skins; drizzle with melted butter and a dash of paprika. Bake at 350° for 15 to 20 minutes.

Mrs. Walker Connally (Guilford)

❈ ❈ ❈ ❈ ❈ ❈ ❈ ❈ ❈ ❈ ❈ ❈ ❈

Use natural ham stock to season vegetables. Refrigerate ham stock to congeal the fat. Discard most or all of the fat, and cook raw vegetables in the stock.

For calorie counters, try using chicken bouillon to flavor canned green beans instead of bacon drippings or fatback.

To peel a tomato easily and make it pretty for serving, dip it in boiling water for 20 to 60 seconds. The skin will slip off easily.

For lighter mashed or creamed potatoes, use hot milk.

TWICE-BAKED POTATOES
A great make-ahead dish

Oven: 450° 1 hour   Yield: 10 servings
     350° 15 to 20 minutes

10 medium baking potatoes	2 teaspoons salt
2 sticks butter	3/4 teaspoon pepper
1/4 cup chopped onions	1 cup shredded mild cheese
1 cup half and half cream	

Scrub potatoes, dry, and pierce. Bake without foil at 450° for about 1 hour on oven rack. Melt butter and sauté onion until clear and tender. Cut a lengthwise slice from top of each potato, scoop out pulp, and mash pulp with cream, salt, pepper, and sautéed onions with butter until fluffy in consistency. Fill reserved shells with the mixture and top with shredded cheese. Potatoes may now be refrigerated or frozen until ready for use. Bake at 350° for 15 to 20 minutes (longer, if frozen).

Mrs. John N. White (Martha)

SPINACH SOUFFLÉ
Very rich and delicious

Oven: 350° 25 to 30 minutes   Yield: 4 servings

1 (10-ounce) package frozen chopped spinach	1 cup Parmesan cheese
1 tablespoon grated onion	1 tablespoon flour
2 eggs, beaten	2 tablespoons butter
1/2 cup sour cream	Dash nutmeg
	Salt and pepper to taste

Cook spinach with onion in small amount of water until thawed. Drain. Add the remaining ingredients to the cooked spinach. Pour into a 1-quart greased casserole and bake at 350° for 25 to 30 minutes or until center is set.

Mrs. James J. Goodrum (Frances Lee)

535

CRUNCHY SPINACH CASSEROLE
A prize of a recipe

Oven: 325° 20 to 30 minutes   Yield: 8 serving

3 (10-ounce) packages
  frozen chopped spinach
1 (8-ounce) package cream
  cheese
1/2 stick butter
Juice of 2 lemons
Salt
Black pepper

Ground nutmeg
1 (3-ounce) package cream
  cheese
1/2 cup dairy sour cream
White pepper
1 1/2 cups dry herb stuffing
  mix
1/2 stick butter

Cook the spinach in salted water according to package directions for approximately 5 minutes. Drain very thoroughly

Combine in a saucepan the 8-ounce package of cream cheese, 1/2 stick of butter, all but 1 teaspoon of the lemon juice, salt, black pepper, lots of ground nutmeg, and the drained spinach. Stir together over low heat until butter and cream cheese are melted, and mixture is thoroughly smooth. Divide in half and set aside.

In the top of a double boiler, combine the 3-ounce package of cream cheese, 1/2 cup sour cream, 1 teaspoon lemon juice, and white pepper. Stir over hot water until smooth.

Place one half of the spinach mixture in a well-buttered 2-quart casserole. Top with all the cream cheese mixture. Add the second half of the spinach.

Sprinkle the stuffing mix over the top and drizzle over the stuffing the remaining 1/2 stick of butter that has been melted

Bake casserole at 325° for about 20 to 30 minutes or until bubbly and brown on top.

Mrs. John Dunn (Teresa

SPINACH CRÊPE CASSEROLE

Oven: 375°   Yield: 10 servings

Cream Sauce:

4 tablespoons butter	Pepper and nutmeg
5 tablespoons flour	1/4 cup heavy cream
2 3/4 cups hot milk	1 cup coarsely grated
1 teaspoon salt	Swiss cheese

Casserole:

1 1/2 cups cooked, chopped	1 cup diced mushrooms,
spinach	sautéed in butter with 2
1 cup cream cheese or	tablespoons scallions added
cottage cheese	24 (6 or 7-inch) crêpes
1 egg	

CREAM SAUCE: Melt butter and stir in flour; cook slowly for 2 minutes, then remove from heat. Beat in milk, salt, pepper, and nutmeg to taste. Boil, stirring, for 1 minute, then beat in cream and all but 2 tablespoons Swiss cheese. Simmer a moment and correct seasonings.

ASSEMBLING AND BAKING: In a bowl, blend several tablespoons of cream sauce into the spinach; season to taste and set aside. In another bowl, beat cream cheese or cottage cheese with egg, mushrooms, and several tablespoons of cream sauce to make a thick paste; season to taste and set aside. Reserve remaining cream sauce.

Lightly butter a casserole, then center a crêpe in the bottom. Spread with spinach, cover with another crêpe, spread with a layer of cheese-mushroom mixture. Continue this layering with remainder of crêpes, spinach, and cheese-mushroom mixture; end with a crêpe on top. Pour reserved cream sauce over top and sprinkle with the remaining 2 tablespoons Swiss cheese. Dot with 1 tablespoon of butter.

Refrigerate until 30 minutes before serving. Place in upper two-thirds of preheated 375° oven until bubbly and cheese has browned lightly.

Mrs. Peter F. Hoffman (Ree)
Atlanta, Georgia

SPINACH TART
Good brunch dish served with ham or bacon

Oven: 350° 30 minutes   Yield: 6 to 8 servings

1 onion, chopped
3 tablespoons margarine
1 tablespoon flour
2 (10-ounce) packages frozen,
  chopped spinach, cooked
  and drained well
4 eggs

1 1/2 cups cream, scalded
Salt and nutmeg to taste
3/4 cup grated Parmesan or
  Swiss cheese
1 deep dish pastry shell, partially baked — about
  10 minutes

Sauté onion in margarine until limp. Sprinkle flour over onions. Add well-drained spinach. Beat eggs slightly and, slowly, add cream to eggs. Add egg mixture to spinach mixture and blend. Add seasonings. Pour into partially baked pastry shell. Sprinkle with cheese and bake at 350° for 30 minutes or until firm.

Mrs. Benny Grant (Diane)

★   FRIED SQUASH BALLS
Different!

Yield: 8 servings

8 to 10 yellow squash,
  chopped
1 onion, finely chopped
Salt and pepper to taste
1 cup Rice Krispies

1 egg, beaten
Dash of worcestershire
  sauce (optional)
Corn meal
Cooking oil

Boil squash with onion and salt to taste until tender. Drain and mash. Add next 3 ingredients and blend. Refrigerate a few hours. Shape mixture into balls, roll in corn meal, and fry in hot oil until brown.

Mrs. Warren Budd (Courtenay)

★ **AUNT FANNY'S BAKED SQUASH**

Oven: 375° 1 hour   Yield: 6 to 8 servings

3 pounds yellow summer   1/2 teaspoon black pepper
   squash   1 teaspoon salt
1/2 cup chopped onions   2 eggs, beaten
1/2 cup cracker meal or   1 tablespoon sugar
   bread crumbs   1 stick butter

Wash and cut up squash. Boil until tender, drain thoroughly, then mash. Add all ingredients to squash except half of the butter. Salt and pepper may be increased to suit taste. Melt remaining butter. Pour squash in baking dish, then spread melted butter over top and sprinkle with cracker meal or bread crumbs. Bake at 375° for about 1 hour or until brown on top.

Aunt Fanny's Cabin
Smyrna, Georgia

★ **GRATED SQUASH CASSEROLE**

Oven: 325° 35 to 40 minutes   Yield: 6 to 8 servings

1 medium onion, minced   1 egg, slightly beaten
2 tablespoons butter   1/4 cup whipping cream or
2 pounds squash (4 cups),   evaporated milk
   coarsely grated   Salt and pepper to taste
1/2 cup Velveeta cheese,   1/2 cup crushed potato chips
   coarsely grated

Sauté onion in butter until transparent. Add coarsely grated squash to butter and onions; cook 5 to 10 minutes, stirring constantly. Combine with cheese, egg, cream, and seasonings. Put in buttered 2-quart casserole and sprinkle chips over top. Cover and bake at 325° for 35 to 40 minutes. Uncover for last 2 or 3 minutes to brown.

Mrs. Joe Bohannon (Mary)

BUTTERNUT SQUASH CASSEROLE
Freezes well

Oven: 350° 45 minutes   Yield: 6 servings

3 cups cooked butternut   1 stick margarine
squash   Ginger to taste
3 eggs   Round buttery crackers,
1 cup sugar   crumbed

Combine all ingredients except crumbs. Place in buttered 2-quart casserole and top with crumbs. Bake at 350° until brown, approximately 45 minutes.

Mrs. Wright Lipford (Faye)
Peachtree City, Georgia

★   SQUASH CASSEROLE I
A delicate dish; freezes well

Oven: 350° 20 minutes   Yield: 6 to 8 servings

2 to 3 cups cooked squash   1 to 1 1/2 cups cracker
1 egg, slightly beaten   crumbs, divided
1/2 stick margarine, sliced   Dash cayenne pepper
1/2 cup mayonnaise   Salt and pepper
1 tablespoon sugar   Herbs (optional)
1 cup grated Cheddar cheese,
divided

Put well-drained, hot squash in large mixing bowl. Add egg, margarine, mayonnaise, sugar, half of cheese, and half of cracker crumbs. Season with cayenne pepper, salt, pepper, and herbs (oregano is especially good in this dish). Mix all ingredients well. Put into buttered 1 1/2-quart casserole and top with remaining cheese and crumbs. Bake at 350° for 20 minutes. Crookneck squash or a mixture of crookneck and zucchini may be used.

Starr Lang

★ ## SQUASH CASSEROLE II

Oven: 375° approximately 20 minutes   Yield: 6 to 8 servings

1 quart frozen squash, cooked	3/4 pint sour cream
1 medium onion, chopped	Salt and pepper to taste
1/2 bell pepper, chopped	1 stick margarine, melted
1 jar chopped pimiento	3/4 package herb stuffing mix
1 (10 3/4-ounce) can cream of chicken soup	

Cook together squash, onion, and bell pepper until soft. Drain. Add pimiento, soup, sour cream, salt, and pepper. Stir and mash together. Stir seasoned bread crumbs into melted margarine. Place half of crumbs in the bottom of a greased casserole dish. Place squash mixture on top of crumbs. Top with remainder of bread crumbs. Bake at 375° until hot, bubbly, and browned.

Mrs. Ray Sewell (Edith)

✳✳✳✳✳✳✳✳✳✳✳✳

Serve an attractive all-in-one vegetable dish. Separately cook zucchini slices, small whole carrots, and small whole onions (or use canned ones). Heat all vegetables together with butter, salt, pepper, and a little orange juice. Arrange zucchini around edge of serving platter, then make a ring of carrots next to the zucchini. Pile onions in the center.

Quickie potato salad: slice canned white potatoes thinly; add diced celery, green onions, hard-cooked eggs, salt, pepper, and mayonnaise or Thousand Island dressing. Garnish with pimiento, if desired.

Cook sliced carrots until tender then drain. Blend 1 tablespoon butter and 2 1/2 tablespoons honey and pour over carrots. Heat until glazed.

★ ## SQUASH CASSEROLE III
May be prepared the day before and re-heated.

Oven: 350° 30 minutes   Yield: 12 servings

4 cups fresh, cooked squash
  or 2 (16-ounce) cans
  drained squash
2 medium carrots, grated
1 medium onion, finely
  chopped

1 (2-ounce) jar pimiento strips
1 (10 3/4-ounce) can cream
  of chicken soup
1/2 pint sour cream
1 stick margarine
1 package Pepperidge Farm
  cornbread dressing mix

Mash squash and mix with carrots, onion, pimiento, soup, and sour cream. In separate pan, melt the margarine and toss with dressing mix. Spread a thin layer of dressing mix in bottom of 9x13-inch casserole or 2 (8x8-inch) casseroles. Alternate layers of squash mixture and dressing mixture. End with a thick layer of dressing mixture on top. Bake at 350° for 30 minutes.

Mrs. Joe W. Wray (Sara)
Atlanta, Georgia
Mrs. Robert H. Shell (Mary)
Mrs. D. M. Worth (Judi)
Mrs. A. L. Fuller (Kate)

❋❋❋❋❋❋❋❋❋❋❋❋❋

Quick seasoning tricks for more tasty vegetables:
—sprinkle snipped parsley or chives into the butter or cream sauce.
—sprinkle with celery, caraway, or dry-toasted sesame seeds.
—sprinkle a tiny bit of crushed thyme, oregano, or marjoram on tomatoes or greens; sprinkle freshly snipped tarragon or chervil on peas, beans, or other greens.

For a quick and easy vegetable sauce, combine the desired amount of mayonnaise with enough curry powder to give it a bright yellow color. Serve over broccoli, asparagus, or other vegetables.

★   ## SQUASH CASSEROLE IV

Oven: 350° 35 minutes   Yield: 6 servings

1 (28-ounce) can cut squash,   2 eggs
  drained, or   Salt and pepper to taste
  1 1/2 pints fresh squash, 1 cup bread crumbs,
  cooked   buttered
1/2 cup chopped onion   1/2 cup grated cheese
3 tablespoons margarine, melted

Mix squash, onion , margarine, eggs, salt, and pepper in buttered 1 1/2-quart casserole. Cook 20 minutes at 350°. Remove from oven and sprinkle grated cheese and bread crumbs on top. Return to oven and continue cooking until well browned, 10 to 15 minutes.

Mrs. Raybon McLain (Harriett)

★   ## SQUASH CASSEROLE V

Oven: 350° 30 minutes   Yield: 4 servings

1 pound squash, cut up   1 egg, beaten
1 onion, chopped   1/2 cup sharp cheese, grated
1 slice white bread,   Salt and pepper
  broken into pieces   Ritz cracker crumbs
1/2 cup milk

Cook squash with onion in salted water until tender. Drain. Soak bread pieces in milk; add beaten egg, cheese, salt, and pepper; then mix with squash. Pour all into a greased 1-quart casserole, top with Ritz cracker crumbs, and bake at 350° for 30 minutes or until set.

Mrs. Annie Pearl Cook

★ ## SQUASH CASSEROLE VI

Oven: 300° 30 minutes   Yield: 6 servings

2 pounds yellow squash
1 small onion
Salt and pepper
  to taste
3/4 cup water

1/2 (3-ounce) jar pimiento
  pepper (or to taste)
1/2 cup slivered almonds
1 (10 3/4-ounce) can cream
  of chicken soup

Dice squash in large pieces and onion in small pieces. Add salt and pepper to taste. Put on to cook in boiler with 3/4 cup of water over medium heat until just tender. Drain squash, butter a casserole dish, and layer squash, pimiento pepper, almonds, and 1/2 of cream of chicken soup. Repeat with another layer and sprinkle cracker crumbs on the top. Place in 300° oven for about 30 minutes or until bubbly.

Mrs. J. L. Weddington, III (Mary)

★ ## SQUASH PARMESAN

Oven: 350° 1 hour   Yield: 6 servings

2 pounds crookneck squash
2 (16-ounce) cans stewed
  tomatoes
1 teaspoon garlic powder
2 teaspoons flour
1 teaspoon salt

2 teaspoons sugar
1 teaspoon paprika
1/8 teaspoon pepper
1/8 teaspoon basil
8 ounces mozzarella cheese
1/2 cup Parmesan cheese

Boil squash about 10 minutes or until tender. Drain. Combine next 8 ingredients and simmer until slightly thickened. In 2-quart casserole alternate layers of squash and mozzarella cheese. Pour tomato mixture over each layer and sprinkle with Parmesan cheese. Cover and bake for 1 hour at 350°.

Winnie Cook

★ SQUASH OR EGGPLANT WITH TOMATOES

Good for surplus garden vegetables

Oven: 350° 10 minutes   Yield: 6 servings

1 onion, chopped	4 tomatoes, coarsely chopped
2 green peppers, chopped	2 teaspoons salt
1/4 cup cooking oil	Pepper to taste
1 medium eggplant, cubed, or	1/2 cup crumbled Cheddar
3 yellow crookneck or	cheese
3 zucchini squash, cubed	

In medium skillet, cook onion and pepper in cooking oil until golden and tender. Push aside; sauté cubed eggplant or squash. Put chopped tomatoes in with other vegetables and season to taste. Cook slowly, uncovered, for some of tomato liquid to evaporate. Top with cheese and continue cooking until cheese melts. Serve "as is" or put vegetable mixture in 1 1/2-quart casserole, top with cheese, and bake at 350° about 10 minutes, or until cheese melts.

Mrs. William R. Miller (Miriam)
Moreland, Georgia

★ STUFFED SQUASH

Oven: 350° 10 minutes   Yield: 4 servings

4 squash	Bacon drippings
1 medium onion, chopped	Bread crumbs
Salt and pepper to taste	Butter
1 slice bacon, cooked	

Boil squash 5 minutes in salt and water. Cut hole in squash and remove pulp. Boil pulp and chopped onion until done. Drain squash shells and pulp mixture. Season pulp with salt, pepper, bacon, and bacon drippings. Mash. Stuff into squash shells. Top with bread crumbs and dot with butter. Put into broiling pan with small amount of water. Bake at 350° for 10 minutes.

Mrs. Charles Woodroof (Minerva)

★ BOURBON SWEET POTATOES

A good Thanksgiving dish

Oven: 375° 20 minutes   Yield: 10 to 12 servings

6 to 8 sweet potatoes, or
   1 (30-ounce) can, drained
2 eggs
6 tablespoons margarine,
   melted
1 cup brown sugar

3 tablespoons bourbon
1/3 cup sweetened condensed
   milk
1 (8-ounce) can crushed
   pineapple with juice

Topping:

2 cups Grape-Nuts (cereal)
1/3 cup chopped nuts

1/4 cup melted margarine

If using raw sweet potatoes, cook, peel, and mash. In blender or mixmaster, put potatoes, eggs, margarine, sugar, bourbon, and condensed milk. Blend well. If using canned potatoes, there will be some lumps. Add pineapple last to avoid liquifying. Pour into 2-quart oblong casserole and top with cereal mixture. Bake at 375° for 20 minutes or until set.

NOTE: Especially good with ham.

Mrs. T. C. Moss (Virginia)
Cameron, South Carolina

❅❅❅❅❅❅❅❅❅❅❅❅❅

Adding 1/2 teaspoon sugar when cooking vegetables such as corn, carrots, or peas will help bring out their flavor, especially if they happen to be a day or two old. Adding salt to water for cooking some vegetables, corn for example, will make the vegetables tough.

Heat a slice or two of garlic in butter for a few minutes; remove the garlic and season vegetables with the butter.

Fruits and vegetables will ripen faster when wrapped in a paper bag and stored in a cabinet or drawer.

★ ## GRATED SWEET POTATO CASSEROLE

Oven: 450° 1 hour   Yield: 10 to 12 servings

1 1/2 cups sugar
1/2 cup milk
3 cups grated raw sweet
  potatoes
2 eggs

1 stick margarine
3/4 cup buttermilk
1/8 teaspoon soda
1/2 cup pecans
1/2 teaspoon cinnamon

Mix sugar and milk in large bowl; add potatoes. Beat eggs; add butter. Combine two mixtures. Add other ingredients and mix. Pour into 2-quart casserole and bake for 1 hour at 450°.

NOTE: Old-fashioned and rarely used but especially delicious during holidays with turkey and ham.

Mrs. Lindsey Barron (Genet)
Mrs. A. L. Fuller (Kate)

★ ## GRATED SWEET POTATO PUDDING
Good with ham

Oven: 350° 60 minutes   Yield: 4 servings

2 cups of grated sweet
  potatoes
  (1 large sweet potato makes
  approximately 2 cups
  grated)
1/2 stick butter or margarine,
  melted

1/4 cup brown sugar
1/4 cup dark corn syrup
1/4 teaspoon salt
1/2 cup powdered sugar
1/4 teaspoon cinnamon
1/4 teaspoon nutmeg
1 egg

Place all ingredients in a bowl and mix well. Pour into a greased 24-ounce casserole. Cook at 350° about 1 hour. Stir when it has cooked about 1/2 hour.

NOTE: Topped with whipped cream, this dish may also be served as a unique Southern dessert.

Mrs. Henry Reese (Alice)

★ ## CANDIED SWEET POTATOES
A Southern treat

Oven: 350° 1 hour   Yield: 8 to 12 servings

6 to 8 sweet potatoes   1/2 cup water
1 cup light brown sugar   Pinch salt
1 cup maple syrup   Marshmallows (optional)
1/2 cup sugar   Chopped pecans (optional)
2 tablespoons butter

Boil sweet potatoes until almost tender. Drain and cool. Peel and slice into thick pieces. Make syrup of light brown sugar, maple syrup, sugar, butter, water, and salt. Boil slowly about 10 minutes. Cover bottom of large, shallow baking dish with half the sweet potato slices. Cover with half of the syrup. Add another layer of potatoes and syrup. Bake in 350° oven about 1 hour, basting occasionally. A topping of marshmallows and pecans may be added before removing from oven.

Mrs. Robert D. Royal (Sue)

****

Zucchini is marvelous boiled with sliced onions until just done. Drain and toss zucchini and onions with melted butter, a dash of garlic powder, and a little grated Parmesan cheese.

Stuff a tomato with caviar seasoned with lemon juice. Garnish with sieved egg yolk and egg white.

Broiled tomato slices are a scrumptious side dish. Sprinkle tomato slices with bread crumbs. Top each with a pat of butter and half a pitted prune. Broil and serve hot.

For a quick, delicious summer salad, peel a fresh tomato and stuff it with a mixture of finely chopped green pepper, celery, green onions, and mayonnaise, preferably homemade. Serve on a lettuce leaf.

SENATOR RUSSELL'S SWEET POTATO CASSEROLE
Great for company

Oven: 350° 30 minutes   Yield: 8 servings

3 cups mashed sweet potatoes   1 tablespoon vanilla extract
1 cup sugar   1/2 cup butter, melted
2 eggs

Topping:
1 cup brown sugar, packed   1 cup chopped nuts
1/2 cup flour   1/3 cup butter

Mix sweet potatoes, sugar, eggs, vanilla, and butter thoroughly. Pour into a buttered 1-quart casserole. Mix all the topping ingredients together with a fork. Sprinkle the crumbs on top of the casserole. Bake for 30 minutes at 350˘.

Mrs. Irwin H. Pike (Helen)
Mrs. Wynn Vineyard (Margaret)
Winder, Georgia
Mrs. C. A. Moody (Virginia)

****

To prevent baked Irish potatoes from being soggy, prick several times with a fork when removing them from the oven.

Save margarine wrappers to wrap baking potatoes.

If vegetables are too salty, drop in a few slices of a raw, peeled potato and cook a little longer. The potato will absorb the extra salt.

Bell peppers; hot peppers, and mushrooms are three fresh vegetables that can be frozen. Place in plastic bag and store in freezer.

★ **SWEET POTATO CASSEROLE I**

Delicious topping adds an extra zip to sweet potatoes

Oven: 350° 30 minutes   Yield: 10 to 12 servings

3 cups sweet potatoes,   2 eggs
  cooked and mashed   1/3 stick of margarine
1 cup granulated sugar   1 teaspoon vanilla extract

Topping:
1 cup brown sugar   1/3 cup margarine
1 cup nuts   1/3 cup self-rising flour
1 cup coconut

In a 2-quart casserole, mix sweet potatoes, sugar, eggs, margarine, and vanilla. Mix brown sugar, nuts, coconut, margarine, and self-rising flour. Top the sweet potatoes with this mixture. Bake at 350° for 30 minutes.

Mrs. Bryan B. Sargent (Ellen)

****

When grating the rind of a lemon or orange, be careful to get just the colored part. The white beneath is bitter; the colored part is called the zest.

A lemon can be a handy household aid:

Fruit stains may be removed from fabrics by dipping up and down in really boiling water. If the stain is on a table cloth, put a bowl under the stain and pour boiling water into the bowl. If stubborn, apply lemon juice as well.

For rust spots, nothing is better than lemon juice plus salt and sunshine.

To clean ivory handles on knives and forks when they have become yellow, dip a piece of lemon in salt and rub over them.

★   **SWEET POTATO CASSEROLE II**

Oven: 350° 25 minutes   Yield: 8 to 10 servings

cups cooked, mashed   2 eggs, well beaten
  sweet potatoes   1/3 cup milk
 cup sugar   1 teaspoon vanilla extract
/2 cup margarine, melted

Topping:
/2 cup brown sugar   2 1/2 tablespoons margarine
/4 cup all-purpose flour   1 cup chopped pecans

    Combine potatoes, sugar, margarine, eggs, vanilla, and milk. Mix well. Put into baking dish. Mix all topping ingredients. Sprinkle on top of potato mixture before baking. Bake at 350° for 25 minutes.

Mrs. J. E. Rainwater (Culley)
Moreland, Georgia

❉❉❉❉❉❉❉❉❉❉❉❉❉

For more lemon juice, soak the lemon in cold water before squeezing. Placing the lemon in hot water or a heated oven might produce more juice, but the juice is inferior in taste and nutrients.

If raisins dry out and become hard, soak them in hot water for 3 minutes before using them.

To prevent raisins, dates, and other fruits from sticking together in a solid mass when put through a food chopper, place fruit in a strainer and hold under the cold water tap before chopping.

When cutting sticky food, dip the knife in cold water often. Rub butter on scissors before cutting marshmallows or fruit to prevent sticking.

551

★ **SWEET POTATO CASSEROLE III**

Freezes well

Oven: 350° 45 minutes   Yield: 8 or 10 serving

1 (32-ounce) can sweet   1 teaspoon cinnamon
   potatoes, mashed   1 cup chopped pecans
1 cup sugar   1 jigger or 2 ounces
1 stick margarine, melted   bourbon or
1 teaspoon salt   1 teaspoon vanilla extract
2 eggs, beaten
1 (5.33-ounce) can
   evaporated milk

Topping:

1 cup flour   1 cup pecans
1 cup brown sugar   1 stick margarine, melted

Mix all ingredients together and spread in a large, shallow casserole. Mix topping ingredients with a fork and crumble over top of casserole. Bake at 350° for 45 minutes.

Mrs. W. Y. Ellis (Ida Lee)

✳✳✳✳✳✳✳✳✳✳✳✳✳

To open a coconut more easily, place it in a warm oven for a few minutes.

To tint coconut, blend 1 teaspoon of milk or water with a drop or two of food color. Add 1 1/3 cups flaked coconut. Toss with a fork until blended or put in a jar and shake.

To freshen shredded coconut, soak in fresh milk with a dash of sugar a few minutes before using or place in a sieve, set over boiling water, and steam until moist.

When selecting pineapples, pluck a leaf from the pineapple's crown. If the leaf pulls out easily, the fruit is ripe and ready to eat.

★ **SWEET POTATO OR BUTTERNUT SQUASH
A LA CHARLESTON**

Oven: 300° to 325° 45 minutes   Yield: 6 to 8 servings

3 1/2 cups mashed, cooked   1/2 teaspoon nutmeg (scant)
   squash or sweet potatoes   2 tablespoons sherry
1 stick butter   2 tablespoons bourbon
9 heaping tablespoons sugar   or brandy
Juice of 1 lemon plus   1/2 teaspoon salt
   grated rind   4 eggs
1 teaspoon mace

Mix first nine ingredients well. Beat eggs and add to squash or potato mixture. Mix well. Bake in greased casserole at 300° to 325° about 45 minutes. To freeze, line casserole with clear plastic wrap. Freeze. Lift out of casserole and wrap well. Keep in freezer. Before baking, remove plastic wrap, put into casserole dish, and let thaw.

Mrs. Joe Bohannon (Mary)

★ **SWEET POTATO SOUFFLÉ I**
Families will love this creamy dish!

Oven: 350° 45 minutes   Yield: 8 to 10 servings

3 cups cooked, mashed,   1/4 cup orange juice
   sweet potatoes   1/2 cup margarine, melted
1 teaspoon vanilla extract   1 teaspoon cinnamon
1 cup sugar   1 cup raisins (optional)
1 egg   1 cup nuts, chopped (optional)
1/4 cup milk   Miniature marshmallows
3 tablespoons flour

Combine all ingredients except marshmallows in mixing bowl. Mix well. Pour into greased 2-quart casserole. Bake at 350° for 30 to 35 minutes; remove from oven, top with miniature marshmallows and return to over for 10 to 15 minutes. This soufflé may be frozen before or after cooking.

Mrs. William Donald Tomlinson (Jane)

553

★ SWEET POTATO SOUFFLÉ II

Oven: 400° 35 minutes

Yield: 6 to 8 servings

3 cups cooked, drained, and
  mashed sweet potatoes
1 1/4 cups sugar
2 eggs
3/4 stick margarine, melted

1/2 cup milk
1/2 teaspoon nutmeg
1/2 teaspoon cinnamon
1/2 cup chopped pecans

Topping:

3/4 cup crushed cornflakes
1/2 cup brown sugar

3/4 stick margarine, melted
1/2 cup chopped pecans

In large bowl of electric mixer, combine all ingredients well. Bake in a 2 1/2-quart casserole dish for 25 minutes at 400°.

TOPPING: Mix all ingredients. Spread on top of baked mixture and return to oven for 10 minutes.

NOTE: A 32-ounce can of sweet potatoes may be used. Do not cook.

Mrs. David L. Parrott (Carol)

★ SCALLOPED TOMATOES

Oven: 350° 45 minutes

Yield: 6 servings

1 quart tomatoes
6 tablespoons brown sugar
1 stick margarine

1 1/2 cups bread crumbs
1/2 teaspoon basil

Bring the tomatoes and brown sugar to a boil; boil a few minutes, stirring. Melt margarine and pour over bread crumbs. Combine the tomatoes and bread crumbs. Add basil and mix well. Bake in a 1 1/2-quart casserole for 45 minutes at 350° uncovered.

Mrs. Hendree Harrison (Carol)

BOHEMIAN TOMATOES
Very good with grilled chicken or steak

Oven: 375° 1 hour   Yield: 4 servings

1 (1 pound) can of tomatoes   1/4 cup butter
1 cup diced celery   1 teaspoon salt
1 large onion, chopped   1/8 teaspoon pepper
1/4 cup chopped green   1/2 cup buttered bread
  pepper   crumbs

Mix all ingredients except bread crumbs and place in buttered casserole. Top with crumbs and bake uncovered in a moderate oven 375° for 1 hour or until it is cooked down and soft.

Mrs. Jett M. Fisher (Carol)
Mrs. Hugh A. Farmer (Zoe)

FRIED GREEN TOMATOES

Yield: 4 servings

4 large green tomatoes   Pinch of black pepper
2 cups plain corn meal   1/2 cup shortening or
1 1/2 tablespoons salt   cooking oil

Wash the tomatoes and pat dry. Cut tomatoes in 1/4-inch slices. Sprinkle with salt and pepper. Dip each slice in corn meal and lay aside on waxed paper. Heat oil. Fry tomato slices until golden brown. Drain on paper towels. Serve hot.

Mrs. Henry Reese (Alice)

NOTES:

Special Features

SPECIAL FEATURES

Special Features Chapter Design: Britannia Hopper Coffee Mill (1910), Milk Boiler (1883)

A Guide to Appetizer Trees

An hors d'oeuvre tree is a great way to add fun to a party table. Let the tree be the appetizer course for a dinner or the eye-catcher on a buffet table. Guests simply help themselves. The tree can be re-used year after year and may be decorated to fit any party theme or season. Let the imagination be the guide!

Purchase a 12 to 18-inch tall Styrofoam cone. Give it a firm base by forcing the base of an 8 or 10-inch angel food cake pan two inches or more into the bottom of the cone. Anchor pan base to a heavy plate or mirror with florist's clay so the tree won't tip over when bites are picked from the tree. A round, footed mirror makes a pretty base to which to attach the tree.

Cover tree and metal base with green foil or green wrapping paper. Decorate around the base with greenery to suit the season or occasion. Attach favorite hot or cold hors d'oeuvres or prepare the tree in one of the following ways:

TOMATO TREE: Tape or staple sprigs of holly at 2-inch intervals over entire cone. Insert one end of toothpick into stem-end of cherry tomato and other end into tree among the holly. Cover whole tree in a random or spiral pattern. Decorate base with holly and holly berries. (Use holly for Christmas party; use other greenery for other occasions.)

MIXED VEGETABLE TREE: Attach greenery if desired, or leave tree with green foil covering. Using toothpicks, attach radish roses or accordians, cauliflower bites, cucumber rounds, celery curls, carrot flowers or curls, cherry tomatoes, or any other crisp, raw vegetables. For variety, also add small cheese cubes, small salami circles, and tiny ham rolls. Place bowls of vegetable dip near the tree.

SHRIMP TREE: Tape or staple parsley sprigs to the covered Styrofoam cone in a random or spiral pattern. Using toothpicks, attach cleaned, cooked shrimp to the tree.

CHEESE AND FRUIT TREE: Using toothpicks, attach cheese cubes and various fruits to the tree. Fruit suggestions: pears, apples, strawberries, pineapple chunks, or substitute sausages for fruit.

STRAWBERRY TREE: Using toothpicks, attach fresh whole strawberries, stems still attached. Decorate the base with fresh greenery and strawberries. Place a bowl of powdered sugar nearby for dipping.

A Guide to Cake Decorating

CAKE DECORATING BASICS

1. Most pound cakes, regular cake mixes, etc., can be baked in almos any gelatin mold.

2. Many containers found in the kitchen can be used for baking as lon as they are oven-proof. These include casserole dishes, metal or Pyre mixing bowls, and clay flower pots. Adjust baking time and test cak for doneness.

3. To decorate with packaged icing mixes, just add 1/3 less liquid tha package directions specify. This may be substituted for boiled o buttercream decorator's icing.

4. To clean decorator tips or tubes when frosting a cake, add 1 teaspoo cream of tartar to 1 cup water in a small pan. Boil tips in th solution until they are clean and clear of frosting. Rinse with clea water and drain on a paper towel.

5. When decorating a cake with decorator tubes, substitute a simila tube if the one called for is not available. Most decorator tubes fal into this general category division:
   numbers 1 through 5-writing tubes
   13 through 32-star tubes
   65 through 70-leaf tubes
   101 through 104-rose tubes

6. Most of the cakes described in this section may be iced using a knif to give a smooth finish or with decorator tubes to give a more detail ed finish.

NURSERY RHYME CAKES

MARY, MARY QUITE CONTRARY

Bake cake in medium or large oven-proof mixin bowl. Place cake on plate or on top of a 9-inc round cake. Frost head and face with white c flesh-tinted icing. Pipe on hair with tube 32; mak hair blonde or brown (chocolate). Spread on blu eyes with a knife tip. Use tube 103 to make flower on hair and around cake; or use tube 16 for flowe clusters. Pipe on green leaves with tube 67.

Ice the round cake green (Mary's "garden") Buy little plastic bells and attach with green leaves pipe a white collar (tube 104) around Mary's nec and a white border around bottom of green roun cake using any tip.

VARIATION: All icing may be spread smoothly with a knife; pull for through icing for hair texture.

560

(Continued

LITTLE MISS MUFFET

Bake cake as for "Mary, Mary". Ice face white or flesh color. Using tube 2, pipe on outline and fill in the following; red mouth, blue eyes, brown lashes. Pipe on yellow hair with tube 32. Ice a cupcake white and attach with icing to head. Place white doily around cupcake base to form a brim. Pipe a blue ribbon around cupcake base with tube 47. Fashion a spider with four 4-inch pieces of wire; knot in the center. Place on hat and touch up with black icing.

CAKE PRESENT

Bake cake batter in one large or several tiny loaf pans. Ice to look like a wrapped gift. Pipe on a contrasting-color ribbon and bow using any decorator tip.

VARIATION: Pipe each child's name (tip 1 through 5) on small cakes and present each guest at the party with his own special cake at refreshment time.

BABY SWEATER AND BOOTIES

Bake 1 cake mix in a square pan for baby sweater (or in a 9x13-inch pan for baby gown). Freeze cake, then cut. To ice, use tube 30 in a circular motion; do the right side, looping icing to the right, then the left, looping to the left. This gives a "knitted" effect. Or use star tube 16 all over for a "crocheted" effect. Use tube 32 for buttons and tube 104 for white ribbon and bows at neck and on booties. Ice in pink, blue, or yellow.

REAL FLOWER POTS

Wash small clay pots in dishwasher to sterilize. Place an Oreo cookie in the bottom of each pot. Hold a straw in the center and fill the pot with ice cream. Cut off straw level with ice cream. Serve with a real flower inserted in the straw. Crush extra Oreo cookies and sprinkle over the top of ice cream for "dirt". Or sprinkle with green-tinted coconut for "grass".

SNOWMAN

Bake one 8-inch and one 9-inch round cake layer. Ice smoothly with white frosting, or use tube 16 and cover entire snowman. Using tube 16, pipe on a blue scarf. Use candy (life-savers, chocolate kisses, candy corn, etc.) for eyes, nose, mouth, and buttons. Red licorice may be used for mouth. Top with a black construction paper hat.

561

(Continued)

BASEBALL GLOVE AND BALL

Bake one 9-inch round cake and cut as illustrated for glove. Bake as many cupcakes as desired for baseballs. Scoop out palm of glove slightly and frost with chocolate icing. Trim cupcakes to give a more rounded look. Frost with white icing. Pipe thin black laces on each baseball with a small writing tube, or use thin black licorice. Place one baseball on glove and arrange remaining baseballs around glove. Insert candles in baseballs if desired.

TRAIN CAKE

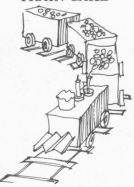

Use 4 to 6 small (4 1/2x2 1/2x2) loaf pans. Fill each pan only half full. Bake at 350° for 20 to 25 minutes. Ice cars any color(s) desired-red caboose, brown engine. Before icing engine, place a marsh-mallow on top for smoke stack and ice over. Use life-savers or small cookies for wheels. Connect cars with short pieces of licorice.

VARIATIONS: To indicate "cargo", sprinkle one of the following on the top of each car: redhots, peanuts, crushed peppermint, colored sugars, non-pareils, etc. If cake is for a birthday party, put candles on top of the cars. Insert each candle in a dollop of icing or a lifesaver.

BUTTERFLY CAKE

Bake one 9x12x2-inch cake or one 8 or 9-inch round cake depending on which pattern is to be used. Cut cake as illustrated. Decorate with tube 16 or simply frost with a knife. Make antenna with tube 2. Ice butterfly bright green, yellow, and brown. Pipe on any markings desired. Or decorate with life-savers, gumdrops, and other candies.

VALENTINE CAKE

Use two cake mixes and bake one in an 9-inch round pan and one in a 9-inch square pan. Cut cooled cake as illustrated. Ice entire cake a soft shade of pink. Then decorate cake with a white ruffle (tube 104), roses (tube 104), or other flowers, and green leaves (tube 67). Make flower shades of darker pink.

CUPCAKES

Cupcakes have always been a favorite with children. Not only are they easy for little hands to handle, but children enjoy having their own "special" cakes.

CUPCAKE CONE

Buy square-bottom ice cream cone cups. Fill each cone with cake batter to within 1 inch of top rim. Place cones in muffin tins and bake at 300° for 15 to 20 minutes (or as cupcake recipe directs). When cool, ice as ice cream cone, or frost and decorate top with icing flowers.

SIMPLE HOLIDAY CUPCAKES

Cut designs from construction paper and secure to toothpicks, then insert in cupcakes. Glue or tape a red heart to a toothpick for a Valentine cupcake; a shamrock for St. Pat's Day; tiny reindeer, stocking, or holly sprigs for Christmas.

CUPCAKE CLOWNS

Turn cupcake upside down and ice. With tube 32, pipe on 2 legs and feet, arms and hands. Buy clown head picks at a bakery supply store and insert in top.

CUPCAKE PARTY

For birthdays and the brave Mother! Provide the small guests with unfrosted cupcakes and plenty of brightly colored frosting. Let them decorate the cupcakes with small items such as M & M's, raisins, miniature marshmallows, gumdrops, cherries, etc. Make sure aprons are available. After they're finished, guests eat their own creations!

EASTER BASKET CUPCAKES

Bake cupcakes in pastel-colored cupcake liners. Frost with white icing and sprinkle center with green coconut. (To tint coconut, place shredded coconut in a jar with a few drops of green food coloring. Screw on lid and shake until coconut is uniformly colored.) Place small colored jelly beans on coconut. Bend a pipe cleaner into a "U" shape for the handle; insert along each side. Tie a pastel ribbon on the top of the pipe cleaner handle.

FLOWER CUPCAKES

Use a 3 or 4-inch clay flower pot. Sterilize in dishwasher. Line the bottom with foil and fill with vanilla ice cream. Place a pepermint candy stick in the center of the ice cream filling. Freeze until firm. Make cupcakes and frosting. Tint frosting pastel pink and yellow; tint coconut the same colors. Frost cupcakes and sprinkle sides and bottoms with matching colored coconut. When ready to serve, stick cupcake (upside down) on the candy stick. Sprinkle ice cream with chocolate curls and add green leaves. Serve at once.

A Guide to Cheeses
Cheese Selection Guide

CHEESE	COLOR, FLAVOR, AND TEXTURE	LIFE SPAN	USED FOR
Bleu (France)	White; spicy and piquant; semi-soft with blue-green veins	3 to 8 months	Appetizers, snacks, salads, dips, dessert
Brick (U.S.)	Yellow to orange; mild, less sharp than Cheddar; semi-soft, smooth	4 weeks	Snacks, sandwiches, salads, melts well
Brie (France)	White edible crust, soft yellow body; mild but definite and distinctive flavor; soft-ripened white mold cow-milk cheese	4 weeks	Dessert cheese-with wine, fruit, French bread
Camembert (France)	White crust, yellow body; mild to pungent; creamy	4 weeks	Dessert cheese-excellent with tart apple slices
Cheddar (England-American)	White, yellow, or orange; mild to sharp; smooth, firm texture	2 to 12 months	Snacks, cooking, dessert, toppings, grating (versatile)
Cottage Cheese (U.S.)	White; mild, slightly acid taste; soft, moist, large or small curd	2 weeks	As a spread, in salads, dips, cooked foods

(Continued)

Cheese Selection Guide (Cont.)

eam Cheese (U.S.)	White; mild, slightly acid taste; soft, smooth, buttery	2 weeks	As a spread, in sandwiches, on crackers, in salads
am (Holland)	Red wax rind, creamy yellow body; mild nutty flavor; semi-soft to firm	6 months	Table cheese, snacks, with fresh fruit, seafood sauces
uda (Holland)	Red wax rind, creamy yellow body; mild nutty flavor (like Edam); Semi-soft to firm-softer than Edam	6 months	Fresh fruits, with beer or wine, in salads, dessert cheese
uyere (Switzerland)	Light yellow body, tan crust; mild, sweetish nut-like flavor (similar to Swiss); firm to hard with tiny holes	2 years	Fresh fruit, dessert, fine cooking cheese (melts well), fondue
ederkranz (U.S.)	Light orange edible rind, deep yellow body; strong flavor and aroma; creamy, soft	4 weeks	Dessert with light wine, on dark bread with beer
nburger (Belgium)	White crust and interior; very strong and aromatic; soft, smooth, creamy	4 to 6 months	Snack with crackers or dark bread with beer or hearty red wine
ozzarella (Italy)	Pale ivory body; mild delicate flavor; semi-soft, mild, creamy	2 weeks	The "pizza" cheese-Italian foods, uncooked sandwiches, melts easily, good topping
uenster (Germany)	Creamy white-body; mild to mellow; semi-soft, smooth	5 weeks	Dessert, table cheese, snacks, sandwiches, breads
rmesan (Italy)	Light yellow body; sharp, piquant flavor and aroma; hard, brittle body	3 years or more	Grating cheese-for seasoning soups, salads, casseroles, meats, vegetables, etc.

(Continued) 565

Cheese Selection Guide (Cont.)

Port du Salut (France)	Creamy yellow body; mellow to robust, depending on age; semi-soft, firm, and buttery texture	7 weeks	Dessert and table cheese, snacks, cocktails, fresh frui
Provolone (Italy)	Yellow to dark crust, pale yellow body; mild to sharp and often smoked; hard, often flaky texture	2 to 3 years	Up to 9 month as table or sna cheese; aged, use for grating on pizza, pasta, etc.
Ricotta (Italy)	White, rindless cheese like cream cheese; mild semi-sweet, nutty flavor; creamy, slightly bland	2 weeks	Important ingredient in ma Italian dishes, used also as a filling for pastries
Roquefort (France)	White, marbled with blue-green mold; sharp, spicy, piquant, semi-soft, pasty, and sometimes crumbly	3 months	Salad dressing, dessert, dips, or with robust red wine, dark bread
Swiss or Emmentaler (Switzerland)	Pale yellow body; mild, sweetish, nutlike flavor; large holes, hard smooth texture	Over 2 years	Sandwiches, snacks, salads, fondues, desse cooking, toppi wine, beer, fruit

GOOD CHEESE ADVICE

1. As a rule, don't freeze cheese. Freezing will affect the body and te ture of most cheeses. They may be suitable for cooking, but wi appear crumbly or mealy.
2. To keep in optimum condition for longer life spans, cheeses should t kept in a cool, dry place and wrapped in air-tight bags. Bleu chees are an exception; leave a bit of air space in the wrapping.
3. Cheeses- should be turned every few days to keep natural oils distr buted.
4. Don't be afraid of mold on cheese. Many cheeses are mold. Ju scrape the mold off and serve as usual.

(Continue

SERVING CHEESE

Cheeses, except cream and cottage cheese, should be served at room temperature. This softens the texture and maximizes the flavor. Allow about an hour out of the refrigerator for most cheeses-longer for some soft cheeses like Camembert and Brie.

Cheese is very compatible with natural surroundings. When serving, a wooden cheese board or a slab of fine marble may be used.

Do not crowd too many cheeses on a board. It's easier for guests to serve themselves from an uncluttered board. Avoid placing strong and mild cheeses next to each other. The flavor of delicate cheeses should be respected and not overpowered by strong beverages or highly seasoned crackers.

Serve cheeses simply. Avoid knickknacks or fruit or crackers on the cheese board. Serve cheeses without their wrappers, no matter how colorful they may be. For a formal tasting, do label cheeses. Also use several kinds of breads-French, rye, pumpernickle, black bread, etc. Seasoned or salty crackers are not good choices; cheeses should never be inferior to other flavors.

The classic way to serve cheese is with fruit, and/or beverages such as beer, wine, ale, cider, or even milk. The milder the cheese the milder the beverage should be, and vice-versa.

Don't pre-cut cheese for guests. It exposes too much surface to the air, which dries it out and robs the cheese of its dignity and identity.

When serving cheese for dessert, provide each person with a small plate and knife. Cheese may be eaten with the fingers, but in formal atmospheres it is eaten with a fork.

Cheese is very versatile and goes with many kinds and combinations of foods. As a last course, it enhances most dinners or luncheons. Exceptions are menus containing rich meat or poultry, and following a rich creamed or cheese dish. It should not be used with dishes from those countries where little cheese is eaten. Cheese is inappropriate following a Chinese or Japanese dinner, or a hot Indian curry.

A Guide to Frozen Punch Rings

Follow these simple instructions to create an absolutely spectacular punch ring that can be easily changed to suit any occasion!

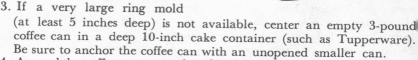

1. Combine one (46-ounce) can of unsweetened grapefruit juice and 1 (46-ounce) can of water.

2. Set aside 1 cup of juice-water mixture for later use.

3. If a very large ring mold (at least 5 inches deep) is not available, center an empty 3-pound coffee can in a deep 10-inch cake container (such as Tupperware). Be sure to anchor the coffee can with an unopened smaller can.

4. Around the coffee can, pour 1 to 2 inches of the juice-water mixture. Freeze until solid.

5. Continue adding and freezing 1 to 2 inches of the juice-water mixture on top of the previously frozen mixture until a frozen ring approximately 4 inches in depth is formed. When complete, the ring will be composed of 2 to 4 separate frozen layers.

6. Without removing the coffee can from the center of the frozen ring, place a design of fruit around the top of the ring. Make sure the top is completely covered. Suggested fruits include grapes, strawberries, oranges and lemons (sliced or whole), kumquats, plums, etc.

7. Pour the 1 cup of reserved juice-water mixture over the fruit arrangement. Freeze.

8. After the fruit is frozen, pour hot water into the coffee can and slowly remove the can from the center of the ring.

9. Run hot water around the outside edge of the cake container and, placing hand in the center of the ring, gently lift out the ring. Place it on foil, and carefully cover the ring making sure that the fruit is not crushed.

10. Store in freezer until ready to use. Properly wrapped, rings may be kept frozen for months.

11. Fruit will frost itself when it is removed from freezer.

Alternate ways to decorate rings:

A. **Holly Wreath**. Holly leaves and berries gently washed with hot water and placed around the frozen ring make a beautiful holly wreath for festive Christmas punches. (Don't forget to anchor holly with reserved juice-water mixture as in Step 7 and freeze before using.)

(Continued)

B. **Floating Flowers**. Small plastic holders may be purchased from a local florist and frozen into the rings. Just before floating ring in the punch bowl, place fresh flowers in holders. Make sure flowers that will not wilt quickly are chosen. Small orchids are beautiful.

A Guide to Garnishes

Food is tastier and more festive when it is served with a flair. Turn a buffet, hors d'oeuvre table, or even a sandwich plate, into a delicious treat for the eye. These vegetable garnishes are relatively simple to make and are guaranteed conversation pieces!

ADVANCE PREPARATION AND STORAGE OF FLOWER GARNISHES

Daffodils, Daisies and Zinnias may be prepared three days in advance. To store, line a large plastic container with a tight-fitting top with damp paper towels. Gently place flowers in container, being careful not to crush them. Snap on lid tightly and refrigerate.

Cheese rosebuds may be prepared five days in advance. To store, line a cookie tin or similar container with waxed paper. Gently place rosebuds in container. Put on lid tightly and refrigerate.

Special Tools Needed (Daffodils, Daisies, Zinnias)

Corrugated-Edge Slicer

Vegetable Cutter

SCULPTURED MUSHROOMS

1. Gently rinse large mushroom caps and pat dry.
2. Slice off stems. Do not pull off.
3. Make 6-8 equally spaced cuts around the mushroom cap, starting about 1/4 inch from center, and cutting through the mushroom.
4. Repeat the procedure, making a second cut to the left of the first cut, resulting in a △ -shaped slice.
5. Gently remove slices between the cuts.
6. Sauté the mushrooms, cap side down, in melted butter mixed with a small amount of lemon juice. (1-2 min.) Turn, and sauté 30 seconds more.

DAFFODILS

Materials required:
Thin-slice vegetable cutter
Corrugated-edge vegetable or egg slicer
1 large turnip (potatoes **not** suitable)
Thimble
1 carrot-cleaned
Toothpicks
Yellow food coloring
Scissors

1. Using a thin-slice vegetable cutter, cut a very thin slice of white turnip.
2. Using the pattern, trace the outline on the turnip slice. Cut it out with scissors. (The size of the pattern may be scaled down, depending on the size of the turnip.)
3. With a thimble, cut the center hole.
4. Place the cut slice in a shallow bowl of ice water with yellow food coloring.
5. Cut a second turnip slice.
6. With a corrugated-edge cutting tool, flute the outside edge of the turnip slice, all the way around.
7. Place fluted-edge turnip slice in another bowl of ice water.
8. Cut 2 to 3 thin strips of carrots, about 2 inches long, and 1/8 inch thick.
9. Wrap the fluted-edge slice around finger, and insert it into the center hole of the yellow slice. Insert carrot strips into the center, and secure the flower by passing a toothpick through the fluted slice on the underside of the flower.

CHEESE ROSEBUDS

Materials required:
Mild Cheddar cheese
Stuffed olives
Scissors
Toothpicks
Red food coloring

1. Allow mild Cheddar cheese to soften at room temperature. Grate.
2. Using fingers, shape a small amount of cheese into a double cone.

3. Remove pimiento from stuffed olives.
4. With scissors, cut olive to form base of rosebud.
5. Insert cheese cone into olive cup, leaving half out to form the bud. Shape with fingers.
6. Using a toothpick or a fine brush, gently streak on a small amount of red food coloring.

Suggestions for use:
1. Using "frilly" toothpicks, stick cheese rosebud on toothpick, and use to garnish a luncheon plate.
2. Using the cheese rosebuds on "frilly" toothpicks, cover a grapefruit to resemble a nosegay. Great for cocktail parties.
3. Using washed hedge greenery from the yard, arrange in a suitable container and stick rosebuds on the tips of the stems. A "delicious" centerpiece which guests will both admire and enjoy!

ZINNIAS

Materials required:
Thin-slice vegetable cutter
Corrugated-edge vegetable or egg slicer
Scissors
Large turnips (potatoes **not** suitable)
Small carrots-cleaned
Toothpicks
Food coloring

1. Using a thin-slice vegetable cutter, cut 3 thin slices of white turnip, varying about 1/3 inch in size.
2. With scissors, cut approximately 12 petals in each slice. Round off the corners.
3. Place cut turnip slices in a bowl of ice water containing food coloring of your choice.
4. Using a corrugated-edge slicer, cut a small carrot cross-wise into slices about 1/2 inch thick.
5. Stick a toothpick into one end of the carrot, and then slide on the smallest turnip slice, the next largest, and the largest, pushing them all close together.

571

FIELD DAISIES

Materials required:
Thin-slice vegetable cutter
Turnip (potatoes **not** suitable)
Corrugated-edge vegetable or egg slicer
Small carrot-cleaned
Toothpicks
Scissors
Optional: Yellow food coloring

1. With a thin-slice vegetable cutter, cut a thin slice of white turnip. *
2. Using a corrugated-edge slicer, cut a small carrot cross-wise into slices ½ to 1-inch thick.
3. Stick the carrot slice on one end of a toothpick.
4. Pass the toothpick through the center of the turnip slice, so the carrot rests on top of the turnip slice.
5. Using scissors, cut about 16 petals in the turnip slice, to within ¼ inch of the carrot center. Cut a thin wedge from each side of the petal.
6. Daisies are more natural looking with two turnip petal layers rather than just one. Repeat steps 1, 4, and 5.

*OPTIONAL: Place turnip slice in a shallow bowl of ice water with yellow food coloring. Obtain variety by leaving some white, and coloring others.

RADISH ROSEBUDS

1. Wash radishes and remove a small, thin slice from each end of the radish.
2. Form petals by cutting v-shaped slits, all the way around the radish, starting at the top, and cutting down about two-thirds the length of the radish.
3. Using the tip of the knife, carefully cut around the inside edge of the radish, to free the petals.
4. Gently remove the v-shaped portions of the radish peel, between the petals.
5. Store in ice water in refrigerator, up to three days.

A Guide to Napkin Folding

The ancient art of napkin folding provides the modern hostess with a gracious, festive way to make her dinner parties and family celebrations uniquely her own. Simple designs are easy to create and are available in folds that co-ordinate with the most formal as well as the most casual table setting.

Square, fabric napkins are best suited for folding, but take care that they are well pressed and lightly starched if too soft for folding. Colorful print napkins are charming when folded; however a formal, elegant look can be achieved with lace-trimmed, embroidered, or very tailored linen napkins.

BASIC FOLD
(extremely easy)

Perfect fold for napkins with an embroided corner

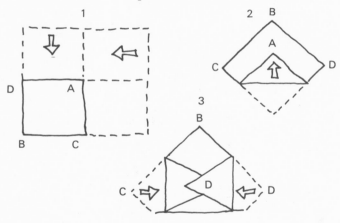

1. Fold napkin in half and then into quarter size (ACBD).
2. Turn up folded corner (A) three quarters of the way to point (B).
3. Fold points (C) and (D) toward center and overlap.
4. Turn napkin over. Make sure sides are even and point (B) is in the center.
5. Use as is or turn down corners at point (B) to reveal lace or embroidered corner.

(Continued) 573

CROSSTIE
(Very simple)

Print napkins are especially effective

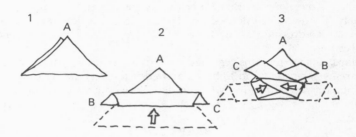

1. Fold napkin into a large triangle with center point (A) at top.
1. Turn fold at base of triangle up 1/4 from bottom. Fold up an additional 1/4.
3. Cross point (B) and point (C). Pretty placed in the center of a dinner plate.

BUFFET KNOT

Handsome on a buffet table

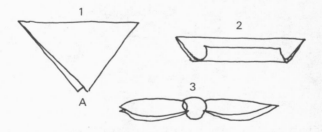

1. Fold napkin into a triangle with center point (A) at bottom.
2. Roll napkin up beginning at point (A).
3. Tie a knot at the center of rolled napkin.

BUFFET SILVER SERVER

Ideal for holding silver when serving a crowd!

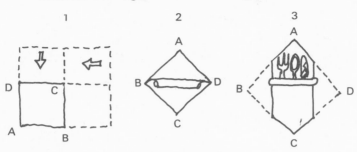

1. Fold napkin in half and then into quarter size (ABCD).
2. Roll two of the four top flaps (A) halfway down the napkin.
3. Fold point (B) and point (D) under. Make sure points (A) and (C) are in the center of the folded napkin. Silver may be placed in the pocket.

STANDING CROWN
(Very formal)

Stand this stately creation on a dinner plate.

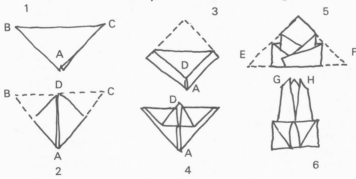

1. Fold napkin into a triangle with the center point (A) at bottom.
2. Fold point (B) and point (C) to meet center point (A).
3. Fold top corner (D) down to within one inch of center point (A)
4. Turn the folded point (D) back to upper edge.
5. Turn napkin over. Fold and overlap left corner (E) and right corner (F). Place one corner inside the other one.
6. Stand up as is or create a flower effect by folding down upper corners (G) and (H).

A Guide to Table Setting

Breakfast Setting

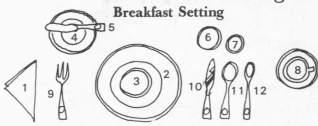

1. Napkin
2. Plate
3. Cereal dish
4. Bread-and-butter plate
5. Butter knife
6. Water glass
7. Juice glass
8. Cup and saucer
9. Fork
10. Knife
11. Cereal spoon (cream-soup spoon)
12. Coffee or tea spoon

Luncheon/Informal Dinner Setting

(First Course in Place)

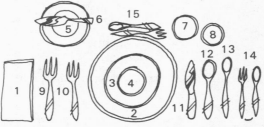

1. Napkin (should be placed across dinner plate if first course is omitted)
2. Plate
3. Liner plate for first course
4. Soup or seafood or fruit service
5. Bread-and-butter plate
6. Butter knife
7. Water glass or goblet
8. Wine goblet
9. Fork
10. Salad fork (may be placed to left of main course fork if salad is served before the main course)
11. Knife
12. Soup spoon (used if soup is served)
13. Coffee or tea spoon (may be brought in with coffee service)
14. Seafood fork or fruit cocktail spoon (used when a first course of seafood or fruit replaces soup)
15. Dessert silver (may be brought in with dessert service)

Formal Dinner Setting

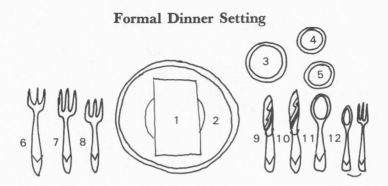

1. Napkin (should always be placed across plate)
2. Plate
3. Water goblet
4. White-wine goblet
5. Red-wine goblet
6. Fish fork
7. Main-course fork
8. Salad fork (may be placed to left of main course fork if salad is served before main course)
9. Main-course knife
10. Fish knife
11. Soup spoon
12. Fruit cocktail spoon or seafood fork
    Note: Dessert silver is brought with dessert service.
    Coffee spoon is brought with coffee service.

A Guide to Kitchen Metric Math

In all probability, the United States will be converting to the metric system of weights and measures before very long. If this does happen, many measurement changes will be made in the American kitchen. Kitchen metric measures are presently being proposed that will be somewhat different in size from the customary spoon and cup measures used in the American kitchens of today. For example, the present 1 cup measure equals 237 milliliters (the metric unit of volume). However, the amount of 237 milliliters would be awkward to work with when recipes must be divided or multiplied. Thus, in order to simplify the process of division and multiplication in recipes, the proposed measurement container comparable to the present 1 cup measure will hold 250 milliliters instead of 237 milliliters.

The table that follows shows at a glance how the sizes of present kitchen measures compare with the sizes of their proposed metric counterparts. Note that in most cases, the size of the metric container will be slightly larger than the present measure.

Present USA Measure	Exact Metric Translation	Proposed Kitchen Metric Measures
¼ teaspoon	1.2 milliliters	1 milliliter
½ teaspoon	2.5 milliliters	2 milliliters
1 teaspoon	5.0 milliliters	5 milliliters
1 tablespoon	14.8 milliliters	15 milliliters
¼ cup	59.2 milliliters	50 milliliters
½ cup	118.4 milliliters	125 milliliters
1 cup	236.8 milliliters	250 milliliters
1 pint	473.6 milliliters	500 milliliters
1 quart	947.2 milliliters	1000 milliliters (1 liter)

SIMPLIFIED METRIC CONVERSION FORMULAS	
Liquid ounce x 30	= milliliter
Liquid pint x 0.47	= liter
Liquid quart x 0.95	= liter
Dry ounce x 28	= gram
Dry pound x 0.45	= gram

Use this quick chart to convert present kitchen measurement (liquid and dry) to the new metric measurement.

OVEN TEMPERATURE CONVERSION TABLE
Fahrenheit (°F) and Celsius (°C)
Boiling (at sea level) 212°F. 100°C

Very slow oven	250° to 275°F.	120°C.
Slow oven	300° to 325°F.	150°C.
Moderate oven	350° to 375°F.	180°C.
Hot oven	400° to 425°F.	200°-220°C.
Very hot oven	450° to 500°F.	230°-260°C.

Recipes in this book have been tested and perfected for use at sea level. Between sea level and 2,500 feet, they will need no modification. However, at higher altitudes adjustments needed in the preparation of these recipes may be obtained from local Extension Home Economists or Utility Home Economists.

NOTES:

Kitchen Charts

KITCHEN CHARTS

Kitchen Charts Chapter Design: Graniteware Cruet Set (circa 1900), Wooden Masher (circa 1900)

COMMON KITCHEN PANS

Name	Size (inches)	Capacity
Loaf Pan	7-3/8x3-5/8x2¼	4 cups
	8½x3-5/8x2-5/8	6 cups
	9x5x3	8 cups
Spring-Form Pan	8x3	12 cups
	9x3	16 cups
Cake Pan	8x1¼	4 cups
	9x1½	6 cups
Square Pan	8x8x2	8 cups
	9x9x2	10 cups
Ring Mold	8½x2¼	4½ cups
	9¼x2¾	8 cups
Brioche Pan	9½x3¼	8 cups

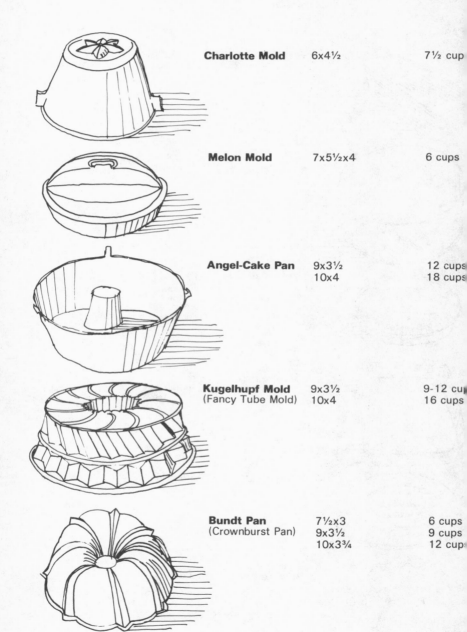

Charlotte Mold	6x4½	7½ cup
Melon Mold	7x5½x4	6 cups
Angel-Cake Pan	9x3½	12 cups
	10x4	18 cups
Kugelhupf Mold (Fancy Tube Mold)	9x3½	9-12 cup
	10x4	16 cups
Bundt Pan (Crownburst Pan)	7½x3	6 cups
	9x3½	9 cups
	10x3¾	12 cups

KITCHEN CHARTS

BAKED CRUMB CRUSTS

Oven: 375° 8 to 10 minutes   Yield: 1 (9-inch) crust

Kind	Cups of Crumbs	Granulated Sugar	Margarine
Graham crackers (crushed) 24 squares	1½	¼ cup	1/3 cup
Vanilla wafers (crushed) 36 (2-inch)	1½	none	¼ cup
Chocolate wafers (crushed) 18 (2¾-inch)	1-1/3	none	3 tablespoons
Gingersnaps (crushed) 30 (2-inch)	1½	none	1/3 cup
Corn or wheat flakes (crushed)	1½	none	1/3 cup
Chocolate creme filled cookies (crushed) 20	1½	none	¼ cup
Flaked or shredded coconut	2	none	¼ cup

BAKING INSTRUCTIONS: Preheat oven to 375°. Combine crumbs, sugar, and melted butter until well mixed. Press into bottom and up sides of a 9-inch pie pan. Bake 8 to 10 minutes or until golden brown. Cool.

NOTE: The graham cracker, vanilla wafer, gingersnap, and chocolate cookie crusts may be chilled without baking, if desired.

CAKE SERVINGS

Size of Cake	Servings
9x5x3-inch loaf cake	8
8-inch square cake	8 to 9
9-inch square cake	9
8-inch double layer cake	10 to 12
9-inch double layer cake	12 to 16
9x13x2-inch cake	12 to 16
10-inch bundt or tube cake	10 to 12
10-inch jelly roll	10

585

KITCHEN CHARTS

CAN SIZES

Can Size	Approximate Net Weight	Approximate Cups
No. ¼	4 to 4½ ounces	½ cup
No. ½	8 ounces	1 cup
No. 1	9½ to 13 ounces	1¼ cups
No. 1 (tall)	16 ounces	2 cups
No. 2	20 ounces	2½ cups
No. 2½	29 ounces	3½ cups
No. 3	3 pounds 3 ounces	5¾ cups
No. 10	6½ to 7 pounds 5 ounces	12 to 13 cups
6 ounce	6 ounces	¾ cup
8 ounce	8 ounces	1 cup
12 ounce	12 ounces	1½ cups
No. 300	14 to 16 ounces	1¾ cups
No. 303	16 to 17 ounces	2 cups

ALTERNATE CAKE PANS *

If a recipe calls for:	Use:
Two 8x1 1/2-inch round pans	18 to 24 (2 1/2'') cupcake pan cups
Three 8x1 1/2-inch round pans	Two 9x9x2-inch square pans or One 13x9x2-inch oblong pan
Two 9x1 1/2-inch round pans	Two 8x8x2-inch square pans or One 13x9x2-inch oblong pan
One 9x5x3-inch loaf pan	One 9x9x2-inch square pan
Two 9x5x3-inch loaf pans	One 10x4-inch tube pan
One 8x4x3-inch loaf pan	One 8x8x2-inch square pan
One 9x3 1/2-inch angel cake pan	One 10x3 3/4-inch bundt pan or One 9x3 1/2-inch fancy tube pan

*This chart applies to butter cakes only. Chiffon, pound, sponge, and angel food cakes are best baked in the pans specifically called for in recipes.

EQUIVALENT MEASURES

If measure called for is:	Its equivalent is:
A few grains, dash, pinch, etc. (dry)	Less than 1/8 teaspoon
Dash (liquid)	2 to 3 drops
1 teaspoon	60 drops
3 teaspoons	1 tablespoon
2 tablespoons	1 fluid ounce, 1/8 cup
4 tablespoons	¼ cup, 2 fluid ounces
5-1/3 tablespoons	1/3 cup, 4 fluid ounces
8 tablespoons	½ cup
10-2/3 tablespoons	2/3 cup
12 tablespoons	¾ cup, 6 fluid ounces
16 tablespoons	1 cup, 8 fluid ounces
½ cup	½ gill
1 cup	½ pint
2 cups	1 pint, 16 fluid ounces
4 cups or 2 pints	1 quart, 32 fluid ounces
4 quarts (liquid)	1 gallon
8 quarts or 2 gallons	1 peck
4 pecks or 32 quarts	1 bushel
16 ounces	1 pound
32 ounces	1 quart
1 ounce (liquid)	2 tablespoons
8 ounces (liquid)	1 cup
16 ounces	1 pound

KITCHEN CHARTS

EQUIVALENT AMOUNTS

If ingredient called for is:	Its equivalent is:
APPLES	
1 pound	3 medium (3 cups sliced)
BAKING POWDER	
5½ ounces	1 cup
BANANAS	
1 pound	3 medium (2½ cups sliced)
BERRIES	
1 pint	1¾ cups
BREAD	
1 slice	½ cup soft bread crumbs
2 slices	1 cup soft bread crumbs
1 pound loaf	12 to 16 slices
BUTTER AND SHORTENING	
Butter or margarine, 1 ounce	2 tablespoons
Butter or margarine, ½ stick	¼ cup
Butter or margarine, 1 stick	½ cup
Butter or margarine, 1 pound	2 cups
Vegetable shortening, 1 pound	2½ cups
CANDIED FRUIT	
½ pound, chopped	1½ cups
CHEESE	
American cheese, 2-2/3 cups cubed	1 pound
American cheese, 4 cups shredded	1 pound
Cottage cheese, 8 ounces	1 cup
Cream cheese, 3-ounce package	1/3 cup or 6 tablespoons
Cream cheese, 8-ounce package	1 cup
CHOCOLATE	
1 ounce	1 square
COCOA	
4 cups, ground	1 pound
COCONUT	
3½-ounce can, shredded	1-1/3 cups
1 pound	5 cups
COFFEE	
5 cups, ground (80 tablespoons)	1 pound
CORNMEAL	
3 cups	1 pound
CORNSTARCH	
3 cups	1 pound
CRACKER CRUMBS	
Soda crackers, 23	1 cup
Graham crackers, 15	1 cup
CREAM	
Cream, ½ pint	1 cup
Heavy or whipping cream, 1 cup	2 cups whipped cream
Sour cream, 8 ounces	1 cup

588

(Continued)

f ingredient called for is:	Its equivalent is:
DATES	
1 pound, whole	2¼ cups
1 pound, chopped	1¾ cups
EGGS	
8 to 10 whites (large eggs)	1 cup
12 to 14 yolks (large eggs)	1 cup
5 to 6 whole eggs	1 cup
1 whole egg	4 tablespoons liquid
FIGS	
1 pound, whole	2¾ cups
1 pound, chopped	2-2/3 cups
FLOUR	
All-purpose flour, 1 pound	4 cups sifted all-purpose
Cake flour, 1 pound	4¾ to 5 cups sifted cake flour
Whole-wheat flour, 1 pound	3½ to 3¾ cups unsifted whole-wheat flour
Rye flour, 1 pound	4½ to 5 cups
GELATIN	
Unflavored envelope, ¼-ounce	1 tablespoon
Flavored package, 3¼-ounces	½ cup
LEMON	
1 medium lemon	3 tablespoons juice
1 medium lemon	1 tablespoon grated rind
5 to 8 medium lemons	1 cup juice
LIME	
1 medium lime	2 tablespoons juice
MARSHMALLOWS	
¼ pound	16 large marshmallows
MILK	
Evaporated milk, 1 cup	3 cups whipped
Evaporated milk, 5-1/3 to 6-ounce can	2/3 cup
Evaporated milk, 13 to 14¼-ounce can	1¼ to 1-1/3 cups
Milk, 1 quart	4 cups
Heavy cream, 1 cup	2 cups whipped
NUTS	
Almonds, 1 pound unshelled	1¼ cups shelled
Almonds, 1 pound shelled	3 cups
Brazil nuts, 1 pound unshelled	1½ cups shelled
Brazil nuts, 1 pound shelled	3¼ cups
Filberts, 1 pound unshelled	2 cups shelled
Filberts, 1 pound shelled	4 cups
Peanuts, 1 pound unshelled	2 cups shelled
Peanuts, 1 pound shelled	4 cups
Pecans, 1 pound unshelled	2¼ cups shelled
Pecans, 1 pound shelled	4 cups
Walnuts, 1 pound unshelled	2 cups shelled
Walnuts, 1 pound shelled	4 cups
ONION	
1 medium, chopped	¾ to 1 cup

KITCHEN CHARTS

If ingredient called for is:	Its equivalent is:
ORANGE	
1 medium	1/3 to ½ cup juice
1 medium	2 to 3 tablespoons grated peel
PASTA	
Macaroni, 1 cup uncooked	2 cups cooked macaroni
Macaroni, 1 pound uncooked	5 cups cooked macaroni
Spaghetti, 1 cup uncooked	2 cups cooked spaghetti
Spaghetti, 1 pound uncooked	5 cups cooked spaghetti
Noodles, 1 cup uncooked	2/3 cup cooked noodles
POTATOES	
White, 1 pound	3 medium
Sweet, 1 pound	3 medium
PRUNES	
1 pound, whole	2-1/3 cups
1 pound, chopped and cooked	3 cups
RAISINS	
1 pound	3 cups loosely packed
RICE	
Rice, 1 pound uncooked	2-1/3 cups cooked rice
Quick-cooking rice, 1 cup uncooked	2 cups cooked rice
Converted rice, 1 cup uncooked	3 to 4 cups cooked rice
Long-grain rice, 1 cup uncooked	4 cups cooked rice
Wild rice, 1 cup uncooked	3 to 4 cups cooked wild rice
SUGAR	
Granulated, 1 pound	2 cups
Brown (light or dark), 1 pound	2¼ cups firmly packed
Powdered, 1 pound	3 to 3½ cups sifted
SYRUP	
Corn syrup, 16 ounces	2 cups
Maple syrup, 12 ounces	1½ cups
TEA	
2 ounces	7/8 cup
1 pound	6 cups
TOMATOES	
1 pound	3 medium

TABLE OF SUBSTITUTIONS

tead of:	Use:
AKING POWDER 1 teaspoon baking powder	¼ teaspoon baking soda **plus** ½ teaspoon cream of tartar
READ CRUMBS 1 cup bread crumbs	¾ cup cracker crumbs
ROTH 1 cup chicken or beef broth	1 bouillon cube or 1 teaspoon powdered broth or 1 envelope powdered broth base dissolved in 1 cup boiling water
UTTER (OR MARGARINE) 1 cup butter or margarine (for shortening)	1 cup hydrogenated fat with ½ teaspoon salt
HOCOLATE 1 square (1-ounce) unsweetened chocolate 6 ounces semi-sweet chocolate	3 tablespoons cocoa **plus** 1 tablespoon butter or margarine 2 ounces unsweetened chocolate **plus** 7 tablespoons sugar and 2 tablespoons fat
ORNSTARCH 1 tablespoon cornstarch (for thickening)	2 tablespoons all-purpose flour
CORN SYRUP 1 cup corn syrup	¾ cup sugar **plus** ¼ cup water
REAM 1 cup light cream 1 cup heavy cream	7 / 8 cup milk **plus** 3 tablespoons butter ¾ cup milk **plus** 1 / 3 cup butter
GGS 1 whole egg (for baking)	2 egg yolks **plus** 1 tablespoon water
GARLIC 1 clove fresh garlic	1 teaspoon garlic salt or 1 / 8 teaspoon garlic powder
FLOUR 1 tablespoon flour (for thickening) 1 cup all-purpose FLOUR 1 cup cake flour 1 cup self-rising flour	½ tablespoon cornstarch or ½ tablespoon arrowroot starch or 1 tablespoon granulated tapioca 1 cup **plus** 2 tablespoons cake flour or Up to ½ cup bran, whole wheat flour, or corn meal **plus** enough allpurpose flour to equal 1 cup 1 cup **minus** 2 tablespoons all-purpose flour 1 cup all-purpose flour **plus** 1 teaspoon baking powder and ½ teaspoon salt

Instead of:	Use:
HERBS	
1 tablespoon fresh herbs	1 teaspoon dried herbs, ground or crushed
HONEY	
1 cup honey	1¼ cups sugar **plus** ¼ cup liquid or 1 cup molasses
MILK	
1 cup skim milk	4 tablespoons nonfat dry milk **plus** 1 cup water
1 cup sour milk or 1 cup buttermilk	1 tablespoon vinegar or lemon juice or 1¾ teaspoons cream of tartar **plus** homogenized milk to equal 1 cup (let stand 5 minutes)
1 cup sweet milk (homogenized)	1 cup sour milk or buttermilk **plus** ½ teaspoon baking soda
1 cup whole milk	¼ cup powdered skim milk **plus** 2 tablespoons butter and 1 cup water or 4 teaspoons powdered whole milk **plus** 1 cup water or ½ cup evaporated milk **plus** ½ cup water or 1 cup skim milk **plus** 2 tablespoons butter or margarine
MUSTARD	
1 tablespoon prepared mustard	1 teaspoon dry mustard
MUSHROOMS	
1 pound fresh mushrooms	6 ounces canned mushrooms
ONION	
2 teaspoons minced onion	1 teaspoon onion powder
SOUR CREAM	
1 cup commercial sour cream	1 tablespoon lemon juice **plus** evaporated milk to make 1 cup.
SUGAR	
1 cup granulated sugar	1 cup brown sugar or 2 cups corn syrup (reduce liquid) or ¾ cup honey (reduce liquid)
TAPIOCA	
2 teaspoons tapioca	1 tablespoon flour
TOMATOES (canned)	
1 cup canned tomatoes	1-1/3 cups fresh, cut-up tomatoes, simmered 10 minutes
1 cup tomato juice	½ cup tomato sauce **plus** ½ cup water
YEAST	
1 cake compressed yeast	1 package (2 teaspoons) active dry yeast
YOGURT	
1 cup yogurt	1 cup buttermilk or sour milk

Index

A

B

M

NEWNAN JUNIOR SERVICE LEAGUE
ACTIVE MEMBERS
1994-1995

Mrs. David Asher (Tammy)
Mrs. Randy Beckom (Ginger)
Mrs. Hank Blanton (Brenda)
Mrs. Tommy Brevelle (Suzy)
Mrs. Michael Booth (Laurie)
Mrs. Mark Brown (Toni)
Mrs. Brad Byrum (Elizabeth)
Mrs. David Clark (Anne)
Mrs. Jimmy Craft (Polly)
Mrs. Joe Crain, Jr. (Sandee)
Mrs. Paul Davis (Angela)
Mrs. Scott Douglas (Julianne)
Mrs. Craig Duncan (Romelle)
Mrs. Randall Duncan (Beth)
Mrs. Frank Eldridge (Edie)
Mrs. Craig Evans (Suanne)
Mrs. Allen Farrish (Rudy)
Mrs. John Fountain (Jeaneane)
Mrs. David Frank (Carol)
Mrs. Tom Freeman (Michelle)
Mrs. Preston Fulmer, Jr. (Ivey)
Mrs. Richard Gunnels (Melinda)
Mrs. Brit Hall (Jennifer)
Mrs. Larry Harkleroad (Jennifer)
Mrs. Steve Harris (Frances)
Mrs. Peter Hayes (Natalie)
Mrs. Steve Hendrix (Chris)
Mrs. Wesley Howard (Mary)
Mrs. Chris Huey (Gay)
Mrs. Alan Huckaby (Josie)
Mrs. Glen LaForce (Jill)

Mrs. David LaGuardia (Jane)
Mrs. Rick LaGuardia (Cathy)
Mrs. Gary Lawrence (Julie)
Mrs. James Lawson (Peggie)
Mrs. H. Russell Lester, III (Elizabe
Mrs. Joe Lowery (Cathy)
Mrs. Jim Luckie (Cindy)
Mrs. William McGuire (Ginny)
Mrs. Dan McManus (Molly)
Mrs. Mac McKinney (Julie)
Mrs. Steve McLain (Patty)
Mrs. Wayne Martin (Stacia)
Mrs. Rick Melville (Rita)
Mrs. Edmond Miller (Frances)
Mrs. William Miller (Tammy)
Mrs. John Myers (Robin)
Mrs. Lee Pettet (Kelly)
Mrs. Don Phillips (Ann)
Mrs. Stan Price (Kern)
Mrs. Steve Register (Susan)
Mrs. Wayne Robertson (Carol)
Mrs. Albert Sealey (Margaret)
Mrs. Earl Smith (Melanie)
Mrs. Eric Stipe (Kathy)
Mrs. Frank Sullivan (Lynne)
Mrs. Jim Taylor (Sally)
Mrs. Lee Troutman (Nan)
Mrs. Keith Troxler (Beth)
Mrs. John Tucker (Carol)
Mrs. Winn Wise (Kim)
Mrs. Mark Wood (Becky)

PROVISIONAL MEMBERS
1994-1995

Mrs. Weston Arnall (Caroline)
Mrs. Jeff Belcher (Beth)
Mrs. Cliff England (Michelle)
Mrs. Preston Foy (Frances)
Ms. Tracey Hammett
Mrs. Kyle Keene (Lori)
Ms. Kim Lavoie

Mrs. Larry Liebe (Sharon)
Mrs. George MacNabb (Michelle)
Mrs. Paul Meyer (Donna)
Mrs. Steve Pelham (Sarah)
Ms. Geri Pike
Mrs. Joe Traylor (Lynn)
Mrs. Michael Worth (Barbara)

NEWNAN JUNIOR SERVICE LEAGUE
SUSTAINERS
1994-1995

Mrs. Jimmy Adams (Brenda) (85)
Mrs. Joe Almon (Deena) (88)
Mrs. Cliff Arnett (Carol) (84)
Mrs. William Banks (Betty) (88)
Mrs. Michael Barber (Julia) (91)
Mrs. William Berry, III (Anne) (91)
Mrs. Duke Blackburn (Lynn) (93)
Mrs. Jerry Boren (Nelda) (87)
Mrs. Tony Brogdon (Wendy) (90)
Mrs. Charlie Brown (Pam) (87)
Mrs. Tim Carrol (Beth) (93)
Mrs. Thomas Carson (Nancy) (90)
Mrs. Ned Chambless (Jane) (87)
Mrs. Roddy Clifton (Connie) (92)
Mrs. Robert Cordle (Mitzi) (90)
Mrs. David Cotton (Pat) (93)
Mrs. Robert Cox (Louise) (86)
Mrs. John Herbert Cranford (Carolyn) (93)
Mrs. Larry Deason (Sharon) (90)
Mrs. Joseph Distel (Pat) (84)
Mrs. Steve Fanning (Diane)
Mrs. Frank Farmer (Melody) (94)
Mrs. Herman Fletcher (Anne)
Mrs. Fred Gilbert (Ann)
Mrs. Jack Giles (Pam) (86)
Mrs. Mitch Ginn (Mary Jane)
Mrs. Richard Glover (Debbie) (86)
Mrs. Peter Gosch (Lisa) (92)
Mrs. Joe Harless (Carol) (86)
Mrs. Bill Hartselle (Joan) (92)
Mrs. Hugh Heflin, Jr. (Julia) (92)
Mrs. Larry Huggins (Missy) (88)
Mrs. Alan W. Jackson (Leigh) (91)
Mrs. E.H. Johnson, II (Marie) (86)
Mrs. Stanley Lanier (Debbie) (89)
Mrs. Walter Lonergan (Ginny) (92)
Mrs. Tery Lunsford (Frances) (91)
Mrs. Frank Marchman (Beth) (91)
Mrs. Scott Markham (Carol) (92)
Mrs. Dennis McEntire (Sally) (92)
Mrs. Robert Merrell (Sam) (93)

Mrs. Robin Miller (Alice) (86)
Mrs. Stephen Mitchell (Linda) (92)
Mrs. David Morgan (Linda) (86)
Mrs. Thomas Morningstar (Donna)
Mrs. Joseph Morris (Linda) (86)
Mrs. Harry Mullins (Susan) (87)
Mrs. Hutch Murphey (Mary Jane) (93)
Mrs. Andrew Muzio (Eileen) (91)
Mrs. James Palmer (Maude) (85)
Mrs. Jim Parks (Betty)
Mrs. David Parrott (Carol) (84)
Mrs. Joe Powell (Cathy) (92)
Mrs. Scott Reeves (Sammy) (89)
Mrs. Mayo Royal, Jr. (Nancy) (90)
Mrs. Bob Sandlin (Pam) (92)
Mrs. Rhodes Shell (Kathy) (85)
Mrs. Neal Shepard (Jodie) (84)
Mrs. Mitchell Sherwood (Cindy) (94)
Mrs. Lee Simpson (Sey) (87)
Mrs. Charles V. Slomka (Tricia) (92)
Mrs. Donald Sprayberry, Jr. (Terri) (89)
Mrs. Stephen Sprayberry (Colleen) (94)
Mrs. Bob Stitt (Valorie) (88)
Mrs. Linda Stone (88)
Mrs. Larry Strickland (Montie) (91)
Mrs. Jim Stripling (Debbie)
Mrs. Kyle Tatum (Kathy) (92)
Mrs. Earnest Taylor (Jan) (84)
Mrs. Robert W. Teller (Nancy) (86)
Mrs. Gene Terrell (Joyce) (85)
Mrs. Robert Tumperi (Barbara) (88)
Ms. Lisa Van Houten (93)
Mrs. Phil Vincent (Mary Anna)
Mrs. Donald Walls (Leigh) (92)
Mrs. Jimmy Whitlock (Clare) (88)
Mrs. Shirley Widner (89)
Mrs. Hal Williams (Penny) (90)
Mrs. Gary Wright (Leroyce) (86)
Mrs. Pat Yancey, III (Julie) (90)
Mrs. Bill Yeager (Cindy) (93)

NEWNAN JUNIOR SERVICE LEAGUE
GOLDEN SUSTAINERS
1994-1995

Mrs. Frances Arnall (W)
Mrs. William Arnall (Linda)
Mrs. Sam Banks (Mary Willie) (W)
Mrs. C.M. Barron (Lavinia)
Mrs. Harold Barron (Catherine)
Mrs. Lindsey Barron(Genet)
Mrs. Thomas W. Barron(Margaret)
Mrs. James Beavers, Jr.(Alice)
Mrs. Marion Beavers (Ann)
Mrs. Duke Blackburn(Julia) (W)
Mrs. Brack Blalock(Eleanor) (W)
Mrs. Keith Brady (Katie)
Mrs. Bill Breed (Ann)
Mrs. Herb Bridges (Eleanor)
Ms. Barbara Brown
Mrs. David R. Brown (Rita)
Mrs. R.A. Brown , Jr. (Lynn)
Mrs. Everett Bryant (Mary) (W)
Mrs. Warren Budd (Courtenay)
Mrs. Robert Campbell (Fran)
Mrs. John J. Cenkner (Sandra)
Mrs. Ed Cole (Sarah Gray)(W)
Mrs. Frank Cole, Jr. (Louise)(W)
Mrs. Madison Cole (Martha) (W)
Mrs. Charles Connally (Rosa)
Mrs. Ed Craft (Brenda)
Mrs. Ellis Crook (Pat)
Mrs. Molly Davis
Mrs. Richard Day (Gayle)
Mrs. Ronald Duffey (Lynn)
Mrs. Willis Edwards (Catherine) (W)
Mrs. W.Y. Ellis (Ida) (W)
Mrs. Charles Farmer (Elsie)
Mrs. Hugh Farmer, Jr. (Charlsie)
Mrs. Jett Fisher (Carol) (W)
Mrs. Oliver Gentry (Florine)
Mrs. Herman Glass (Catherine)
Mrs. Cliff Glover (Inez)
Mrs. Howard C. Glover, Jr.(Margaret)
Mrs. J. L. Glover, Sr. (Margaret)
Mrs. John Gray (Alice)
Mrs. John Goodrum (Marsha)
Mrs. Larry Hansen (Karen)
Mrs. James Hardin (Louise)
Mrs. Will Haugen (Evelyn)
Mrs. William Headley (Anita)
Mrs. R.B. Hubbard (Eleanor) (W)
Mrs. Tom Johnson
Mrs. Babe Jenkins

Ms. Julie Jones
Mrs. R.O. Jones (Evelyn) (W)
Mrs. Aaron Keheley (Alberta) (W)
Mrs. Wilkins Kirby, Jr. (Alice)
Mrs. Ed Klein (Winnie Boone) (W)
Mrs. Nathan Knight (Ann)
Mrs. Billy Lee (Susan)
Mrs. Bobby Lee (Pam)
Mrs. Bob Lines (Alice)
Mrs. Wright Lipford (Faye)
Mrs. Howard McCullough (Barbara)
Mrs. Bill McWaters (Linda)
Mrs. V.E. Manget, Jr. (Catherine) (W)
Mrs. Bob Mann (Frances)
Mrs. James Mann (Frances) (W)
Mrs. Taft Mansour (Marguerite) (W)
Mrs. Clarence Moody (Virginia) (W)
Mrs. Parnell Odom (Pat)
Mrs. Terry Overton (Mary)
Mrs. Gene Owen (Judy)
Mrs. James Owens (Elon)
Mrs. Henry Payton (Rosemary)
Mrs. Lavergne Peterson (W)
Mrs. Irwin Pike (Helen) (W)
Mrs. Bill Pinson (Ola)
Mrs. J.H. Powell (Skeez)
Mrs. Roy Power (Judy) (W)
Mrs. Oliver Reason (Annette)
Mrs. Howard Royal (Mary)
Mrs. Robert Royal (Sue)
Mrs. Leigh Sanders (Martha)
Mrs. Walter Sanders (Clara Berry) (W)
Ms. Inez Slaton
Mrs. Charles Smith (Lynn)
Mrs. Michael Smith (Debbie)
Mrs. Maurice Sponcler (Dot)
Mrs. Tommy Strother (Frances)
Mrs. John Stucky (Sandy)
Mrs. Steve Threlkeld (Genny)
Mrs. Don Tomlinson (Jane)
Mrs. Dan Umbach (Marie)
Mrs. Jean Wagner
Mrs. Jimmy Weddington (Mary)
Mrs. John White (Martha)
Mrs. Bruce Williams (Sandra)
Mrs. Carl E. Williams (Eddy)
Mrs. Minerva Woodroof
Mrs. Pat Yancey, Jr. (Jeanne)

(W) Widow

A Taste of Georgia
Newnan Junior Service League, Inc.
P.O. Box 1433
Newnan, Georgia 30264

ease send_____ copies of **A Taste of Georgia**
$16.95* per book plus $3.00 for postage and handling for
ch book. Georgia residents add $1.02 sales tax per book.

ame _____

ddress _____

ty _____ State _____ Zip _____
ke checks payable to **A Taste of Georgia**. *All Previous coupons void.

A Taste of Georgia
Newnan Junior Service League, Inc.
P.O. Box 1433
Newnan, Georgia 30264

ease send_____ copies of **A Taste of Georgia**
$16.95* per book plus $3.00 for postage and handling for
ch book. Georgia residents add $1.02 sales tax per book.

ame _____

ddress _____

ty_____ State _____Zip _____
ke checks payable to **A Taste of Georgia**. *All Previous coupons void.

A Taste of Georgia
Newnan Junior Service League, Inc.
P.O. Box 1433
Newnan, Georgia 30264

ease send _____ copies of **A Taste of Georgia**
$16.95* per book plus $3.00 for postage and handling for
ch book. Georgia residents add $1.02 sales tax per book.

ame _____

ddress _____

ty_____ State _____ Zip _____
ke checks payable to **A Taste of Georgia**. *All Previous coupons void.

A Taste of Georgia, Another Serving is a fresh innovative companion to our first cookbook. Professionally produced in the tradition of *A Taste of Georgia*, it too is destined to become a best-seller throughout the nation.

This volume contains recipes tested and selected using the same discriminating system that produced *A Taste of Georgia*. We have added an excellent children's section and easy reference pages for lowfat, microwave and grill recipes. The artwork is interesting and informative, featuring flatware and silver pieces from a southern manor. The book features a beautiful lay-flat, hardcover, wire-o binding.

A Taste of Georgia, *Another Serving*
Newnan Junior Service League, Inc.
P.O. Box 1433
Newnan, Georgia 30264

Please send_____copies of **Another Serving** at $14.95* per book plus $2.50 for postage and handling for each book. Georgia residents please add $.90 sales tax per book.

Name _____

Address _____

City_____ State _____Zip _____
Make checks payable to **A Taste of Georgia.** *All Previous coupons void.

A Taste of Georgia, *Another Serving*
Newnan Junior Service League, Inc.
P.O. Box 1433
Newnan, Georgia 30264

Please send_____ copies of **Another Serving** at $14.95* per book plus $2.50 for postage and handling for each book. Georgia residents please add $.90 sales tax per book.

Name _____

Address _____

City_____ State _____ Zip _____
Make checks payable to **A Taste of Georgia.** *All Previous coupons void.